CONTROVERSY
IN
MARKETING
THEORY

CONTROVERSY
IN
MARKETING
THEORY

FOR REASON, REALISM, TRUTH, AND OBJECTIVITY

SHELBY D. HUNT

M.E. Sharpe
Armonk, New York
London, England

Library of Congress Cataloging-in-Publication Data

Hunt, Shelby D.
    Controversy in marketing theory : for reason, realism, truth, and objectivity / by
Shelby D. Hunt
       p. cm.
    Includes bibliographical references and index.
    ISBN 0-7656-0931-3 (cloth: alk. paper) — ISBN 0-7656-0932-0 (pbk.: alk. paper)
    1. Marketing. 2. Philosophy and science. I. Title.

HF5415 .H868 2003
658.8′001—dc21   2002030894

Printed in the United States of America

The paper used in this publication meets the minimum requirements of
American National Standard for Information Sciences
Permanence of Paper for Printed Library Materials,
ANSI Z 39.48-1984.

∞

BM (c)	10	9	8	7	6	5	4	3	2	1
BM (p)	10	9	8	7	6	5	4	3	2	1

This book
is dedicated to
my daughter, Michelle,
of whom I am
very proud.

CONTENTS

PREFACE

This book is the companion volume to *Foundations of Marketing Theory: Toward a General Theory of Marketing* (Hunt 2002a). That volume, as did Hunt (1976a), Hunt (1983b), and Part 1 of Hunt (1991a), focused on the traditional philosophy of science topics in marketing theory. That is, *Foundations* focused on such topics as the morphology of scientific explanations, scientific laws, and theories. It also argued that resource-advantage theory is *toward* a general theory of marketing.

In contrast, *Controversy in Marketing Theory: For Reason, Realism, Truth, and Objectivity* focuses on what have been called the "philosophy debates" in marketing. That is, as did Part 2 of Hunt (1991a), *Controversy* uses historical method to investigate controversies in marketing concerning various philosophical "isms," including: logical positivism, logical empiricism, classical empiricism, classical rationalism, classical realism, idealism, relativism, and so forth. Specifically, Chapters 2–5 of this volume trace the historical development of the various philosophical "isms," and Chapters 6–9 use the historical material to analyze, in detail, specific controversies in marketing theory. Therefore, *Controversy* and *Foundations*, when used together, provide a complete package for marketing theory courses and seminars.

All those who have attempted to find publishers for works that have small markets know the difficulty of the task. Therefore, I should like to thank M.E. Sharpe for agreeing to publish this work. In particular, I wish to thank Harry Briggs, Executive Editor, for encouraging me to revise *Marketing Theory*, once again.

In an extraordinary display of intercollegial generosity, numerous philosophers of science agreed graciously to review drafts of the Hunt (1991a) versions of Chapters 2–6. These philosophers include: Robert L. Causey (University of Texas, Austin), Martin Hollis (University of East Anglia, United Kingdom), Evan K. Jobe (Texas Tech University), John Kekes (State University of New York at Albany), Michael Krausz (Bryn Mawr College), Jarrett Leplin (University of North Carolina at Greensboro), Michael E. Levin (City

College, City University of New York), Steven Lukes (Oxford University), Paul E. Meehl (University of Minnesota), Jack W. Meiland (University of Michigan), Dennis C. Phillips (Stanford University), Hilary Putnam (Harvard University), Israel Scheffler (Harvard University), and David Stove (University of Sydney). Given the ambitious nature of Chapters 2–6, these reviewers' assistance and encouraging comments are most appreciated. Indeed, they significantly improved the book by correcting numerous errors. Although any remaining errors are my responsibility alone, I gratefully thank all these philosophers for their help.

One philosopher of science, more so than any other, has influenced the content of this book. That philosopher is Harvey Siegel (Philosophy Department, University of Miami). My own work has benefited enormously from Professor Siegel's many writings. His incisive analyses of extraordinarily complex issues in the philosophy of science are exemplary examples of true scholarship.

Many colleagues have encouraged me to write this (final?) edition of *Marketing Theory* and provided suggestions as to specific topics to be included, excluded, or revised. I gratefully acknowledge the encouragement, comments, and suggestions of Dennis Arnett (Texas Tech University), Danny Bellenger (Georgia State University), Adam Finn (University of Alberta), David Gardner (University of Illinois), Michael Hyman (New Mexico State University), Robert Morgan (University of Alabama), William Pride (Texas A&M University), Arturo Vasquez-Parraga (University of Texas, PanAmerican), Scott Vitell (University of Mississippi), and Arch Woodside (Tulane University).

Over the years, my doctoral students, as well as my students in theory courses at other universities, have provided numerous helpful suggestions. I thank them all. Finally, but very importantly, thanks go to Raylynn Dorny, Bessie Jones, Jill Stephens, and Jennifer Taylor for their extensive assistance in manuscript preparation.

S.D.H.

CONTROVERSY
IN
MARKETING
THEORY

1 INTRODUCTION

Science is, above all else, a reality-driven enterprise. Every active investigator is inescapably aware of this. It creates the pain as well as much of the delight of research. Reality is the overseer at one's shoulder, ready to rap one's knuckles or to spring the trap into which one has been led by overconfidence, or by a too-complacent reliance on mere surmise. Science succeeds precisely because it has accepted a bargain in which even the boldest imagination stands hostage to reality.

—Paul R. Gross and Norman Levitt (1994)

Controversy in marketing theory is longstanding. In the early part of the twentieth century, marketers debated whether their subject should be approached from the perspective of marketing functions, commodities, or institutions (Bartels 1976). Those advocating the functional approach prevailed, and most early textbooks stressed the activities that were believed to be the essential components of all marketing systems. Later, controversy in marketing theory centered on questions such as: (1) Should marketing be taught from a managerial rather than a functional perspective? (2) Should marketing be guided by the marketing concept? (3) Is marketing (can it be) a science? (4) What is the role of theory in marketing research? (5) Should (can) marketing have its own general theory? (6) Should marketing theory be developed deductively or inductively? (7) Are marketing laws (or lawlike generalizations) possible? (8) What does it mean to explain a marketing phenomenon? (9) Is marketing an applied discipline? (10) Who are the clients of the marketing discipline? (11) Can (should) marketing be broadened to include nonprofit organizations? (12) What is the role of strategy in marketing research? (See Kerin 1996.)

This book is titled *Controversy in Marketing Theory*. Yet the controversies referred to in the title are not the dozen just cited. Instead, the controversies are those, often referred to collectively as the "philosophy debates," that arose in the early 1980s and continue in many different guises today (e.g., controversies in marketing involving relativism, postmodernism, interpretivism, humanism, and feminism) (Easton 2002). Examples of specific controversies in the philosophy debates include: (1) Does science (and, therefore, *marketing* science) differ from nonscience in any fundamental way (or ways)? (2) Does "positivism" (i.e., logical positivism and logical empiricism) dominate marketing research? (3) Does positivism imply quantitative methods? (4) Would positivist research be causality-seeking, adopt the machine metaphor, adopt realism, be deterministic, reify unobservables, and adopt functionalism? (5) What is philosophical relativism? (6) Is relativism an appropriate foundation for marketing research? (7) Does relativism imply pluralism, tolerance, and openness? (8) Should qualitative methods (e.g., naturalistic inquiry, humanistic inquiry, ethnographic methods, historical method, critical theory, literary explication, interpretivism, feminism, and postmodernism) be more prominent in marketing research? (9) Do qualitative methods imply relativism? (10) What is the philosophy known as "scientific realism"? (11) Is scientific realism an appropriate foundation for marketing research? (12) Are true theories, as emphasized by realism, an appropriate goal for marketing research? (13) Is objective research in marketing possible? (14) Should marketing pursue the goal of objective research?[1]

The controversies addressed in this book that prompt its title are those that have been prominent and contentious in marketing's philosophy debates. Our analyses of the controversies will reflect the subtitle of the book; they reflect what the book argues *for*. That is, this work's analyses of the controversies argue *for Reason, Realism, Truth, and Objectivity*. This book argues for a reasoned approach to marketing's controversies, for realism as a foundation for marketing theory and research, and for truth and objectivity as goals for marketing to pursue and regulative ideals for marketing to maintain. These "fors," in turn, stem from the foundations of the philosophy underlying our method of analysis. These foundations are seven (Hunt 2001).

First, the book's philosophical foundations hold that Plato's "critical discussion" (see section 2.1.2) is essential for knowledge development. In this view, the pursuit of truth is furthered by proposing penetrating, highly critical questions, which are to be followed by equally insightful, thoughtful answers. Second, civility in critical discussion is a virtue. For example, the use of *ad hominem* is proscribed: Discussion should always be directed at the ideas of people, not at the people themselves. Third, the use of sophistry is prohibited: It is impermissible to employ disingenuous argumentation, even when such arguments might be persuasive to one's audience. Fourth, one should respect reason and evidence: The fallibility of all research methods implies that one must be open to all alternative views that provide well-reasoned arguments and evidence. Fifth, clarity in scholarship is a virtue: To be obscure should never be confused with being profound. Sixth, of all the "isms" in the philosophy of science, scientific realism seems to make the most sense for marketing: No other philosophy is coherent (without being dogmatic), is critical (without being nihilistic), is open (without being anarchistic), and, at the same time, can account for the success of science.

Seventh, and finally, the philosophy underlying this work emphasizes critical pluralism. "Critical pluralism" is a label originally suggested by Siegel (1988) to characterize how scholars should view their own and others' theories and methods. The "pluralism" part reminds us that dogmatism is antithetical to science; we should adopt a tolerant, open posture toward new theories and methods. The "critical" half stresses that nonevaluational, nonjudgmental, or noncritical pluralism (which would view the supposed encapsulation of rival theories and alternative methods as thwarting comparison and evaluation) is just as bad as dogmatism. All methods, theories, and their respective knowledge claims can (and must) be subjected to critical scrutiny; nothing is exempt. Critical pluralism, therefore, implies that the philosophy underlying the book is open-minded, but not empty-headed.

1.1   THE BASIC THESIS

The basic thesis of this book is that marketing's philosophy debates—like those in the social sciences, as discussed in Fiske and Shweder (1986) and Phillips (1987)—have been (and are) muddled, at least in part, because they have been uninformed as to the "isms" of the philosophy of science. That is, the debates are less productive than they might be if the debates' participants understood the nature of, and differences among, logical positivism, logical empiricism, historical relativism, historical empiricism, and scientific realism. However, understanding these "isms" requires at least some understanding of their historical predecessors, that is, idealism, classical rationalism, classical realism, classical positivism, and classical empiricism. Therefore, Chapters 2 through 5 adopt a qualitative method, that is, historical method, to explicate the philosophical "isms" that have figured, and continue to figure, so prominently in marketing's philosophy debates. As shown in Figure 1.1, the relevant "isms" begin with Platonism, which traces to 600 B.C., and culminate in today's historical empiricism and scientific realism.

The objectives of Chapters 2 through 5 are to provide an initial analysis of some of the controversies in the philosophy debates, and to develop the historical groundwork for detailed examination of the debates in Chapters 6 through 9. Furthermore, Chapters 2 through 5 provide readers with historical references and other materials that would be useful for future analyses of philosophical controversies in marketing. As readers will note, the analyses in Chapters 6 through 9 will refer extensively to the historical materials in Chapters 2 through 5 (often by section number).

Figure 1.1   **Philosophy of Science Time Chart**

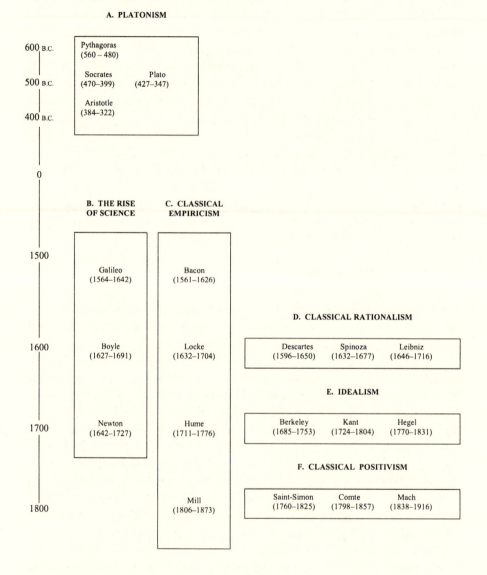

1.2   A LOOK AHEAD

Chapter 2 traces the history of the philosophy of science and the scientific
method from its Grecian origins with Platonism to the latter part of the nineteenth century and the triumph of German idealism. Specifically, the chapter

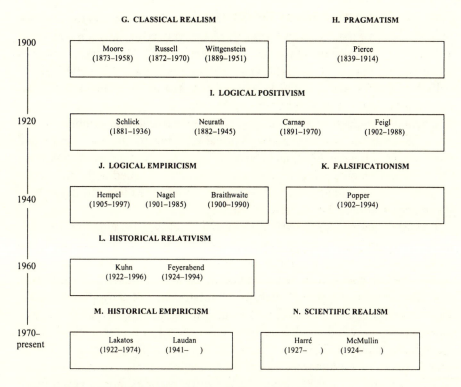

Source: Hunt (2002b). Reprinted by permission of the author.

discusses Platonism; the rise of modern science in the sixteenth and seventeenth centuries; the classical empiricism of Bacon, Locke, Hume, and Mill; the rationalism of Descartes, Spinoza, and Leibniz; the ascendence of idealism, as argued for by Berkeley, Kant, and Hegel; and the classical positivism of Conte and Mach, before concluding with a discussion of the methodological contributions of Frege. As will be discussed in Chapter 2, Socrates, in his debate with the sophists, developed a version of the "self-refutation" argument against relativism that modern philosophers of science also find useful in evaluating relativism.

Chapter 3 begins with the emergence of classical realism, as argued for by Moore, Russell, and Wittgenstein. The chapter then turns to the origins of the logical positivist movement and shows how it was stimulated by developments in Einsteinian relativity and quantum mechanics. The chapter then discusses the flaws in the logical positivists' research program and how those flaws led to the development of logical empiricism and Popperian falsificationism. The chapter concludes with discussions of scientific progress, scientific knowledge, the doctrine of foundationalism, and the philosophers' fallacy.

Chapter 4 chronicles the rise and fall of historical relativism in the philosophy of science. First, the chapter distinguishes between relativism and absolutism. After identifying the various kinds of relativism, the chapter discusses and evaluates both Kuhnian relativism and the relativism of Feyerabend. Finally, the chapter speculates as to why relativism was so enthusiastically, almost unthinkingly, embraced in the 1960s.

Chapter 5 discusses the three major post-relativistic philosophies of science. These include two kinds of historical empiricism, that of Lakatos and the version of Laudan. Although both versions of historical empiricism are shown to have merit, both versions are shown to be plagued with fatal flaws. Chapter 5 then introduces the philosophy of scientific realism and shows how it can accommodate the success of science.

Chapter 6 begins the specific analyses of controversies in the philosophy debates in marketing. First, the chapter evaluates the "nature of science" controversy. It is shown that, despite marketing's relativists not wishing to embrace nihilistic conclusions regarding science, their premises *imply* nihilism. The chapter then discusses "weak-form" relativism and shows how it, also, fails the test of reason. Chapter 6 then turns to the positivism versus qualitative methods controversy. Positivism is shown not to be the same thing as quantitative methods. Likewise, positivist research is shown not to imply the search for causal explanations, not to be guided by the machine metaphor, not to have a realist view with respect to scientific theories, not to be guilty of reification, and not to be functionalist in its view of explanations. The chapter concludes that marketing is not dominated by either logical positivism or logical empiricism. Therefore, the "positivism versus qualitative methods" controversy has been muddled, at least in part, because the controversy has a demonstrably false, initial premise.

Chapter 7 evaluates the controversy regarding truth in marketing theory and research. First, the chapter discusses the nature of truth, and how scientific realism maintains that truth is (1) not an entity, (2) not known with certainty, and (3) not equal to pragmatic success. The chapter then introduces the concept of relativistic truth, and evaluates the various relativist arguments maintaining that marketing should abandon the goal of truth in theory and research. It is found that those who argue against truth, among other things, commit the philosophers' fallacy. After discussing the concept of relativistic reality, the chapter concludes that *trust* provides a major reason for maintaining the pursuit of truth as a major objective of marketing theory and research.

Chapter 8 evaluates the controversy over objectivity in marketing research. First, after discussing the nature of objectivity, the concept of objectivity is distinguished from objectivism. Then, the issue of whether the social sciences are inherently subjective is analyzed. After discussing the historical relativist view of objectivity, five different relativist arguments against objectivity are reviewed and analyzed. The results show that there is no reason to believe that objective marketing research is not possible. Finally, the positive case for objectivity in marketing research is put forth, and, like the case for truth as a goal, the positive case for objectivity focuses on the importance of trust.

Chapter 9 extends the discussion of scientific realism begun in Chapter 5. The chapter argues that realism merits marketing's consideration as a foundation for marketing theory and research. Four fundamental tenets of scientific realism are developed, and the implications of scientific realism for physics, biology, marketing, and the social sciences are discussed. After examining two versions of critical realism, the chapter concludes with the development of a realist theory of empirical testing. This theory, it is argued, has important implications for marketing and social science.

The controversies in marketing theory await. Let's get started.

NOTE

1. For a brief introduction to the history of the philosophy debates in marketing, see Hunt (2001).

2 NATURAL PHILOSOPHY AND THE RISE OF SCIENCE: FROM PLATO TO HEGEL

The need for justifying rationality arises out of the context of a longstanding conflict between faith and reason. Some defenders of faith contend that in the last analysis no belief or action can be rationally justified. They argue that the standards upon which the supposed justifications rest do, themselves, need justification. But this justification cannot be provided because the processes of justifying one standard by another must lead either to infinite regress, or to nonrational commitment to some standard. Opposed to this is the view to be defended here: that the rational justification of beliefs and actions is possible.

If it were true that nothing could be justified by reason, then all honestly held convictions would have an equal claim upon general acceptance, and argument would, indeed, be replaced by "passionate intensity." This would be a dangerous and undesirable situation, for the inevitable conflicts could then be settled only by force. The civilizing restraint of debate and criticism would disappear. If rationality is abandoned, then either "anarchy is loosed upon the world," or dogmatism supported by brute force would prevail.

—John Kekes (1976)

This chapter traces the history of the philosophy of science and the scientific method from its origins in ancient Greece, with Platonism, to the triumph of German idealism in the latter part of the nineteenth century. Figure 1.1 in the previous chapter shows the various "isms" to be discussed. As we shall see, philosophy and science were "one" throughout most of this 2,500-year period. Furthermore, we shall see that many of the current debates in marketing and the social sciences were argued (perhaps better) in Plato's time. Thus, we begin with Platonism.

2.1 PLATONISM

Any history of the philosophy of science (at least, Western philosophy of science) must begin with the ancient Greeks.[1] Indeed, the very word "philosophy" comes from the two Greek words *philo*, meaning "love," and *sophia*, meaning "wisdom." Therefore, the term "philosophy" has its origins in the "love of wisdom." However, *sophia* in ancient Greek had a slightly different meaning than the English "wisdom." *Sophia*, when combined with *philo*, actually connoted something closer to the "love of intellectual curiosity" than to the love of wisdom in the sense of "sage" philosophy (see section 2.1.2).

2.1.1 Pythagoras

Although Thales of Miletus, founder of the Ionian school of philosophy in about 580 B.C., is often referred to as the "father of philosophy," little is known about him. Therefore, our study begins with Pythagoras (570–520 B.C.), who was the first scholar to actually refer to himself as a "philosopher" (Guthrie 1962). Much of what we know about Pythagoras comes from Plato. We know that Pythagoras founded a school of scholars in southern Italy that required all members to take vows of secrecy. The school taught its members to spurn such things as fame and worldly possessions and to focus, instead, on seeking "truth by contemplation."

The Pythagoreans made significant contributions to the development of mathematics. In fact, they believed that numerals had an almost mystical significance and were the keys to understanding the universe. Even today, when one speaks of a philosopher as having a "Pythagorean orientation," one implies that the person believes there is a "mathematical harmony" present in nature. Thus, the sixteenth-century astronomer Kepler believed that God had created the solar system in a regular mathematical pattern, and Kepler explained the internal radii of each of the six planets (known at that time) by showing that within each planet just one of the five "regular" solids would fit. For example, a regular cube fits within the sphere of Saturn, a tetrahedron within Jupiter, a dodecahedron within Mars, and so on in a "nest" (Losee 1980, p. 46). To the Pythagoreans, experience and observation played an inconsequential role in inquiry.

2.1.2 Plato

The philosophy of Plato (427–347 B.C.) was very consistent with that of Pythagoras. The historian, John Losee, notes that "Plato described the creation of the universe by a benevolent Demiurge, who impressed a mathematical pattern upon a formless primordial matter" (Losee 1980, p. 18). Plato's significance to Western philosophy cannot be overemphasized. Plato defined knowledge as "justified true belief," and, for him, the method of "truth by contemplation" (in the manner of Pythagoras) fell far short of the goal. Rather, true philosophical wisdom, according to Plato, must pass the "test of critical discussion." That is, truth will reveal itself through the Socratic method of vigorously critical questions, followed by equally thoughtful answers (the Socratic dialogues). In Plato's Greece, these dialogues or debates had formal rules governing permissible conduct for both questioner and answerer. Furthermore, critical discussion through the Socratic method was to be conducted for the purpose of the pursuit of truth, in contrast to the Sophists who, Plato claimed, were interested solely in the pursuit of victory in argument.

In essence, Plato's views on the nature of philosophy (the pursuit of truth) and its method (critical discussion) have dominated the Western philosophical world for over 2,000 years. As Popper noted in his classic work, *The Logic of Scientific Discovery*, "there is a method which might be described as 'the one method of philosophy' . . . *rational discussion* . . . stating one's problem clearly and examining its various proposed solutions *critically*" (1959, p. 16; italics in original).

Recall that the meaning of *sophia* in ancient Greek was closer to "intellectual curiosity" than to the English "wisdom." It is worth noting that Eastern philosophy, instead of adopting a critical discussion method, developed along "sage" lines (Ben-David 1984). In sage philosophy, true knowledge is to be obtained by studying and interpreting the pronouncements of the master, or *sage*. If there is to be critical discussion in sage philosophy, it is on how to most appropriately interpret the truths of the master. Sage philosophy, by its very nature, cannot be cumulative or progressive, because the knowledge of the student cannot go beyond that of the master. Also, it has the distressing tendency to deteriorate into cultism or mysticism. The dominance of truth-through-critical-discussion in Western philosophy, in contrast to the dominance of sage philosophy in the East, is one reason why science became institutionalized in seventeenth-century Europe, rather than in countries such as China and Russia (Ben-David 1984, p. 28). We shall return to the subject of the institutionalization of science in seventeenth-century Europe in section 2.2.

Plato's philosophical inquiry focused on issues such as the nature of justice, human pleasure, values, politics, and ethics. He did not delve into topics that would normally be included today within the natural or physical sciences. Nevertheless, one of his most controversial theories, the "theory of forms," has implications for science. Enamored with the abstract nature of mathematics and numerals, Plato theorized that there was an independent realm of "forms" (abstract ideas or essences) that had a real existence outside space and time. These forms, he theorized, had an ultimate reality indepen-dent from being perceived by any human mind. The objects that we perceive through our senses are just imperfect copies of these ultimate forms. For ex-ample, there is an ultimate form called "man" that exists in some autonomous realm. Individual men in the perceived world are simply imperfect copies of this ultimate form. Given that knowledge is *justified true belief* and that ob-jects in the external world are only imperfect copies of these perfect forms, *genuine* knowledge was possible only about Plato's idealized forms and not about the existing world revealed to our senses. Today, we may note, the mod-ern relativist/constructionist view claims that scientists "construct" the ideal-ized reality they seek to explain (Peter and Olson 1983; Olson 1987; Lincoln and Guba 1985). Because Plato's idealized forms were independent of the human mind, his theory was very different from the modern relativist/ constructivist view, but both share the common element called "idealism" (see section 2.4).

2.1.3 Socrates on Relativism

The position that truth could be gleaned from critical discussion earned Plato the enmity of the Sophists, who had a relativist conception of truth that differs very little from the versions of modern-day relativists. Protagoras of Abdera was a Sophist who earned his livelihood by going from city to city in the Greek world offering instruction to the young on rhetoric and politics. In *Theaetetus*, Plato presents a dialogue between Protagoras and Socrates that analyzes and evaluates the notion of "relativist truth" that Protagoras put for-ward. According to the dialogue, Protagoras held that:

> Man is the measure of all things . . . [and that any given thing] is to me such as it appears to me, and is to you such as it appears to you . . . [Then] each one of us is a measure of what is and what is not . . . to the sick man his food appears sour and is so; to the healthy man it is and appears the opposite. Now there is no call to repre-sent either of the two as wiser—that cannot be—nor is the sick man to be pro-nounced unwise because he thinks as he does, or the healthy man wise because he thinks differently . . . in this way it is true . . . that no one thinks falsely. (Hamilton and Cairns 1961, pp. 152a, 160c, 166d, 167d, and 170a)

Following the analysis of Siegel, the relativism proposed by Protagoras "denies the existence of any standard or criterion higher than the individual by which claims to truth and knowledge can be adjudicated," because "knowl-edge and truth are relative to the person contemplating the proposition in question" (Siegel 1986, p. 226). For Protagoras a proposition is true if it seems so to the observer; and false if it seems so to the observer, and "that is the end of that." Socrates attacks relativism through several arguments, including:

> If what every man believes as a result of perception is indeed to be true for him; if, just as no one is a better judge of what another experiences, so no one is better entitled to consider whether what another thinks is true or false, and . . . every man is to have his own beliefs for himself alone and they are all right and true—then . . . where is the wisdom of Protagoras, to justify his setting up to teach others and to be handsomely paid for it, and where is our comparative ignorance or the need for us to go and sit at his feet, when each of us is himself the measure of his own wisdom? . . . To set about overhauling and testing one another's notions and opinions when those of each and every one are right, is a tedious and monstrous display of folly, if the Truth of Protagoras is really truthful. (Hamilton and Cairns 1961, p. 162a)

Thus, Socrates contends that Protagorean relativism is self-defeating, making it incoherent (the various claims are inconsistent). Siegel (1986, p. 226) paraphrases the argument of Socrates in the following succinct fashion:

1. Protagoras claims to show his students how to assess the warrant and justification of knowledge-claims ("overhauling and testing one another's notions and opinions").
2. The thesis of Protagoras (that "man is the measure of all things") undermines the task Protagoras sets out to do since, if his thesis is correct, no proposition can ever be judged unjustified or unwarranted.
3. Consequently, if knowledge is relative, then it is useless to ever engage in the task that Protagoras is engaging in ("overhauling and testing one another's notions and opinions").
4. Therefore, "if Protagoras' thesis is right, it cannot be right, for it undermines the very notion of rightness."

Although Plato may have thought that the various arguments in *Theaetetus* destroyed conclusively the doctrine of relativist truth, in hindsight we know that such was not to be the case. Nevertheless, Siegel (1986) and other writers maintain that the arguments of Socrates are as powerful and definitive now as they were in the time of Plato. For example, Vallicella (1984, p. 462), following Socrates, notes that a "consistent relativist, on pain of contradiction, must hold that the thesis of relativism is itself only relatively true." That is, a consistent relativist cannot hold that *it is absolutely true* that "all truths are relative (to social classes, historical epochs, whatever)." Therefore, a consistent relativist must hold that "it is *relatively true* that all truths are relative." But what does it mean to say that "it is relatively true that all truths are relative"? Such a statement is highly ambiguous and quickly degenerates into incoherent assertions like "it is true that for everyone (for every class, epoch, group) that all truths are relative" or that "*it is only true for relativists* that all truths are relative." Vallicella closes his analysis with "we must conclude, then, that relativized relativism is just as incoherent as absolute relativism" (1984, p. 463).

As an aside, analysts of *ethical* relativism have also questioned whether a coherent (i.e., not self-refuting) version of *it* is possible. Lyons analyzes the various forms of ethical relativism and concludes: "The only clear reason that we seem to have for resorting to relativistic analyses of moral judgments is that this will save the vulnerable forms of relativism from the scrap heaps of incoherence. As I suggested earlier, a theory that avoids incoherence by arbitrary modifications, that lacks independent theoretical justification, cannot command our respect" (Lyons 1982, p. 224). (See section 4.1.1 for more on moral relativism.)

2.1.4   Aristotle

Plato's greatest student was undoubtedly Aristotle (384–322 B.C.). Whereas Plato restricted the study of philosophy to a narrow range of topics, Aristotle expanded philosophical inquiry into the study of virtually everything. He studied and wrote not only on topics such as ethics, politics, rhetoric, and metaphysics, but also on areas such as astronomy, physics, zoology, psychology, and the formal nature of logic (Ben-David 1984). Thus, Aristotle added the study of all the elements of *natural philosophy* to the traditional subjects of moral philosophy, political philosophy, and metaphysics. Stated differently, Aristotle expanded philosophy to include what we now call *science*. In fact, the English word "science" was coined in the latter half of the nineteenth century. Prior to that time the closest English word to "scientist" was "natural philosopher" (Ben-David 1984 , p. xii).

Aristotle disagreed vigorously with Plato's theory of forms. In today's terms, Aristotle was both an *empiricist* and a *realist*. Plato's extreme distrust of any claims to knowledge stemming from sense-perceptions (observations) led him to postulate the existence of an independent, autonomous realm of objectively perfect "forms." Not only did this autonomous realm include perfect forms such as "man" and "tree," but also, perfect forms such as "good" and "beauty." The nature of these transcendent forms could not be grasped by observation, but only by the power of intellectual intuition.

Aristotle argued that Plato had committed the logical error of treating the *property* of an object as the object itself. That is, the fact that it is meaningful to claim that a woman is *beautiful* (an attribute of a woman) is logically different from claiming that "beauty" has an existence independent of the object (the woman). Thus, Aristotle adopted a form of *realism*, proposing that the outside world consists only of individual objects, such as women (who may have the attribute "beauty") and trees, and not the idealized perfect forms of "woman" and "tree." It is easy to see how Aristotle's rejection of Plato's theory of forms was a necessary prerequisite for his empirical work in natural philosophy, because that work was heavily observation-based.

Aristotle not only *did* science, he was also the first *philosopher* of science. As Losee (1980, p. 6) notes, Aristotle "created the discipline [of the philosophy of science] by analyzing certain problems that arise in connection with scientific explanation." In fact, much of Aristotle's philosophy of science survives to this day in one form or another. First, Aristotle is usually credited with developing what is now referred to as "syllogistic" logic. He proposed that science *begins* with observations in the real world, progresses through inductive processes to explanatory principles, and then uses these explanatory general principles to deduce (syllogistically) observations. These views presaged by almost 2,000 years those of Sir Francis Bacon.

Aristotle also analyzed the nature of scientific explanations and mathematics. He proposed that satisfactory explanations must be developed in syllogistic form, with *true* general premises, deductive logic, and conclusions. Thus, the deductive-nomological model of scientific explanation developed by Hempel has its origins in Aristotle (Laudan 1968, p. 12). Aristotle also recognized that there was something different fundamentally between mathematics and empirical science. In today's terms, he was interested in a *demarcation* issue. Aristotle maintained that, whereas the subject matter of empirical science changes in character through time, the subject matter of mathematics is "that which is unchanging" (Losee 1980, p. 12). The changing/unchanging demarcation of Aristotle bears a striking similarity to today's analytic/synthetic distinction between mathematics and empirical science.

Most important, Aristotle merged Plato's method of knowledge-through-critical-discussion with the empiricist method of careful observation. However, Aristotle's method of inquiry did not include the testing of hypotheses through experimentation. He was an observer of nature, not an intervener or experimenter. As Durant (1954, p. 71) puts it: "It is again the absence of experiment and fruitful hypothesis that leaves Aristotle's natural science a mass of undigested observations." Nevertheless, many claim that Aristotle's works remain:

> [T]he most marvelous and influential system of thought put together by a single mind. It may be doubted if any other thinker has contributed so much to the enlightenment of the world. Every later age has drawn upon Aristotle, and stood upon his shoulders to see the truth. (Durant 1954, p. 72)

2.1.5   Philosophy After Aristotle

After the death of Aristotle in 322 B.C., Greek philosophy was heavily influenced by several strains of cultism and mysticism. For example, the Phoenician merchant Zeno introduced Stoic philosophy into Athens about 310 B.C. Unlike the optimistic philosophy of Aristotle, Stoicism emphasized the apathetic acceptance of defeat. The study in Greece of subjects such as natural philosophy and the philosophy of science virtually disappeared. Nor did the situation improve with the subjugation of Greece by Rome in 146 B.C. As Durant puts it so eloquently:

> The glory that had been Greece faded now in the dawn of the Roman sun; and the grandeur that was Rome was the pomp of power rather than the light of thought. Then that grandeur decayed, that little light went almost out. For a thousand years darkness brooded over the face of Europe. All the world awaited the resurrection of philosophy. (Durant 1954, p. 74)

The reawakening of philosophy in Western civilization began within the Roman Catholic Church. Over a period of several hundred years, the wealth and power of the Church had been growing steadily. In fact, it was the single unifying institution in Europe, and by the thirteenth century owned approximately one third of the landmass of Europe (Durant 1954, p. 79). Returning from the Middle East, the Church's crusaders brought back copies of Aristotle's works in Latin, Greek, Arabic, and Hebrew. At first, the Church resisted Aristotle's philosophy and forbade its teachers to lecture on his works. However, primarily through the efforts of Thomas Aquinas, the works of Aristotle were absorbed gradually into official Church teaching. As a result, "by 1260 A.D. he was *de rigueur* in every Christian school, and Ecclesiastical assemblies penalized deviations from his views" (Durant 1954, p. 73).

Alas, the Church had turned Aristotle into the Western equivalent of an Eastern sage. Now, knowledge about the world was not to be had through methods of Platonian critical discussion or Aristotelian observation. Rather, truth about the world was to be found through properly interpreting the works of Aristotle. (Thirteenth-century scholars are known to have consulted Aristotle's writings to determine whether oil would congeal if left out in the cold at night.) The pursuit of knowledge degenerated into scholastic interpretation. Though the Church had revived philosophy, the revival of the philosophy of science awaited the scientific revolution that occurred in seventeenth-century Europe. We turn now to the nature of this revolution and its causes.

2.2   THE RISE OF MODERN SCIENCE

The period beginning in approximately A.D. 1550 and stretching through A.D. 1700 encompasses the rise of modern science. In fact, the achievements of science were so spectacular and their impact on society so great that the label "scientific revolution" aptly applies. Butterfield (1958, p. vii) claims that the Scientific Revolution "outshines everything since the rise of Christianity and reduces the Renaissance and the Reformation to the rank of mere episodes, mere internal displacements, within the system of Medieval Christendom."

Consider the enormous achievements during the span of only 150 years: Kepler (1571–1630) developed his laws of planetary motion (among them, that the orbits of the planets around the sun are elliptical); Gilbert (1544–1603) did his pioneering work in the areas of magnetism and electricity; Vesalius (1514–1564) expanded the frontiers of knowledge in anatomy; Harvey (1578–1657) discovered and demonstrated that blood circulates throughout the human body; Boyle (1627–1691) experimented on gases, showing that the pressure of a gas and its volume are inversely related (i.e., Boyle's laws); Galileo (1564–1642) experimented with falling bodies, demonstrating the "law of descent" (i.e., the distance that a body falls is directly proportional to the square of the time of its descent); finally, and most important, Newton (1642–1727) developed his laws with respect to the motions of all physical objects and published them in *Principia* in 1687. *Principia* provided a theoretical framework for synthesizing the works of Kepler, Galileo, and others. In Newton's laws, scientists believed for over 200 years that they had discovered genuine *episteme* (proven knowledge or knowledge with certainty), similar to the certainty previously provided by the authority of the Church.

The rise of modern science in Europe in the seventeenth-century has been well studied. One of the most authoritative works on the subject was written by Ben-David (originally published in 1971 and revised in 1984). Ben-David explores the lack of continuous scientific growth throughout the world before seventeenth-century Europe:

> Rapid accumulation of knowledge, which has characterized the development of science since the 17th century, had never occurred before that time. The new kind of scientific activity emerged only in a few countries of Western Europe, and it was restricted to that small area for about two hundred years. (Since the 19th century, scientific knowledge has been assimilated by the rest of the world.) This assimilation has not occurred through the incorporation of science into the cultures and institutions of the different societies. Instead it has occurred through the diffusion of the patterns of scientific activity and scientific roles from Western Europe to the other parts of the world. (Ben-David 1984, p. 21)

Four features characterize the rise of modern science in the seventeenth-century. First, there was a *rapid growth* in knowledge. The rapidity in the growth of knowledge justifies calling it a "revolutionary," rather than an "evolutionary" phenomenon. Second, the rapid growth in knowledge occurred across many different areas, including medicine, biology, anatomy, electricity, mechanics, and astronomy. Third, rather than natural philosophers (scientists) "starting from scratch" and building free-standing, complete philosophical systems, they took the works of other philosophers and built upon them. The *cumulative* nature of their work was (in today's terms) both verificationist and falsificationist. The work of Galileo built upon the efforts of Kepler and Copernicus (verificationist), and *refuted* the work of Ptolemy (falsificationist). Similarly, the work of Newton built upon Galileo, and the discoveries of Vesalius in anatomy refuted the official Church position of Galen (A.D. 129–200). (The Church endorsed the Galenic view that the heart, brain, and liver have their own *independent* systems of arteries, nerves, and veins.)

The fourth feature characterizing the rise of modern science was its *method*. The "new philosophy" rejected emphatically the position that knowledge was to be restricted to the proper interpretation of the ancient canonical trio of Aristotle, Ptolemy, and Galen. First, the new philosophy brought back the knowledge-through-critical-discussion criterion of Plato. Second, the new philosophy retained the strong emphasis on logic and observation, as expounded by Aristotle. Third, it resurrected the notion from Pythagoras that much of the external world can be expressed in terms of mathematical relationships. To the methods of Plato, Aristotle, and Pythagoras, the method of the new philosophy added a new and key component: the belief in experimentation. Not only was the knowledge generated by the new philosopher-scientist to be logical, consistent with observation, and capable of passing the tests of critical discussion, but also the truth-content of the knowledge should be capable of empirical testing through experimentation, as emphasized by Galileo.

The importance of adding experimentation to the natural philosopher's methodological "tool kit" in the seventeenth-century cannot be overestimated. Experimentation plays a significant role both in the discovery of hypotheses about the world and in their justification. For example, Galileo's experiment leading to the law of descent has been described as one of the twenty "great scientific experiments" that changed our world (Harré 1984). Galileo used a polished bronze ball rolling down a groove in an inclined wooden beam to determine that the distance a freely moving object would travel would be directly proportional to the square of the duration of time. (Interestingly, one of Galileo's "clocks" was his pulse rate.) Historians differ as to whether Galileo's experiment was only a test of his hypothesis (justification) or whether he actually derived his "time-squared" hypothesis from observing balls rolling down inclined planes (discovery). Galileo's own working notes suggest that he conducted numerous (over 100) experiments with balls rolling down inclined planes. He used some of them to generate inductively the "time-squared" relationship, and other experiments to demonstrate and test it (Harré 1984, p. 78).

The preceding paragraphs on the rise of modern science adopt a rationalist perspective that there has been a *genuine* accumulation of knowledge as a result of the rise of modern science. The opposite position, or irrationalism, claims the contrary. For example, Stove reviews the works of those he calls the "modern irrationalists," including Kuhn and Feyerabend, and notes:

> Much more is known now than was known fifty years ago, and much more was known then than in 1580. So there has been a great accumulation or growth of knowledge in the last four hundred years. This is an extremely well-known fact, which I will refer to as (A) . . . . So a writer whose position inclined him to deny (A), or even made him at all reluctant to admit it, would almost inevitably seem, to the philosophers who read him, to be maintaining something extremely implausible. . . . Everyone would admit that if there has *ever* been a growth of knowledge it has been in the last four hundred years, so anyone reluctant to admit (A) must, if he is consistent, be reluctant to admit that there has ever been a growth of knowledge at all. But if a philosopher of science takes a position which obliges him, on pain of inconsistency, to be reluctant to admit *this*, then his position can be rightly described as irrationalism. (Stove 1982, pp. 3, 4)

Stove (1982) goes on to explore the literary devices that modern irrationalists use to seduce even highly trained philosophers (not to mention unwary, casual readers) into the relativistic thesis that our knowledge of the external world has not truly progressed in the past 400 years. The subjects of irrationalism, relativism, and scientific progress will be examined in detail in Chapters 4 and 5. For now, we need to explore the rather formidable barriers in the seventeenth-century that inhibited the development of modern science.

2.2.1   Opposition to the Rise of Science

Four institutions and societal groupings fought vigorously the development of modern science: organized religion, the universities, mechanicians (engineers), and the speculative metaphysicians. Each will be discussed, in turn.

The antipathy of organized religion toward the development of modern science is well documented and has been much discussed. The rise of modern science, with its claims to produce knowledge about the external world through critical discussion, observation, logic, and experimentation, challenged the authority of the Roman Catholic Church over temporal things. By challenging the authority of the Church concerning sources of knowledge about how the world "works," science threatened to weaken the Church's power as the dominant institution in Europe.

The most celebrated case of the religious suppression of science was, of course, the silencing of Galileo in 1633. In his *Dialogue Concerning the Two Chief World Systems*, Galileo compared the relative merits of the Copernican universe (with the planets revolving around the Sun) and the Ptolemaic system (with the Sun revolving around the Earth). Galileo's book was harshly critical of the Church-approved Ptolemaic system, and, consequently, the Inquisition found him guilty of heresy. He spent the last nine years of his life under house arrest (which was a rather lenient sentence, because he could, like countless others, have been burned at the stake). Only in 1820 did the Church admit that Copernicus was right (Worrell and Currie 1978, p. 6). And only in the latter part of the twentieth century did the Church begin to admit that it may have made a mistake in silencing Galileo. In 1980, Pope John Paul II commissioned a panel of scholars to reexamine the evidence and verdict. In 1992, the Church admitted that it had erred, and it formally rehabilitated Galileo.

Many current writers forget that the uneasy truce between science and religion is primarily a product of the twentieth century. Not only have religious leaders distrusted science, but, as recently as 1874, the Catholic University in Ireland refused to allow the physical sciences to be taught at all (Gieryn 1983, p. 784). Similarly, in the late 1800s, it was still the practice of the prime minister of England, when facing a national crisis such as a cholera epidemic or a cattle plague, to seek primarily the assistance of Anglican Church leaders, rather than science. The Church leaders would then call for a "national day of prayer" to ask for divine intervention to solve the crisis. Such practices prompted the superintendent of the Royal Institution (of science) in London to challenge Church leaders to conduct a "prayer gauge" experiment (Gieryn 1983). The proposed experiment involved selecting a hospital that would be the focus of national prayer, and comparing the mortality rate before and after the day of supplication. Although the experiment was never conducted, the fact that the challenge caused such an uproar illustrates the high tension and distrust between the religious and scientific communities that existed as recently as the latter half of the nineteenth century (Gieryn 1983).

The universities in the seventeenth-century constituted a second institution openly hostile to the development of modern science. Formal universities emerged in Europe in the thirteenth century, with the University of Paris (about 1210) and Oxford University (in 1284). One obvious reason for their hostility to science was that almost all universities were sectarian in nature. For example, it was not until 1870 that a non-Anglican could study at either Oxford or Cambridge (Brubacher and Rudy 1958).

Although natural philosophy was taught in the universities, the curriculum was oriented primarily toward the humanities and the professions of law, politics, and medicine. Further, the dominant method of inquiry was Scholasticism; that is, knowledge was to be found through the proper interpretation of the writings of others, primarily the ancient Greeks. In fact, the modern notion of the university professor as a scholar engaging in original research that creates new knowledge is of very recent origin. The first universities to emphasize science and research were those in Germany in the early part of the nineteenth century, with the University of Berlin in 1810 being the forerunner. Only much later was the concept of the professor-as-researcher accepted in England. It was not until 1917 that Oxford University granted its first Ph.D. (Brubacher and Rudy 1958).

The Scholasticism of the Middle Ages survives today in the form of "hermeneutics." Hermeneutics in the nineteenth century focused on the interpretation of holy and sacred writings, with the intent of finding their *real* meaning. However, in the twentieth century, following the works of Heidegger, proponents of hermeneutics expanded its scope to include the interpretation of all literary works. Furthermore, they have, in the main, abandoned the belief that there is any such thing as the real meaning of a text. Rather, they now emphasize the "meaning for the subject" (Palmer 1969).

Although the universities were openly hostile to the development of science and refused to disseminate the knowledge that science generated, this does not imply that they had no positive impact. On the contrary, most of the natural philosophers who engaged in empirical science in the seventeenth-century were university trained. The university training in logic and mathematics was definitely beneficial to the seventeenth-century natural philosophers. Not surprisingly, Hall (1959, p. 5) analyzed the backgrounds of those who were members of England's Royal Society (of science) in 1663 and found that 57 percent definitely had attended a university, and another 30 percent had probably done so.

The mechanicians (engineers) also resisted the development of science (Ben-David 1984, p. 26). The mechanicians were non–university-educated people who saw little relationship between the explorations of science and their own practical problems of building bridges, constructing buildings, and designing machinery. Many doubted that science would ever contribute anything to practical technology (Gieryn 1983, p. 785). Even by the time of the Industrial Revolution in eighteenth century England, the link between science and technology had not yet been firmly established, which led one prominent engineer to conclude: The scientist's "deep thinking [is] quite out of place in a world of railroads and steamboats, printing presses and spinning-jennies" (Houghton 1957, p. 114). (Of course, the debate over "theory" and "practical research" continues today in marketing; the reader should note the parallels.)

The speculative metaphysicians of the seventeenth-century also resisted the development of science (Ravetz 1971, p. 18). The speculative metaphysicians sought to develop comprehensive philosophies through reasoning alone, unaided by observation, measurement, or experiment. The hostility of metaphysicians toward empirical science continues to this day, influenced largely by Hegel (1770–1831), whose works will be examined later (see section 2.4.3).

The question "Why did science develop in Western Europe in the seventeenth-century and not elsewhere"? is often asked. Ben-David (1984) proposes that the question is ill-formed. Recalling the powerful institutions that opposed vigorously the development of science, he notes that these institutions would exist in *all* societies, and they would probably have similar animosities toward science. He notes that religious institutions provided purpose and meaning to people's lives, and, therefore, were *needed*. Mechanicians provided buildings, roads, and machines; all *needed*. Metaphysicians provided grand philosophies of the universe to all who required grandiose explanations of the world. Magicians and astrologers provided wonderment and sweeping prophesy. Universities provided training for physicians, lawyers, and ministers. Against the backdrop of these groups and institutions, the activities, methods, and objectives of seventeenth-century science must have seemed pale, indeed. In short, empirical science was, simply, not needed. The properly formed question, Ben-David suggests, is not "Why didn't science develop in places other than 17th century Europe"? Rather, he insists, "What needs explanation is the fact that science ever emerged [anywhere] at all" (Ben-David 1984, p. 31).

But we know that science *did* successfully take root in seventeenth-century Europe. The scientific revolution *did* succeed. Those institutions and groups that resisted the rise of modern science *were* unsuccessful. Why?

2.2.2   Factors Contributing to the Rise of Science

Several factors combine to explain the almost miraculous success of the scientific revolution. Chronologically, the first factor is the Renaissance. The Renaissance is a label usually applied to the period 1350–1600 when there was in Europe a rebirth of interest in art, literature, and learning. Furthermore, there was a dramatic increase in general economic activity and in trade with the East. Through this interaction, the East played a critical role in the development of science in the West. Trading ships brought back not only Eastern goods, but also copies of ancient manuscripts. In particular, Renaissance scholars rediscovered the works of Plato, and, through him, Pythagoras. From reading Plato, Renaissance scholars reintroduced the concept that knowledge could be gained by means of critical discussion, rather than *only* from authority. Stimulated by Pythagoras, Renaissance scholars made significant achievements in the development of both pure and applied mathematics. For example, it was during this period of time that the concept of the "equals sign" in mathematics was formally developed.

The European traders also brought back cheap paper from Egypt, which, when combined with the development of printing presses, made books no longer the sole province of monks in monasteries. In fact, numerous technological achievements both contributed to, and were absolutely necessary for, the rise of modern science. The achievements of Galileo would have been impossible without the invention of the telescope in the early seventeenth century (Russell 1945, p. 535). Similarly, the invention of the microscope in the latter part of the seventeenth century was a necessary precursor for the study of microbiology.

In addition to (1) the Renaissance, (2) contacts with the East, and (3) the rise of technology, the Protestant Reformation gave significant impetus to the development of modern science. The Reformation did so by breaking the hegemony of the Roman Catholic Church over intellectual activity throughout Europe. Of the many Protestant sects, the beliefs of the Puritans were particularly hospitable to modern science. First, the Puritans believed in social welfare, or the good of the many, as an important *religious* objective. Furthermore, they believed that "the experimental study of Nature to be a most effective means of begetting in men a veneration for God" (Merton 1968, p. 232). Not surprisingly, many Puritans were prominent members of England's Royal Society (of science) in the seventeenth century (Merton 1968, p. 30).

However, not all Protestant sects were equally tolerant. In fact, many small, self-contained Protestant communities had no appreciable class of intellectuals except their clergymen, and, therefore, "would not tolerate anything approaching Heresy" (Ben-David 1984, p. 71). Fortunately, in most of Europe, Protestants were not able to effectively form closed religious communities, and, therefore, there was no single religious authority to enforce religious dogma. Moreover, Protestant leaders began to realize that the persecution of scientists (such as Galileo) by the Roman Catholic Church offered them excellent opportunities to gain converts: "As a result, official Protestant authorities on several occasions adopted policies of supporting science, and eventually in Commonwealth England they came very near to the acceptance of the scientistic utopia as a basis for their official educational policy" (Ben-David 1984, p. 71). Thus, one answer to the problem of science being "not needed" is that the Protestants needed science in their struggle with the Roman Catholic Church.

Another answer to the "not needed" problem can be found in the political and social structures of seventeenth-century Europe. At that time, there were numerous groups throughout Europe seeking to change European political and social structures by making them more pluralistic, open, and future-oriented. These groups became benefactors and supporters of science because, Ben-David (1984, p. 170) suggests, they needed science to provide a "cognitive structure consistent with their interests." That is, they viewed the scientist as:

a person studying nature rather than the ways of God and man, and using as his intellectual tools, mathematics, measurements and experiment, instead of relying on the interpretation of authoritative sources, speculation, or inspiration. He was a person viewing the state of knowledge in his time as something to be constantly improved on in the future rather than something to be brought up to the standards of a golden age in the past. (Ben-David 1984, p. 170)

So the Renaissance gave science Plato's method of critical discussion and improvements in mathematics. The rise of technology gave science instruments with which to conduct experiments. The Protestant Reformation needed science, as did those who wanted to change the political and social structures of Europe. In addition, the specific behaviors and activities of the practitioners and proponents of the new philosophy also contributed to the successful rise of modern science. Although the new philosophy was inherently concerned with *understanding* (theory) rather than *doing* (practice), many scientists attempted to demonstrate the science-technology link by working on problems having practical consequences. For example, Merton (1968) quantitatively analyzed the papers offered to England's Royal Society in the seventeenth century and found a preponderance of papers focusing on practical problems in mining, navigation, and warfare.

Scientists also attempted to assuage the fears of clerics by demonstrating that the knowledge gained through science was not necessarily antithetical to religion in general or to the existence of God in particular. Such efforts are unsurprising, because most natural philosophers in the seventeenth century were confirmed deists. For example, Newton's first law (a body will remain at rest unless acted upon by an outside force) denies that motion is *inherent* to matter. It, therefore, retains for God the role of "prime mover." In fact, standard attacks by Marxists on Newton, such as those by Hessen (in Werskey 1971) include the criticism that Newton "left room" for God.

The development of scientific academies also helped assure the success of the scientific revolution. Scientists formed England's Royal Society (of science) in 1660 and France's *Académie des Sciences* in 1666. With the inception of the academies, science now became institutionalized in the sense of having its own set of procedures and norms and in "the acceptance in a society of a certain activity as an important social function valued for its own sake" (Ben-David 1984, p. 75).

The most important factor favoring the success of the scientific revolution (though, most certainly, not *assuring* it) was the very power of the idea of the "scientific method" itself. The scientific method of combining critical discussion, logic, and mathematics with observation and experimentation was definitely an idea whose time had come. It has been referred to by many writers as "the most significant intellectual contribution of Western civilization"

(Morris 1955, p. 63). Natural philosophers in the seventeenth-century were truly inspired when they conjoined (1) the emphasis on logic and speculation implicit in Plato's method of critical discussion, (2) the powerful tool of mathematics, as proposed by Pythagoras, (3) the belief in systematic observation and syllogistic logic of Aristotle, and, very important, (4) the reliance on experimentation advocated by Galileo (and subsequently articulated by Sir Francis Bacon). As long as societies were mired in the morass of purely speculative philosophy, "sage" philosophy, and knowledge from interpreting authority, genuinely cumulative knowledge about the external world was unlikely.

Given the rise of the "new philosophy," with its emphasis on the development of knowledge through the scientific method, there was a need to articulate and explicate the characteristics of this method. That is, there was a need for the activity we refer to now as the philosophy of science. The first great debate over the fundamental nature of the scientific method was between two groups, one group called "empiricists," the other, "rationalists."

2.3   THE EMPIRICISM-RATIONALISM DEBATE

The empiricism-rationalism debate focused on the scientific method and the best procedures to ensure scientific progress. We shall use the term "classical empiricism" to identify a group of philosophers (most notably Bacon, Hume, Locke, and Mill) who believed that science should start from observations of the real world and inductively develop its generalizations, laws, and theories. The modifier "classical" is used to remind the reader that we are examining the specific beliefs of a specific philosophical movement. Although all current philosophers who refer to themselves as "empiricists" would hold observation and experience in high regard, few would completely embrace all the positions of the classical empiricists. All the classical empiricists shared the following fundamental tenet: *Experience and observation are the fundamental sources or "foundations" of our knowledge of the external world.*

Opposing the empiricists were the classical rationalists, as exemplified by Descartes, Spinoza, and Leibniz. The fundamental tenet of the classical rationalists was that *a priori reason alone is the fundamental source or "foundation" of our knowledge of the external world.* Again, the modifier "classical" is used to indicate that we are referring to a specific philosophical movement and to differentiate it from other forms of rationalism. Although there are numerous uses of the term "rationalism" (both in general philosophy and the philosophy of science), they all share the common concept of "reason." For example, the Age of Enlightenment, usually associated with certain developments in Europe in the eighteenth century, is often called the "Age of Reason." The rationalism of the Enlightenment implied a deep conviction that mankind, through human reasoning (contrasted with superstition, mysticism, and religious faith) could comprehend the nature of the world and that this comprehension would result in cumulative progress toward a better life for all. Therefore, the rationalism of the Enlightenment in the eighteenth century was a distinctly optimistic and uplifting philosophy that drew in part upon the success of science in the seventeenth century. What was necessary for mankind to progress, it was argued, was the release of the power of reason from the shackles of superstition, mysticism, and religious and political dogma.

As mentioned in section 2.2, Stove (1982, p. 4) notes that the works of Kuhn and Feyerabend necessarily imply an extreme form of "irrationalism." In doing so, Stove does *not* mean that Kuhn and Feyerabend are opposing what we are referring to here as "classical rationalism" (reason is the *primary* source of knowledge). Rather, Kuhn and Feyerabend are irrationalists to Stove and others because they believe that mankind's reasoning ability is incapable of gaining knowledge about the nature of the world. Irrationalism contends that reason (combined with anything) is incapable of producing genuine knowledge about the world at all, in the past, present, or future. It is in this sense that such standard reference books as the *Dictionary of the History of Science* use Kuhn and Feyerabend as typical examples of prominent irrationalists (Bynum et al. 1981, p. 360).

2.3.1   Classical Empiricism

Both the classical empiricists and the classical rationalists were sympathetic toward the development of science. Indeed, unlike today where most academic philosophers of science are not practitioners of science (Laudan 1981b, p. 7), *all* the classical empiricists and rationalists were *both* philosophers and practitioners. Although sharing a positive view toward science and its progress, the different fundamental tenets of the classical empiricists and rationalists led them along very different paths. We begin with the empiricists.

Sir Francis Bacon. Many scholars refer to Sir Francis Bacon (1561–1626) as England's first great philosopher. Left penniless at an early age by the death of his father, Bacon studied the law and earned a seat for himself in the House of Commons, after which he was knighted and became Lord Chancellor of England (Anderson 1948). Although Bacon (as a practitioner of science) made no great scientific discoveries, his literary skills made him a powerful advocate of both science and the scientific method. His most important work, *Novum Organum*, was published in 1620. In it, Bacon propounded his theory of "inductive ascent," which holds that science starts with observations and inductively proceeds (like bricks in a pile) in a steady, gradual process to general principles that would be known with the certainty of their foundations, that is, simple, direct observations. What is generally not recognized is that Bacon was firmly committed to the inductive-deductive scientific procedure advocated by Aristotle (Losee 1980, p. 62). That is, the *inductively* developed generalizations were to be tested through *deductively* generated hypotheses. Bacon bitterly opposed the Aristotelian scholasticism of his day, which used only deductive logic to properly interpret the truths of the "master," Aristotle. Bacon decried the fact that even when practitioners of Aristotelian science relied on observation, they did so in an entirely too casual fashion (generalizing too quickly and avoiding systematic experimentation). Bacon emphasized that the "first principles" from which useful deductions can be made should be arrived at through his "inductive ascent," rather than from Church authority.

Given Bacon's belief that experience and observation are the fundamental sources of knowledge of the external world, he devoted much of his writings on the scientific method to developing procedures for careful observation and experimentation. Primary among these procedures were his three Tables of Investigation. After amassing large quantities of observational and experimental data on a given phenomenon, Bacon suggested that the data be categorized in Tables of Affirmation, Negation, and Degrees. Basically, these three tables would reveal when one phenomenon was positively associated with another phenomenon (Affirmation), or negatively associated with the existence of another phenomenon (Negation), or changes in one phenomenon were associated with changes in another phenomenon (Degrees). To help investigators further analyze the Tables of Investigation, Bacon offered twenty-seven techniques for finding important relationships in the data. Of these "Prerogative Instances," the most important was the "Instance of the Fingerpost," to which he gave the label "crucial experiment." Such an experiment could be decisive, he argued, in choosing between two rival hypotheses.

Finally, to do good research, Bacon urged investigators to purge themselves of their own biases and prejudices about the phenomenon under investigation. He called these biases and prejudices "Idols" and urged investigators to rid themselves of Idols of the "Tribe," "Den," "Market Place," and "Theater." The Idols of the Theater earned for Bacon the enmity of philosophers, for these Idols included the metaphysical philosophical systems of his day, which, he contended, were like "stage plays" and did not give a true picture of the real nature of the world.

Consistent with the Enlightenment, Bacon sought to encourage scientists to work on projects that would lead to control over nature for the betterment of mankind and a higher quality of life. He likened the speculative metaphysicians to "spiders," spinning webs of marvelous ingenuity out of their own bodies, but having no contact with reality: "Bacon's hostility [toward the scholastics and metaphysicians] reflects *moral* outrage—Aristotle's philosophy not only had not led to new works to benefit mankind, but also had thwarted those few attempts that had been made" (Losee 1980, p. 68).

John Locke. Our second empiricist, John Locke (1632–1704), was an English physician and lecturer on philosophy at Oxford University. His primary contribution to the empiricism-rationalism debate came with the publication of his *Essay Concerning Human Understanding*, published in 1690. In it, Locke attacked vigorously the rationalist conception of "innate ideas." The rationalists argued that many of our concepts or ideas (both within and outside of science) are present at birth. Locke argued powerfully and persuasively the empiricist position that all ideas come from either "sensation" (the interaction of the senses with the environment) or "reflection" on sensations. Therefore, all knowledge of the external world must come from experience and observation, or reflection on the same. Not only did his *Essay* further the empiricist cause in science, but it also provided a major philosophical foundation for the Enlightenment of the eighteenth century. Locke's view that the human mind at birth is truly a *tabula rasa* on which experience is imprinted justifies the liberal view of the Enlightenment that the education of the young can improve society and the quality of life.

David Hume. David Hume (1711–1776), our third empiricist, was a Scottish philosopher who dropped out of Edinburgh University at the age of fifteen to devote full time to the pursuit of philosophy. His first major work, *A Treatise of Human Nature* (1739), was very poorly received and, therefore, he published a revised version in 1748 entitled *An Enquiry Concerning Human Understanding*. Whereas Bacon and Locke had analyzed science from the viewpoint of the coexistence of the properties of various phenomena, Hume extended the empiricist approach to the investigation of the *sequences* of phenomena through time. He also attacked the rationalist belief that science could produce "necessary truths" about the external world.

Hume divided all knowledge statements into two, mutually exclusive, categories: "relations of ideas" and "matters of fact." Consistent with Locke (and contrary to the views of the rationalists), Hume claimed that "matters of fact" can be known only from sense impressions. On the other hand, some kinds of "relations of ideas" are "necessary truths" because they are "intuitively certain." For example, the axioms of Euclidean geometry were to Hume intuitively certain. Therefore, any theorems derived deductively from the axioms of Euclidean geometry were "necessary truths" because they were demonstrably certain by means of deductive logic.

Hume next proceeded to analyze the kinds of relations of ideas called "causal relations." He concluded that, unlike geometrical relations, causal relations cannot reach the status of "necessary truths," because they cannot be known with certainty. In other words, the observation that phenomenon *X* has always in the past been succeeded by phenomenon *Y* does not imply *deductively* that phenomenon *X* will always in the future be succeeded *necessarily* by phenomenon *Y*. Given that all our knowledge of the external world comes from sense impressions, there is no way to establish the "necessary connection" between the phenomena.

The preceding argument on necessary truths is usually referred to as "Humean skepticism," or in Laudan's (1981, p. 80) terms, the "plebeian problem of induction." Hume's argument was devastating to the rationalist position that science *could* produce and *did* produce certain knowledge through pure reason alone. However, to those who were content with science producing "highly probable" knowledge or "highly warranted" knowledge, Humean skepticism posed no insurmountable problem. Indeed, Hume himself summarily dismissed his own skepticism, believing that inferring causality inductively was essential for scientific knowledge and was justified by custom and habit:

> Custom, then, is the great guide of human life. It is that principle alone which renders our experience useful to us—without the influence of custom we should be entirely ignorant of every matter of fact beyond what is immediately present to the memory and senses. (Hume 1927, p. 45)

As we shall see later, although Hume saw no problem with Humean skepticism, many subsequent writers have either explicitly or implicitly adopted his skeptical position. Prominent among these adopters of skepticism have been Popper, Kuhn, and Feyerabend. (See sections 3.2.3, 3.3.4, and 3.6.2.)

John Stuart Mill. Our final empiricist, John Stuart Mill (1806–1873), authored *The System of Logic* (1843) and *Utilitarianism* (1863), and was probably the most influential philosopher (empiricist or otherwise) in the English-speaking world during the nineteenth century. All his writings were driven by a deep commitment to foster both scientific and social progress. The "intuitionism" of the classical rationalists, he held, inhibited the progress of science toward understanding the true nature of the world. Similarly, intuitionism in ethics, by inhibiting progress toward the liberal ideal of individual freedom and human happiness, should be replaced with his utilitarianism.

With respect to our sources of knowledge, Mill took empiricism to its logical extreme. Rejecting the Humean dichotomy of knowledge about "matters of fact" and "relations of ideas," Mill claimed that even the fundamental axioms of geometry were simply highly confirmed generalizations from experience (Laudan 1968, p. 31). (He did, however, recognize that the *theorems* of geometry were "necessary truths" by deductive logic.) Thus, all genuine knowledge in science comes from generalizing inductively from experience. Mill's justly famous "canons of induction" included the methods of agreement, difference, concomitant variation, residues, and the "joint method" of agreement and difference. Mill made the incredibly strong (and demonstrably incorrect) assertion that, historically, all the causal laws in science had been generated from the application of one or more of his methods. Of the five methods, Mill held the "method of difference" to be most important, claiming that only the method of difference could conclusively separate true causal laws from merely accidental regularities. Unfortunately, like his contemporaries, Mill constantly confused *discovery* with *verification*. Thus, he writes that *induction* is "the operation of *discovering* and *proving* general propositions" (Mill, as quoted in Laudan 1968, p. 33). (See Bagozzi [1979] for a discussion of the application of Mill's methods to marketing.)

But, if all the laws of science are to be generated inductively from experience, what is the *justification* for these inductive procedures? Mill's answer to Humean skepticism was to postulate a principle of universal causation, which provided that every phenomenon is preceded invariably and unconditionally by some particular set of antecedent circumstances. Recognizing that his principle of universal causation could be justifiably attacked as metaphysical speculation, Mill claimed that the principle could be empirically justified by "simply enumerating" the enormously large number of cases that affirmed his principle and the complete lack of contradictory instances.

2.3.2   Classical Rationalism

Both the classical empiricists and rationalists opposed scholasticism and were generally sympathetic toward the development of science. Nevertheless, whereas the empiricists criticized scholasticism for its lack of empirical foundations, the rationalists criticized the implausibility of the underlying laws or "first principles" of scholasticism. They believed that the knowledge-claims of empirical science could be made with the same degree of certainty as the claims of mathematics (which for them were indeed certain), if only science would but emulate Euclidian geometry and start with first principles whose truth-status was incontrovertible. Science would then contain "necessary truths" in the sense that the claims would be true in both this world and all possible worlds. That is, the nature of the world could be nothing other than the way science claims it to be.

René Descartes. The first great rationalist was the Frenchman René Descartes (1596–1650).[2] Although university trained in the law, his inherited wealth enabled him to spend a lifetime on philosophical inquiry. His pioneering works on theoretical mathematics lay the foundations for modern analytic geometry, and his most famous work was his 1641 *Meditations on First Philosophies* (often referred to as, simply, "Meditations").

Descartes's procedure for developing his "first principles" was the "method of doubt." He started by examining introspectively all the things that he thought to be true, and he then proceeded to eliminate systematically all beliefs about which he had any doubt. Finally, he was left with one, absolutely incontrovertible, undeniably true, belief: *cogito ergo sum* (I think, therefore I am). The fact that he was thinking *necessarily* implied that he existed, and he could not possibly be in error about his thinking because "to be in error" would necessarily imply that he was thinking. From *cogito ergo sum* Descartes attempted to derive deductively the existence of God. Maintaining that God was the "first cause" of all motion, he deduced that a Perfect Being would necessarily want the motion in His creation to continue in perpetuity (otherwise, like a human clock, the universe would run down). From the principle that a Perfect Being would want to conserve all of the motion in His universe, Descartes derived his three general laws of motion and seven rules governing the impact of objects when they collide.

Unfortunately, several of his laws and rules could be (and were) easily refuted by empirical tests. For example, his fourth rule of impact states that, regardless of the speed of an object, a body of smaller size cannot move a body of larger size. Such easily refuted principles caused massive problems for both Descartes's science and his philosophy. Although Descartes retained for experience and observation a minor role in determining such things as the "boundary conditions" for the general laws, empirical refutation of such general laws was impermissible since the principles were *necessary truths*. Further, since "God is no deceiver," the world of sense perceptions could be consistent only with his deductively derived laws of science. Therefore, empirical testing was unnecessary.

Descartes believed that many of our "ideas," such as "tree," "flower," and "table," stem directly from sense-perceptions. A second genus of ideas is *formed* by the human mind as a result of reflecting on our sense-perceptions. For example, some trees are "larger" than other trees. However, Descartes maintained that a third group of ideas had to be "innate" because they did not exist in the world of sense-perceptions and were used by people temporally *prior* to the opportunity for people to generate them by "reflection." An example would be the concept of "infinity." As will be recalled, Descartes's claim for the existence of innate ideas was attacked by Locke. His *Essay* refuted Descartes by noting that, as a matter of fact, small children have no conceptualization of ideas like "infinity" until they receive instruction on the topic. Therefore, Locke argued, such concepts cannot be innate but must come from "reflection" on sensations.

Benedict de Spinoza. The second great rationalist philosopher was the Dutch metaphysician, Benedict de Spinoza (1632–1677). Trained as a rabbi, he was expelled from his synagogue for his unorthodox beliefs and had to earn his living by grinding and polishing lenses. His principal philosophical works include *Tractatus Theologico-politicus* (1670) and *Ethics* (published posthumously in 1677).

Spinoza's philosophy was a completely self-contained, deductive metaphysical system that used the structure of Euclidian geometry as its model. Like Hegel after him, Spinoza claimed that his system came to him through a mystical experience. As with Descartes, the starting point for Spinoza's system was theological in character. Completely rejecting the Judeo-Christian concept of anthropomorphic God, Spinoza proclaimed that God and nature are "one" (*Deus sive Natura*). All of Spinoza's beliefs about science, ethics, and politics derive from his belief that "God" and "nature" are simply two different terms applied to the same infinite, eternal, and self-sufficient reality. Spinoza's pantheism, thus, led him to proclaim as absurd the belief of Descartes and the Scholastics in "divine teleology," the notion that God had purposes for the world. Divine teleology would imply that God wished to bring about some state of affairs in the world that did not yet exist. However, such a situation would necessarily imply, Spinoza reasoned, the absurdly contradictory belief that there was something God lacked, but which He needed or desired. It is easy to understand how Spinoza's pantheism was decried as a thinly disguised atheism by his clerical critics and why he was expelled from his synagogue.

Spinoza's philosophical system included a severely deterministic perspective both in natural science and in the areas of ethics, political economy, and social science. All physical and mental activities are strictly determined; nothing can be other than it is. In *Ethics*, Spinoza contended that authors of conventional moral codes believed fallaciously in free will. In *Politics*, Spinoza accepted the Hobbesian belief that "have the right to" means the same as "have the power to." Thus, Spinoza's works, along with those of Hegel, provided a philosophical/historical foundation for Marxist social philosophy. The Russian historian Georgi Plekhanov (1940) viewed Spinozism as one of the direct, historical forerunners of Marxist dialectical materialism.

Gottfried Leibniz. The last of the great trio of classical rationalists was Gottfried Leibniz (1646–1716). A German philosopher, mathematician, lawyer, and diplomat, Leibniz was a tireless worker for scientific cooperation throughout the nations of Europe. He maintained active memberships in all three of the major European scientific academies: the Royal Society (of England), the French Academy, and the Prussian Academy.

Consistent with the liberal views of the Enlightenment, Leibniz was an optimist with respect to human reasoning and scientific progress (Popper 1963, p. 69). Although he was a great reader and admirer of Spinoza, Leibniz, being a confirmed deist, rejected emphatically Spinoza's pantheism: God and nature, for Leibniz, were *not* simply two different "labels" for the same "thing."

Leibniz held that the world was a harmonious whole produced by God for divine ends and could be described and understood in a clear and consistent way through the "language" of mathematics. Extending Descartes's view of innate ideas, Leibniz proposed that we are also born with "innate principles." For example, insofar as the most fundamental principles of syllogistic logic can neither be inferred from experience and observation, nor deduced (by definition) from more fundamental principles of logic, they must necessarily be with us at birth, or *innate*.

In addition to God, the other fundamental entity in Leibniz's philosophy was the "monad." Like the original conceptualization of "atom," monads were the smallest, indestructible units of the cosmos. Yet, unlike the materialistic conceptualization of the atom, monads contained their own distinct, divinely inspired purposes. Therefore, each monad is not only *distinct*, but also *unique*. Leibniz developed a complete philosophical system using the tools of logic and mathematics, together with his fundamental entity, the monad.

Although Leibniz's philosophical system based on monads has not survived in modern science, his work on mathematics endures. For many centuries, mathematicians had struggled with procedures to handle processes and problems that contained units of change that were infinitesimally small. Inspired by the work of his predecessors on summations of series and differences, Leibniz proposed both the basic procedure and the specific notation for modern differential and integral calculus. He also tackled the problem of reducing mathematics to logic, and provided the basis for the later work in this area by Frege in the nineteenth century and Russell in the twentieth. (See sections 2.5.2 and 3.1.2.)

2.3.3   The Quest for Certainty and the Grand Synthesis

Understanding the empiricism-rationalism debate requires an appreciation of the aims or objectives of the participants. Both the empiricists and the rationalists accepted "foundationalism" as their objective, that is, the development of a method for producing knowledge from foundations that would *invariably* produce *certain* knowledge. This infallibilist orientation had characterized philosophy since the time of Aristotle and Plato (Laudan 1981 p. 185). As Popper (1963, p. 103) put it, the science of Galileo wanted to establish the truth of its theories "beyond all reasonable doubt." Indeed, epistemology, the branch of philosophy that studies the warrant for knowledge-claims, has its roots in the Greek word *episteme*, meaning "indubitable knowledge," as contrasted with *doxa*, meaning "opinion." However, since the time of Aristotle and Plato, philosophers also knew of the "fallacy of affirming the consequent" (the truth of the consequence or predictions of a theory or law does not, according to deductive logic, imply that the theory or law is true).

Therefore, the "method of hypothesis" (what would now more commonly be called the "hypothetico-deductive" method of verification) was highly suspect in that it could not yield *certain* knowledge.

In medieval times the Church provided the necessary authority for those seeking knowledge with certainty in both things-spiritual and things-temporal. Both the empiricists and the rationalists sought a method or logic for producing knowledge with certainty equal to that previously provided by the authority of the Church. The empiricists (many strongly influenced by Sir Issac Newton) recognized the fallacy of affirming the consequent and believed that knowledge with certainty could be produced by generalizing inductively from observations. The rationalists in their quest for certainty were highly suspicious of the accuracy of observational processes and also recognized the fallacy of affirming the consequent. Therefore, seeing in mathematics and geometry a kind of certainty similar to that of the Church, they searched earnestly for indubitably true first premises on which to base their scientific knowledge (e.g., the *cogito ergo sum* of Descartes). As Nickles (1985, p. 180) phrases it, for both the empiricists and rationalists, "the correct method of discovery = correct method of verification."

The empiricist's logic of discovery (inductive generalizations) began to crumble when it became apparent that many scientific discoveries were being made through conjectural, rather than inductive-empirical means. For example, the wave theory of light and the theory of the atom involved inherently unobservable entities that were not and could not have been produced through inductive generalizations (Laudan 1981, p. 187). The rationalists' logic of discovery (i.e., start from indubitable first principles) was damaged by the development of non-Euclidian geometry. (Because Euclidian geometry is not true with certainty, that is, *True*, how can geometrical methods produce infallible truths [*Truth*] in empirical science?) Furthermore, the rationalists could not rely exclusively on mathematical methods, given Hume's analysis of the purely analytical or formal nature of mathematics. As Einstein (1923, p. 28) later phrased it: "As far as the laws of mathematics refer to reality, they are not certain; and as far as they are certain, they do not refer to reality."

The empiricism-rationalism debate resolved into what has been described by van Fraassen (Churchland and Hooker 1985, p. 263) as the "Grand Synthesis" of John Herschel (1792–1871) and William Whewell (1794–1866). Herschel's *Preliminary Discourse on Natural Philosophy* (1830) has been described as "the most comprehensive and best balanced work on the philosophy of science" at that time (Losee 1980, p. 115). Herschel was the first to distinguish clearly between the "context of discovery" and the "context of justification" in science (see Hunt 2002a, section 1.5). He noted that "we must not, therefore, be scrupulous as to how we reach a knowledge of such general facts, i.e., laws and theories; provided only we verify them carefully when once discovered, we must be content to seize them wherever they are to be found" (Herschel 1830 , p. 164).

Herschel stressed that the quest for certainty of the earlier empiricists and rationalists was hopeless. The best that science can do is to produce fallibilistic knowledge that is highly likely or very probable. Furthermore, there was no single logic of discovery. Rather, both inductive and hypothetico-deductive methods can be fruitful in developing the hypotheses, generalizations, and theories of science. Nevertheless, "Herschel emphasized that agreement with observations is the most important criterion of acceptability for laws and theories" (Losee 1980, p. 118). That is, with respect to the contexts of discovery and justification, Herschel's views correspond well to those prevailing today. Nevertheless, although the grand syntheses of Herschel and Whewell were highly influential, they did not dominate philosophical thought in the nineteenth century. Philosophy turned its back on science and embraced the philosophy of *idealism*.

2.4   THE ASCENDANCE OF IDEALISM

Although the classical rationalists and empiricists disagreed vigorously over the best procedures for ensuring scientific progress, each was decidedly sympathetic toward both the works of scientists and their developing social institution. We turn now to a group of philosophers who, with the exception of Kant, were generally hostile to science. The common characteristic of these philosophers is a commitment to *idealism*, whose central tenet is that *the external world does not exist independently of its being perceived.*

Basically, idealism is an ontological position relating to what philosophers usually refer to as the "mind-body problem." That is, to what extent is the conscious, perceiving mind separate from the material body within which it is housed? At one extreme lies *materialism*, which holds that *only* material objects (the mind being one such object) constitute reality. At the other extreme lies *idealism*, holding that the only things that are real are the ideas housed in some perceiving mind.

As an aside, some may note that many writers advocating the relativist/constructivist position in the social sciences seem unaware that they are advocating a form of idealism. Such is not the case, however, with Olson. He states:

> Some people—realists—believe in an objectively knowable world that exists independently of themselves. . . . If you don't believe in an independent reality (or for purposes of doing science, you pretend you don't believe in that), then your *idealistic* perspective will probably lead you in entirely different directions. . . . Since I believe in the latter perspective, I guess I am a relativist. (Olson, p. 14 in Bush and Hunt 1982; italics added)

Versions of idealism can be traced back at least to the works of Plato. As will be recalled, his theory of forms postulated an independent realm of abstract ideas or essences that had a real existence outside space and time. However, in contrast with the views of the major idealist philosophers we shall discuss (i.e., Berkeley, Kant, and Hegel), Plato's idealized "forms" did not depend for their existence on the perceiving mind, a most important difference.

2.4.1 Berkeley

George Berkeley (1685–1753), whose name is pronounced as if it were "Barkley," was an Irishman of English heritage who, after studying at Trinity College in Dublin, became an Anglican bishop and founded a college on the island of Bermuda. His major philosophical writings include the *Treatise Concerning the Principles of Human Knowledge* (1710) and *Three Dialogues Between Hylas and Philonous* (1713). Berkeley is often acknowledged as the originator of philosophical idealism, even though he gave the label "immaterialism" to the central thesis of his philosophy. Bishop Berkeley was alarmed by the theological skepticism implicit in many scientific works and in other writings of those associated with the Enlightenment, as is evidenced by the following subtitle of his 1710 book: *Wherein the chief causes of error and difficulty in the sciences, with the grounds of skepticism, atheism, and irreligion, are inquired into.*

A summarized version of Berkeley's idealism is his phrase "to be is to perceive or to be perceived" (Losee 1980, p.161). How did Berkeley come to the conclusion that reality consists only of perception? He started by observing that no one would contend seriously that an idea such as "pain" or "itching" could exist independently from the one who experienced it. (Trees neither itch nor experience pain.) Similarly, ideas like "red" and "sweet" are inherently objects of perception. His *Treatise* challenges the skeptical reader to attempt to conceive of any object existing unperceived, as for example, a chair or tree. Berkeley contended that it was impossible to conceive of a tree existing unperceived in that the person who perceived it, by the very fact of doing so, "constructed" the tree and brought it into "existence." Therefore, "to be is to perceive or to be perceived." Berkeley then had to address an issue that confronts every philosopher who contends that all reality is of the "constructed" variety: how to account for the "apparent" stability in the external world. That is, are chairs and trees annihilated and then recreated during intervals when they are not being perceived? Berkeley's answer was most ingenious. Because, to him, nothing could exist without its being perceived, in the time intervals when chairs and trees are not being perceived by human beings, they must exist in some other mind, which, for him, was the mind of

God. Moreover, the lawlike regularities among perceptions that are discovered and verified in science are simply the manifestations of God's purpose for the world. Therefore, Berkeley's idealistic philosophy could, he claimed, prove the existence of God, and science could prove God's purpose.

Berkeley's idealism led him directly to embrace what we would now call an instrumentalist view of laws and theories. This view holds that scientific laws and theories are merely instruments to make computations or predictions. They do not in any significant sense describe *truly* the real world. Section 2.2.1 discussed the silencing of Galileo by the Church in 1633. In that celebrated case, the Church was quite willing to allow Galileo to extol the virtue of the Copernican universe as a, perhaps, better *computational* device (an instrumentalist position). Galileo's "mistake" was to insist that the Copernican system was both a better computational device and a better model of how the universe *actually was* (a *realist* position). Berkeley chastised Newton on precisely the same grounds that the Church had silenced Galileo. Berkeley maintained that Newton's references to "attractive forces," "cohesive forces," and "dissolutive forces," as describing truly the external world were misleading, because these forces are mathematical entities only (Losee 1980, p. 161). For Berkeley, because only *ideas* were real, only *they*, not such things as "forces," could be causal agents. Given Berkeley's idealism and instrumentalism, it is easy to understand how Popper (1959, p. 29) would conclude that Berkeley opposed "the very idea of rational scientific knowledge" and that "he feared its advance."

2.4.2 Immanuel Kant

Immanuel Kant (1724–1804) was born in Königsberg in East Prussia, studied at its university, and spent his entire life there, teaching physics, mathematics, physical geography, and philosophy. Kant was aroused, in his words, from a "dogmatic slumber" by the radical implications of Humean skepticism, which Kant believed destroyed the intellectual foundations of both religion and science. Being both a confirmed deist and a sympathetic supporter of science, Kant's philosophy attempted, through the *Critique of Pure Reason* (1781) and other works, to save both religion and science from skepticism. To understand how Kant saved science, one must start with how he saved mathematics.

Hume had contended that mathematical truths were both *analytic* and *a priori*. That is, the truths of mathematics depend only upon how terms and relationships are defined (i.e., they are *analytic*), and they cannot be established or refuted by experience (i.e., they are *a priori*). On the other hand, to Mill the truths of mathematics were *synthetic* (about the real world) and *a posteriori* (inductive generalizations from the real world that can be established or refuted by experience). Kant contended that the truths of mathematics and (Euclidian) geometry were *synthetic a priori*. Kant proposed that mathematical truths, such as "7 + 5 = 12," are *synthetic* because "12" contains "more knowledge" than "7 + 5." These truths were also *a priori because* they were "necessary truths" in the sense that mathematical and geometrical truths were true both in this world and in all possible worlds. Thus, Kant's philosophy, he claimed, "saved" mathematics, and, in the process, "saved" classical rationalism, because pure reason alone could generate both mathematical and geometrical truths.

Kant dismissed summarily what he referred to as Berkeley's "dogmatic idealism." The external world could not consist entirely of "mere imaginations," because, he argued, no one could possibly become aware of himself unless there were enduring material substances with which he could compare his own sense-perceptions. Our sense-perceptions *reflect* these enduring material substances. Therefore, all scientific knowledge of the real world must (consistent with the classical empiricists) *come from* or have their origin in sense-perceptions. However, although "coming from" the world, sense-perceptions alone do not *constitute* scientific knowledge. These sense-perceptions must be organized, analyzed, and interpreted by the active consciousness of the human mind, and *only* organized sense-perceptions deserve the status of *knowledge*.

What could possibly justify or legitimize the organizing, analyzing, and interpreting of the human mind? At this point, Kant was ready to contend with the Humean skepticism that had aroused him from "dogmatic slumber." Recall that Hume believed his own skepticism would not and could not be taken seriously because inferring causality from the constant conjunction of events (an unobservable inferred from observables) was firmly established or justified by "habit and custom." Further recall that Mill believed the concept of "cause" was justified as the most general of all inductive generalizations. Kant (and scores of philosophers since Kant) took Humean skepticism seriously and sought a stronger justification for causality than Hume's habit and custom or Mill's induction. Kant proposed that there were certain "categories" of ideas or concepts that were *synthetic a priori*, examples being "cause," "unity," "reciprocal relation," and "necessity." Just as *empirical* concepts, like "tree," *arrange* sensations from the real world, these "transcendent" categories of concepts enable us to arrange, analyze, and interpret empirical concepts to create scientific knowledge. Transcendent concepts like "cause" are *synthetic a priori* because they relate to the real world of sense-perceptions (synthetic), and, contended Kant, the very fact of the possibility of perceptual experience presupposes concepts like "cause." Thus, a concept like "cause" was *a priori* and *necessarily* true because one cannot even imagine the existence of a world of empirical events in which such events are uncaused.

But where do *synthetic a priori* concepts like "cause" come from, if not from habit and custom à la Hume, or inductively derived from experience, à la Mill? Kant's answer was to propose the existence of the "transcendental self." (Hence, Kant's idealism is referred to as "transcendental idealism.") The transcendental self provides us with categories of concepts such as "cause" and "necessity." However, nothing can be known about this "transcendental self" because it is a precondition for knowledge to exist, and, therefore, could not possibly become an object of investigation for that knowledge. Thus, said Kant, science is "saved" from Humean skepticism.

In his day, Kant was known as the "all-destroyer." The rationalists felt betrayed because Kant concluded that pure reason alone could generate *only* mathematical and geometrical truths and not knowledge about the external world of objects and phenomena. The speculative metaphysicians were likewise infuriated by Kant's demonstration that metaphysics, because it relied only on pure reason, could not generate knowledge. Kant proposed that the truths of metaphysics (to the extent that there were any) should be accepted on "faith," an entirely unsatisfactory prospect for the metaphysicians. Empiricists were upset at the introduction of idealistic concepts such as the "transcendental self" into the justification of science. Finally, in the area of ethics, Kant himself claimed to have destroyed "utilitarianism" (although the doctrine would not acquire that label until the time of Mill) with his categorical imperative: Act only according to those maxims you could wish to become universal law.

Unfortunately for Kant's physical safety, his works deviated from orthodox Lutheran Protestantism. In particular, Kant's attacks on rationalism and metaphysics necessarily implied that the existence of God could not be proved by the standard ontological methods of rationalism. Although Kant claimed to have saved theology by showing that the existence of God could not be *disproved* by rationalist methods, and he claimed that the existence of God could be accepted as a practical commitment of morality, such a defense was unpersuasive to the Lutheran hierarchy. As a consequence, Kant received the following order from the Prussian government:

> Our highest person has been greatly displeased to observe how you misuse your philosophy to undermine and destroy many of the most important and fundamental doctrines of the Holy Scriptures and of Christianity. We demand of you immediately an exact account, and expect that in the future you will give no such cause of offense, but rather that, in accordance with your duty, you will employ your talents and authority so that our paternal purpose may be more and more obtained. If you continue to oppose this order you may expect unpleasant consequences. (Paulsen 1910, p. 49)

Kant reflected on the precise nature of the threatened "unpleasant consequences," and, as Galileo had done before him, accepted the silencing.

2.4.3 Hegel

When philosophers and historians of philosophy speak of "German idealism," they generally refer not to the transcendental idealism of Kant, but to the idealism of Hegel. In fact, "Hegelian philosophy" is often used synonymously with "German philosophy": "He ruled the philosophic world as indisputably as Goethe the world of literature, and Beethoven the realm of music" (Durant 1954, p. 222). Many twentieth-century philosophies owe their origins to Hegel. For example, the underlying philosophies of fascism (the myth of the "chosen race") and Marxism (the myth of the "chosen class") spring directly from Hegel (Popper 1966, p. 9). Who was Hegel and how could his ideas become so powerful that his very name would be equivalent to the central philosophy of an entire nation?

Georg Wilhelm Friedrich Hegel (1770–1831) was born to a family of modest means in Stuttgart, Prussia, studied the ministry at the University of Tübingen, and wrote two of his most important books, *The Phenomenology of Mind* and *Logic*, before being appointed in 1817 to the Chair of Philosophy at the University of Heidelberg. Hegel was upset by the liberal democratic views of the Enlightenment and the destruction of metaphysics by Kant. The nature of his philosophical system came to him through a "mystical experience" that compelled him to reveal the "truths of idealism" to the world.

Essentially, Kant's transcendental idealism had held that we can comprehend the external world because the active mind forms or molds our sense-perceptions, that is, because "reality" is "mind-like." Hegel's idealism claimed not that the world was "mind-like," but that the mind is the world: There is only one reality of minds and matter, which is a holistic unity, called the "Absolute" mind, or *Geist*. "The rational is the real and the real is the rational" claims Hegel's "philosophy of the identity of reason and reality." Proclaiming *only* reason (the rational) to be "real," gave Hegel the license, he argued, to construct a metaphysical philosophical system comprised of pure reason alone. Knowledge about Absolute mind could not be gleaned from the method of science with its emphasis on observation and experimentation, because only reason is "real," and reason is unobservable. Therefore, Hegel articulated and developed his alternative method, the method of dialectic. In many respects Hegel's system and method was a direct descendant of medieval scholasticism (Neurath et al. 1955, p. 7).

Hegel was a firmly committed historicist. Because only "ideas" are "real," what needed explaining was the history of the progression of ideas. Central to

Hegel's dialectic was the concept of contradiction or contradictory ideas. (Actually, the reader will note, Hegel's "contradictions" are often better described as "polar opposites.") From the empirical observation that the history of ideas is filled with contradictory (polar opposite) concepts (e.g., freedom and slavery, democracy and totalitarianism, good and evil), Hegel propounded the radical *causal* proposition that every idea (or thesis) *produces* its contradiction (or antithesis) (Popper 1966, p. 315). The contradictory theses and antitheses engage in conflict and struggle, producing *syntheses* that contain elements of both contradictions. Therefore, a good idea never wins over a bad idea and a true idea never refutes a false one, the synthesis is always an inexorable (Hegel is deterministic) combination of the two. For example, in any struggle between democracy and totalitarianism, one side cannot "win"; the conclusion (or synthesis) *must* contain elements of both. Each dialectical process produces a synthesis, which, in turn, becomes a thesis and produces its *own* antithesis.

According to Hegel, all the great writers in the history of ideas had been producing theses and antitheses like "stones on a pile." Because the process was inexorable and determined strictly by the *Zeitgeist* (the spirit of the age), the ideas could neither be objectively true nor objectively false, but only products of the spirit of the age. However, the dialectical progression of the history of ideas (the "pile of stones") comes to its final conclusion in Hegel's philosophical system, because he had "the good fortune to come last, and when he places his stone the arch stands self-supported" (Durant 1954, p. 225).

2.4.4 The Triumph of German Idealism

The firestorm of German idealism swept through the Western philosophical world and completely dominated it from 1850 to 1900. Even that bastion of empiricism, the British Isles, fell under the idealistic onslaught. The empiricism of Galileo, Bacon, Locke, Hume, Mill, and Newton was considered so much rubbish to be swept from the idealist house of intellect. Indeed, claimed the idealists, how presumptuous of these scientists and philosophers to believe that knowledge about the external world could be gained from a method that conjoined hypothesis development with mathematics, observation, experiment, and "old logic" (as contrasted with the new logic of dialectic)? German idealism seemed to solve the major philosophical problems of such diverse groups as the speculative metaphysicians, organized religion, right-wing monarchists, and left-wing revolutionaries. That such a philosophy could serve well such diverse groups attests to its obtuseness. As Schopenhauer (1788–1860), Hegel's contemporary, noted:

But the height of audacity in serving up pure nonsense, in stringing together senseless and extravagant mazes of words, such as had previously been known only in
madhouses, was finally reached in Hegel, and became the instrument of the most
bare-faced general mystification that has ever taken place. (Schopenhauer 1969,
p. 429)

A major problem of the speculative metaphysicians had been their disen-
franchisement from the productive activity of knowledge-creation by both
the rapid advances of practicing scientists and the philosophical works of
Kant. The metaphysicians could now rejoin the knowledge-generating enterprise by pejoratively attacking the knowledge-claims of science. After all,
because only the "rational is real," only rationalist metaphysics could explore
the "real" or important problems of knowledge. Examples of such "real" issues included: Is the Absolute beyond time? Does the Absolute transcend
thought? Is it personal? Is it moral? Is it beautiful? Metaphysicians, such as
Francis Bradley (1846–1924), perhaps the most prominent English advocate
of idealism, explored issues such as these in his famous work, *Appearance
and Reality*. I offer the reader the following long passage from Bradley's book
as an example of how the nineteenth century idealists attempted to demonstrate that relationships between entities in the external world were "mere
appearances," rather than "reality":

But how the relation can stand to the qualities is, on the other side, unintelligible. If
it is nothing to the qualities, then they are not related at all; and, if so, as we saw,
they have ceased to be qualities, and their relation is a nonentity. But if it is to be
something to them, then clearly we shall require a *new* connecting relation. For the
relation hardly can be the mere adjective of one or both of its terms; or, at least, as
such it seems indefensible. And, being something itself, if it does not itself bear a
relation to the terms, in what intelligible way will it succeed in being anything to
them? But here again we are hurried off into the eddy of a hopeless process, since
we are forced to go on finding new relations without end. The links are united by a
link, and this bond of union is a link which also has two ends; and these require each
a fresh link to connect them with the old. The problem is to find how the relation can
stand to its qualities, and this problem is insoluble. (Bradley, as quoted in Russell
1929, p. 14)

Note the obtuseness of the preceding argument. Russell (1929 p. 14) concludes that "most people will admit, I think, that it [Bradley's argument] is
calculated to produce bewilderment rather than conviction, because there is
more likelihood of error in a very subtle, abstract, and difficult argument than
in so patent a fact as the interrelatedness of the things in the world."

In addition to the metaphysicians, organized religion warmly embraced
Hegel's idealism. As will be recalled, Kant had argued that rationalist metaphysics could neither prove nor disprove the existence of God, because all
knowledge has its foundations in sense-perceptions. Hegel's claim that "the

rational is the real," when combined with the concept of the Absolute, provides a rationalist "proof" for the existence of God. For organized religion, Hegel's Absolute became simply another label for God. Hegel himself encouraged religious leaders to so interpret his Absolute and late in his life attempted to destroy an earlier writing on religion (his *Life of Jesus*) that might have troubled them (Durant 1954, p. 221).

Right-wing monarchists also endorsed Hegelian idealism. Instead of focusing on "the rational is the real" (as did the metaphysicians), the monarchists emphasized "the real is the rational," because it implies that whatever state of affairs presently exists, exists because it is *necessarily* so and *ought* to exist. All existing governments are completely justified because none could be other than it is. Hegel had allied himself with the Prussian king and despised liberal democracy, as the following passage shows:

> To hold that every single person should share in deliberating and deciding on political matters of general concern on the ground that all individuals are members of the state, that its concerns are their concerns, and that it is their right that what is done should be done with their knowledge and volition, is tantamount to a proposal to put the democratic element without any rational form into the organism of the state although it is only in virtue of the possession of such a form that the state is an organism at all. (Hegel, as quoted in Brodbeck 1968, p. 563)

Note how Hegel's argument depends so heavily on the view that the state is "real" (it has "rational form") and individual people are "unreal" by comparison (the "democratic element [is] without rational form"), a thesis which was later to be forcefully argued by Bosanquet, the English idealist philosopher. The reader is urged at this point to pause and reflect on the implications, especially the moral implications, of *any* philosophy that claims individual people to be "unreal."

Left-wing revolutionaries also found solace and inspiration in Hegelian idealism. Eastern Marxist philosophers, such as Plekhanov, have historically downplayed the importance of idealistic concepts such as the Absolute in their use of Hegelian philosophy. On the other hand, Western Marxist philosophers, such as Lukacs and Mannheim, have *emphasized* the idealistic component that dominates much of Marx's writings. In any respect, Marx himself, in the preface to the second edition of *Das Kapital*, indicated he was "the pupil of that mighty thinker" Hegel, and all Marxist writers have adopted Hegel's "method of dialectic." The idealistic ontology of Hegel's philosophy, as stated in "the real is the rational," argued for the status quo of the Prussian monarchy. Marx recognized that, on the contrary, Hegel's epistemology, as rooted in the "method of dialectic," argued for continuous revolutionary activity. Writing on the dialectical method in Marxism, Engels (as quoted in Popper 1963, p. 333) notes, "What therefore is the negation of the negation?

An extremely general . . . law of development of nature, history and thought; a law which holds in the animal and plant kingdoms, in geology, in mathematics, in history, and in philosophy." For Marx, the dialectic implied that the monarchy (thesis) would give rise to, or produce, its own "contradiction" (antithesis). Thus, the monarchy and its contradiction, or "negation," would produce a new synthesis, and so on. Hegel thought the dialectical process ended with his own philosophy. Similarly, the dialectical materialism of Marx proposed that the history of political economy is an inexorable process ending with the ultimate socialist state.

Marxist philosophers have made great use of the concept of "contradiction" from Hegelian idealism, and they, also, confuse "contradiction" with "polar opposite." Critics of Marxist philosophy in particular and German idealism in general often point out numerous instances of logical contradictions. That is, critics point out instances where such philosophies proclaim loudly that the statement "*x* is true" and the statement "*x* is false" are *both* "true" at the same time. As Popper (1963, p. 328) cogently observes, when confronted by their critics with such obvious logical fallacies, Marxists and other idealists claim that the "criticism is mistaken because it is based on logic of the ordinary type instead of on dialectic." Thus, if German idealism in general and Marxist philosophy in particular cannot be attacked on either logical grounds (because normal logic is "old logic" in contrast with the "new logic" of dialectic) or on empirical grounds (because only the "rational is real"), the reader should ponder the grounds that might remain (force? power? coercion?).

As noted previously, science grew out of general philosophy and for centuries scientific inquiry was a subdivision of philosophical inquiry. Scientists were in fact called natural philosophers until about 1800. By the middle of the nineteenth century, German idealism had driven a mighty wedge between the child (science) and its parent (philosophy). Scientists viewed philosophical writings as irrelevant, at best, or mystical, metaphysical nonsense, at worst. Philosophers, following Hegel, viewed mathematics with contempt and scorned empirical science. This "dangerous gulf," in Popper's terms (1963, p. 69), between science and philosophy continued until the rise of realism and logical positivism in the early part of the twentieth century. But to understand the rise of these philosophies, we must first examine briefly the writings of Comte, Mach, and Frege, for they paved the way for realism and logical positivism.

2.5   CLASSICAL POSITIVISM

During the early part of the nineteenth century, there arose in France a movement known as "social positivism" that had as its central objective the promotion of a more just society through the application of the knowledge generated by science and the scientific method. The movement was closely associated with the philosopher Saint-Simon (1760–1825), who coined the term "positivism." Saint-Simon's ideas greatly influenced August Comte (1798–1857), the French philosopher, mathematician, and historian. Comte's major work, the six-volume *Cours de Philosophie Positive*, elaborated and popularized the "positive philosophy of science," viewed by Laudan as "the most important single development in the last century" as to theories of the scientific method (Laudan 1968, p. 29).

Comte was a confirmed historicist, who believed that there were certain inexorable laws of history with respect to the stages of thinking that all disciplines go through (Popper 1963, p. 338). All sciences go inevitably through three stages of development: the theological, the metaphysical, and the "positive" (Keat and Urry 1975, p. 72). In the theological stage, all events are caused by the exercise of the will of the gods, or the will of God. In the metaphysical stage, abstract concepts, such as "essence," replace the will of the gods. In the final, or positive stage, the discipline gives up the quest for absolute knowledge in the sense of "final will" or "first cause," and, instead, turns toward attempting to discover the lawlike relationships of coexistence and succession by using the methods of observation, experimentation, and comparison.

Comte arranged the sciences in the hierarchy of (from bottom to top): astronomy, physics, chemistry, biology, and sociology. Comte, though a mathematician, viewed mathematics as a fundamental tool to be used in all the sciences, and, therefore, was not "in" the hierarchy. Each discipline had either *gone* through the stages (like astronomy), or would have to *go through* the stages in the future (like sociology). Comte believed that social phenomena (when properly investigated) would follow lawlike patterns, coined the term "sociologie" to identify the scientific study of social phenomena. Thus, Comte is considered the "father of sociology" (Merton 1973, p. 299). His "sociologie," however, was not to emphasize statistics, as did the "social physics" of his day (Comte 1877, p. 15). Sociology is at the top of Comte's hierarchy because it gave meaning and purpose to the other sciences and because of the fundamental tenets of the social positivist movement. That is, scientific knowledge was not sought for its own sake, but to bring about a better life for all and a more just society by means of, among other things, the prediction and control of phenomena.

Many aspects of Comte's positivist philosophy were to influence the logical positivists in the next century. These aspects include: the emphasis on the explanation and prediction of observable phenomena, the disavowal of the search for "deeper" or "final" causes, the rejection of metaphysics, and the view that scientific knowledge and the use of the scientific method could be useful in bringing about a better society. In fact, the "verificationist theory of meaning" of the logical positivists has its roots in Comte: "Any proposition which is not reducible to the simple enunciation of the fact, either particular or general, can have no real or intelligible meaning for us" (Comte, as quoted in Keat and Urry 1975, p. 73).

2.5.1   Ernst Mach

Our second nineteenth-century positivist, Ernst Mach (1838–1916), was an Austrian physicist and philosopher, who was born in Moravia (now the Czech Republic). While occupying a chair of physics at Prague University, he wrote his best known work, *The Science of Mechanics*, in which he attempted to reformulate Newtonian mechanics using a phenomenalist or sensationalist perspective.

Smitten with the quest for certainty, Mach insisted that science should purge itself of metaphysical concepts. Because, for Mach, the only knowledge-claims that can be known with certainty are those related directly to sense-perceptions, or "sensations," science should restrict itself to laws and theories dealing directly with sensations. Mach held that "the aim of a theory is to correlate the facts, given that the process of correlation must take one beyond the facts, it should do so without postulating any other entities or processes that are not necessary for that task of correlation" (Laudan 1981, p. 208). Stated succinctly, Mach held that the purpose of laws and theories ought to be to give the most economical description of the phenomena. Thus, Mach (like Berkeley) embraced an *instrumentalist* view of scientific theory: The statements of a theory are mere instruments for summarizing phenomena in an efficient fashion. Laws and theories are not meant to be true descriptions of how the world is actually constructed, nor are the theoretical (nonobservable) concepts in a theory to be construed as having a real existence.

As is well known, Mach bitterly opposed the introduction of the concept of the atom into physics. He did so, not because of some objection that the atom could not be observed or that statements involving the atom could not be inductively generated from sense-data. Indeed, "contrary to popular mythology, there was nothing in 19th century positivism that was hostile to speculative theory construction." In fact, "all the major positivists from Comte to Mach, Poincaré, and Duhem enthusiastically accepted Kant's point about the active knower and were thoroughly contemptuous of that 18th-century brand of empiricism and inductivism which imagined that theories would somehow emerge mechanically from the data" (Laudan 1981, p. 207). Mach opposed the introduction of the atom into physics because he believed that all the known laws about physics could be stated more economically without using the concept "atom." Thus, Mach was not opposed to the introduction into science of *all* concepts that transcend sensory experience. He himself considered "oxygen," "heat," and "center of gravity," as useful scientific concepts going beyond sensations. Rather, Mach believed that such concepts should be added to scientific knowledge only when necessary for the economical and efficient description of sensations (Laudan 1981, p. 204). As we shall see in Chapter 3, the logical positivists relied heavily on Mach's instrumentalist view of theories and his sensationalist epistemology. Further, we shall see that Mach's positivism influenced Einstein in developing his theories of relativity.

2.5.2   Gottlob Frege

Our third philosopher, the German mathematician Gottlob Frege (1848–1925), was not, strictly speaking, a classical positivist—his philosophical orientation was decidedly realist. Nevertheless, Frege's nineteenth-century work in the area of the philosophy of mathematics was enormously influential on twentieth-century logical positivism. Therefore, it seems appropriate to discuss his views in this section, along with his nineteenth-century colleagues.

Three fundamental questions have dominated the philosophy of mathematics for hundreds of years: (1) What is the fundamental nature of mathematics (the ontological question)? (2) How do we know mathematical truths (the epistemological question)? and (3) Why is it the case that mathematics is useful in empirical science (the pragmatical question)? Three different general approaches to these fundamental questions have been employed: intuitionism, formalism, and logicism (Kyburg 1968, p. 201).

Kant was one of the foremost exponents of the *intuitionist* approach. Kant believed that the sequence of natural numbers ("1," "2," "3," etc.) is a *synthetic a priori* concept provided by our intuition. That is, in some meaningful sense, mathematical numerals have a "real existence" (synthetic) and are known to us without the benefit of sense-perceptions (*a priori*).

Uneasiness about relying on vague concepts such as "intuition" to explain the fundamental nature of mathematics has led many philosophers in the direction of *formalism*. Vigorous efforts to formalize the arithmetic of natural numbers culminated with the successful formulation of the Italian mathematician Giuseppe Peano (1858–1932) in 1899. As discussed in Chapter 7, section 3 of Hunt (2002a), an axiomatic formal system (or calculus) contains elements, formation rules, definitions, transformation rules, and axioms. Peano showed that the fundamental nature of mathematics can be represented as a formal system with a minimum set of five axioms containing three primitive or undefined elements: "0," "number," and "successor" (Wartofsky 1968, p. 148). Thus, Peano's answer to the fundamental nature of mathematics question was that mathematics was an uninterpreted formal system, or calculus. Further, Peano's answer to how we know the truths of mathematics was that we deductively derive them from the formal system. However, why should it be the case that mathematics should be useful to empirical science? Given that uninterpreted systems, by definition, "say nothing" about the real world, and given the fact that there are an infinite number of formal systems that could be constructed that would in fact be of little use to empirical science, is it simply an incredibly fortuitous occurrence that this particular formal system (mathematics) is so useful to empirical science? Or, alternatively, were the Pythagoreans correct that the gods had used mathematics as the pattern from which the cloth of the universe was cut? Now enter *logicism* and Gottlob Frege in an attempt to answer simultaneously all three fundamental questions concerning mathematics.

Systematic efforts to show the strong relationship between mathematics and logic go back at least as far as the English mathematician George Boole (1815–1864). However, Boole's works always contained expressions that most writers would identify as purely mathematical, rather than logical in fundamental character. In a series of three famous publications, beginning with *Begrisschrift* in 1879, Gottlob Frege explored the fundamental nature of mathematics by showing that all mathematical concepts and operations could be replaced by purely logical concepts, while maintaining the truth-content of mathematical proofs. Frege maintained that the central notion for the conception of all cardinal numbers ("1," "2," etc.) is captured in the expression "just as many as there are things of some standard kind." Further, Frege defined the number "zero" as the "number of objects not identical with themselves." Thus, Frege's answers to the three fundamental philosophical questions about mathematics were: (1) the fundamental nature of all mathematics is logic; (2) we know the truths of mathematics because they can be derived from the truths of logic; and (3) mathematics is useful to science on the same grounds that logic is useful to science. That is, it is inconceivable that science could exist without logic, because science necessarily includes statements containing both logical terms ("and," "or," etc.) and logical operations (e.g., syllogistic reasoning). However, more important for our purposes than Frege's concepts and definitions was his method of analysis. In order to analyze the logical character of mathematics, he found it necessary to create an entire system of notation and procedures that has come to be known as "mathematical logic," "modern logic," "symbolic logic," or, simply, "formal logic."

Another way of stating Frege's *methodological* achievement is to say that he *formalized* ordinary logic by explicitly creating a system of logical symbols (elements), rules for combining symbols meaningfully (formation rules), and rules for deriving certain combinations of symbols from other combinations (transformation rules). (See Hunt 2002a, section 7.3.) But why should he do this and what is its significance? The impetus for the formalization of logic stems from the impreciseness of logic as stated in any "ordinary" natural language. For example, English (a "natural" language), with its immense vocabulary (over twice the number of words as most other modern languages), is extraordinarily precise. Nevertheless, many English sentences containing logical terms are notoriously *imprecise*. For example, consider the following sentence: "Shopping goods or convenience goods may be used in the experiment." What is the meaning of "or" in the sentence? Does it mean "either/or" or "and/or"? One does not know unless given further information. Formal logic uses the symbol "v" to stand for the disjunctive connective "or." Therefore, because the symbol "v" is *always* used to mean "and/or," the meaning of any expression containing "v" is much more precise than an English sentence containing the word "or."

Frege's reduction of mathematics to logic was not to stand the test of time.[3] In a personal letter to Frege in 1901, Bertrand Russell pointed out a serious contradiction in one of Frege's axioms. This contradiction meant that the theorem stating that the series of natural numbers is infinitely large could no longer be proved in Frege's formal system. Nevertheless, Frege's work strongly influenced Russell's attempt to reduce mathematics to logic in his classic, *Principia Mathematica*. And Frege's method, formal logic, was to be adopted as a principal tool of analysis by the logical positivists in the twentieth century.

This section has focused on the classical positivists in the nineteenth century, Comte and Mach, and the work of Frege in symbolic logic and mathematics. The reader should be reminded, however, that these philosophers did not dominate philosophical thought in their time. Rather, the philosophical world continued to be dominated by German idealism through the latter half of the nineteenth century. Only with the rise of classical realism, as exemplified by philosophers such as Moore, Russell, and Wittgenstein, accompanied by the pragmatism of Peirce, did the influence of German idealism begin to wane.

QUESTIONS FOR ANALYSIS AND DISCUSSION

1. The epigraph at the beginning of Chapter 2 by John Kekes states: "If rationality is abandoned, then either 'anarchy is loosed upon the world,' or dogmatism supported by brute force would prevail." Why is this the case? What does this have to do with the "fear" that many scholars have of relativism?

2. Section 2.1.2 contends that "Sage philosophy, by its very nature, can-

not be cumulative . . . because the knowledge of the student cannot go beyond that of the master." It also points out that Sage philosophy "has the distressing tendency to deteriorate into cultism or mysticism." What do we mean by "cumulative"? Given your definition, under what circumstances can inquiry be cumulative? There is an underlying value judgment in the word "deteriorate." What is this value judgment? Do you agree or disagree with it? Why?

3. Summarize the argument that Socrates used against Protagoras and his version of relativism that is discussed in section 2.1.3. What does it mean for an argument to be self-refuting? Why should we care whether an argument is self-refuting? Would your answer differ if you believed that science is "just another game"?

4. Someone has said that "the key to understanding many of the silly statements that are made about the 'demarcation issue' in science is to recognize that the term 'science' should be approached from a *taxonomical* perspective, rather than a *definitional* perspective. In particular, 'scientific method' should be approached this way." Evaluate this view. Hint: See Hunt (2002a, section 8.1) on monothetic vs. polythetic classifications.

5. Compare and contrast the views of the "mechanicians" concerning their opposition to the rise of science with the views of many marketing practitioners and their beliefs about the purpose of marketing research and marketing science.

6. Many people seem to define the purpose of others exclusively in terms of some particular role. For example, many children never see their mothers and fathers as *people*. Rather, their mothers and fathers exist only as *parents*. To what extent can this help us understand why there will always be conflict between marketing practitioners and marketing academicians? To what extent does the fault lie with both groups?

7. It is often pointed out that all research involves "interpretation." Section 2.2.1 pointed out that the "hermeneutics" of today derives from the "scholasticism" of the Middle Ages. Select a recent article in marketing. To what extent does "interpretation" enter into the research? Where? To what extent is the research *exclusively* "interpretation"? If one chooses to claim that an instance of "interpretation" is "incorrect," what could be the various bases for such a claim? Is all research *just* "interpretation"? (For more on this issue, see the Calder and Tybout article and Hirschman's "Afterword" in Hirschman 1989).

8. Classical empiricism claims that experience and observation are the fundamental sources or "foundations" of our knowledge of the external world. On the other hand, classical rationalism claims that *a priori*

reason alone is the fundamental source or "foundation" of our knowledge of the external world. What do we mean by "fundamental source"? Suppose we had a child who, most unfortunately, was born without any of the "five senses." Could such an individual gain knowledge of the external world? Consider, next, a child born with all the five senses but with absolutely zero reasoning capability. Could such a child gain knowledge? How does "foundationalism" as a doctrine differ from "all research has foundations"?

9. Summarize the empiricism-rationalism debate. To what extent does the "discovery/justification" (see Hunt 2002a, section 1.5.1) distinction help us understand the debate? To what extent does the "fallible/ infallible" distinction help us? In your judgment, which "side" of the debate had the better case?

10. What is "foundationalism"? Why should we be interested in distinguishing between "knowledge" and "opinion"? If all knowledge-claims are, ultimately, based on "faith," then are not all knowledge-claims "merely opinions"? Evaluate.

11. What is idealism? How does idealism relate to relativism? Many ethicists attack idealism on the basis that it is "morally corrupt." What does "morally corrupt" mean? Evaluate the thesis that idealism is morally corrupt.

12. What is Hegel's "philosophy of the idea of the identity of reason and reality"? Why does such a philosophy *necessarily* imply that observation and experimentation are useless for gaining knowledge? What is the relevance for epistemology of Russell's argument against idealism: "There is more likelihood of error in a very subtle, abstract, and difficult argument than so patent a fact as the interrelatedness of the things in the world"? How does this relate to sophistry?

13. What is classical positivism? What is its relationship to the Enlightenment? Why did the classical positivists reject metaphysical concepts? Should they have? Should we?

NOTES

1. For an introduction to Eastern philosophy of science, see Snyder (1978), especially his Chapter 6.

2. It is worth noting that Raftopoulos (1995) argues that the standard philosophical interpretation of Descartes—which is reviewed here—is misguided. He maintains that Descartes never believed that science could proceed without observation. Raftopoulos interprets Descartes as using "a priori" to mean "cause and effect," not "without observation."

3. The modern view in the philosophy of mathematics is that mathematics can be formalized into second-order logic. (Frege and Russell used fiirst-order logic.) The issues at debate are whether second-order logic is properly called "logic" and the implications of such a formalization for the epistemology of mathematics (Putnam 1979, p. 386).

3 THE DEVELOPMENT OF THE PHILOSOPHY OF SCIENCE DISCIPLINE: FROM CLASSICAL REALISM TO LOGICAL EMPIRICISM

Insofar as the revolt against science condemns science for making of itself the instrument of power, looks with dismay on the devastation to which science-based technology has given rise, rejects a world made grey by standardization or a world in which the individual counts for less and less, and seeks to reinstate the imagination and direct sensual enjoyment, one can sympathize with its motives even when one believes that its accusations rest on a misunderstanding of science. But the attack on disciplined thinking, the revival of occultism with its doctrine of "hidden truths" to be revealed by magical means, the demand for instant gratification in every area of human life, the rejection of the idea of learning, of discipleship, of tradition—these, I freely confess, fill me with horror and dismay. And it is not only science which suffers but all the activities which particularly distinguish human society, as compared with a society of bees and ants—art, history, philosophy, social innovation, technological achievement, the spirit of critical inquiry.

—John Passmore

After having given birth to science in the seventeenth century, philosophy became estranged from science in the latter half of the nineteenth century. In fact, philosophy adopted an antiscience orientation as a result of its entanglement in Hegelian idealism. This chapter traces the decline of idealism in philosophy under the attacks on it by the (classical) realists and the reconciliation of science with philosophy brought about by the logical positivists and logical empiricists. The chapter closes with a discussion of scientific knowledge and its progress.

3.1   THE EMERGENCE OF REALISM

As will be recalled, Western philosophy at the beginning of the twentieth century had been dominated by German idealism for over fifty years. Hegel's dictum "the Real is the Rational" guided philosophical inquiry. Arguing that "all cognition is judgment," idealists denied the existence of the world of tangible objects and phenomena, and claimed that only Absolute Mind is real. The "doctrine of internal relations" also buttressed the case for idealism. This doctrine held that the nature of anything must be grounded in and constituted by the relations it has with other things. That is, the "parts" cannot exist independently from their relatedness to some "whole." Therefore, objects cannot exist independently from their "relation" to the mind that knows them, and *the external world does not exist independently of its being perceived* (the central tenet of German idealism).

The revolt against idealism was led by many philosophers who, themselves, had been seduced by idealism in the early parts of their careers. In this section, we shall discuss the emergence of classical realism, whose central tenet maintains, contra idealism, that *the external world exists independently of its being perceived.* Note that the realism being advocated by philosophers at the turn of this century was primarily ontological (the nature of existence) rather than epistemological (the nature of knowledge) in character. Modern philosophers of science who characterize themselves as "scientific realists" usually adopt realism in *both* an ontological and epistemological sense. We shall return to the issue of scientific realism in Chapters 5 and 9. For now, we shall examine the arguments that realist philosophers, such as Moore, Russell, and Wittgenstein, employed in their debate with German idealism.

3.1.1   G.E. Moore

The opening salvo fired in the idealism/realism debate was the publication of Moore's "The Refutation of Idealism" (1903). George Edward Moore (1873–1958), professional philosopher, ethicist, Cambridge University lecturer, and close friend of Bertrand Russell, had been a dedicated idealist in the early part of his career. In one of his early papers entitled "In What Sense, if Any, Do Past and Future Time Exist"? (1897), Moore argued that time does not exist and that if this conclusion outraged common sense, then common sense is simply wrong. By 1903, Moore's analysis of language led him to conclude that idealism was fundamentally mistaken. In fact, Moore's method of analysis presaged modern linguistic analysis, because he delved constantly into the nature of meaning (in both its ordinary and philosophical senses). Both he and his realist contemporaries used several arguments to refute idealism. First,

Moore claimed that sentences like "I think of X" describe (1) mental acts and (2) objects related to but distinct from those acts. Once the object of a mental act—the distal stimulus (see section 9.3)—is distinguished from the awareness of it, there is no reason to deny the existence of the object independently from its being perceived. Idealism simply confused the act of perception with the object being perceived. Moreover, if the perception or the awareness of an object cannot provide satisfactory evidence of the object's existence, no awareness is ever awareness of anything, for we could not be aware of other persons or even of ourselves and our own sensations. That is, *the very concept of "awareness" presumes that there are objects independent of that awareness.*

Moore's second argument against idealism concerned the concept "real." The realists argued that idealism used the concept "real" in ways that violated fundamental principles of intelligible discourse. That is, the fundamental meaning of the term "real" derives from such standard examples as "this chair is real" and "this table exists." To deny the fundamental examples that give meaning to a term and at the same time, to continue to use the term in other contexts, produces unintelligible speech. To continue to create pseudosentences, containing terms stripped of their meanings, constitutes farce, not profundity. (Some writers in marketing and the social sciences today, it must unfortunately be admitted, employ the same technique.)

His third argument against idealism had a distinctly pragmatic character to it. The argument stemmed from the inconsistency between stated beliefs and actual behaviors. Realists claimed that idealists were disingenuous in their claimed beliefs. Although idealists would claim that objects like tables and chairs do not exist, their actual behaviors belied their claims. When idealists entered rooms, they approached and sat on chairs, just as if the chairs actually existed. When idealists ate their meals, they pulled their chairs to tables, just as if the tables actually existed. Thus, the elaborate argumentation of idealism points toward sophistry and hypocrisy, rather than genuine belief.

3.1.2   Bertrand Russell

Whereas G.E. Moore was a philosopher/ethicist, our second realist, Bertrand Russell (1872–1970), was a philosopher/mathematician at Cambridge University. Russell argued powerfully and persuasively in a series of papers (later published as *Our Knowledge of the External World* [Russell 1929]) that there are nonmental facts that are independent of any mind becoming aware of them. He further argued (contra the doctrine of internal relations) that these facts are "atomic" in the sense that the truth-content of propositions containing them could be determined "in isolation" on the basis of whether the propositions *correspond* with observations. His arguments were so forceful and conclusive that he is often credited with bringing about the downfall of idealism throughout Europe (German philosophy excepted) (Popper 1963, p. 69).

Russell's "logical atomism" (his ontology) licensed his philosophical method, that is, his method of analyzing philosophical problems by breaking them into their constituent parts or elements. Idealism had maintained a kind of "hermeneutical circle" view, in which the analysis of anything was impossible because to understand the nature of a part is impossible without already knowing how it fits into the whole. Therefore, one had already to comprehend the whole, or "Absolute," in order to understand each part. Russell called his method "logical constructionism," which, stated briefly, entailed the following steps: (1) identify a body of knowledge about which there are unresolved philosophical questions concerning the status of the entities involved in the knowledge and the justification for the knowledge-claims about the entities; (2) demonstrate how the body of knowledge could be reformulated in terms of simpler, more undeniable entities; and (3) analyze the philosophical problems in the original body of knowledge in terms of the language of the simpler, more rigorous, "ideal" language. The objective of the procedure would be to solve the philosophical problems by converting the problematic to the unproblematic, and the obscure to the clear. The method of "logical constructionism"—not to be confused with the reality relativism of *today's* constructionism (see section 4.1.3)—implies that the philosophical problems in the original, complex body of knowledge were "constructed" from simpler entities.

Russell, together with Alfred North Whitehead (1861–1947), applied the method of logical constructionism with vigor to mathematical knowledge. In the classic set of works *Principia Mathematica* (1910–1913), they proceeded to take up Frege's work of reformulating all of pure mathematics in terms of logic alone. The Russell-Whitehead notation for formal logic survives today as one of a handful of notational systems. Based on the primitive term "class," they defined (or "constructed") numbers as "classes of classes." The number "0" was defined as the "class of all empty classes," and the number "1" was defined as the "class of all classes each of which is such that any member is identical with any other member."

More important than the details of how Russell translated mathematics into logic was what has come to be known as "Russell's paradox," and how Russell solved it. As will be recalled from the previous chapter, Russell had found a contradiction in the fifth axiom of Frege's efforts to reduce mathematics to logic. The contradiction had to do with the concept "class," and, in particular, the "class of all classes which are not members of themselves." Referring to this class as "X," Russell asked whether "X" was, or was not, "a member of itself." Either way the question is answered, a paradox arises: If "X" is a member of itself, then it satisfied the defining condition of such members, so it is not a member of itself; and if it is not a member of itself, it belongs to the class of such classes and so is a member of itself.

Russell solved the paradox (and showed how the same procedure could solve a large number of such paradoxes) by showing that the paradox stemmed from a vicious circle arising when we propose a collection of objects containing members definable only by means of the collection as a whole. In other words, the contradiction involved the treatment of *classes* as being on a par with the treatment of their constituent *members*. Russell's "theory of types" maintained that there was a hierarchy existing among the types of entities in his mathematical logic and that, if this hierarchy were violated, contradictions would result from the ill-formed expressions.

By now, most readers are probably thoroughly confused. And for good reason. The reader has been asked to attempt to understand sentences such as "Is the class of all classes that are not members of themselves a member of itself"? Russell showed that the statements in the "paradox" are neither true nor false, but ill-formed or *meaningless* expressions. Readers, therefore, have been asked to comprehend (make meaningful) the incomprehensible (the meaningless). Could it be the case that most philosophical puzzles were *meaningless* in the same sense as Russell's paradox, and could it be the case that using logical constructionism would make the supposed problems of philosophy disappear? Could it be the case that most of the problems of philosophy resulted, simply, from philosophers phrasing their propositions and questions in an ill-formed, inconsistent, meaningless manner? Enter Ludwig Wittgenstein.

3.1.3   Ludwig Wittgenstein

Ludwig Wittgenstein (1889–1951), born in Vienna, Austria, studied engineering at the Technische Hochschule in Berlin and the University of Manchester in England. Upon reading Bertrand Russell's *Principles of Mathematics* (not to be confused with *Principia Mathematica*), he became enthusiastic about mathematics and transferred to Cambridge in 1912. There, he studied under, and was greatly influenced by, Bertrand Russell. Wittgenstein's sole published work during his lifetime was *Tractatus Logico-philosophicus* (published in German in 1921, followed by an English translation in 1922). His only other published work was *Philosophical Investigations* (1953), published posthumously (at his request). In a terse eighty pages, *Tractatus* explicated a philosophy that was to be enormously influential in the twentieth century. (As we shall see, his 1953 *Philosophical Investigations* represented a critique and rejection of *Tractatus*, and it also has been enormously influential.) This section will focus exclusively on the content of *Tractatus*; *Philosophical Investigations* will be discussed in Chapter 4.

Tractatus starts with a theory of meaning and winds up being a comprehensive theory of philosophy. Historically, the philosophy of language has been concerned with the following question: "What are we saying about a linguistic expression when we specify its meaning"? (Alston 1964, p. 10) The many theories that have been advanced to answer the question of meaning can be grouped loosely into three types: referential, ideational, and behavioral. *Referential* theories identify the meaning of a word or expression with that to which the word or expression refers. For example, the word "cat" refers to a certain kind of animal existing in the world. *Ideational* theories indicate that the meaning of a word is equivalent to the ideas in the human mind that the word "stands for." The classic statement of the ideational theory was given by John Locke in his *Essay Concerning Human Understanding*: "The Use, Then, of Words is to be Sensible Marks of Ideas; and the Ideas They Stand For Are Their Proper and Immediate Signification" (Locke, in Alston 1964, p. 22). Drawing upon the stimulus-response theories of psychology, *behaviorist* theories of meaning specify the meaning of a linguistic form to be identical with "the situation in which the speaker utters it [the linguistic form] and the response which it calls forth in the hearer" (Bloomfield 1935, p. 139).

Central to understanding *Tractatus* is comprehending Wittgenstein's picture theory of meaning. As previously indicated, Wittgenstein was heavily influenced by Bertrand Russell. Russell's version of realism implied a referential theory of meaning. (In fact, at one time Russell believed that even logical terms, such as "and" and "or," had referents in the world of objects and phenomena.) Wittgenstein's picture theory of meaning specifies that the meaning of any linguistic form is a "picture in the mind" that refers to reality. Moreover, the pictures are not restricted to individual words, but, most important, all meaningful sentences and propositions are pictures of reality. Thus, Section 4.01 of *Tractatus* states: "A proposition is a picture of reality. A proposition is a model of reality as we think it to be." Note that Wittgenstein does not simply state that a sentence was *like* a picture. Rather, he believed a sentence to be *literally* a "picture in the mind."

Wittgenstein justified his picture theory of meaning as the only sensible way to explain the fact that people can understand the meaning of a sentence that is composed of familiar words, even though they have never seen the sentence before, nor had it explained to them. To Wittgenstein, a sentence must be a picture in the mind because the sentence "shows its sense." A sentence composed of familiar words is able to communicate a new state of affairs by virtue of being a picture of that supposed state of affairs.

The implications of the picture theory of meaning were enormous. First of all, for an elementary, basic, or "atomic" linguistic expression to have meaning or sense, its picture must either represent reality truly or falsely (Baker and Hacker 1984, p. 41). That is, the meaning of a linguistic expression is *construed* to be either a true or false "picture" of reality. Because, for Wittgenstein, the logical terms in a language were "operators" that showed how meaningful atomic linguistic expressions could be combined to form complex sentences or propositions, complex linguistic expressions were likewise meaningful. Therefore, all *significant* sentences or propositions could be analyzed by means of truth-functional combinations of their atomic constituents.

The means by which all significant propositions in a language could be analyzed in terms of their atomic constituents was the method of *truth-tables*. Wittgenstein's method of truth-tables can be illustrated through a simple example. The following is a truth-table for the linguistic expression "P & Q":

	P	Q	P&Q
1.	T	T	T
2.	T	F	F
3.	F	T	F
4.	F	F	F

For example, the first row of the truth-table indicates that "if P is true and Q is true, then P & Q is also true." Other rows are similarly interpreted. Wittgenstein proposed that all meaningful propositions, no matter how logically complex, could be broken into their constituent parts, displayed in truth-tables, and *if those constituent parts were meaningful*, the meaningfulness (truth-content) of the complex proposition could be unequivocally determined.

Wittgenstein's *Tractatus* claimed to have solved all the problems that had confronted philosophers from the dawn of time. All philosophical problems were dissolved, he contended, by showing them to be ill-formed, pseudo, or meaningless *answers* to ill-formed or meaningless *questions* or *pseudoquestions*. As Baker and Hacker put it, Wittgenstein claimed to dissolve philosophical puzzles by showing that:

> The cardinal proposition of philosophy, conceived since the dawn of the subject as revealing ultimate truths about the nature of reality, the metaphysical structure of the world, transpire to be ill-formed propositions which violate the rules of logical syntax. They are not bi-polar, since they are conceived as *necessary* truths about reality. But only bi-polar propositions picture reality; and only Tautologies are necessary truths, and they say nothing about the world. The typical philosophical "propositions" employ illegitimate categorial concepts (substance, property, concept, etc.) as if they were genuine names, but analysis reveals them to be variables, not names. Consequently these metaphysical pronouncements are no more than pseudo-propositions. (Baker and Hacker 1984, p. 45)

But, if all the world's philosophical puzzles are nothing more than pseudo-answers to pseudoquestions, what is the function of philosophy in the modern world? Wittgenstein gives his answer in Section 4.0031 of *Tractatus*: "All philosophy is a critique of language."

Wittgenstein was cryptic, to say the least. He wrote in aphorisms and even spoke aphoristically (Munz 1987). In many respects, Wittgenstein was much like an Eastern "sage" philosopher. Indeed, entire careers have been made in philosophy in the pursuit of interpreting and reinterpreting Wittgenstein. Nevertheless, on two points there is philosophical consensus: Wittgenstein's *Tractatus* shifted the course of philosophical analysis toward the analysis of language (Baker and Hacker refer to his work as "the watershed" (1984, p. 39)), and Wittgenstein strongly influenced the movement that would come to be known as logical positivism. Who were the logical positivists, what were their beliefs, and why were they so influential in the twentieth century? The next section addresses these questions.

3.2   EINSTEINIAN RELATIVITY, QUANTUM MECHANICS, AND LOGICAL POSITIVISM

Science in the nineteenth century was characterized not only by the quest for certainty with respect to scientific knowledge, but also by the widespread belief that science had indeed achieved that ambitious goal. Scientific discoveries increased exponentially, based upon the absolutely secure bedrock of Newtonian physics. However, Einstein's special theory of relativity, formulated in 1905, and general theory of relativity, formulated in 1916, combined with quantum mechanics, struck the foundations of physics like a lightning bolt.

Greatly influenced by Mach's positivism (see section 2.5.1), Einstein became suspicious of the "absolute" nature of Newtonian physics (Manicas 1987, p. 248; Leplin 1986, p. 35). Newtonian physics held that space, time, and mass were absolutes in nature; Einstein proposed that all three were relative. Therefore, Newton's laws of motion would hold only for velocities that are small compared with the speed of light. Whereas Newtonian physics held that energy and mass were separate entities, relativity held that energy and mass were *aspects* of the *same* reality, related through the equation, $E = mc^2$. Quantum mechanics also rejected the intuitive distinction between particulate matter and wave-like light, and accepted the "wave-particle duality," which holds that under certain conditions light mimics the characteristics of waves and under other conditions behaves like particulate matter. The wave-particle duality is expressed in Heisenberg's indeterminacy principle that the position and momentum of a particle may not simultaneously be measured to arbitrary accuracy. Thus, the nature of subatomic particles appears to be fundamentally discontinuous (in quantum units), rather than continuous; indeterministic, rather than deterministic.

The fall of Newtonian mechanics and the rise of Einsteinian relativity and quantum mechanics sent shock waves through the scientific and philosophical communities, particularly those in Germany. At the turn of the century, four philosophies coexisted in the German philosophical and scientific communities: mechanistic materialism, Hegelian idealism, neo-Kantian idealism, and Machian neo-positivism (Suppe 1977b, pp. 8–10). Mechanistic materialism, with its commitment that all the laws of physics must be strictly deterministic in character, was incompatible with quantum mechanics. Hegelian idealism, the "official philosophy of the German state and the state universities," (Suppe 1977b, p. 8). held that the world does not exist independently of its being perceived, and, therefore, whatever is "known" is "relative to the mind that knows it." Because Hegelian idealism was hostile to science in general and mathematics in particular, it could not provide a satisfactory foundation for the mathematical ontology of "new physics." As the nuclear physicist Mermin points out, quantum mechanics is just mathematics, that is, it is *just* a series of equations (this is the meaning of the expression "mathematical ontology"):

> The fact is that although the underlying quantum mechanical view of the world is extraordinarily confusing—Bohr is said to have remarked that if it doesn't make you dizzy then you don't understand it—quantum mechanics as a computational tool is entirely straightforward . . . the problem is that although the formalism of the quantum theory fits nature like a glove, nobody, not even Bohr or Heisenberg, has ever really understood what it means. The only concise picture the formalism offers the world prior to an act of measurement is the formalism itself. (Mermin 1983, pp. 655–56)

The dominant philosophy of the German scientific community was neo-Kantian idealism, which held that there is an ideal world structure that exemplifies itself in structured phenomena, and the job of science is to discover the structure of this ideal world. But, the deterministic orientation of neo-Kantianism "virtually precluded acceptance of both relativity-theory and quantum-theory" (Suppe 1977b, p. 9). Finally, there was a small minority of scientists (primarily in the Göttingen and Berlin schools) who embraced Machian neo-positivism, with an epistemology based on "sensations." However, strict Machian positivism did not allow for the high place that quantum theory gave to mathematics. Clearly, a crisis in both philosophy and science had emerged. Stove succinctly summarizes the situation:

> The crucial event was that one which for almost 200 years had been felt to be impossible, but which nevertheless took place near the start of this century: the fall of the

> Newtonian empire in physics. This catastrophe, and the period of extreme turbu-
> lence in physics which it inaugurated, changed the entire climate of the philosophy
> of science. Almost all philosophers of the 18th and 19th centuries, it was now clear,
> had enormously exaggerated the certainty and the extent of scientific knowledge.
> What was needed, evidently, was a far less optimistic philosophy of science, a rigor-
> ously *fallibilist* philosophy, which would ensure that such fearful *hubris* as had been
> incurred in connection with Newtonian physics should never be incurred again. (Stove
> 1982, p. 51)

The philosophy that was to emerge that could accommodate what the physicist Mermin calls the "bizarre" nature of Einsteinian relativity and quantum
mechanics came to be called "logical positivism" (a label coined by Feigl)
(Meehl 1986). It had its chronological origin with an informal discussion
group at the University of Vienna in 1907.

3.2.1   The Origins of the Logical Positivist Movement

Following Ayer's historical account, logical positivism should be construed
as a *movement* (Ayer 1959, p. 3). As such, the logical positivist movement has
an identifiable beginning, a specifiable group of members, a program of action, and an identifiable end. The movement began with an informal discussion group, formed in 1907, which was composed of the mathematician Hans
Hahn, the physicist Philipp Frank, and the social scientist Otto Neurath. All
three were on the faculty at the University of Vienna (hence, the group later
referred to itself as the "Vienna Circle"), and they discussed the desultory
state of affairs in philosophy and its estrangement from science. Although at
one time science (under the designation "natural philosophy") had been a
subdivision of philosophy, science and philosophy were now not only independent of each other but also openly hostile. Science was progressing by
developing and empirically testing theories; philosophy seemed mired in the
metaphysical speculation of German idealism. Two questions dominated the
discussion group in Vienna: (1) Does philosophy have anything to contribute
to the progress of the scientific enterprise, especially in light of recent developments in Einsteinian relativity and quantum mechanics? (2) If philosophy
could contribute to the scientific enterprise, what methods could be employed
to make the contribution?

In 1922, the physicist Moritz Schlick joined the faculty at Vienna and the
discussion group. Schlick immediately became a major discussion leader of
the group, and under his leadership it added the following members: Friedrich
Waismann (a mathematician), Edgar Zilsel (a sociologist), Bela von Juhos (a
physicist), Felix Kaufmann (a lawyer), Herbert Feigl (a physicist and chem-
ist), Victor Kraft (a historian), Karl Menger (a mathematician), Kurt Gödel (a
mathematician), and Rudolph Carnap (a mathematician). Recognizing that

the views of the members of the discussion group were similar to those of Ernst Mach, the discussion group formally became the Ernst Mach Society in 1928. All the members of the society were German-speaking, and most were trained in logic, mathematics, and/or physics. No member was a "pure" or "professional" philosopher in the German idealistic tradition. In the main, these were philosophically oriented *scientists*, not scientifically oriented *philosophers*. Although Ludwig Wittgenstein, Bertrand Russell, and Karl Popper were not formal members of the society, they interacted extensively with its members and strongly influenced their views. In 1926, the group studied Wittgenstein's *Tractatus*, and, though its mysticism was disquieting, "they accepted it, and it stood out as the most powerful and exciting, though not indeed the most lucid, exposition of their point of view" (Ayer 1959, p. 5).

In 1929, the society published its manifesto entitled *Wissenschaftliche Weltauffassung, Der Wiener Kreis* (*The Scientific World View: The Vienna Circle*). The manifesto proclaimed a new philosophy of science that eschewed the metaphysical excesses of German idealism in order to "further and propagate a scientific world view" (Joergensen, in Neurath et al. 1970, p. 850). The manifesto traced the historical origins of the new philosophy and set forth its program. As a result of the manifesto, the society came to be known as the "Vienna Circle." The label "logical positivism" was later coined by Herbert Feigl to identify the views of the circle. "Logical" signified the tremendous importance placed by members of the circle on using formal logic to analyze philosophical problems, and "positivism" associated the circle with the views of such classical positivists as Comte and Mach.

Logical positivism quickly became a truly international movement, and the members of the Vienna Circle began to propagate their views. They established a new journal (*Erkenntnis*) in 1930, and held world congresses in 1934 (Prague), 1936 (Copenhagen), 1937 (Paris), 1938 (Cambridge), 1939 (Harvard), and 1941 (Chicago). The congresses were heavily attended by both practicing scientists and philosophers. The Vienna Circle also helped establish the Philosophy of Science Association and its journal, *Philosophy of Science*. The lead article in the inaugural issue of *Philosophy of Science* in January 1934, Rudolph Carnap's "On the Character of Philosophic Problems," proposed the logical positivist perspective. Moreover, the inaugural issue's editorial stated a positivist objective: "Philosophy of science is the organized expression of a growing intent to clarify, perhaps unify, the programs, methods and results of the disciplines of philosophy and science" (Churchman 1984, p. 20).

Logical positivism and its legatee, logical empiricism, came to dominate Western philosophy of science in the first half of this century. Only (but very important) German philosophy stayed firmly committed to idealism. Formally speaking, logical positivism as a movement and the Vienna Circle as an organized group disintegrated in the 1930s. Although the members of the circle were not generally politically active, their views on freedom and scientific objectivity were incompatible with Nazism. Many members of the circle escaped the clutches of the Nazis only by migrating to England and the United States. The Ernst Mach Society was formally dissolved in 1938; *Erkenntnis* was moved in 1938 to The Hague, where it took the name of *Journal of Unified Science*; it was discontinued in 1940 (to be revived in the 1970s). The Third Reich made publications of the Vienna Circle illegal. By 1940, the doctrines of logical positivism had been merged into, or had become, mainstream empiricism. Although the logical positivists did not develop their complete program, the views of the circle changed the topography of the philosophical landscape. The precise nature of the circle's program is our next topic.

3.2.2   The Logical Positivist Program

From the time of Aristotle to the nineteenth century, all inquiry was philosophy: Philosophy housed both our methods of inquiry and their applications. Philosophy gave us methods such as critical discussion, syllogistic logic, mathematics, observation, experimentation, and formal logic. Philosophy also applied its methods to areas as diverse as moral philosophy, political philosophy, social philosophy, and natural philosophy. Gradually, these application areas, the "children" of philosophy, matured and developed separate identities of their own: mathematics, physics, chemistry, sociology, political science, and so forth. One science after another separated from the mother, philosophy (Neurath, in Neurath et al. 1955, p. 10). As a response to the maturation of its children, philosophy in the latter half of the nineteenth century turned toward endless speculation about the ultimate nature of reality, that is, German idealism. Even here, Einstein's theory of relativity seemed to tell us much more about the ultimate nature of reality than did the "theories" proposed by idealist metaphysicians (compare $E = mc^2$ with "the first cause of the world is the Unconscious," or "there is an entelechy which is the leading principle in living being"). Given that philosophy and science were no longer coterminous, and given that science the child had coopted the methods of philosophy the parent, was there any continuing role that the parent could play that would further assist the child's development? Stated succinctly, what could or should be the purpose of philosophy in the age of modern science? The logical positivists believed they had found the answer to this question in the works of Wittgenstein and Russell. Section 4.111 of Wittgenstein's *Tractatus* stated:

> The object of philosophy is the logical clarification of thoughts. Philosophy is not a theory, but an activity. A philosophical work consists essentially of elucidations.

> The result of philosophy is not a number of "philosophical propositions," but to make propositions clear. Philosophy should make clear and delimit sharply the thoughts which otherwise are, as it were, opaque and blurred.

Thus, the logical positivists followed Wittgenstein and claimed that the purpose of *philosophy* should be the logical clarification of language, and the purpose of the philosophy of *science* should be to clarify the language of science. In the lead article in the inaugural edition of *Erkenntnis* (1930), Schlick discussed the "turning point in philosophy." He contended that "philosophy is not a system of statements; it is not a science." Indeed, he proclaimed, "the great contemporary turning point is characterized by the fact we see in philosophy not a system of cognitions, but a system of *acts*; philosophy is that activity through which the meaning of different statements is revealed or determined. By means of philosophy statements are explained, by means of science they are verified" (Schlick, as quoted in Ayer 1959, p. 56).

How was the logical clarification of the language of science to be accomplished? To buttress the traditional method of critical discussion, two tools were proposed for the task. First, following Wittgenstein's lead, the positivists proposed the "verification theory of meaning" as an Ockham's razor to expunge all metaphysical entities and propositions from the language of science. One formulation of the verifiability principle stated that "the meaning of a proposition is the method of its verification." The phrase "the meaning of a proposition" is customarily interpreted as equating with "the meaningfulness of a proposition." Given the positivists' penchant for clarity of expression, this ambiguous and vague formulation of their principle was both surprising and unfortunate, or as Feigl later reminisced, "brash and careless" (Feigl 1969, p. 5). Essentially, the verifiability principle claimed that all the propositions, or statements, in science could fall into only one of three potential categories:

1. statements that are cognitively meaningful and true,
2. statements that are cognitively meaningful and false, and
3. statements that are meaningless.

Similar to Russell's "logical atomism," all cognitively meaningful statements, no matter how complex, could be subdivided into their elemental components that could be verified conclusively as either true or false. These elemental components could then be displayed in the truth-tables of Wittgenstein to determine the truth or falsity of the complex proposition. All statements, either elementary or complex, that could not be recast in the preceding manner were held to be meaningless, or "empty talk."

The second tool to be employed in the clarification of scientific language was formal logic, as originally developed by Frege and extended by Bertrand Russell in *Principia*. Given the notorious imprecision of natural languages (e.g., English, French, etc.), the precision of formal logic would enable the positivists to clarify the language of science in general, and its theories in particular, by reconstructing it from a natural, imprecise language into an ideal, precise one.

What would be the outcome of the clarification of the language of science through ridding it of meaningless assertions by means of the verifiability principle and reconstructing it through formal logic into a precise, ideal language? The ultimate outcome, the Vienna Circle believed, was to be an *Einheitswessenschaft*, that is, "a unified science comprising all knowledge of reality accessible to man without dividing it into separate unconnected special disciplines, such as physics and psychology, natural science and letters, philosophy and the special sciences" (Joergensen, in Neurath et al. 1970, p. 850).

The logical positivists rejected the notion of Comte that there was a hierarchy of sciences. Rather (following Mach), they embraced the "unity of science" thesis, which provided that, though there were numerous differences in terms of subject matter and techniques among the various sciences, they all shared a common belief that their knowledge-claims should be intersubjectively certifiable through empirical testing. Disciplinary objectives (i.e., the explanation of phenomena through laws and theories) separate the sciences from art and the humanities; its method of verification (intersubjectively certifiable tests) separate the sciences from pseudosciences, such as astrology, palmistry, and phrenology (see section 6.1).

A second aspect of the "unity of science" thesis was that "scientists of different disciplines should collaborate more closely with each other and with philosophers than they usually do" (Ayer 1959, p. 29). This is why the positivists organized numerous congresses where they could bring together both philosophers and scientists from all disciplines for the purpose of discussing common interests. (It is worth noting that most philosophy of science conferences today are attended almost exclusively by philosophers, historians, and sociologists of science, rather than practicing scientists.) The positivists believed that many of the problems separating the different sciences were brought about because practitioners in the various sciences were using concepts and terminology that inhibited communication. Therefore, they believed it very important that the unification of the various "special" sciences should take place through the formation of a universal language of science (Joergensen, in Neurath et al. 1970, p. 922).

Finally, the "unity of science" thesis entailed the objective of working toward "reducing" all the special sciences into a "unitary or monistic set of explanatory premises" (Feigl 1969, p. 21). In this regard, the positivists were encouraged by the partial success of reducing chemistry to physics, of reducing biology to physics and chemistry, and of reducing psychology to neurophysiology. To further all the goals of the unity of science movement, the positivists planned an ambitious program of developing an *International Encyclopedia of Unified Science*. The encyclopedia was planned for twenty-six volumes and was to be a forum "where scientists of the special sciences and philosophers worked together in harmony, although being completely free to express varying opinions on questions of doubt" (Joergensen, in Neurath et al. 1970, p. 928). Because of the war and other problems, only two volumes (Neurath et al. 1955, 1970) of the encyclopedia were ever finished. (Interestingly—ironically—the second volume housed Kuhn's "Structure of Scientific Revolutions.") Obviously, although the Vienna Circle rejected idealism in the sense of a philosophy identified with speculative metaphysics (German idealism), they were nonetheless "idealistic" in the sense of having lofty goals and noble ambitions. They were visionaries.

Stated succinctly, the logical positivists viewed the purpose of philosophy of science to be the clarification of the language of science through critical discussion, formal logic, and the verifiability principle in order to create a unified science. In doing so, the positivists fostered the development of the academic discipline of the philosophy of science in the 1920s and 1930s. By 1950, the professionalization and institutionalization of the discipline in university philosophy departments had become complete (Losee 1980, p. 174).

3.2.3 Implementing the Logical Positivists' Program

The first phase of implementing the logical positivists' program included the destruction of the metaphysics of German idealism. This phase was led by Carnap (1932, 1936, 1950, 1956, 1962, 1966). Historically, the hostility of German idealism toward science had been returned in kind by both practitioners and philosophers of science. Hume's beliefs about metaphysics are captured in the following famous quotation from his *Enquiry Concerning Human Understanding*:

> When we run over to libraries, persuaded of these principles, what havoc must we take? If we take in our hand any volume; of divinity or school metaphysics, for instance; let us ask, *Does it contain any abstract reasoning concerning quantity or number?* No. *Does it contain any experimental reasoning concerning matter of fact and existence?* No. Commit it then to the flames: for it can contain nothing but sophistry and illusion.

The positivists' position on metaphysics was similar to Hume's. They believed that the verification theory of meaning, when combined with formal logic, would be sufficient to show that all metaphysics was comprised of meaningless pseudosentences that should be "committed to the flames."

In order to understand the assault on Hegel and his idealist successors, it is useful to have an example of exactly what was being argued against. The following passage comes from Heidegger's 1929 book entitled *Was Ist Metaphysik?* as reproduced in Carnap's famous article "The Elimination of Metaphysics Through Logical Analysis of Language":

> What is to be investigated is being only and—*nothing* else; being alone and further —*nothing*; solely being, and beyond being—*nothing. What about this Nothing? ... does the Nothing exist only because the Not, i.e. the Negation, exists? Or is it the* other way around? *Does Negation and the Not exist only because the Nothing exists? ...* We assert: *the Nothing is prior to the Not and the Negation ... where do we seek the Nothing? How do we find the Nothing ... we know the Nothing ... anxiety reveals the Nothing. . . that for which and because of which we were anxious, was "really"—nothing. Indeed: the Nothing itself—as such—was present. . . . What about this Nothing?—the Nothing itself nothings.* (Carnap 1932, p. 69; italics in original)

What should be made of the preceding paragraph? Is it profound truth, or odious falsity? Carnap and other positivists claimed that it was as senseless to believe the quoted passage to be true as it was to believe it to be false. Rather, as Hume proposed, the passage should be "committed to the flames" as meaningless. Carnap's analysis was basically as follows.

According to the members of the Vienna Circle, all languages contain a vocabulary (words) and a syntax (rules for forming meaningful combinations of words, or sentences). Essentially, the positivists adopted a referential theory of the meaning of words. That is, words have meaning because they are associated with things in the external world to which they refer, that is, "observables." All meaningful words either refer directly to these observables or can be explicitly defined through "correspondence rules" or "reduction sentences" in terms of the observables. By way of illustration, Carnap asks the reader to suppose "that someone invented the new word 'teavy' and maintained that there are things which are teavy and things which are not teavy" (Carnap 1932, p. 64). Carnap suggests that "in order to learn the meaning of this word, we ask him about its criterion of application: How is one to ascertain in a concrete case whether a given thing is teavy or not"? (1932, p. 64). If the inventor of the new word could not provide "empirical signs of teaviness," the word would be described as meaningless. Using this line of reasoning, Carnap claimed as meaningless such familiar concepts of German idealism as: "the Idea," "the Absolute," "the Unconditioned," "the being of being," "thing in itself," "being-in-itself," and "being-in-and-for-itself."

Given that many of the concepts used in metaphysics were meaningless, all statements comprised of such concepts would be equally meaningless.

Nevertheless, the more insightful and original aspect of Carnap's assault on the metaphysics of idealism as meaningless lay not in sentences composed of meaningless words. Much more interesting was his claim that, even though all the terms might be meaningful, many of the statements in metaphysics were meaningless because the statements violated certain *syntactical* considerations. For example, all speakers of English would recognize the following (grammatically correct) sentence as meaningless: "Julius Caesar is a prime number." The sentence is meaningless because it violates Russell's—see section 3.1.2—"type confusion" of terms; in this case, names of people and names of numbers belong to different logical types. Thus, although the sentence is grammatically "correct," it is nevertheless meaningless. It is as senseless to *deny* that "Julius Caesar is a prime number," as it is to affirm it.

Returning now to the passage by Heidegger concerning "the Nothing," Carnap proceeded to demonstrate, using formal logic and meaning analysis, that Heidegger's entire passage was meaningless on *syntactical* grounds. Although the English word "nothing" is meaningful, Heidegger had combined it with other words to form syntactically impermissible statements. That is, the very meaning of the word "nothing" implies nonexistence and, therefore, to assert (in a seemingly profound fashion) the existence of nonexistence, and discuss its relationship with other concepts is as syntactically unintelligible as to assert "Caesar is a prime number."

The positivists were well aware of the fact that the word "meaning" can have several different *meanings*. In particular, they differentiated between *cognitive* meaning (designative or referential) and noncognitive meaning (expressive or emotive). Thus, they compared the works of the metaphysicians to poetry and art, but "Metaphysicians are musicians without musical ability" (Carnap 1932, p. 80). The danger of the metaphysics of German idealism was that their works of (bad) poetry and art were claimed by their proponents to have *cognitive* meaning and assertive force, representing a higher, more profound kind of "understanding" than science. Thus, Heidegger asserted (as being cognitively profound) statements such as: "[I]f thus the power of the *understanding* in the field of questions concerning Nothing and Being is broken, then the fate of the sovereignty of 'logic' within philosophy is thereby decided as well. But will sober science condone the whirl of counter-logical questioning"? (Heidegger, in Carnap 1932, p. 72). Although positivist philosophers believed their arguments against the illogicality and meaninglessness of idealism to be conclusive (as did Socrates—see section 2.1.3—in his arguments against the relativism of the sophists), as we shall see in Chapter 4, such was not to be the case.

A second part of implementing the logical positivists' program centered on examining the nature of science. In particular, how could a philosophy of science be constructed that would be compatible with both the lessons of the metaphysical excesses of German idealism and the overthrow of the Newtonian empire by Einsteinian relativity and quantum mechanics? To understand how the positivists interpreted the "lessons" requires an understanding of what Watkins refers to as the "security pole," and its counterpart, the "depth pole," in science (Watkins 1984, p. 133).

Ever since the time of Bacon and Descartes, science has embraced two aims that often appeared to conflict with each other. On the one hand, science strived toward developing theories about the world whose knowledge-claims could be known with absolute certainty (the "security pole"). On the other hand, science strived toward developing theories whose knowledge-claims progressed toward ever deeper, more fundamental, explanations (the "depth pole"). For the positivists, the lesson to be learned from both idealism and the fall of Newtonian mechanics was that science should, essentially, abandon the depth pole and move decisively toward the security pole. Only by adopting the very conservative procedure of restricting the knowledge-claims of science to directly observable phenomena and relationships among those phenomena could another Newtonian debacle be prevented. As the 1929 manifesto of the Vienna Circle emphasized, "in science there are no 'depths'; there is surface everywhere" (Watkins 1984, p. 137). Thus, the positivists adopted a form of *radical* empiricism with regard to science. (The positivist version of radical empiricism was similar to, but conceived and developed independently of, the version known as "operationalism," as discussed in Hunt (2002a, section 7.5.2.)

Suppe's (1977b) summary indicates that the radical empiricism of the Vienna Circle contained the following view of scientific theories. First, scientific theories should be capable of being axiomatized in accordance with the formal logic of Bertrand Russell. Second, the terms in theories should be composed of (1) logical and mathematical terms, (2) theoretical terms, and (3) observational terms. Logical and mathematical terms were justified on the basis of their acceptance of Kant's analytic/synthetic dichotomy (see Hunt 2002a, section 5.3) and the reduction of mathematics to logic by Frege and Russell (see sections 2.5.2 and 3.1.2). Although "theoretical terms" were allowed, such terms were not to be in any sense "metaphysical." All theoretical terms must be explicitly definable through correspondence rules with "observable terms." The *correspondence rules* guaranteed the cognitive significance of the theoretical terms and specified the admissible experimental procedures for applying a theory to phenomena (empirical testing) (Suppe 1977b, p. 102).

As a major "lesson" to be learned from Einsteinian relativity and quantum mechanics, the logical positivists, led by Schlick, proposed that both theories and their constituent theoretical terms were to be interpreted in a Machian *instrumentalist*, rather than *realist*, manner (Friedman 1984). Although the positivists accepted the classical realist position that the world exists independently of its being perceived (Schlick referred to it as "empirical realism" [Manicas 1987, p. 247]), they rejected the much stronger thesis of *scientific realism* that theories may contain theoretical terms that (1) are in principle unobservable and (2) cannot be reduced through definitions or correspondence rules to observable terms. Whereas scientific realism holds that theories, including the postulated relationships among constituent theoretical terms, truly represent in some significant fashion how the world really is constituted, the positivists held that *only* relationships among observables "truly represent." Because it was believed (and continues to be held according to the "Copenhagen interpretation" in physics today—see Mermin 1983) that, in principle, there could not be anything in reality corresponding to the formalisms in quantum mechanics (the wave-particle duality), quantum theory must be interpreted instrumentally. That is, quantum theory is *just* a series of equations that can serve as an instrument to economically summarize the results of experiments. Because the "Copenhagen" version of quantum mechanics is that the equations are to be interpreted instrumentally, the "lesson" for the logical positivists was (in a colossal act of inductive *hubris*) that *all* theories should be interpreted instrumentally.

As Bergmann has observed, a fundamental, unifying belief of the positivists was the adoption of the Humean view of causality (Bergmann 1967, p. 2). The Humean view of causality and induction also suggests a strictly instrumentalist perspective of scientific theories. Hume (see section 2.3) observed that metaphysical concepts such as "cause" can never be inferred logically from the observation of a series of correlated events. Thus, it is impossible to go logically (deductively) from a series of observable antecedents and consequents to any "unobservable," such as "cause." Because no amount of empirical support could possibly confirm a theory with certainty (here *certainty* implies the same degree of warrant as proof by deductive logic), theories should be construed as instruments to summarize observations economically, rather than be postulated as truly representing the actual "hidden structure" of the world. Or, as we have previously noted, Humean analysis suggests science should stay as close as possible to the "security pole," as it is described by Watkins (1984).

If the "lesson" of quantum mechanics for the positivists was to embrace instrumentalism for all scientific theories (and not just quantum mechanics), such has definitely not been the view of scientists in general. Nor was it the view of the physicists who actually *developed* quantum mechanics. Physicists such as Planck, Einstein, Rutherford, Bohr, Heisenberg, and Schrodinger believed that the world existed independently of its being perceived (ontological or classical realism) and that the purpose of science was to develop theories that in some meaningful sense explain truly how the world *really* is (a tenet scientific realism). (Of all the sciences, only the behaviorist branch of psychology embraced radical empiricism in preference to scientific realism.) To the developers of quantum theory, throwing out scientific realism for *all* science because of the problems inherent in quantum mechanics would be analogous to "throwing out the baby with the bath water." In today's vernacular, throwing out scientific realism because of the anomaly of quantum mechanics would be tantamount to "naive" falsificationism (see section 5.1).

Although the "early" Einstein was *positivistic* in perspective, in a famous letter to Schlick, the "mature" Einstein emphatically expressed his *realist* views:

> I tell you straight out: Physics is the attempt at the conceptual construction of a model of the real world and its lawful structure . . . in short, I suffer under the unsharp separation of Reality of Experience and Reality of Being . . . you will be astonished about the "metaphysicist" Einstein. But every four- and two-legged animal is de facto in this sense a metaphysicist. (Einstein 1930, as quoted in Holton 1970, p. 188)

The year after Einstein's letter, Planck expressed the same view:

> Now the two sentences: 1) There is a real outer world which exists independently of our act of knowing and 2) the real outer world is not directly knowable form together the cardinal hinge on which the whole structure of physical science turns. And yet there is a certain degree of contradiction between these two sentences . . . therefore, we see the task of science arising before us, an incessant struggle toward a goal which will never be reached, because by its very nature it is unreachable. It is of a metaphysical character, and, as such, is always and again beyond our achievement. (Planck 1931, as quoted in Holton 1970, p. 189)

The reader should note that Planck is specifically stating that the ultimate goal of science is, in principle, unrealizable. This position is in sharp contrast to those modern philosophers and historians of science who believe that all of the cognitive aims of science must be *realizable* if they are to be legitimate. Thus, Laudan argues against the acceptance of "utopian" aims in science (1984, p. 52). We shall return to this issue in section 7.4.3.

As previously indicated, logical positivism was a *movement*. It had its inception with a discussion group at the University of Vienna in the early 1920s; it peaked in the late 1920s with the manifesto; and it ended in the middle 1930s with the dissolution of the Vienna Circle under the onslaught of Nazism. The legacy of logical positivism was not a movement, but what might be called a "research program" or "research tradition" (Brown 1977, p. 26). Many of the members of the Vienna Circle continued to explicate the nature of science with critical discussion through logical analysis, using both formal logic (or "mathematical" logic in the spirit of Russell) and informal logic (or "traditional" logic in the spirit of Moore). They were joined in their efforts by scores of other philosophers of science, including, most prominently, Carl G. Hempel (e.g., 1965b), Ernest Nagel (e.g., 1961), and Richard B. Braithwaite (e.g., 1968). Their writings dominated the philosophy of science literature in the 1940s and 1950s, and their views came to be known as *logical empiricism*. Neurath suggested in 1938 that "empirical rationalism" should be the preferred term because the approach represented a kind of synthesis of the rationalism of Descartes, Spinoza, and Leibniz (with its emphasis on deductive logic) and the empiricism of Bacon, Locke, Hume, and Mill (with its emphasis on observation) (Neurath, in Neurath et al. 1955, p. 1). Much of the logical empiricist research program involved not only the explication of science, but also a retreat from the rigid positions of the radical empiricism inherent in logical positivism. The next several sections will discuss how the logical empiricists modified the rigid positions of the logical positivists. (Chapters 4 and 5 discuss how, in turn, the views of the logical empiricists were attacked by advocates of scientific realism, historicism, and relativism.)

3.3 THE DEVELOPMENT OF LOGICAL EMPIRICISM

The logical empiricists shared many of the fundamental beliefs of the logical positivists concerning the nature of the world, science, and the philosophy of science. Indeed, many of the logical empiricists had themselves been members of the logical positivist movement. Most important, the logical empiricists shared beliefs with their positivist predecessors concerning the purpose of the philosophy of science and its appropriate method of inquiry. That is, the purpose of the philosophy of science was to clarify, or explicate, the language of science, using a method that conjoined critical discussion with formal logic. To understand logical empiricism and how it differs from logical positivism, we shall explore how the logical empiricists explicated four key concepts in the language of science: laws, explanation, theories, and verification.

3.3.1 Explicating Scientific Laws

Given the influence of Mach, the logical positivists had, quite naturally, given high status to the importance of science discovering and justifying laws and lawlike generalizations. Such laws were generally construed to be universal conditionals relating observable phenomena to other observable phenomena: "Every time phenomenon X occurs, then phenomenon Y will occur."

The positivists' construal of scientific laws as universal conditionals posed for them an embarrassing dilemma. Because the "verifiability principle" implied that all cognitively meaningful statements must be *verifiable* (the ability to be shown conclusively true or false), all scientific laws must be cognitively meaningless. This is because all statements having the form of universal conditionals *cannot* be conclusively verified. (Although observations in the past may have conformed to the universal conditional, it is always *possible* that some disconfirming observation might occur in the future.) Either the positivists would have to give up the verifiability principle or assert that scientific laws are meaningless. They, of course, chose to give up the verifiability principle.

Carnap, in his 1936 paper entitled "Testability and Meaning," specifically addressed the problem that scientific laws posed for the verifiability principle and suggested that it be replaced with the more liberal "testability criterion" (Carnap 1936). Brown suggests that Carnap's article "can reasonably be viewed as the founding document of logical empiricism" (Brown 1977, p. 23). As stated by Feigl, the testability criterion indicated that "the differences between an assertion and its denial must in principle be open to at least partial and indirect observational tests, otherwise there is no factual meaning present in the assertion" (Feigl, in Cohen 1981, p. 13).

Recall that the logical positivists, as a reaction to the downfall of the Newtonian empire and the rise of relativity and quantum mechanics, had sought to secure the foundations of scientific knowledge in observable phenomena. Statements concerning only observable phenomena had been thought to be capable of conclusive verification. According to Carnap, the adoption of the testability criterion implied necessarily the substitution of "gradually increasing confirmation" as a requirement of the knowledge-claims of science. However, the abandonment of verification meant also that the knowledge-claims of science could no longer be considered *positive*. Hence, Carnap's 1936 article provides the genesis of the label "logical empiricism" as a successor for "logical positivism." For the members of the Vienna Circle "positive knowledge" had implied a kind of knowledge capable of being known with the same certainty associated with the simple, atomistic assertions of Russell and Wittgenstein; for example, "the cover of the Hunt (1983b) book is red."

How the logical empiricists explicated Carnap's concept of "gradually increasing confirmation" will be addressed in section 3.3.4. For now, we need to discuss the logical empiricist approach to scientific explanation, for their approach to scientific laws influenced their views on explanation.

3.3.2 Explicating Scientific Explanation

Much of the work of the logical empiricists focused on the nature of scientific explanation. Indeed, they held that "the distinctive aim of the scientific enterprise is to provide systematic and responsibly supported explanations" (Nagel 1961, p. 15). Building upon the models of scientific explanation implicit in the works of Hume (1911) and Kant (1783), Hempel and Oppenheim in their 1948 article entitled "Studies in the Logic of Explanation" developed the deductive-nomological, or "covering law," model of explanation (see Hunt 2002a, section 3.3). Briefly, the covering law model of explanation proposes that a phenomenon is to be explained by showing that it can be *deduced* from a set of universal laws and a set of initial characteristics associated with the particular situation. Hempel and Oppenheim showed that the covering law model of explananation conforms well to many classical views on the topic. For example, Kant had referred to "the laws from which reason explains the facts" (Kant 1783, p. 18).

Although the deductive-nomological model conforms well to many explanations in science, the logical empiricists came to realize that many scientific explanations involve statistical laws, rather than laws in the form of universal generalizations. Therefore, either they had to claim that explanations such as quantum mechanics based on statistical laws are not scientific, or another model that incorporated statistical laws would be required. Hempel's 1962 article (in Feigl 1962) entitled "deductive-nomological vs. statistical explanation" developed the deductive-statistical and inductive-statistical models of explanation (see Hunt 2002a, sections 3.4.3 and 3.4.4). However, because statistical laws do not deductively imply the phenomenon to be explained, Hempel added the requirement that the statistical laws should confer a "high probability" on the likelihood of the occurrence of the phenomenon to be explained. The issue of what "high probability" implies will be returned to later.

Hempel and Oppenheim's original 1948 article also proposed that scientific explanation and scientific prediction had the same logical form. The "thesis of structural symmetry" (as it came to be called) asserted that (1) every adequate explanation is potentially a prediction, and (2) conversely, every adequate prediction is potentially an explanation (see Hunt 2002a, section 4.1; Hempel 1965b, p. 367). Articles by, among others, Scheffler (1957) and Scriven (1959) attacked Hempel's thesis of structural symmetry. The attacks centered on several fundamental issues, including the observation that if "adequate" means "accurate," then there are many instances where one can accurately predict the occurrence of a phenomenon that science would not claim as truly explanatory. (One such example was predicting the stock market through the rise and fall of the hemlines in women's skirts.) Hempel's 1965 book reviewed the charges of his critics, acknowledged that their criticisms posed significant problems for (at least) the second subthesis, but only concluded that the second subthesis must "be regarded here as an open question" (Hempel 1965, p. 376).

The reason why Hempel and other logical empiricists could not simply deny the second subthesis in the "symmetry" argument was that they were firmly committed to the logical positivist view that the concepts "cause" and "causal" were metaphysical and superfluous to science. That is, they could not deny it because they were firmly committed to the Humean view of causality (Bergman 1967; Keat and Urry 1975, p. 12). For example, Brodbeck defended the thesis of structural symmetry in 1962 by noting that critics had adopted the "causal idiom" and that the truth-content of "statements like 'C is the cause of E' is problematic" (Brodbeck, in Feigl and Maxwell 1962, p. 250). Discussing the concept of causal explanations, Hempel concludes, "it is not clear what precise construal could be given to the notion of factors 'bringing about' a given event, and what reason there would be for denying the status of explanation to all accounts invoking occurrences that temporally succeed the event to be explained" (Hempel 1965, pp. 353–54). As we shall see, the influence of Hume was also strongly evident in how the logical empiricists explicated the concept of theory.

3.3.3   Explicating Theory

The logical positivists had held that theories should be comprised of (1) logical and mathematical terms, (2) theoretical terms, and (3) observational terms. Lawlike relationships between observational terms, or "observables," came to be called "empirical laws," and lawlike relationships between theoretical terms, or "theoreticals," came to be called "theoretical laws" (Nagel 1961). However, all theoretical terms, in order to be cognitively meaningful, had to be explicitly definable through correspondence rules with "observables." The historical origin of the thesis that theoretical terms must be defined through observable terms traces back to Russell and Hume (Manicas 1987).

Hume had contended (the "Humean problem of induction") that it was improper to infer the existence of an "unobservable" (like "cause") from observations, because such a procedure was inconsistent with *deductive* logic. Russell, in a very influential 1914 essay entitled "The Relation of Sense-Data to Physics," accepted the Humean view that "correlation does not deductively imply causation" as necessarily implying that "whenever possible, logical constructions are to be substituted for inferred entities" and that "we may succeed in actually defining the objects of physics as a function of sense-data" (Russell, as quoted in Manicas 1987, p. 250). Following the positions of Hume and Russell, the logical positivists adopted a very limited realism as their ontology—the classical realism discussed in section 3.1. On this view, observational terms have a real existence, but, because theoretical terms were nonobservational terms (or the "inferred entities" of Hume and Russell), they were not accorded the status of *real*. Therefore, in order for the theoretical laws to be cognitively meaningful, all theoretical terms must be explicitly definable through observational terms. The explicit definitions would make the relationship between the theoretical terms and observational terms *purely analytic*. Thus enters the analytic/synthetic dichotomy into the construction of theories. (See Hunt 2002a, section 5.3.)

The reader should note that the preceding on "correspondence rules" is not the same thing as *measuring* a construct, or identifying empirical indicators of a construct. Because the logical positivists believed that theoretical terms, or nonobservational terms, did not have a real existence, such terms could not in principle be measured in the customary sense. Rather, theoretical terms represented logical constructions, or a shorthand way of talking about "observables." Those readers familiar with structural equation modeling and modern measurement theory will recognize that the logical positivists assumed a view similar to that of a *formative* measurement model, rather than a *reflective* measurement model, as a basis for understanding the relationships among the theoretical terms and the observables (Diamantopoulos and Winklhofer 2001; Fornell and Bookstein 1982; Howell 1987). For example, a reflective measurement model of the concept "intelligence" would claim that the concept is in some meaningful sense *real* and can be measured through a variety of instruments. On the other hand, a formative measurement model might claim that intelligence is whatever the Stanford-Binet IQ test measures and nothing *more* than what the test measures.

The logical empiricists recognized that there were at least three major problems with the criterion that required all theoretical terms to be defined explicitly by means of correspondence rules and observation terms. We shall call these problems the problems of (1) extension, (2) dispositionals, and (3) theoretical dispensibility, and we shall discuss each in turn.

The problem of *extension* points out that a major characteristic of *good* theories is that they be capable of predicting new phenomena. However, if the entire cognitive content of all theoretical terms is captured by a unique set of observational terms, then the theoretical laws would obviously be incapable of predicting new phenomena. In fact, the "explicit definition" requirement would imply logically that every time a theory predicts a new phenomenon (a new "observable"), the "meaning" of the theoretical terms has changed, and, therefore, we have "new" concepts and a "new" theory. As the reader will no doubt note, this is exactly the argument that Hempel used in his 1950 and 1954 articles (reprinted in his 1965 book) that demonstrated the poverty of the underlying philosophy of operationalism. (See Hunt 2002a, section 7.5.2.)

The second problem, the problem of "dispositional terms," was addressed by Carnap in his 1936 article entitled "Testability and Meaning." Carnap noted that there were many theoretical terms that could not in principle be defined explicitly through observables using the formal logic of *Principia*. For example, terms like "soluble" and "magnetic" state that certain entities have a dispositional ability, and such an ability could not be explicitly defined in terms of observables. Carnap's suggestion was that the explicit definition criterion should be abandoned and replaced with "partial interpretation." He proposed that theoretical terms were meaningful if they were partially interpreted through "reduction sentences" to observable terms. Rather than providing general definitions of dispositional terms, the reduction sentences would show how such terms could be introduced in specific test conditions (Brown 1977, p. 41).

The third problem, theoretical dispensibility, focused on the role of theoretical concepts in theory construction and is summarized in Hempel's famous article, "The Theoretician's Dilemma" (1958, reprinted in his 1965 book). Hempel quotes the behaviorist psychologist B.F. Skinner, stating that theoretical terms are unnecessary in science because all meaningful theoretical terms can be replaced with observation terms. In short, paraphrasing Hempel, the "dilemma" is that if all theoretical terms can be explicitly defined or reduced to observation terms, then theoretical terms are "unnecessary," because they can be eliminated. On the other hand, if theoretical terms cannot be explicitly defined or reduced to observation terms, then they surely are "unnecessary" because they are meaningless! Hempel resolves the dilemma by concluding:

> The theoreticians dilemma took it to be the sole purpose of a theory to establish deductive connections among observation sentences. If this were the case, theoretical terms would indeed be unnecessary. But if it is recognized that a satisfactory theory should provide possibilities also for inductive explanatory and predictive use and that it should achieve systematic economy and heuristic fertility, then it is clear that theoretical formulations cannot be replaced by expressions and terms of observables only; the theoreticians dilemma, with its conclusion to the contrary, is seen to rest on a false premise. (Hempel 1958, reprinted 1965, p. 222)

Why does Hempel not resolve the dilemma by affirming that, even with Carnap's reduction sentences, the cognitive content of a theoretical term cannot be captured by defining it by means of observables? Again, the influence of Hume on the logical empiricists is evident. To argue that theoretical terms are meaningful, yet undefined by observable terms, is tantamount to admitting that theoretical terms are "real." In Hempel's words, "to assert that the terms of a given theory have a factual reference, that the entities that they purport to refer to actually exist, is tantamount to asserting that what the theory says is true" (Hempel 1958, reprinted in his 1965, p. 221). Again, the reader should note the pervasive impact of Hume and the Newtonian debacle. Hempel is concerned that to accept a realist interpretation of theoretical concepts would be "tantamount to inferring" (improperly accordingly to Hume) that an empirically well-confirmed theory is true (and thus risking another Newtonian disaster, should the theory later be disconfirmed).

By 1970, the logical empiricist version of scientific theories had concluded that the total cognitive content of theoretical terms could not be captured through any definitional system of correspondence rules or reduction sentences. Thus, Feigl proposed that the theoretical concepts are implicitly defined by the theoretical postulates or laws in which they occur, and they are "linked" by correspondence rules to observable concepts. His "orthodox view of theories" provides that there is an "upward seepage of meaning of the observational terms to the theoretical concepts" (Feigl, in Radner and Winokur 1970, p. 7). Hempel provides an even more liberal view of the problem of the meaningfulness of theoretical terms. He notes that there has been a "steady retrenchment of the initial belief in, or demand for, full definability of all scientific terms by means of some antecedent vocabulary consisting of observational predicates or the like." But if we do not come to understand the meaning of theoretical terms through explicit definitions, how do we? Hempel responds:

> We come to understand new terms, we learn how to use them properly, in many ways besides definition: from instances of their use in particular contexts, from paraphrases that can make no claim to being definitions and so forth. The internal principles and bridge principles of a theory, apart from systematically characterizing its content, no doubt offer the learner the most important access to an "understanding" of its expressions, including terms as well as sentences. (Hempel, in Radner and Winokur 1970, p. 162–63)

3.3.4   Explicating Verification

As discussed in section 3.3.1, the fact that scientific laws are often expressed in terms of universal conditionals implied necessarily that the "verifiability principle" would have to be modified. Carnap proposed that, rather than verifiability, the requirement ought to be that all scientifically meaningful assertions must be empirically testable. Therefore, verification should give way to "gradually increasing confirmation." The logical empiricists then began the explication of "confirmation."

The epistemic problem of confirmation can be stated as a question: "How is it possible that observing a finite number of instances of a generalization (law or theory) can enable one to know that the generalization holds in all the unexamined cases (of which there normally is potential infinity)"? (Suppe 1977b, p. 624). For the logical empiricists the question had both a qualitative and a quantitative dimension.

Qualitatively, what kind of observation or "instance" is to count as a bona fide confirmation? Analyzing this question from a purely logical, syntactical perspective generated the "paradoxes of confirmation" concerning ravens and "grue." Hempel's 1945 paper developed the paradox of the ravens, which (paraphrased) states that the proposition P "all ravens are black" is logically equivalent to the statement $P*$ "all nonblack things are nonravens." Further, any observation or instance that tends to confirm $P*$ *must* tend logically to confirm P. Therefore, the fact that one observes a nonblack object (e.g., a red object) and determines that the nonblack object is a nonraven (the red object is a rose) must "tend to confirm" logically statement P that "all ravens are black."

Goodman in 1953 (reprinted in 1965) proposed the paradox of "grue." Again briefly, Goodman starts by inquiring whether the observation that a particular emerald is green would be an instance of confirming the generalization "all emeralds are green." Goodman continues by defining the adjective "grue" as applying anytime an object is green before some arbitrary time t and blue after the arbitrary time t. Goodman notes that, because all observations of emeralds will occur before the arbitrary t, the observation that a particular emerald is green *equally* confirms both "all emeralds are green" and "all emeralds are *grue*." The "grue" paradox generated, according to Goodman, "a new riddle of induction" (Goodman 1965, p. 59).

Both the raven and "grue" paradoxes spawned a large number of papers that attempted their resolution. Specific efforts at resolution need not detain us here. Rather, we should note that the paradoxes stemmed in large measure from the general approach to confirmation that the logical empiricists used, that is, approaching confirmation as a syntactical and logical problem. Even more specifically, one of the reasons the paradoxes occur is that "one of the characteristic features of *Principia* logic is that it is an extensional logic, that it does not take into account the *meaning* of the proposition involved in an argument" (Brown 1977, p. 33). That is, just as using mathematics as a tool for analyzing certain problems in empirical science will, by itself, create problems, so will the use of *mathematical logic*.

Much more important than the qualitative dimension of confirmation, as exemplified in the "paradoxes," was the quantitative dimension. The logical empiricists interpreted the problem of finding a quantitative "degree of confirmation" that observed instances would confer on a generalization to be equivalent to solving the Humean problem of induction, or "Humean skepticism." In order to understand the logical empiricist approach, it is time to formally state the basic propositions underlying Humean skepticism.

Following the approach of Watkins (1984), Humean skepticism is not to be confused with "academic" skepticism, which states that "there is but one thing that one can know, namely, that one can know nothing else." Neither is it Pyrrhonian skepticism, which claims that one cannot even know that one cannot know anything. Rather, Humean skepticism allows that each of us can have genuine knowledge about our own beliefs, feelings, and perceptual experiences, in addition to allowing that logical and mathematical truths are possible. However, Humean skepticism "denies that one can progress by logical reasoning from perceptual experience to any genuine knowledge of an external world, if there is one" (Watkins 1984, p. 3). Stated more formally, Humean skepticism denies that genuine knowledge of the external world can proceed from perceptual experience by asserting the following three fundamental propositions (Watkins 1984, p. 3):

HS1.   There are no synthetic *a priori* truths about the external world.
HS2.   Any genuine knowledge we have of the external world must ultimately be derived from perceptual experience.
HS3.   Only deductive derivations are valid.

The three propositions of Humean skepticism are sometimes referred to as the *anti-apriorist* thesis (HS1), the *experientialist* thesis (HS2), and the *deductivist* thesis (HS3). As will be recalled, Kant's answer to Hume was to deny HS1 and assert that there exist concepts (like "cause") that are both synthetic and *a priori*. Further, Mill's answer to Hume was that "cause" is the most general of all inductive generalizations. That is, Mill denied HS3. We should note that Hume did not take his own skepticism seriously, but denied it on the grounds of "habit and custom." The logical empiricists took Humean skepticism seriously and attempted to overcome it by modifying HS3 with the claim that "probability logic, or the logic of partial entailment, is a legitimate extension or generalization of classical logic" (Watkins 1984, p. 4). That is, the logical empiricists attempted to develop the logic of probability so that they could show that finite instances of observable evidence could be combined in a logical fashion to generate a probability number between zero and one, such that the number would be related logically to the intuitive notion that instances of observable evidence, more or less strongly, confirm a generalization.

The authors who are most closely associated with the attempt to develop probability theory into a logic of confirmation are Reichenbach (1949), Carnap (1950), and, more recently, the Finnish mathematicians Hintikka and Niiniluoto (1976). Reichenbach's approach to the problem used what are referred to as "self-corrective" procedures; Carnap's approach focused on system probabilities determined by state descriptions and structure descriptions; whereas Hintikka's approach was to modify the system of Carnap. Suppe reviews the effort to develop the logic of probability as a logic of confirmation and concludes:

> What is common to all the approaches to inductive logic is that in one way or another they make only a finite number of instances relevant to the testing of universal generalizations, and such means ultimately rest on various assumptions about the sorts of regularities characteristic of the world. Thus it would appear that one can obtain non-zero probability measures for generalizations only if one makes certain fairly metaphysical assumptions to the effect that certain patterns of regularity are characteristic of the world. Burks argues that such assumptions are pragmatic presuppositions of induction which can be established on neither *a priori* nor empirical grounds . . . initially, logical positivism was concerned with global induction: Reichenbach's self-corrective method and Carnap's analytic inductive method were attempts to prove the truth of probabilistic induction hypotheses which would enable us to obtain general knowledge; both failed to do this. More recent work in inductive logic [e.g., Hintikka] has given up the attempt to develop a more global inductive logic. (Suppe 1977a, p. 630)

Suppe points out that most of the recent works, rather than focusing on global induction, focus on "local induction." In these efforts, one attempts to justify generalizations inductively in the context of specific scientific inquiries, given "deeply held metaphysical presuppositions or beliefs" (Suppe 1977a, p. 630).

The logical empiricists approached Humean skepticism as a problem to be solved, and a problem that *could* be solved, by means of the development of the logic of probability. Our next philosopher of science assumed that Humean skepticism was irrefutable, and he made it the basis for his entire philosophy. That philosopher is Sir Karl Popper.

3.4   POPPER, CRITICAL RATIONALISM, AND FALSIFICATIONISM

Sir Karl Popper (1902–1994) was born in Austria and studied mathematics, physics, and philosophy at the University of Vienna. Although not a member of the Vienna Circle, he interacted frequently with its members. The German edition of his first book, *The Logic of Scientific Discovery*, was published in Vienna in 1935. He accepted a position as senior lecturer at Canterbury University in New Zealand in 1937, moved to England in 1945 to teach at the London School of Economics, and was knighted in 1964. At various times, and by numerous people, he has been called a logical positivist, a logical empiricist, an irrationalist, a relativist, and a realist. While he refers to his philosophy as "critical rationalism," others refer to it as "falsificationism." The reasons why different people come to different conclusions concerning Popperian philosophy will become evident as we trace the development of its major themes.

As a student of physics, Popper was immersed in the development of Einstein's theories of relativity. He recalls being "thrilled" at the results of Eddington's test of Einsteinian theory (Popper 1959, p. 34). Popper noted that

Newtonian mechanics had been overthrown, or in his words "refuted," by Einsteinian theory even though Newtonian mechanics had been "confirmed," or "verified," by literally millions of observations over a span of time exceeding two hundred years. Popper also experienced, observed, and was greatly upset by, the rising tide of irrationalist philosophies in Europe, most notably, fascism and Marxism. He saw both of these political philosophies as logical outgrowths of Hegelian idealism and its notion of the historical inevitability of social events and structure. On the one hand, fascism claimed that it was inevitable historically that the "chosen race" should rule. On the other hand, Marxism claimed the historical inevitability of the success of the "chosen class" (Popper 1966, p. 9). Tracing Hegelian idealism and its irrationalism and historicism back to Plato, Popper was later to argue forcefully that such closed societies "are not inevitable; the future depends on ourselves" (1966, p. 2). For Popper, the key to combatting totalitarianism and for maintaining an "open society" was the maintenance of a belief in reason, or rationalism, because "beginning with the suppression of reason and truth, we must end with the most brutal and violent destruction of all that is human" (Popper 1966, p. 200).

But was not the theory underlying Marxist philosophy scientific? Did it not explain thousands of observable social phenomena? In fact, was it not the case that *all* social phenomena could be explained by Marxist theory? Before turning eighteen, Popper had formulated his answer to all those who claimed that theories could be verified by means of their confirming instances. He set about developing a book on the topic, which culminated in 1931 with a manuscript so massive that it was never to be published in that form. However, Popper's basic thesis concerning falsifiability was published in a letter to the editor of *Erkenntnis* in 1933. In this letter he attacks the logical positivists' "verifiability principle" and puts forth his own criterion of falsifiability (Popper 1959, p. 311). A shortened version of the 1931 manuscript was published in Vienna as *Logik der Forschung* (The Logic of Scientific Discovery), which was translated into English in 1959.

Given the pervasive concern of philosophy with Humean skepticism, it is not surprising that the very first section in Chapter 1 of *The Logic of Scientific Discovery* is "The Problem of Induction." Popper discusses the "widely accepted view" that the fundamental characteristic of the empirical sciences is that they use "inductive methods." These methods are usually considered to be procedures that allow one to go from "observations or experiments to universal statements, such as hypotheses or theories" (Popper 1959, p. 27). Therefore, according to this widely accepted view, what is necessary is to find a procedure for justifying inductive inferences or a "principle of induction" that would enable us to "put inductive inferences into a logically acceptable form" (Popper 1959, p. 29). Popper believed it was impossible to find a suitable principle of induction. Why? Because "I found Hume's refutation of inductive inference clear and conclusive" (Popper 1963, p. 42). Popper notes that "I regard Hume's formulation and treatment of the logical problem of induction . . . as a flawless gem . . . a simple, straightforward, logical refutation of any claim that induction could be a valid argument, or a justifiable way of reasoning" (Popper 1982, pp. 86, 88).

At this point, the reader should carefully note Popper's words. He rejects inductive arguments because they could not be "valid arguments." In this case, he is using "valid" as synonymous with "deductive arguments." That is, Popper rejects inductive arguments because they are not valid, and they are not valid because they are not deductive arguments. But inductive arguments, by definition, are not deductive arguments. More important, note the phrase "or a justifiable way of reasoning." All reasoning in order to be legitimate must be deductive in nature. Popper would have us equate "good reasons to believe" in the truth of a proposition with "reasons that accord with deductive logic." We shall return to this issue later and shall see how restricting "good reasons" to "deductive logic" (ironically) leads Popper to irrationalism, rather than rationalism (Stove 1982).

Popper dismissed the logical empiricists' program that attempted to find a probability formulation for the "degree of confirmation" of a lawlike generalization. (Indeed, over 25 percent of the original text of *The Logic of Scientific Discovery* was devoted to examining and refuting the position that the degree of confirmation could be equated with a probability.) Popper next considered whether the logical positivist verifiability principle could solve the "problem of demarcation" between science and pseudoscience. Popper points out, as he did in his letter to *Erkenntnis* in 1933, that the verifiability principle as a method of demarcation is untenable because lawlike generalizations cannot be verified in the sense of being shown *deductively* true. (It is on the basis of the *Erkenntnis* letter pointing out the deficiencies of the verifiability principle and on the *Logic of Scientific Discovery* that Popper justifies the claim that he "killed" logical positivism. It is also why Popper deeply resented the fact that many of his critics called him a "positivist.")

Popper concludes that, because neither verifiability nor probability-confirmation will work, "the *falsifiability* of a system is to be taken as a criterion of demarcation." In other words, "it must be possible for an empirical scientific system to be refuted by experience" (Popper 1959, pp. 40–41). As will be recalled, Popper refers to his philosophy as critical rationalism, and it is precisely the doctrine of falsifiability that to him justifies the label of "critical" in his philosophy.

Popper proposed that the *objectivity* of science is maintained through the falsifiability principle: "The objectivity of scientific statements lies in the fact that they can be inter-subjectively tested" (Popper 1959, p. 44). But a scientific statement is not testable because one can find confirming instances. Rather, a statement is "more testable" the more things that it excludes from happening. (Some "theories" exclude nothing from happening, and, therefore, are not testable. In particular, Popper held that devices such as the concept of "false consciousness" made all social phenomena consistent with Marxist theory, and, therefore, prevented it from being falsifiable.)

Theories, for Popper, cannot be confirmed, they can only be "corroborated." But corroboration is not to be found in terms of the number of times a theory has withstood attempts at falsification. Nor can the degree of corroboration be associated with a specific probability. Rather, a theory is corroborated more highly to the extent that it has passed *severe* tests (Popper 1959, p. 267).

Popper is often accused of proposing a "dogmatic falsificationism," in which a theory must be ruthlessly rejected on the basis of a single falsifying test (see Lakatos 1970, p. 181). Popper's writings belie that interpretation. Consider the following: "No conclusive disproof of a theory can ever be produced; for it is always possible to say that the experimental results are not reliable" (Popper 1959, p. 50). Also, "a few stray basic statements contradicting a theory will hardly induce us to reject it as falsified" (p. 86). Furthermore, Popper recognized that we attempt to falsify "basic statements," and it is always possible in principle to deduce even *more* basic statements for further test (p. 104). Therefore, for Popper, we "corroborate" that a theory is not false by subjecting it to numerous severe tests, carefully examining the experimental requirements and characteristics of each test, and examining whether the basic statements being exposed to testing are truly the most appropriate.

How does science progress? By means of "bold conjectures and refutations" is Popper's answer (Popper 1963). In this regard, Popper noted, Marxism is filled with bold conjectures (e.g., capitalism will result in the absolute impoverishment of the working class, the first socialist revolution will occur in the most industrially developed country, and socialism will be free of revolutions). It was also abundantly clear to Popper that all the bold conjectures had been refuted and that Marxism could be "saved" from further refutations only by its advocates putting forth ex post, ad hoc, auxiliary hypotheses.

Popper's philosophy is decidedly realist as to the aims of science and the ontology of the concepts in its theories. It is not the "*possession* of knowledge, of irrefutable truth, that makes the man of science, but his persistent and recklessly critical *quest* for truth" (Popper 1959, p. 281). Furthermore, theories are "genuine conjectures—highly informative guesses about the world which although not verifiable . . . can be submitted to severe critical tests. They are serious attempts to discover the truth" (Popper 1959, p. 115). Popper rejects the instrumentalist view of theories and the entities in them. He attributes the current allure of instrumentalism to the "Copenhagen interpretation" of quantum mechanics. Popper accepts the position that we cannot know both the position and the momentum of a subatomic particle, but he rejects the assertion that a subatomic particle cannot *have* both a position and a momentum (Popper 1982). Is the Hegelian idealist position correct that the world does not exist independently of its being perceived? No, claims Popper: "Some of these theories of ours can clash with reality; and when they do, we know that there is a reality; that there is something to remind us of the fact that our ideas may be mistaken. And this is why the realist is right" (Popper 1959, p. 117). But, because we never know for certain that our theories are correct, we should *proliferate* our theories as much as possible to encourage the growth of scientific knowledge. This proliferation of theories will lead to an "open society."

We opened this section on Popper with the observation that he and his philosophy have been called many, often contradictory, names. For Popper, falsifiability made his philosophy "critical," and the strong emphasis on conjectures made his philosophy similar to the rationalists. Hence, he refers to it as "critical rationalism." Even though Popper claims to have "killed" positivism by pointing out the problems of the verifiability principle, many writers, such as Barone (1986) continue to refer to Popper as a positivist. Similarly, writers such as Laudan (1979) refer to Popper as a logical empiricist, even though Popper strongly opposed the reliance on formal logic of the logical empiricists and their program of formalizing scientific theories in terms of mathematical logic. He also sharply opposed the instrumentalist's view of theories held by most logical empiricists, and he clearly identified his falsifiability criterion as not being a "theory of meaning" (unlike the testability criterion of Carnap and Feigl). However, Popper did interact extensively with both the logical positivists and the logical empiricists and shared many of their values and views. In particular, he shared their views with respect to the unity of science, the importance of observation in science, the rationality of science, and the progress of science. In fact, the shared belief in the progress of science of Popper and the logical empiricists is of such importance that their concept of scientific progress warrants more detailed explication.

3.5   THE CONCEPT OF SCIENTIFIC PROGRESS

Implicit (and sometimes explicit) in the views of Popper and the logical empiricists was the belief that science progressed through four different means: (1) the development of new theories for phenomena not previously explained, (2) the falsification of existing theories and their replacement with new theories, (3) the expansion of the scope of a theory to include new phenomena, and (4) the reduction of specific theories into more general theories. We shall discuss each of these means of progress.

3.5.1   New Theories

With respect to the first method of progress (the development of new theories for phenomena not previously explained), the logical empiricists believed that this was beyond the scope of their endeavors. Specifically, the logical empiricists, following Whewell (1840) and Reichenbach (1938), made a sharp distinction between the "context of discovery" and the "context of justification." They believed that there was no *logic* of discovery, but that the discovery of new hypotheses and theories was an inherently psychological/sociological process, and the study of that process properly belonged within the psychology of science and/or the sociology of science. A second aspect of the discovery/justification thesis was that discovery was irrelevant to justification: "It is one thing to ask how we arrive at our scientific knowledge claims and what sociocultural factors contribute to their acceptance or rejection; and it is another thing to ask what sort of evidence and what general, objective rules and standards govern the testing, the confirmation or disconfirmation, and the acceptance or rejection of knowledge claims of science" (Feigl 1965, p. 472). Popper agreed that "the question how it happens that a new idea occurs to a man—whether it is a musical theme, a dramatic conflict, or a scientific theory—may be of great interest to empirical psychology; but it is irrelevant to the logical analysis of scientific knowledge" (Popper 1959, p. 31).

It is fashionable among many writers to deny the discovery/justification distinction. The reasons cited for denying the distinction usually fall under one or more of the following arguments: (1) the "argument from understanding science" (Suppe 1977b, pp. 125–26), (2) Kuhn's "context of pedagogy" and "subjective factors arguments" (Kuhn 1977, p. 327), and (3) Quine's argument for "naturalizing epistemology" (Quine 1969). Seigel reviews and analyzes the various arguments that the discovery/justification distinction should be abandoned and concludes that "these distinctions are necessary for our overall understanding of the complexities of scientific knowledge—and, in particular, for our understanding of the way in which scientific claims purport to *appropriately* portray our natural environment" (Siegel 1980a, p. 321). Similarly, Hoyningen-Huene reviews the status of the discovery/justification debate and points out that "philosophers of the historicist orientation felt compelled, in order to legitimize their philosophical child, to argue against the distinction" (Hoyningen-Huene 1987, p. 501). He traces the historical origins of the distinction, analyzes the arguments both in favor and against it, and concludes: "It is striking that none of the attacks on the context distinction has been directed against the distinction between the factual and the normative. But this difference seems to be the core of the context distinction as intended by its proponents" (Hoyningen-Huene 1987, p. 511). Stated simply, Hoyningen-Huene is pointing out that "is does not imply ought."

The issue of the discovery/justification distinction has arisen in the marketing literature. For example, Peter and Olson claim that the "positivistic/empiricist" view of science is that "only the logic of justification is needed to understand science" (Peter and Olson 1983, p. 119). Obviously, this is a straw man distortion of the actual views of the logical empiricists, for they simply restricted *their own studies* to justification.

3.5.2   Falsification of Theories

Continuing our discussion of the ways that science progresses, the second way is the falsification of prior theories and their replacement by successors. A common example is the falsification of the view of Ptolemy that the Sun revolves around the Earth and its replacement with the Copernican view that the Earth revolves around the Sun. Essentially, this is a major part of the Popperian view of scientific progress. But, if science is an endless series of conjectures and their refutations, in what meaningful sense can we say that science has made *progress*? Indeed, this is a serious issue for strict falsificationists. In mature sciences, such as physics, the issue seems to hinge on how one should answer the following question: "Is it more meaningful to claim that Newtonian physics was *false* and superseded by Einsteinian relativity; or is it more meaningful to claim that Newtonian physics was in some sense 'approximately true' or 'true within certain boundaries'"? On the one hand there are philosophers such as Laudan who claim that "I am aware of no sense of approximate truth according to which highly successful, but evidently false, theoretical assumptions could be regarded as 'truth like' " (Laudan 1981, p. 35). Others, in both physics and philosophy, contend that Newtonian physics is in some sense "approximately true" within its boundary conditions, and citing as examples that it was the predictive accuracy of Newtonian physics that put man on the moon, rather than Einsteinian relativity. For example, Rohrlich and Hardin argue that "superseding theories do not falsify established theories" as long as the "validity limits" of the theories are appropriately identified (Rohrlich and Hardin 1983, p. 603).

Recall that the logical empiricists adopted an instrumentalist, rather than realist, approach to theories (one of the "lessons" of the downfall of Newtonian mechanics). The fact that the existence of particular theoretical terms in a theory was demonstrated to be false would pose no insurmountable problem to a logical empiricist conception of "approximate truth" so long as the "directly testable consequences were close to the observable values" (Laudan 1981, p. 33).

3.5.3 Expansion of Theories

A third method for science to progress is to expand the scope of a theory by showing that it can explain more, or different, phenomena. The logical empiricists believed that the formalization of theories through mathematical logic might be helpful in this regard. The formalization would clearly identify the underlying structure of the theory and perhaps show how the theory could be expanded to cover additional phenomena. An example of this kind of procedure is the extension of classical particle mechanics to rigid body mechanics (Suppe 1977b, p. 53).

3.5.4 Reduction of Theories

The fourth way that science progresses is the subsumption of specific theories (reduction) into more general theories. For example, "Galileo's *Two New Sciences* was a contribution to the physics of freely falling terrestrial bodies; but when Newton showed that his own general theory of mechanics and gravitation (when supplemented by appropriate boundary conditions) entailed Galileo's laws, the latter were incorporated into the Newtonian theory as a special case" (Nagel 1960, p. 39). A strict or "naïve falsificationist" would claim that the reduction of Galileo's laws to Newton's would not be an example of progress because Galileo's laws cannot be derived *deductively* from Newton's laws. (Galileo's laws provide that a body falls to the earth with constant acceleration; Newton proposed that acceleration is inversely proportional to the square of the distance of the body to the center of the earth.)

The underlying issue concerning scientific progress is the *cumulativity* of scientific knowledge. Perhaps the most fundamental question facing science and the issue of scientific progress today is: To what extent, if any, is scientific knowledge cumulative? To what extent, if any, do we know more about the world as a result of the activities of science over, say, the past 400 years? Should we characterize Galileo's laws as "false" and Newton's laws as "false," and *generalizing* (inductively) that all of science is, simply, an endless succession of replacing "false" theories with *equally* "false" theories? Under such a construal, it would indeed be difficult (but perhaps not impossible) to make the case that science is cumulative, or even partially cumulative. Conversely, is it more meaningful to claim that we genuinely *knew more* about the world after Galileo's laws than before? Similarly, did we *know* more after Newton's laws? Note that the issue here is not whether over the past 400 years all the knowledge-claims of science have been *strictly* cumulative, analogous to bricks in a pile. Nor is the issue whether science has established, or even *could* establish, final or ultimate truths. The question is: Has there been *any* cumulative growth in scientific knowledge at all?

There are some authors who claim, or whose stated views logically imply, that there has been no scientific progress, no cumulativity at all in the knowledge-claims of science. These writers are generally referred to as "historical relativists," and are the topic of the next chapter. But to understand and evaluate the credibility of the historical relativists, we need first to examine more extensively what we mean by "knowledge" and the approaches to justifying knowledge-claims.

3.6   KNOWLEDGE, FOUNDATIONALISM, AND FALLIBILISM

The purpose of this section is to explicate what we mean by scientific knowledge. We start from Plato's conceptualization that knowledge means "justified true belief." We then examine foundationalism, the "K-K thesis," the "philosophers' fallacy," and fallibilism as they relate to scientific knowledge.

3.6.1   Knowledge, Belief, and Theories of Truth

Since the time of Plato, (see section 2.1) philosophy has conceptualized knowledge to be "justified true belief" (Suppe 1977b, p. 701). On this view, knowledge implies belief. That is, (unless the person is lying), a speaker of the English language cannot truthfully claim to "know that *P*" unless they "believe that *P*." Although philosophers have investigated the nature of knowledge and knowledge-claims extensively over thousands of years, they have paid little attention to the nature of belief or belief-claims. Generally, belief-claims have been thought to be nonproblematical. The locus classicus concerning belief was *The Emotions and the Will* written by the Scottish philosopher Alexander Bain in 1859. Bain suggested that to know the beliefs of people is to examine their actions, because people may respond untruthfully to questions about their beliefs, or they may not even know their own beliefs. Therefore, the beliefs of people are to be inferred from examining their actions. For example, if an individual in fact believes that a water-well contains no poison, the person should be willing to drink from the well. As will be recalled, it is precisely this line of reasoning that G.E. Moore used in his attack on idealism, in which he claimed that the stated beliefs of idealists were inconsistent with their behaviors (see section 3.1.1).

A knowledge-claim is more than simply the statement of belief. Knowledge also implies a belief that is in some sense true. That is, if a speaker of the English language claims to "know that *P*" and subsequently claims to "know not *P*," the person does not speak of having previously had "false knowledge" and now having "true knowledge." Rather, the person would claim to have been *mistaken* in claiming to "know that *P*." For example, if a person claims to *know* that a water-well contains no poison and subsequently observes that many people have drunk from the well and immediately died, the person speaks of being mistaken in claiming to know that the well was safe. Therefore, the word "knowledge" in the English language always connotes some sense of the word "true," as well as "belief."

Finally, knowledge is more than a belief that is claimed to be true, it is a belief that can be *justified* as true. Although there have been many theories as to what justifies the truth-content of a belief, almost all fall within three major groupings: the correspondence theory of truth, the coherence theory of truth, and the pragmatic theory of truth. (Strictly speaking, the "consensus theory of truth," held by relativists, is not really a "theory" of *truth*, insofar it simply states that whatever a person or group *believes* to be true, is true, i.e., "belief" equals "truth"—see section 4.1.3.)

The correspondence theory of truth provides that the truth-content of any statement or proposition is the extent to which what the statement refers to, in fact, corresponds with reality. Three problems are evident with any correspondence theory of truth. First, there may be no reality external to the human mind for establishing correspondence. For example, the idealist position is that the external world does not exist unperceived (see section 2.4). Therefore, in Hegelian terms, since only the "rational is the real," one cannot compare knowledge-claims with any external reality. Second, even if one accepts the fundamental premise of classical realism (that the external world exists unperceived), there are knowledge-claims that consist exclusively of terms that appear in principle to have no external referents. For example, the "entities" in mathematics and logic seem to have no reference in the external world, yet areas such as mathematics and logic contain knowledge-claims that have truth-content. Third, again, even if it is conceded that the external world exists unperceived, knowledge of the characteristics of this external world can be gleaned only through human senses. But a problem arises because we know that our perceptual processes are fallible, and, therefore, what is *perceived* to be reality, may in fact be an illusion. One of the most complete expositions and defenses of the correspondence theory of truth in the twentieth century using formal logic was the work of Alfred Tarski (see his 1956 work). Tarski's formal development of the correspondence theory of truth was very influential on Popper (1959, p. 274).

The second theory of truth, the coherence theory, indicates that a statement is true or false to the extent it fits, is consistent with, or "coheres" with another statement or system of statements. This conceptualization of how one justifies the truth of a statement certainly accords with many examples of how people claim to know that a statement is true. For example, we may reject as false the claim that a particular consumer is brand-loyal to two different brands of the same product at the same time on the basis that it fails to *cohere* with our knowledge of how brand loyalty may be measured (e.g., if brand loyalty is defined as purchasing more than 50 percent of one's requirements of a particular product from a particular brand).

Infinite regress poses the major problem with the coherence theory of truth. That is, if statement A is to be justified as true by statement B, and statement B is to be justified by statement C, and statement C is to be justified by statement D, and so on, what is the justification for the statement at the end of the justificatory chain? Sometimes the last statement in the chain is justified through correspondence, as in the correspondence theory of truth. Sometimes the last statement in the chain is justified as a "necessary truth" (true in all possible worlds). For example, the axioms of Euclidian geometry were thought to be *necessarily true*. Similarly, the last statement in the justificatory chain might be a statement that is, on intuitive grounds, indubitably true (true for any normal person "beyond all reasonable doubt"). For example, the statement *cogito ergo sum* was considered by Descartes to be indubitably true (see section 2.3.2). Finally, the last statement in the justificatory chain might, simply, be assumed to be true by stipulation or convention.

The third theory of truth, the pragmatic theory of truth, has its origins in the pragmatism of C.S. Peirce (1839–1914). Pragmatism is often considered to be the only unique philosophical system original to the United States. Peirce developed pragmatism as a rule or procedure for promoting conceptual clarity in science. (Thus, Peirce shared much with the logical positivists.) In his 1878 paper entitled "How to Make Our Ideas Clear," Peirce proposed that the meaning of scientific terms is entailed by their "practical consequences." The totality of practical consequences for a scientific term provides a conditional translation for the term or "sign." All terms for which there are no practical consequences have no "pragmatic meaning" or are "empty." Thus, the pragmatic theory of meaning of Peirce is very similar to the operational definitions proposed by the operationalists several decades later. It also foreshadowed the "verifiability theory of meaning" developed by the logical positivists.

Although Peirce restricted his pragmatic theory of meaning to *experimental* inquiry, William James (1842–1910) generalized pragmatism to a theory of truth. In particular, James proposed that the truth-content of statements must be evaluated on the basis of their "practical consequences," "usefulness," "workability," or "cash value." Thus, in a famous defense of faith, James noted: "On pragmatic principles, if the hypothesis of God works satisfactorily in the widest sense of the word, it is 'true'" (James 1907, p. 299).

The extension of pragmatism to such concepts as "truth" infuriated its originator, C.S. Peirce. In fact, Peirce objected so violently that he coined the label "pragmaticism" to differentiate his own philosophy from the pragmatism of William James. Other philosophers began to assail James's pragmatic theory of truth, most notably, Bertrand Russell and G.E. Moore. For example, Russell (1945) pointed out that the way James used the word "working" is at odds with how scientists use the term. When a scientist says a theory "works," the implication is that the theory, for example, predicts correctly, *not* that the theory is good for the scientist or for society. Furthermore, the pragmatic theory of truth confuses sentences like "It is true that other people exist" with sentences like "It is useful and desirable to believe that other people exist." Although some recent writers (see Phillips 1984, 1987) believe that James was misunderstood, the pragmatic theory of truth has gained little acceptance.

3.6.2   Foundationalism, the K-K Thesis, the "Philosophers' Fallacy," and Fallibilism

The preceding section points out that, at least since the time of Plato, Western philosophy has considered knowledge to be "justified true belief." Further, the truth of a knowledge-claim was to be determined by its correspondence with reality and/or its coherence with other statements that we *knew*. However, in *Theaetetus*, Plato argued that genuine knowledge can be had only of those things that are eternal and unchanging, for example, the entities in geometry and his idealized "forms" (see section 2.1.2). Because the objects in the existing external world were constantly changing and were only "imperfect copies" of the "forms," genuine knowledge of the existing external world could not be had. That is, Plato equated knowledge with true beliefs "justified with certainty." And for Plato, "certainty" meant the degree of certainty found in the truths of geometry.

Plato's view of restricting knowledge to claims "known with certainty" provided the historical genesis for the position known as *foundationalism*. Briefly, foundationalism provides that scientific knowledge must be based on a foundation that is known to be true with absolute certainty (McMullin 1985, p. 124). Consider the classical rationalists. As previously discussed in section 2.3.2., Descartes's "method of doubt" sought unquestionably true first principles for his science and arrived at *cogito ergo sum* for such a foundation. On the other hand, classical empiricists, such as Bacon, believed that direct observation and experience would provide a secure and certain foundation for the development of science. A modern variant of Plato's thesis is the "K-K thesis."

The K-K thesis holds that to "know that *P*" entails "one must *know* that one *knows* that *P*" (hence, "K-K"). In other words, "one cannot know that P unless one knows that one's claim to know that P is correct" (Suppe 1977b, p. 717).[1] Thus, not only must science justify its knowledge claims with good reasons, but it must justify its method of justifying. The tacit acceptance of the K-K thesis has resulted in a slide into skepticism by many philosophers of science through two mechanisms. First, the K-K thesis involves infinite regress. "To know" entails "one must know that one knows," which entails "one must know that one knows that one knows," and so forth. Second, "to know that one knows" has often been interpreted as "to *know with certainty* that one knows."

For example, the K-K thesis underlies Humean skepticism: "The heart of Hume's attack consists in showing that one cannot know the induction hypothesis needed to infer the derivative knowledge that *P* from what one already knows, hence that one does not know that one's evidence is adequate; but this yields his [Hume's] skeptical conclusions only if resort is made to the K-K Thesis" (Suppe 1977b, p. 718). Furthermore, the logical positivists implicitly accepted the K-K thesis, and, therefore, attempted (unsuccessfully) to overcome Humean skepticism with an inductive logic substituting a known probability for "know with certainty." Similarly, Popper accepted the K-K thesis and attempted to meet its resultant skepticism with the falsification doctrine, which, in turn, "fails" because such procedures do not enable one to *know with certainty* that any particular theory is conclusively false. Finally, "the K-K Thesis crucially underlies Feyerabend's and Kuhn's extreme views on scientific knowledge" (Suppe 1977b, p. 719).

Three options for dealing with the K-K thesis are manifest. The first option is to follow in the footsteps of the classical rationalists, classical empiricists, logical positivists, logical empiricists, and falsificationists. This option implies the acceptance of the K-K thesis and to continue the foundationalist search for incorrigible foundations and methods for the development of scientific knowledge. The second option is to reject the K-K thesis and develop fallibilistic models and theories regarding science and the development of scientific knowledge. In this regard, *fallibilism* is an alternative to foundationalism. That is, fallibilism holds not only that scientific knowledge is fallible, but also that genuine scientific knowledge may be built upon foundations that are themselves fallible. As Suppe has observed, the denial of the K-K thesis and the acceptance of fallibilism "appears to accord more closely with the actual means whereby science evaluates putative knowledge claims in the attempt to undergo the objective growth in scientific knowledge" (Suppe 1977b, p. 726). My own position on the K-K thesis is in accord with Suppe: "In science all knowledge claims are tentative, subject to revision on the basis of new evidence. The concept 'certainty' belongs to theology, not science" (Hunt 1991a, p. 201). I believe that the acceptance of fallibilism and its concomitant rejection of the K-K thesis and foundationalism, is the preferred option.

There is a third option that is put forth by many as the preferred path to follow. This option is to (1) accept the K-K thesis, (2) point out that neither science nor the philosophy of science can justify with certainty its own methods of justifying its knowledge-claims, and (3) proceed to accept (reluctantly, as with Thomas Kuhn, or exuberantly, as with Paul Feyerabend) the resultant relativism, skepticism, and irrationalism. This third option represents a classic example of what Harré has labeled the "philosophers' fallacy of high redefinition" (Harré 1986, p. 4). This is the fallacy of defining a concept (e.g., scientific knowledge, truth, falsity, objectivity, or progress) in such a manner (e.g., must be "known with certainty" or "known with probability 'p'") that the concept cannot be realized and then lapsing into relativism, nihilism, or skepticism.[2] To the subject of relativism, we now turn.

QUESTIONS FOR ANALYSIS AND DISCUSSION

1. Explain the relevance of John Passmore's quotation in the epigraph to this chapter to the quest by the ancient Greeks to separate "knowledge" from "opinion." What does Passmore mean when he claims "its accusations rest on a misunderstanding of science"? Evaluate Passmore's thesis that the attack on science is also an attack on art, history, philosophy, and so forth. Do the humanities have a stake in the defense of science? Do the sciences have a stake in the defense of the humanities?

2. What is classical realism? To what extent is classical realism consistent/inconsistent with classical empiricism/rationalism? It is often claimed that all scientists are either classical realists or sophists. Evaluate this position.

3. What is Russell's method of "logical constructionism"? Do experience and observation play any role in logical constructionism? If so, what? If not, is this a deficiency of logical constructionism?

4. What is the "picture theory of meaning" of Wittgenstein? How does this theory of meaning relate to classical realism? How does this theory of meaning relate to Russell's logical constructionism? What is the difference between attempting to build a "philosophical system" and Wittgenstein's claim that "all philosophy is critique of language"?

5. Why was Einsteinian relativity so disastrous for the philosophy of science at the turn of the century? Why could Hegelian idealism not be compatible with quantum mechanics? What problems for Machian

neo-positivism did quantum mechanics pose? How does logical positivism accommodate both Einsteinian relativity and quantum mechanics?

6. What are the fundamental tenets of logical positivism? What is the difference between considering logical positivism to be a movement and considering it to be a research program? To what extent is the movement of logical positivism consistent with the aims of the Enlightenment? Why were the logical positivists so critical of Hegelian idealism? In your judgment, should they have been so critical?

7. What was the major "lesson" that the logical positivists learned from Einsteinian relativity and quantum mechanics? To what extent did the views of logical positivists depart from classical realism? To what extent did the views of logical positivists accord with those of classical realism? Why was the "Humean view of causality" consistent with the "lesson" that the logical positivists learned from Einsteinian relativity and quantum mechanics?

8. How does logical empiricism differ from logical positivism? How does Humean skepticism relate to the views of the logical empiricists concerning scientific explanation? How does Humean skepticism relate to the "theoretical term/observational term" distinction?

9. What is the difference between developing a "correspondence rule" for *defining* a construct and developing a "measure" of a construct? Are there circumstances under which "correspondence rules" and "measures" are identical? Are there research programs that imply that "correspondence rules" and "measures" are identical? *Should* all "measures" of constructs be "correspondence rules"?

10. Summarize Humean skepticism. Why does it require that "only deductive derivations are valid"? Speculate on why the discipline of philosophy has been so obsessed with Humean skepticism. What does Humean skepticism have to do with Plato, his conceptualization of knowledge, and his "theory of forms"?

11. To what extent is Popper's philosophy of "critical rationalism" consistent/inconsistent with the Enlightenment? To what extent does Popper's philosophy rely on Humean skepticism? How do Popper's philosophy and Humean skepticism relate to the Enlightenment?

12. Differentiate between "corroboration" for Popper and "confirmation" for the logical empiricists. Does the claim that theories are not, strictly speaking, *falsifiable* necessarily imply that all theories are "equally false"? Does the claim that theories are not, strictly speaking, *confirmable*, mean that all theories are "equally true"? If so, why? If not, why not? If we cannot show that our theories are true-with-certainty,

or, alternatively, that they are false-with-certainty, should we not (as relativists demand) dispense entirely with the notions of "truth" and "falsity"?

13. What does "scientific progress" imply? Why should we be interested in whether science makes progress or not? Do we really *know* more about marketing now than we did two decades ago? How about four decades ago? In which areas are we making the most progress? What definition of "progress" was implied in your answer to the previous question?

14. What is the difference between the claim that "only the logic of justification is needed to understand science" (Peter and Olson 1983, p. 119) and the claim that "the logical empiricists focused exclusively on the logic of justification." Why is this difference significant? What does it mean to "understand" science? What does the positive/normative dichotomy have to do with this issue?

15. What is the "philosophers' fallacy"? How does it relate to Humean skepticism? How does it relate to the current discussions concerning relativism in marketing and the social sciences? Why is the "philosophers' fallacy" a genuine fallacy? How does the philosophers' fallacy inexorably lead to the destruction of our ability to make judgments on the merits of issues? (Hint: Consider the extent to which the philosophers' fallacy *destroys* language. Remember, Orwell's world of *1984* had no word for "science.")

NOTES

1. I am indebted to Michael Levin, Department of Philosophy, City University of New York for helpful correspondence on the implications of the K-K thesis.

2. I am indebted to David Stove, University of Sydney Philosophy Department, for pointing out that the "fallacy of high redefinition" was first discussed by Paul Edwards in his evaluation of Bertrand Russell's work on induction. See Edwards (1951).

4 THE RISE AND FALL OF HISTORICAL RELATIVISM IN PHILOSOPHY OF SCIENCE

The cruelest fate which can overtake enfants-terribles *is to awake and find that their avowed opinions have swept the suburbs.*

—David C. Stove

In the 1960s, the philosophy of science turned toward historicism, relativism, and irrationalism. Indeed, the pejorative label of "Received View" was coined and used as an epithet to be hurled at anyone who dared hold any view that did not conform with an irrationalistic perspective of science.[1] But, to understand historical relativism requires a basic, working knowledge of *relativism* itself. Therefore, this chapter begins with a discussion of relativism, then examines the versions of historical relativism provided by Kuhn and Feyerabend, and concludes with a discussion of why historical relativism was so quickly and passionately embraced in the 1960s.

4.1 RELATIVISM VERSUS ABSOLUTISM

Although (as was pointed out in section 2.1.3) relativism can be traced to the time of Socrates, modern relativism has its genesis in the works of certain cultural anthropologists at the turn of the twentieth century. Much of the cultural anthropology of the nineteenth century, implicitly or explicitly, accepted the concept of the progressivity of culture, which maintained that cultures progressed from those of primitive tribes and peoples to those of modern societies. Similarly (as with August Comte), science was considered to be an institution that progressed from beliefs based on magic and superstition to beliefs justified by scientific method. As a reaction to what was considered to be cultural ethnocentrism, several anthropologists, led by Franz Boas and M. Herskovits, argued strongly that other cultures should not be evaluated in terms of Western norms. Rather, they argued that we should accept "the validity of every set of norms for the people whose lives are guided by them, and the values they represent" (Herskovits 1947, p. 76). Thus, cultural relativism was born.

4.1.1 Cultural/Moral Relativism

Essentially, the cultural relativism proposed by the anthropologists embodied the acceptance of three theses: (1) the elements embodied in a culture can be evaluated only relative to the norms of that culture; (2) there are no transcultural or culture-neutral norms to evaluate different cultures (or different elements within cultures); and (3) because there are no transcultural norms, no culture (and no element within a culture) can be claimed to be "better" or "more advanced" than any other culture (or any other element within another culture). For relativist anthropologists, cultures and elements within cultures are neither good nor bad, they simply *are*.

Cultural relativism has come to be closely associated with *moral* relativism, so much so, in fact, that the terms are often used synonymously. As Krausz and Meiland put it, "cultural relativism is the position which begins with value relativism—the view that each set of values, *including moral values*, is as valid as each other set—and draws the conclusion that no society has a right to attempt to change or otherwise interfere with any other society" (1982, p. 7, italics added). Moral relativism holds the following:

1. Whether an action is right or wrong can be evaluated only relative to some moral code (held by an individual, group, society or culture).
2. There are no objective, impartial, or nonarbitrary standards or criteria for evaluating different moral codes (across individuals, groups, societies, or cultures).

Therefore, because there are no objective criteria for evaluating codes, the holder of one moral code cannot praise, condemn, or interfere with the actions of another individual, group, society, or culture that has a different moral code.

Cultural relativism was embraced enthusiastically by many liberal colonialists, most notably many British administrators in places such as West Africa (Williams, in Krausz and Meiland 1982, p. 171). Several academic disciplines have, either implicitly or explicitly, embraced cultural relativism. The discipline of social anthropology has come closest to being dominated by the cultural relativist perspective (Hollis and Lukes 1982, p. 1). Furthermore, many writers believe that cultural and ethical relativism are pervasive throughout American society. For example, Bloom believes:

> There is one thing a professor can be absolutely certain of: almost every student entering the university believes, or says he believes that truth is relative. If this belief is put to the test, one can count on the students' reaction: they will be uncomprehending. . . . The danger they have been taught to fear from absolutism is not error but intolerance. . . . The true believer is the real danger. The study of history and of culture teaches that all the world was mad in the past; men always thought they were right, and that led to wars, persecutions, slavery, xenophobia, racism, and chauvinism. The point is not to correct the mistakes and really be right; rather it is not to think you are right at all. If I pose the routine questions designed to confute them and make them think, such as, "if you had been a British administrator in India, would you have let the natives under your governance burn the widow at the funeral of a man who had died"? they either remain silent or reply that the British should never have been there in the first place. (Bloom 1987, p. 25–26)

On Cultural/Moral Relativism: For Reason. So, cultural and moral relativism began with the observation of diversity, was nourished by hostility toward ethnocentrism, and was (often) motivated by a desire for pluralism and an enlightened tolerance toward non-Western cultures. Unfortunately, although individual relativists may advocate pluralism and enlightened tolerance, the *philosophy* of relativism does not *imply* these attributes. In that our focus in this book is on cognitive relativism, we can give only a flavor of the arguments that show the deficiencies of cultural/moral relativism.

First, we examine the claim that relativism leads to an "enlightened" viewpoint toward other cultures. Consider the fact that there still are several societies in the world today where the practice of slavery continues unabated. (The "market price" of a young child has been reported to be $150–250) (Palacios 1987). Or, consider that, in the late 1970s, the Khmer Rouge slaughtered between one and two million of their fellow Cambodians (out of a population of approximately 7 million) (*Time* 1988, p. 32). Or, consider that the Western estimates of "only" 20 million Soviet citizens being murdered during Stalin's purges have been revised upward by the Soviet historian Bestuzhevlada to 38–50 million ("Purge Toll Under Stalin Revised" 1988). (As a consequence of the revelations of Bestuzhevlada and others, the Soviet State Committee on Education, as the collapse of the Soviet Union neared, canceled all traditional history exams so that the history books—which had maintained that, at most, a "few thousand" dissidents had been executed—could be revised to reflect the truth) (Brown 1988, p. 74). This Orwellian approach to the facts of social reality and its accompanying list of atrocities could go on and on. Is it "enlightened" not to condemn such atrocities? Most of us would, rightly, claim "No." Yet, as the ethicist James Rachels has pointed out, cultural/moral relativism implies that none of these heinous actions and practices could be condemned under moral relativism:

> Cultural Relativism would preclude us from saying that any of these practices were wrong. We would not even be able to say that a society tolerant of Jews is *better* than the anti-Semitic society, for that would imply some sort of transcultural standard of comparison. The failure to condemn *these* practices does not seem "enlightened"; on the contrary, slavery and anti-Semiticism seem wrong *wherever they occur. Nevertheless, if we took cultural relativism seriously, we would have to admit that these social practices are also immune from criticism.* (Rachels 1986, pp. 17–18)

When Rachels uses the phrase "if we took cultural relativism seriously," he is pointing out that many who refer to themselves as cultural relativists are engaging in self-delusion or sophistry.[2]

Second, just as cultural/moral relativism does not imply an enlightened perspective, neither does it imply a tolerant pluralism, even though advocates such as Herskovits seem to believe that it does: "In practice, the philosophy of relativism is a philosophy of tolerance" (Herskovits 1972, p. 31). Harrison provides a detailed analysis of why cultural relativism does not imply tolerance (Harrison, in Krausz and Meiland 1982). Briefly, suppose we have two societies, *A* and *B*, both of which are firmly committed to relativism, but which have different religions. Suppose further that society *A* has a norm that states that it has a moral obligation to impose, by force if necessary, its religion on all other societies of different religions. Such a norm, because it is consistent with the rest of its culture, is "right," and, given relativism, the norm cannot be challenged from outside the culture. What logically follows is that society *A* will be morally "correct" in invading society *B* to impose on *B* the religion of *A*. Not only can other countries (e.g., *C* and *D*) not morally condemn society *A* (because it is only following a norm of its culture), but (most ironically) society *B* cannot even condemn society *A* (because *B* is also firmly committed to relativism). In short, not only does relativism not *imply* tolerance, but also, relativism can easily be used to defend the most atrociously intolerant actions. As the sociologist Orlando Patterson observes:

> Relativism, in fact, can be associated just as easily with a reactionary view of the world, and can easily be used to rationalize inaction, complacency, and even the wildest forms of oppression. It is all too easy for the reactionary white South African, or American, to say of the reservation Bantus or Indians, that it is wrong to interfere with their way of life since what might appear to be squalor and backwardness to us, may be matters of great virtue to them. (Patterson 1973, p. 126)

Recognizing that cultural/moral relativism does not deliver on its implied benefits, most ethicists (such as Rachels 1986) reject it. Some ethicists point out that cultural relativism, just like cognitive relativism, is self-refuting and incoherent (Lyons 1982). That is, the conclusion that one cannot (morally) interfere with the actions of another who holds a different moral code is inconsistent (self-refuting) with the thesis that there are no transcultural standards: "Critics find [supposed] moral relativists maintaining the relativity of morals, while at the same time morally condemning in an absolute way any outside interference in other societies" (Krausz and Meiland 1982, p. 9). On the other hand, many ethicists reject relativism on the basis that its second thesis is incorrect. Such ethicists hold that there exist criteria for appraising cultural values and norms, in general, and ethical values and norms, in particular. Such ethicists would subscribe to some form of *absolutism*. One should note that subscribing to the thesis that there exist appraisal criteria for evaluating ethical values (absolutism) does not imply that one must know with certainty that one's appraisal criteria are correct (the position that Siegel (1987) calls "vulgar absolutism"). Such a requirement would be akin to accepting the K-K thesis and falling prey to the "philosophers' fallacy," as discussed in section 3.6.2. In other words, one can hold that there exist appraisal criteria without holding that one *knows* for certain that one's appraisal criteria are true or correct.

Whereas moral relativism deals with matters of *value*, cognitive relativism deals with matters of *fact* (although sharp distinctions may at times be difficult to make) (Hollis and Lukes 1982, p. 2). Both share the *relativity thesis* that "something is relative to something else" and both share the *evaluation thesis* that "there are no objective, impartial, or nonarbitrary criteria to make evaluations *across* the various kinds of 'something else.'" (Absolutism rejects the evaluation thesis, not the relativity thesis.) As we shall see, as with moral relativism, cognitive relativism also has historical roots in cultural relativism.

4.1.2   Rationality Relativism and the "Strong Thesis"

There are numerous kinds of cognitive relativism. For example, Muncy and Fisk discuss subjective relativism, objective relativism, aletheic relativism, conceptual relativism, and social relativism (Muncy and Fisk 1987). However, three major types have the greatest import for marketing and social science: rationality relativism, reality relativism, and conceptual framework relativism. To understand the nature and origins of these kinds of relativism requires a brief discussion of the sociology of science.

The sociology of science can trace its roots back to the French philosopher August Comte. However, most sociologists ascribe to Robert K. Merton the distinction of "founding father of modern sociology of science" (Storer, in Merton 1973, p. xi). Merton's 1935 doctoral dissertation was titled "Science,

Technology, and Society in Seventeenth Century England." As a reaction to the fate of "non-Aryan science" in Hitler's Germany during the 1930s, Merton subsequently focused his attention on the various social conditions under which science can lose its autonomy in a 1937 paper entitled "Science and the Social Order." At that time, he also developed the concept of a "scientific community" that was later to be expanded on by Michael Polanyi and then to become a basic concept in the sociology of science (Storer, in Merton 1973, p. xvii). By 1942, Merton had developed his comprehensive analysis of the ideal norms of the various scientific communities:

1. Universalism (the knowledge-claims of science are to be subjected to preestablished impersonal criteria and are not to depend on attributes of the scientist such as race, nationality, and social class).
2. Communism (the knowledge gleaned from scientific activity is to be made available to all and is not to be the "private property" of the scientist).
3. Organized skepticism (all knowledge-claims are open to doubt and to be exposed to intense scrutiny).
4. Disinterestedness (in providing expert opinions on matters of controversy within the realm of the scientist's domain of knowledge, the scientist is to render an opinion based on the objective facts of the matter and not on the basis of the interests of a particular party in the controversy).

In 1945, Merton laid out a research program for studying the sociology of knowledge in an article entitled "The Paradigm for the Sociology of Knowledge." His program has been enormously influential in guiding the research activities of sociologists of science. An implicit assumption of the program was what Laudan calls the "arationality assumption," which "amounts to the claim that the sociology of knowledge may step in to explain beliefs if and only if those beliefs cannot be explained in terms of their rational merits" (Laudan 1977, p. 202). The arationality thesis has to do with the following question: Are the beliefs and knowledge-claims of science to be explained by examining the *reasons* that scientists give for their knowledge-claims, or are they to be explained as being *caused* by social factors such as race, nationality, social class, social position, and culture? Most sociologists of science have thought it appropriate to explain the knowledge-claims of science by looking for *causes* only when it was evident that there were no rational reasons underpinning the scientists' claims. In recent years, some sociologists of science have put forth the so-called "strong thesis" that all knowledge-claims in science are to be explained as being caused, or determined, by social factors. In the sociology of science literature, "the terms 'relativist' and 'strong thesis' are used almost interchangeably" (Sayers 1987, p. 135).[3]

The "strong thesis," or relativism in sociology, has its origins in the work of Karl Mannheim (1893–1947). Mannheim's most famous work was *Ideology and Utopia*, published in English in 1936. Acknowledging the tremendous influence of Hegel on his views, Mannheim proposed that "a modern theory of knowledge which takes account of the relational as distinct from the merely relative character of all historical knowledge must start with the assumption that there are spheres of thought in which it is impossible to conceive of absolute truth existing independently of the values and position of the subject and unrelated to the social context" (Mannheim, in Brodbeck 1968, p. 123). Given Mannheim's avowed Marxist orientation, it is not surprising that he focused on "values and position of the subject" and the "social context" as factors determinative of knowledge. A second source of Mannheim's view that knowledge was "socially determined" was his realization that the prevailing views of sociology, itself, were so determined:

> As Mannheim concedes, the entire discipline of the sociology of knowledge emerged as a generalization from the features of sociology itself. Early twentieth-century sociologists, examining the history of their own discipline, came to the conclusion that it was full of doctrines which owed more to the social background of their defenders than to their intrinsic rational merits. The general thesis of the sociology of knowledge (to wit, that ideas in most disciplines are socially determined) was founded on the hope that all other forms of knowledge might prove to be as subjective as sociology clearly was. (Laudan 1977, p. 244)

The impact of Mannheim on the development of the "strong thesis" in sociology has been great. Equally great, however, has been the work of the cultural anthropologists on the nature of rationality in primitive cultures. Recall that Merton and Laudan proposed that "social factors" should be used to explain *only* those knowledge-claims in science that could not be justified on rational grounds. However, suppose the canons that we in Western societies call "rational" were found to be a "purely local" formulation? Barnes and Bloor reviewed the works of the cultural anthropologists on primitive cultures and concluded that many such cultures do not exhibit a preference for what, by Western standards, would be called "rational." They, therefore, proposed that *rationality* is relative:

> For the relativist there is no sense attached to the idea that some standards or beliefs are really rational as distinct from merely locally accepted as such. Because he thinks that there are no context-free or super-cultural norms of rationality, he does not see rationally and irrationally held beliefs as making up two distinct and qualitatively different classes of thing . . . hence the relativist conclusion that they are to be explained in the same way. (Barnes and Bloor, in Hollis and Lukes 1982, pp. 27–28)

Our first major kind of cognitive relativism, *rationality relativism*, provides a major underlying rationale for the "strong thesis" that all knowledge-claims are to be treated equally and to be explained through the use of social factors, such as race, class, religion, and position. Thus, rationality relativism claims the following:

1.   The canons of correct, or rational, reasoning are relative to individual cultures.
2.   There are no objective, neutral, or nonarbitrary criteria to evaluate what is called "rational" across different cultures.

Therefore, if what counts as rational, or "good reasons," for accepting a knowledge-claim cannot be evaluated outside the confines of a particular culture, then *all* knowledge-claims are to be "explained" through social factors.

On Rationality Relativism: For Reason. Several lines of criticism have been directed at rationality relativism and the "strong thesis." The first observation about rationality relativism is that it is self-refuting and incoherent. Rationality relativism asserts that there are no objective, impartial, nonarbitrary means to evaluate different canons of rationality across different cultures. We may, therefore, legitimately ask: Is this assertion true? In order to justify the assertion, the relativist will have to provide "good reasons" for believing the assertion. However, if the "good reasons" that demonstrate the truth of the assertion are objective, impartial, and nonarbitrary, then the doctrine of rationality-relativism is false. And if the "good reasons" to demonstrate the truth of rationality-relativism are nonobjective, biased, and arbitrary, then the reasons (being *not good*) beg the question, in that they assume the assertion to be true in their premises. Either way, rationality relativism cannot be justified. Note that this is the same argument that Socrates used against Protagoras (see section 2.1.3) and is similar to the self-refuting argument against moral relativism (see section 4.1.1).

Second, some sociologists have examined the findings of the cultural anthropologists and have concluded, contra Barnes and Bloor, that the similarities between primitive societies' concept of "rationality" and the West's were greater than the differences. Put more simply, the empirical evidence seems to support the assertion that what comes to be known or considered to be rational across diverse cultures is pretty much the same (Ben-David 1984, p. xxiii). The cultural anthropologists Cole and Scribner review the mass of studies that have been conducted on the reasoning processes of different cultures and conclude: "There is no evidence for different *kinds* of reasoning processes such as the old classic theories alleged—we have no evidence for a 'primitive logic'" (Cole and Scribner 1974, p. 170). And why should anyone ever have *expected* that empirical studies of other cultures would yield any other conclusion? Stripped to its essence, the canons of rational thought hold that people can (inductively) learn from experience: We *generalize* (learn) that "alligators are unfaithful swimming companions" from *observing* (and being told others have observed) that "alligators have a penchant for eating humans." Furthermore, we can *act* on the basis of our (deductive) reasoning: If it is true that "alligators are unfaithful swimming companions," then "don't swim with alligators." Thus, those cultures that did not apply so-called Western canons of rational thinking would not have survived to be available for cultural anthropologists to study.

Laudan provides a third argument against rationality relativism. He points out that the historical record undercuts the thesis that major scientific theories can be explained by social factors. There has never existed a specifically "bourgeois mathematics" (contra the Marxists), nor a "Jewish physics" (contra the Nazis), nor a "specifically proletarian version of the special theory of relativity" (contra the Leninists). The reason for the failure of sociologists to make their "social factors" case (among other things) is "that the vast majority of scientific beliefs (though by no means all) seem to be of no social significance whatever" (Laudan 1977, p. 218).

A fourth argument against rationality relativism provides that, even if Western canons of rationality cannot be proved with certainty to be superior to those of primitive tribes, science may choose to work within those canons of rationality on the basis that they represent a significant intellectual achievement of Western civilization (Hacking 1982, p. 52). (Such a posture is much like bumble bees, who, not knowing that it is impossible for them to fly, continue to fly anyway, or, "if others wish to swim with alligators, let them.")

A fifth line of attack has been to deny the assertion that there are no objective, impartial, nonarbitrary criteria for evaluating different conceptualizations of "rationality" across cultures (Hollis 1982, p. 72). The reader should note that rationality relativists, such as Barnes and Bloor, *implicitly* accept the K-K thesis and commit the "philosophers' fallacy." That is, they (1) point out that we cannot know with certainty that our criteria for evaluating different conceptualizations of rationality across cultures are objective and impartial. They then (2) implicitly place the know-with-certainty requirement and the K-K thesis on all efforts to compare concepts of rationality across cultures. Given that we cannot know with certainty that our evaluative criteria are correct, they then (3) conclude that no such criteria exist. However, if we reject the K-K thesis with respect to rationality, we need only have good reasons to believe that our evaluative criteria are objective and impartial to claim that rationality is not relative. Further, even if some cultures *believe* in a different form of rationality, such criteria could still enable us to evaluate the relative merits of the different versions.

The force of arguments such as the preceding ones have resulted in the "strong thesis" remaining a minority view in the sociology of science. Indeed, Barnes and Bloor, themselves, point this out (Barnes and Bloor, in Hollis and Lukes 1982, p. 21).

4.1.3 Reality Relativism

Modern forms of relativism owe much to the later writings of Wittgenstein, notably his *Philosophical Investigations*, which was published posthumously (Wittgenstein 1953). The "early" Wittgenstein was decidedly realist in orientation (see section 2.6.3), and believed that the meanings of words and propositions were pictures in the mind that *referred* to the external world. The "later" Wittgenstein specifically rejects the view that the meanings of words, phrases, and propositions are to be found in their referential properties; rather, their meanings are to be found in the circumstances in which they are used. The idealism inherent in *Philosophical Investigations* provides that all language is a rule-governed activity (i.e., in his words, a "game"). Because language is a vehicle to communicate with someone else, the rules for various languages cannot be "private," they must be shared with other people (i.e., in his words, there are no "private languages"). The use of language to communicate with others is carried out in many different kinds of situations, contexts, or circumstances (i.e., "forms of life"). Within the same language, the particular rules that will govern the meanings of words, phrases, and propositions will vary depending upon the situations, contexts, and circumstances (i.e., there are numerous "language-games" that can be played). Therefore, the meaning of even scientific terms or words changes radically among contexts (among various "language-games").

The "later" Wittgenstein heavily influenced Winch and his 1958 monograph titled *The Idea of a Social Science and Its Relation to Philosophy*, which "like Kuhn's book was short, polemical, provocative, and ambiguous" (Bernstein 1983, p. 25). Winch's book and his 1964 article, "Understanding a Primitive Society," (reprinted in Winch 1972) analyzed the primitive society of the Azande and its reliance on witchcraft, as detailed in the 1930s by works of anthropologist Evans-Pritchard. Using Wittgenstein to analyze the witchcraft practices of the Azande, Winch concluded that (using Bernstein's paraphrase) these "*forms of life* may be so radically different from each other that in order to understand and interpret alien or primitive societies we not only have to bracket our prejudices and biases but have to suspend our own Western standards and criteria of rationality. We may be confronted with standards of rationality about beliefs and actions that are incompatible with or incommensurable with our standards" (Bernstein 1983, p. 27). Thus, to Winch, Western rationality represents, simply, "our standards" and Azande rationality represents, simply, "their standards." Judging other people's standards of rationality by our own standards reveals, for him, our ethnocentrism.

If Wittgenstein is correct that words, phrases, and propositions do not in some meaningful sense *refer* to reality, then what is the nature of reality? Winch answers:

> Our idea of what belongs to the realm of reality is given for us in the language that we use. The concepts we have settle for us the form of the experience we have of the world. . . . The world is for us what is presented through those concepts. That is not to say that our concepts may not change; but when they do, that means that our concept of the world has changed too. (Winch 1958, p. 15).

Essentially, Winch says that what comes to be considered reality is *constructed* by us as a result of the nature of the language we use. Hanson's book *Patterns of Discovery* (1958) comes to a similar conclusion through an analysis of our perceptual processes. Hanson wished to explore perception in science as "seeing," and to distinguish between *retinal-stimulation* and *interpretation*. He argued that scientists who held different theories about the world would "see" different things, even though each might be exposed to the same retinal stimulation. Hanson uses several examples to explore the issue, but he discusses most extensively the following:

> Let us consider Johannes Kepler: imagine him on a hill watching the dawn. With him is Tycho Brahe. Kepler regarded the sun as fixed: it was the earth that moved. But Tycho followed Ptolemy and Aristotle in this much at least: the earth was fixed and all other celestial bodies moved around it. *Do Kepler and Tycho see the same thing in the East at dawn?* (Hanson 1958, p. 5, italics added)

Hanson considered several answers to his question. He rejects the position that the "same retinal stimulation" justifies the claim that they saw the same thing. Hanson uses the Wittgensteinian example of the "duck/rabbit" from Gestalt psychology to argue the case that seeing *inherently* involves interpretation. (In this classic example of Gestalt, subjects are shown an ambiguous drawing in which some people see a duck, others see a rabbit, and some people can switch back and forth, seeing first one and then the other.) Hanson then argued that what scientists *see* (or perceive, or observe) is directly related to their knowledge, theories, and beliefs. He then answered his question concerning Kepler and Tycho:

> Tycho sees the sun beginning its journey from horizon to horizon. He sees that from some celestial vantage point the sun (carrying with it the moon and the planets)

could be watched circling our fixed earth. Watching the sun at dawn through tychonic spectacles would be to see it in something like this way, . . . but Kepler will see the horizon dipping or turning away, from our local fixed star. The shift from sunrise to horizon-turn is analogous to the shift-of-aspect [from "duck" to "rabbit"] phenomena already considered; it is occasioned by differences between what Tycho and Kepler think they knew. (Hanson 1958, pp. 23–24)

The preceding kinds of examples and analyses led Hanson to conclude that all observation in science is formed or directed by theory and, thus, is "theory-laden." Against the obvious response that the "duck" in his example was "really" an *interpretation* of an ambiguous set of pencil lines on paper, Hanson's reply would be that the "duck" is precisely the kind of "seeing" that is entailed in all scientific observation. That is, the "seeing" in all scientific observation *inherently* has an element of interpretation to it and is not "lines on paper."

The arguments of those, like Winch, who proposed that it is our language that determines our reality, and those, like Hanson, who proposed that it is our theories that determine our reality, have led many to what is now referred to as the "constructivist thesis," or *reality relativism*. Reality relativism holds that:

1. What comes to be known as "reality" is constructed by individuals *relative* to their language, group, social class, culture, theory, paradigm, worldview, or *Weltanschauung*.
2. What comes to count as "reality" cannot be objectively, impartially, or nonarbitrarily evaluated across different languages, individuals, groups, social classes, cultures, theories, paradigms, worldviews, or *Weltanschauungen*.

The reader should note that reality relativism is *not* simply that different people perceive the *same* phenomenon differently, for this would mean that the perceptions of some of the people could be right and others could be wrong. Further, reality relativism does *not* mean simply that our theories guide us, or inform us, or direct us in our observations and experiments. Rather, reality relativism implies that we cannot compare or evaluate or adjudicate different conceptualizations of reality across theories (or whatever).

The constructivist thesis, or reality relativism, has been eagerly embraced by many writers. For example, Latour and Woolgar (1979) have investigated the "construction of reality" in biochemistry laboratories. They propose that the purpose of the biochemists was to produce what they call literary inscriptions, "such as diagrams, figures, tables and other items contained in written reports" (Latour and Woolgar 1979, p. 236). These literary inscriptions are constitutive of reality, and the biochemists attempted to persuade their colleagues to accept their literary inscriptions as a scientific fact. How are the arguments among various biochemists settled? Is it not the case that the arguments are settled because one side can show that their "literary inscriptions" correspond better with the real world than do other interpretations? No, according to Latour and Woolgar, "argument between scientists transforms some statements into figments of one's imagination and others into facts of nature," and "*reality was the consequence* of the settlement of the dispute rather than its cause" (1979, p. 236; italics added). That is, scientific reality was constructed in the laboratory independent of any relationship to a world external to the biochemists' "language-game." This conclusion corresponds well with the view of Collins about science: "The natural world *in no way* constrains what is believed to be" (Collins 1981, p. 54; italics added).

Knorr-Cetina opts for a constructivist position very similar to Latour and Woolgar in her book *The Manufacture of Knowledge* (Knorr-Cetina 1981). Knorr-Cetina proposes that "the products of science have to be seen as highly internally structured through the process of production, *independent* of the question of their external structuring through some match or mismatch with reality" (1981, p. 5, italics added). Similarly, the philosopher Nelson Goodman in his *Ways of Worldmaking* (1978) also develops a constructivist thesis: "There are many different *equally* true descriptions of the world, and their truth is the only standard of their faithfulness," and "none of them tells us *the* way the world is, but each of them tells us *a* way the world is" (Goodman 1978, p. 30). (For an evaluation of Goodmanian relativism, see Siegel (1984).)

Several writers in marketing recommend the adoption of reality relativism (Olson 1987). Thus Peter and Olson contend that "science creates many realities" and believe that "adopting the R/C [relativistic/constructionist] approach in marketing could produce more creative and useful theories," when compared with "the outdated P/E [positivistic/empiricist] orientation that currently dominates marketing research" (Peter and Olson 1983, pp. 119, 123). Similarly, Sauer, Nighswonger, and Zaltman suggest: "Because realities are socially and psychologically constructed, the same event may have multiple realities, *each of which is valid*" (1982, p. 18; italics added). Anderson's "critical relativism" rejects the position "that there is a single knowable reality waiting 'out there' to be discovered via *the* scientific method" (Anderson 1986, p. 157). Similarly, Zaltman, LeMasters, and Heffring advocate what they call the "contemporary" view "that 'reality' may be structured in different yet equally valid ways" (1982, p. 5). Hudson and Ozanne believe that interpretivist research in consumer behavior assumes that "reality is essentially mental and perceived," and that it is "also socially constructed" (1988, p. 509). Many of the advocates of naturalistic, humanistic, and interpretivist approaches to research rely heavily on the work of Lincoln and Guba and their contention:

It is dubious whether there is a reality. If there is, we can never know it. Furthermore, no amount of inquiry can produce convergence on it. (Lincoln and Guba 1985, p. 83)

On Reality Relativism: For Reason. Reality relativism is almost indistinguishable from *idealism*, its nineteenth century predecessor, whose central tenet—see section 2.4—was that the external world does not exist unperceived. Thus, those who believe that the world exists unperceived (i.e., realism) and who believe that different conceptualizations of the nature of the world can be objectively, impartially, and nonarbitrarily evaluated (i.e., absolutism) frequently use many of the same arguments developed in sections 3.1.1 and 3.1.2 against this modern version of idealism. Therefore, those arguments (e.g., the sophistry argument) need not be repeated here. Similarly, many of the criticisms leveled at rationality relativism in section 4.1.2 are equally applicable to reality relativism, (e.g., both are self-refuting and incoherent). However, there is one argument against reality relativism that must be developed here—the argument from morality. Given that Hegelian idealism concluded that individual people are "unreal," but the state was "real" (see section 2.4.3), is this modern version of idealism also ethically troublesome?

Reality relativism starts innocently enough with the observation that different people have different perceptions of the real world. Reality relativists then (1) propose that these different perceptions constitute multiple realities, (2) argue that there are no neutral standards for comparing these multiple realities, (3) advance the view that the truth of any of the multiple realities is established by consensus, not by correspondence with any external reality, and (4) conclude that each of the many multiple realities is equally valid. Lincoln and Guba (1985) give numerous examples of such "constructed realities," including: "handicapped children," "social science," "Bobby Knight," "communism," "the Holocaust," "Watergate," and the "Vietnam Era." Each of these realities, they contend, is constructed, although some of them may in some way be related to what they call "tangible entities." As a parenthetical aside, they casually point out that "there are people who have argued, for instance, that the Holocaust never happened, but was merely a political construction to arouse world-wide sympathy for the Jews" (Lincoln and Guba 1985, p. 84). Their cavalier treatment of an issue as sober as the existence or nonexistence of the Holocaust provides a powerful example of the massive problems confronting the morality of reality relativism.

It is indeed true that one of the "multiple realities" that some people hold concerning the actions of the Nazis in World War II is that the Holocaust never occurred, but has been "manufactured," or "constructed," or "created" by those sympathetic to the Jews. An alternative "multiple reality" concerning World

War II is that the Holocaust did in fact occur; the Nazis did in fact slaughter millions of Jews (and others) in their notorious concentration camps; and never again should such an atrocity be allowed to occur. What is to be said of these two "multiple realities"? Which "multiple reality" is correct? Where does truth lie? Sincere (non-sophist) advocates of reality relativism must stand mute when confronted with this question. Contending, as they do, that the two "multiple realities" cannot be objectively, impartially, or nonarbitrarily compared, they cannot evaluate which "reality" corresponds better with what actually occurred. Each is "equally valid." All consistent reality relativists can only (impotently) inquire whether the members of some group agree on a "reality." Thus, reality relativists such as Lincoln and Guba, explicitly advocate a "consensus theory of truth" (Lincoln and Guba 1985, p. 84), and others do so by implication.

In contrast, absolutists have no problem addressing the question of which view of the Holocaust is correct, because they believe that the evidence (e.g., photographs, diaries, eyewitness accounts, concentration-camp records, and the like) can provide an objective, impartial, nonarbitrary basis for evaluating which of the two claimed realities is closer to the truth. This is not to say that absolutists will always be correct when addressing questions such as this, for sometimes the evidence may lead them toward error. (And the task of epistemology in the philosophy of science has historically been that of trying to increase the odds of being right.) To those, and only to those, who prefer the *certainty* of moral impotence over the *possibility* of moral error, reality relativism has something to offer.

Some may think Lincoln and Guba's (1985) example of the Holocaust— and my reporting of it—to be extreme or atypical. But such is not the case. Most of the truly important issues throughout all the social sciences have to do with genuine realities, not "essentially mental" constructs. Consider the many propositions and statements in the social sciences involving constructs such as racism, poverty, freedom, slavery, democracy, totalitarianism, fascism, and hunger. To contend that propositions and statements involving these kinds of constructs are "essentially mental," each being one example of a "multiple reality," and each being "equally valid" is disingenuous, or preposterous, or leads to moral impotence. Although absolutists, when facing the difficult decisions of our age, may at times choose incorrectly, at least they need not stand impotently mute. It is for this reason (among others) that ethicists condemn equally both *moral* relativism and *reality* relativism (note the similarity of the arguments against both). It is also for this reason that ethicists and others fear relativism, and we can note how misguided are those in marketing and the social sciences who, in the manner of Feyerabend, contend that such fears are "unwarranted" (Anderson 1988a, p. 137). In fact, Feyerabend's own works demonstrate the moral impotence of relativism.

Feyerabend clearly saw the logical implications of his reality relativism concerning morality. He notes:

> We certainly cannot assume that two incommensurable theories deal with one and the same objective state of affairs (to make the assumption we would have to assume that both at least *refer* to the same objective situation). . . . [Therefore,] we must admit that they deal with different worlds and that the change (from one world to another) has been brought about by a switch from one theory to another. (Feyerabend 1978b, p. 70)

Feyerabend takes his reality relativism to its logical conclusion in his book, *Farewell to Reason*. He notes: "My refusal to condemn even an extreme fascism and my suggestion that it should be allowed to survive . . . has enraged many readers and disappointed many friends" (Feyerabend 1987a, p. 309). Although he points out that "fascism is not my cup of tea," he finds that his relativism does not allow him to condemn it. He asks, do his feelings toward fascism have "an 'objective core' that would enable me to combat fascism not just because *it does not please me,* but because *it is inherently evil?* And my answer is: we have an inclination—nothing more" (1987, p. 309, italics in original). After recognizing that there are "philosophical systems" (e.g., realism, absolutism, and fallibilism) that might enable some people to justify their "inclinations," his own relativistic philosophy leads him to conclude: "And all I can find when trying to identify some content are different [philosophical] systems asserting different sets of values *with nothing but our inclination to decide between them*" (Feyerabend 1987, p. 309; italics added). Thus, we can see that Feyerabend sincerely believes in his reality relativism and accepts its logical implication of moral impotence.

Why have some philosophers (among many others) allowed themselves to be drawn into the moral morass of reality relativism? The philosopher Frederick L. Will believes that this, what he calls "perverse," position has resulted from philosophers' acceptance of the "relativist illusion." Thus:

> To recognize the role that practices and their governance play in the conduct of investigation [in science] is by no means to depreciate the role that the objects of investigation themselves play, in particular cases, in determining the course of investigation and, eventually, its results. . . . Recognition that knowledge of objects is gained through practices [in science] has led some philosophers to conclude that objects thus known are *produced* by the practices and are thus artifacts somehow dependent for their existence and character upon the practices themselves. Judged in the context of the history of human knowledge, and in particular the fabulous development of physical science in the past four centuries, *this is perverse.* Cognitive practices are designed to *discover and disclose* objects, not to produce them. . . . Of course not all cognitive practices are *well designed* for the purpose; but as is indeed obvious to us *when we are not bemused by some potent philosophical illusion,* they are not all ill designed. (Will 1981, p. 18; italics added)

The third major form of relativism that we need to address is conceptual-framework relativism, alternatively referred to as, simply, conceptual relativism. Conceptual framework relativism holds that:

1. Knowledge or knowledge-claims are relative to conceptual frameworks, theories, paradigms, worldviews, or *Weltanschauungen*.
2. Knowledge or knowledge-claims cannot be objectively, impartially, or nonarbitrarily evaluated across different conceptual frameworks, theories, paradigms, worldviews, or *Weltanschauungen*.

This version of relativism is associated most commonly with those philosophers subscribing to the view known as historical relativism, which can be traced to Thomas Kuhn's (1962) influential book, *The Structure of Scientific Revolutions*. We shall examine the views of the two most influential historical relativists, Kuhn and Feyerabend, in the next section.

4.2 HISTORICAL RELATIVISM

Upon the rise of logical positivism in the 1920s and the birth of the philosophy of science as a distinct academic discipline, philosophers (at least in the Anglo-American tradition) viewed the purpose of philosophy of science as the clarification of the language of science. Although philosophers differed in the extent to which they used formal logic as an analytical tool, they agreed that "critical discussion" in the manner of Plato was the appropriate method for analyzing, evaluating, and, thus, clarifying the nature of scientific concepts such as theory, explanation, laws, and models. The use of history and historical analysis was limited to providing examples for illustrative purposes.

Starting in the 1960s, a philosophical perspective known as historical relativism developed, which had a different set of premises. First, instead of attempting to clarify the language of science, the historical relativists attempted to generate general *theories* of science. The historical relativists believed that from analyzing the historical development of science they could develop theories to explain (much like a social science) how scientists both discover and justify their knowledge-claims. The theories proposed by several of these historically oriented philosophers embraced one version or another of cognitive relativism, with the theories of Kuhn and Feyerabend being the most influential. Because Kuhn is generally given credit for initiating the "historical turn" that philosophy of science took in the 1960s, we begin our discussion with him.

4.2.1   Kuhnian Relativism

Although Thomas S. Kuhn (1922–1996) received his Ph.D. in physics from Harvard University, most of his academic career focused on the history and philosophy of science. In his early years, Kuhn was heavily influenced by the works of Jean Piaget (on the cognitive development of children), the Gestalt psychologists (on perception), W.V.O. Quine (1951) (on the analytic-synthetic distinction), and Ludwyk Fleck (on the sociology of science). After publishing his first major book, *The Copernican Revolution*, in 1953, Kuhn accepted an invitation from the logical empiricists to develop a monograph on his emerging theory of science for inclusion in their *International Encyclopedia of Unified Science*, which came to be retitled as the *Foundations of the Unity of Science* (see Neurath et al. 1970). The resulting work, "The Structure of Scientific Revolutions," first appeared in the *Encyclopedia* in 1962 (Neurath et al. 1970), was reprinted as a free-standing monograph shortly thereafter (Kuhn 1962), and was later revised with a *Postscript* (Kuhn 1970b). Since that time, Kuhn published numerous articles explaining and clarifying his views, many of which are included in his 1977 book of readings, *The Essential Tension* (Kuhn 1977).

The origins of the central tenets of Kuhn's theory illustrate that the process of discovery is seldom neat and tidy. Although the concept of "paradigm" as it relates to the "worldview" or *Weltanschauung* of a community of scientists is usually considered to be the central construct of Kuhnian theory, the concept of "scientific revolution" was developed prior to his notions concerning the worldviews of scientists. In particular, his Chapter IX, titled "On the Nature and Necessity of Scientific Revolutions," was written before he had even begun its predecessors on "normal science." He relates:

> The concept of paradigms proved to be the missing element I required in order to write the book . . . unfortunately, in that process, paradigms took on a life of their own . . . having begun simply as exemplary problem solutions, they expanded their empire to include, first the classic books in which these accepted examples initially appeared and, finally, the entire global set of commitments shared by the members of a particular scientific community. (Kuhn 1977, p. xix)

The preceding illustrates one reason why the concept of paradigm became so ambiguous in the original version of *The Structure of Scientific Revolutions*. Indeed the ambiguity was so great that Masterman found twenty-one separate usages of the term (Masterman 1970). In the 1970 edition of *Structure*, Kuhn recommends that the term paradigm be restricted to what he calls "exemplars," which are the concrete solutions to problems identified as important by the members of a specific scientific community. He suggested using the term "disciplinary matrix" (instead of paradigm) to identify the constellation of beliefs, values, and techniques (or "worldview") of a specific scientific community. In large measure, however, most writers continue to use the term paradigm in its broader context, and we shall follow that tradition in this section.

A paradigm, or *Weltanschauung* ("worldview"), contains three separate kinds of entities. First, there is a content, which includes theories, laws, concepts, "symbolic generalizations" (e.g., $F = ma$), and "exemplars." The exemplars represent standard examples of problems that the content of the paradigm solves. Second, a paradigm contains a methodology, which represents the procedures and techniques by which further knowledge within the paradigm is to be generated. Third, a paradigm contains an epistemology, which represents the set of criteria (Kuhn calls them "values" in his revised addition [Kuhn 1970, p. 205]) for evaluating knowledge-claims.

Kuhn divides the historical development of all disciplines into three stages: the pre-paradigm stage, the normal science stage, and the revolutionary stage. In the pre-paradigm stage, there are many schools of thought within a discipline, none of which can be characterized as a full-fledged paradigm with well-developed "exemplars" that successfully solve important problems. Thus, scientists in the pre-paradigm stage spend much time in disputation regarding philosophical and methodological issues. The absence of well-developed paradigms means that research in this stage has a high random component and exhibits little, if any, cumulativity. Kuhn characterized the social sciences as being pre-paradigmatic (and would have, most assuredly, so characterized the marketing discipline had he been aware of it) (Kuhn 1970, p. 15). Thus, Kuhn believed that his model of scientific change would *not* apply to the social sciences and marketing, which is ironic in that his greatest impact has been in the social, not natural sciences (Suppe 1984).

Building upon his earlier work in the *Copernican Revolution*, Kuhn often uses Ptolemaic astronomy as an example of a paradigm. Kuhn proposed that the normal science stage of development occurs when one particular paradigm is viewed to be more successful than its "competitors in solving a few problems that a group of practitioners had come to recognize as acute" (Kuhn 1970, p. 23). The members of the discipline then gradually coalesce around this single paradigm with its exemplars, and the paradigm uniquely dominates the entire scientific community. New members of the scientific community learn the details of the paradigm through studying its exemplars. That is, the learning of the paradigm is done *implicitly* through interacting with other members of the scientific community and learning how problems are to be solved in a manner similar to the exemplars. During normal science, scientists engage in activities, known as "puzzle-solving," to flesh out the paradigm: "Mopping-up operations are what engage most scientists throughout their careers" (Kuhn 1977, p. 24). Research during periods of normal science is cumulative, but does not aim at the production of novelties of fact or theory. Such novelties are rare and generally unwelcome when they do appear (Kuhn 1970, p. 35).

Genuine scientific discovery occurs only when, contrary to their aims, scientists stumble upon "anomalies," that is, "the recognition that nature has somehow violated the paradigm-induced expectations that govern normal science" (Kuhn 1970, p. 52). For example, although Ptolemaic astronomy was extraordinarily successful in predicting the changing positions of both stars and planets when compared with any of its predecessors, "Ptolemy's system never quite conformed with the best available observations" (1970, p. 68). Although the system was patched-up time and time again, "by the early 16th century an increasing number of Europe's best astronomers were recognizing that the astronomical paradigm [of Ptolemy] was failing in application to its own traditional problems. That recognition was prerequisite to Copernicus' rejection of the Ptolemaic paradigm and his search for a new one" (1970, p. 69). Persistent anomalies will provoke a scientific "crisis" within the community, and it is only during this "crisis" period that all aspects of the dominant paradigm are explicitly examined, evaluated, and discussed. (It is from Kuhn that Shweder and Fiske [1986] draw the label "crisis literature" to describe the philosophy debates in social science.)

During crisis periods, and only then, is there a proliferation of rival theories, including some that are variations of the fundamental principles in the dominant paradigm. Paradigm-debate within any discipline is resolved in one of only three ways: (1) Some modifications of the dominant paradigm make it successful in accommodating the anomalies; (2) the problems presented by the anomalies are simply shelved to be solved by some future generation; or (3) "a crisis may end with the emergence of a new candidate for [the status of dominant] paradigm and with the ensuing battle over its acceptance" (Kuhn 1970, p. 84).

Kuhn likens the change to the new paradigm as a political revolution because both involve choices "between incompatible modes of community life," and both involve techniques of "mass persuasion." Furthermore, there will be "significant shifts in the criteria determining the legitimacy of both problems and proposed solutions," and the advocates of the competing paradigms "will inevitably talk through each other when debating the relative merits of their respective paradigms" (Kuhn 1970, p. 109). One might wonder why techniques of "mass persuasion" would be needed. Why could there not be experimental tests or other investigations conducted to guide the choice between the rival paradigms? For Kuhn, however, a rational resolution would be possible only "if there were but one set of problems, one world within which to work on them, and one set of standards for their solution, [then] paradigm competition might be settled more or less this way" (1970, p. 148). Unfortunately, the two rival paradigms are "incommensurable" in three ways: (1) the list of problems to be solved by the paradigm, (2) how terms and concepts are to be defined, and (3) "in a sense that I am unable to explicate further, the proponents of competing paradigms practice their trades in different worlds" (1970, p. 150). Therefore, relying heavily on the work of Wittgenstein and Hanson (as discussed in the previous section), the shift to the new paradigm is like a "Gestalt switch," from "duck" to "rabbit." Furthermore, "just because it is a transition between incommensurables, the transition between competing paradigms cannot be made a step at a time, forced by logic and neutral experience. Like the Gestalt switch, it must occur all at once . . . or not at all." Indeed, "the transfer of allegiance from paradigm to paradigm is a conversion experience that cannot be forced" (Kuhn 1977, pp. 150–51).

To what extent, for Kuhn, does the shift to a new paradigm after a revolution constitute scientific progress? Is there any meaningful way we can state that we *knew more* after Newton than before? Or, did we know more after Einstein than before? Kuhn answers these questions in two ways. First, the scientific communities have *defined* their revolutions to be progress. As Kuhn notes, "revolutions close with a total victory for one of the two opposing camps," and asks "Will that group [the victor] ever say that the result of its victory has been something less than progress"? (Kuhn 1970, p. 166). He proposes that "the member of a mature scientific community is, like the typical character in Orwell's *1984*, the victim of a history rewritten by the powers that be" (Kuhn 1970, p. 167). However, he believes the Orwellian analogy "is not altogether inappropriate," because "there are losses as well as gains in scientific revolutions, and scientists tend to be peculiarly blind to the former" (1970, p. 167).

The second answer to the progress question is that there is growth in the "list of problems solved by science and the precision of individual problem-solutions" (Kuhn 1970, p. 170). Furthermore, "later scientific theories are better than earlier ones for solving puzzles in the often quite different environments to which they are applied." However, successive theories in science do not "grow ever closer to, or approximate more and more closely to, the truth, . . . there is, I think, no theory-independent way to reconstruct phrases like 'really there'; the notion of a match between the ontology of a theory and its 'real' counterpart in nature now seems to me illusive in principle" (1970, p. 206). Using Darwinian evolution as a metaphor, Kuhn proposes that scientific knowledge is evolving, but it is not evolving toward truly understanding the world: "I can see in their succession no coherent direction of ontological development" (1970, p. 206).

On Paradigms and Weltanschauungen: For Reason. The Kuhnian theory of science was obviously a radical and provocative departure from (in Kuhn's terms) the "image of science" put forth by the logical empiricists and the falsificationists: "Part of the reason for its [the book's] success is, I regretfully conclude, that it can be too nearly all things to all people" (Kuhn 1977,

p. 293). Most regrettably (as previously noted), Kuhn used his central construct, the "paradigm," in so many ways that for several years much discussion and debate focused on how to define this key term. Although Kuhn opted for restricting the term to refer to "exemplars," most other writers continued to use it in a broader context, often like the German construct, "*Weltanschauung*." Used in this manner, to possess a paradigm would imply that a scientist has a particular language where the belief in a certain theory or group of theories *uniquely* determines: (1) the meanings of the terms in the language, (2) the canons of experimental design and control, (3) standards for assessing the adequacy of the theory, (4) the relevance of information to the theory, and (5) which questions or problems the theory is committed to answer.

Suppe (1977b, p. 218) reviews this *Weltanschauung*, or worldview, approach to interpreting the meaning of a Kuhnian paradigm and asks "how plausible is it to suppose that each person working with a theory possesses a *Weltanschauung*"? He notes that a central characteristic of scientific communities is the extreme *diversity* of the backgrounds, beliefs, and cultures of scientists practicing in the same scientific "community." Therefore, it is "exceedingly doubtful whether a *Weltanschauung* can be the joint possession of a group of scientists—as, for example, Kuhn's analysis requires. For there is every reason to suppose that there will be enough individual variation between individuals—even among individuals engaged in close cooperation in research—that no two persons will share exactly the same *Weltanschauung*" (Suppe 1977b, p. 218). Thus, Suppe exhorts his colleagues in the philosophy of science "to eschew *Weltanschauungen* talk and instead speak of languages, theory formulations, experimental canons, standards, and so on" (1977b, p. 220).

Although "strong form" versions of paradigms such as *Weltanschauungen*, or worldviews, are untenable, it is obviously the case that members of scientific communities and subgroups within those communities often share *some* beliefs about theories, methods, objectives, and epistemology. Therefore, it is reasonable to ask whether "weak-form" Kuhnian theory adequately describes the actual history of science, wherein the concept of paradigm is viewed to mean a rough, or approximate, agreement on a set of theories, methods, aims, and evaluation procedures. We must remember that a central complaint of Kuhn (and all other historicists) about the logical empiricists and falsificationists' "image of science" was that it did not adequately *describe* the actual development of science. Although the logical empiricists (adopting as they did a "reconstructionist" approach) neither claimed that their views *described* actual scientific practice, nor agreed that their views could be properly *evaluated* by examining historical events, those who adopt the historical method for understanding science (at the very least) claim that their "image of science" is accurately historical.

How well does Kuhnian theory accurately describe the actual history of science? The answer is: very poorly indeed. For example, consider the Kuhnian notion that there exists a pre-paradigm stage that all the mature sciences passed through. Hull examined the various sciences that Kuhn himself used as evidence for the "stage" and concluded: "The periods which he [Kuhn] had previously described as pre-paradigm contained paradigms not that different from those of normal science" (Hull 1975, p. 397). How about the claim that, during "normal science," there is a single paradigm that is dominant and the subclaim that, during normal science, debate about the fundamental assumptions of the paradigm is absent? Laudan's review of the history of the sciences concludes that "virtually every major period in the history of science is characterized both by the co-existence of numerous competing paradigms, with none exerting hegemony over the field, and by the persistent and continuous manner in which the foundational assumptions of every paradigm are debated within the scientific community" (Laudan 1977, p. 74). Indeed, "Kuhn can point to no major science in which paradigm monopoly has been the rule, nor in which foundational debate has been absent" (Laudan 1977, p. 151). How about the Kuhnian claim that paradigms are always "implicit?" If debate does exist during normal science on fundamental assumptions, then paradigms must have a significant degree of *explicitness*, otherwise such debate could not occur (Laudan 1977, p. 75). Recall that Kuhnian theory claims that there is a cyclical pattern between long periods of "normal science," then a "crisis" and a short period of "revolutionary science." Hull examines the history of science on these counts and concludes "nor does normal science alternate with revolutionary science; both are taking place all the time. Sometimes a revolution occurs without any preceding state of crisis" (Hull 1975, p. 397).

In short, the Kuhnian theory of science fails by its own standard of adequacy: It does not accurately describe the actual development of science nor the individual sciences to any significant extent. Therefore, "Kuhn belongs more to the history of the philosophy of science than to contemporary philosophy of science; for today few philosophers of science . . . believe that Kuhn's views are acceptable or even a near approximation to an adequate account" (Suppe 1984, p. 98).

On Kuhnian Relativism: For Reason. More important for our purposes than the fact that Kuhnian theory is historically inaccurate is his (seeming) adoption of both reality relativism and conceptual-framework relativism. As Kuhn himself has acknowledged, his constant references to scientists who hold different paradigms as living in "different worlds" and phrases like "the world changes according to different paradigms" strongly implied reality relativism (Kuhn 1970, p. 192). Thus, Suppe asks "if one's only approach to the world is always through a disciplinary matrix which shapes and loads the data, how is it that the world, which does not depend on the matrix, exerts an objectifying and restraining influence on what some science accepts? Put more flippantly, if science always views the world through a disciplinary matrix on Kuhn's view, then isn't Kuhn committed to some form of antiempirical idealism"? (Suppe 1977b, p. 151) Similarly, Scheffler claims that, for Kuhn, "reality is gone as an independent factor; each viewpoint creates its own reality," and paradigms "are not only 'constitutive of science' . . . but they are constitutive of nature as well" (Scheffler 1967, p. 19).

Although many current-day advocates of reality-relativism cite Kuhn to justify their positions, Kuhn, himself, explicitly denied this interpretation of his views. In the *Postscript* to the 1970 version of *Structure*, Kuhn states: "We posit the existence of stimuli [distal stimuli, see section 9.3] to explain our perceptions of the world, and we posit their immutability to avoid both individual and social solipsism. About neither posit have I the slightest reservation" (Kuhn 1970, p. 193). (Solipsism is the philosophical view that either the "self" is the only reality or one can claim to have knowledge only about one's self.) Given that Kuhn specifically acknowledged (see Kuhn 1970, p. 167) the Orwellian implications of his theory of science, it is both surprising and sorrowful that he did not repudiate reality relativism in 1962, rather than eight years later.

Although Kuhn defused his critics by denying the charge of reality relativism, the charge of conceptual-framework relativism continues to plague his "image of science." Recall that Kuhn claimed that advocates of rival paradigms during revolutionary science must undergo a "Gestalt switch" (from "duck" to "rabbit") or a "conversion process" because the rival paradigms are *incommensurable*. Thus, Kuhn necessarily implies some form of conceptual framework-relativism, because a "conversion process" would surely be unnecessary if there were paradigm-neutral criteria for adjudicating the conflict between the dominant paradigm and its rivals. That is, Kuhnian theory implies that (1) the knowledge-claims of a paradigm are relative to that paradigm (or conceptual framework), and (2) the claims cannot be objectively, impartially, or nonarbitrarily evaluated across rival paradigms.

Because Kuhnian conceptual-framework relativism depends crucially on his concept of *incommensurability*, various writers began (soon after the publication of his 1962 work) identifying precisely how incommensurability should be interpreted. Space limitations prevent a detailed description of all the interpretations, and their resultant analyses. Rather, we shall identify here only the three most prominent interpretations and point the reader toward the literature that evaluates them.

One of the earliest interpretations was the *meaning-variance* view that scientific terms change meaning from paradigm to paradigm. This view was critiqued by Shapere (1964, 1966), Scheffler (1967, ch. 3), and Kordig (1971, ch. 2, 3). A second analysis, the *radical translation* interpretation, suggests that in some meaningful way the actual terms involved in one paradigm cannot be translated into the language of its rivals. This interpretation was suggested by Kuhn, himself, in his *Postscript* to the 1970 edition of *Structure* (1970, pp. 200–204). The radical translation view has been analyzed by Kitcher (1978), Moberg (1979), and Levin (1979). The radical translation view was also critiqued in my own earlier work (Hunt 1983b, pp. 368–72). A third interpretation of incommensurability has been the *incomparability* view that rival paradigms simply cannot be meaningfully compared. This interpretation was critiqued by Scheffler, Shapere, and Kordig in the references previously cited and also by Laudan (1976), Jones (1981), and Putnam (1981).

Although, as previously mentioned, the details of the analyses cited in the preceding paragraph cannot be developed extensively here, some flavor of the arguments can be presented. For example, consider the *incomparability* interpretation. Most assuredly, incommensurability *cannot* imply incomparability, for to recognize that the "revolutionary" paradigm is incommensurable with the rival "dominant" paradigm—as Siegel (1980, p. 366) has noted—is at the very least to imply that the paradigms can be *compared*. How would one even know that the paradigms are *rival* if they could not be compared in some meaningful way? Two genuinely rival theories *cannot* be just solving self-contained, self-generated, encapsulated "puzzles" because one could not determine if they were rival unless they shared problems.

Similarly, the *radical translation* thesis is fundamentally flawed. As Putnam points out, to contend that the language of one paradigm cannot be translated into the terms of another paradigm "and then to go on and describe [both paradigms] *at length* [in the same language] is totally incoherent" (Putnam 1981, p. 114). Finally, the *meaning-variance* thesis (that some concepts or terms that are used in the revolutionary paradigm have a meaning that is different from how the concepts or terms are used in the dominant paradigm) may present difficulties in communicating, but it surely does not imply *incommensurability* in any meaningful sense. Again, how can the two paradigms be genuinely *rival* paradigms if they are "talking" about different phenomena? Roughly speaking, it is like "Aha! Here we have been arguing and all the time you were discussing apples and I was discussing oranges!"

The many detailed analyses of the concept of incommensurability over several decades led most philosophers of science to agree with the summary evaluation put forward by Hintikka: "The frequent arguments that strive to use the absolute or relative incommensurability of scientific theories as a reason for thinking that they are inaccessible to purely scientific (rational) comparisons are simply fallacious" (Hintikka 1988, p. 38). Ironically, advocates of the *meaning-variance* interpretation of incommensurability have demonstrated the cogency of the logical positivist view of the purpose of the philosophy of science. The logical positivists held that philosophers could and should clarify the language of science, and, therefore, increase the ability of various scientists to talk with each other when working in different "paradigms."

A fundamental flaw of Kuhnian conceptual-framework relativism is its interpretation of the concept of a "theory-neutral observation language." Shapere examines what it means for an "observation-language" to be "theory-neutral" (as summarized in Suppe 1977b) and points out the fatal flaw underlying most of Kuhn's (and his successors') confused discussions on this issue. Briefly, Shapere notes that most writers, since the time of Wittgenstein (1953), have believed that in order for science to be objective and relativism to be avoided, who have (correctly) noted that science needs a theory-neutral observation language to determine the extent to which its theories *correspond* with the external world. Many writers, such as Kuhn and Hanson, then note that our perceptual processes influence, inform, impart, or (more strongly) *determine*, our interpretations of what we observe. Therefore, they have concluded, observation is "theory-laden," and the absence of a "theory-neutral" observation language defeats the claimed objectivity of science, leading to conceptual-framework relativism.

As Shapere (see Suppe 1977a, p. 689) points out, the fatal flaw in the preceding analysis is the presumption that objectivity in science requires an observation-language that is neutral for *all* theories. However, it is *never* the case that the knowledge-claims of a theory are evaluated against *all* theoretically possible alternatives. Rather, the knowledge-claims of a theory are always compared against a limited number of genuine rivals. *What is required for objectivity in science is not an observation-language that is neutral with respect to all potential theories; rather, what is required is an observation-language that is neutral with respect to comparing the theories in question.* That is, what is required for objectivity is an observation-language that does not beg the question, or presume the truth-content, of the specific theories being evaluated.

For example, both the Ptolemaic and Copernican theories base their predictions of the observed position of Mars on the *theory* that a certain light in the sky is actually a physical body millions of miles away that continues to exist when unobserved. However, that "theory" does not assume anything about the orbit of the object in question. So the fact that observations of Mars depend on a "theory of Mars" does not imply that the observations cannot be used to compare, evaluate, or potentially adjudicate between the Ptolemaic and Copernican theories. Thus, the absence of an observation-language that is neutral with respect to all theories in science does not imply cognitive relativism of any kind, nor does it imply that there cannot be objective, impartial, nonarbitrary criteria for evaluating the knowledge-claims across theories or (in Kuhn's case) paradigms. In fact, in the actual practice of science, there appears to be no significant problem in finding theory-neutral terms for adjudicating claims across genuinely rival theories.

Kuhn's response to the many critiques of incommensurability is enlightening. Sensitive to the complex issues raised by the critiques, he attempted to modify his positions accordingly. In his 1970 revision of *Structure*, he claimed that his critics had completely misinterpreted his views on incommensurability when they claimed that he believed "the proponents of incommensurable theories cannot communicate with each other at all; as a result, in a debate over theory-choice there can be no recourse to *good* reasons; instead theory must be chosen for reasons that are ultimately personal and subjective; some sort of mystical apperception is responsible for the decision actually reached" (Kuhn 1970, pp. 198–99; italics in original). That is, the 1970 Kuhn wished to deny his previous rhetoric about "conversions" and "Gestalt-shifts" from "ducks" to ""rabbits." Rather, he wished to emphasize that science relies on "good reasons." Moreover, the reader should note that Kuhn did not just say "reasons," but *good* reasons, which would seem to necessarily imply that there are some paradigm-neutral standards that can be used to assess the adequacy of rival paradigms. (Otherwise, how could the reasons be *good*?) However, Kuhn did not simply stop with advocating *good reasons*. In his 1970 "Reflections on My Critics," he stated:

> What I mean to be saying, however, is only the following. In a debate over choice of theory, neither party has access to an argument which resembles a proof in logic or formal mathematics. (Kuhn 1970, p. 260)

In his 1976 work, he attempted to clarify again his concept of incommensurability and construed it as analogous to the concept of a *mathematical algorithm*:

> Most readers of my text have supposed that when I spoke of theories as incommensurable, I meant that they could not be compared. But "incommensurability" is a term borrowed from mathematics, and it there has no such implication. The hypotenuse of an isosceles right triangle is incommensurable with its side, but the two can be compared to any required degree of precision. What is lacking is not comparability but a unit of length in terms of which both can be measured directly and exactly. (Kuhn 1976, pp. 190–91)

Note that, for Kuhn, incommensurability stems from the inability to adjudicate paradigm choice "exactly" because "any required degree of precision" is not enough; there is nothing resembling "a proof in logic or formal mathematics."

Why was Kuhn so anxious to modify and thereby retreat from his earlier, highly provocative, "Gestalt-shift" position? It is precisely because Kuhn recognized that his earlier position implied relativism and irrationalism:

> My critics respond to my views . . . with charges of irrationality, relativism, and the defense of mob rule. These are all labels which I categorically reject. (Kuhn 1970, p. 234)

Similarly, when Feyerabend defended Kuhn's theory of science as (like Feyerabend's) advocating irrationalism, Kuhn retorted that this was "not only absurd but vaguely obscene" (Kuhn 1970, p. 264).

Given our previous analysis of both moral and cognitive relativism, it is easy to understand why Kuhn would want to disassociate himself from such positions (even though some readers might be offended that Kuhn would characterize such positions as "obscene"). How did one of the most eminent historians of science in the twentieth century get himself into a position that necessitated a retreat from many of the views argued so provocatively in *Structure*? A clue to the answer to this question lies on page 171 of *Structure*. On this occasion, Kuhn discusses the "maze" of problems associated with the nature of science and scientific progress and concludes: "Somewhere in this maze, for example, must lie the problem of induction." In other words, Kuhn sees the Humean "problem of induction" (see section 3.3.4) as underlying his "maze" of problems. A second clue occurs fifteen years after *Structure*, when Kuhn attempts to defend the fact that his views have seemed often to imply relativism and irrationalism. He states: "This is only another way of saying that I make no claim to have solved the problem of induction" (Kuhn 1977, p. 332). Finally, the reader should note carefully that Kuhn's final attempt to define incommensurability as analogous to a mathematical algorithm essentially sets up the standard that we cannot know anything (paradigms are incommensurable) unless our method of knowing has the certainty of a *deductive* mathematical proof ("directly and exactly"). Thus, Suppe notes that "the K-K thesis crucially underlies Feyerabend's and Kuhn's extreme views on scientific knowledge" (Suppe 1977a, p. 719). As we have seen before, Kuhn commits the "philosophers' fallacy." He sets for science an impossible standard: Science must know with certainty (i.e., the certainty of a mathematical proof) that its procedures for justifying its knowledge-claims are correct. He then finds that certainty is unavailable to science and (rather than adopting fallibilism) opts for views that (to his later lament) inexorably lead down the slippery slope to relativism and irrationalism.

Kuhn can be aptly described as a "reluctant relativist." Our next author, Paul Feyerabend, is an *exuberant* relativist.

4.2.2 Feyerabend's Relativism

Paul K. Feyerabend (1924–1994) was born in Austria, served in the German Army (1942–45), in which he received the Iron Cross. He later studied theater, mathematics, history, and physics at the University of Vienna, where he received his doctorate in 1951. While in Vienna, he interacted extensively with Wittgenstein, from whom he got his "first doubts about the identification of science with the explicit features of its theories and its observational reports" (Feyerabend 1987, p. 294). In Vienna he also met Sir Karl Popper, studied under him at the London School of Economics, and was strongly influenced by his philosophy. In 1955, with Popper's assistance, Feyerabend obtained a lectureship in the philosophy of science at the University of Bristol in England, after which he joined the faculty at the University of California, Berkeley, in 1959. There, he interacted with Kuhn, who was also teaching at Berkeley at the time. After 1979, he taught at Berkeley and the Federal Institute of Technology in Zurich, Switzerland. Widely cited as one of the foremost advocates of relativism, Feyerabend forcefully argued his relativistic approach to science in many articles and several major books, including: *Against Method* (1970, 1975) (first presented at a conference at the University of Minnesota in 1966, published in its proceedings in 1970, and turned into a book in 1975), *Science in a Free Society* (1978), and *Farewell to Reason* (1987).

Although Feyerabend's advocacy of the historical method and relativism is widely known, less recognized is that he started his philosophical career as an ardent believer in scientific realism (Feyerabend 1978, p. 113). Thus, one of his earliest papers was a 1958 article entitled "An Attempt at a Realistic Interpretation of Experience." Later, he stated: "I for one am not aware of having produced a single idea that is not already contained in the realistic tradition and especially in professor Popper's account of it" (Feyerabend 1965, p. 251). However, we shall not review Feyerabend's realism; rather, we shall examine his relativistic approach to science.

A key to understanding Feyerabend's relativism is his ongoing attack on rationalism, which he (somewhat idiosyncratically) defines as "the idea that there are general rules and standards for conducting our affairs, affairs of knowledge included" (Feyerabend 1978, p. 16). Throughout Feyerabend's years as a realist, he attempted to find "general rules" that would assist scientists in the conduct of research. However, a discussion with professor C.F. von Weizsäcker in Hamburg in 1965 on the foundations of quantum mechanics convinced Feyerabend that the pursuit of general rules for all science was an illusion, that any such rules would only be "a hindrance rather than a help: a person trying to solve a problem whether in science or elsewhere *must be given complete freedom* and cannot be restricted by any demands, [or] norms, however plausible they may seem to the logician or the philosopher who has thought them out in the privacy of his study" (Feyerabend 1978, p. 117; italics in original). (We again note that a prominent philosopher has drawn a "lesson" from the downfall of Newton and the rise of quantum mechanics.)

Feyerabend believed that the discipline of the philosophy of science had become dictatorial in its relationship with science and *Against Method* was written in part "to defend scientific practice from the rule of philosophical law" (Feyerabend 1987, p. 316). In short, Feyerabend wanted philosophy to "leave science to the scientists!" (1987, p. 317). His disdain for other philosophers of science is, to say the least, strong. He calls them "ratiofascists," "illiterates," "academic rodents," and a "gang of autistic intellectuals" who have gone from "incompetent professionalism to professionalized incompetence" (see Feyerabend 1982, p. 191; 1978, pp. 183, 195, 209; and 1987, p. 315). Notwithstanding his 1965 claim of admiration for Popper, his invective toward Popper in the latter part of his career became particularly strong, referring to him as a "mere propagandist" and his philosophy as an "outhouse," a "dog hut," and a "tiny puff of hot air in the positivistic teacup" (Feyerabend 1978, p. 208; 1987, pp. 282–83).

A major thesis of *Against Method* was that science is not a rule-governed endeavor. It cites numerous examples of rules that Feyerabend believed the philosophy of science had attempted to introduce into the practice of science. These include such things as never using ad hoc hypotheses, never introducing hypotheses that contradict well-established, experimental results, and never introducing hypotheses whose content is smaller than the content of empirically adequate alternatives (Feyerabend 1970, p. 22). Also attacked are rules that are attributed to Popper's critical rationalism, including: (1) "theories of large content are to be preferred to theories of small content," (2) "increase of content is welcome; decrease of content is to be avoided," (3) "a theory that contradicts an accepted basic statement must be given up," and (4) "*ad hoc* hypotheses are forbidden" (1970, p. 73). Feyerabend chronicles several historical examples of actual scientific activity that almost any believer in science would accept as being episodes resulting in scientific progress. Most notably, he focuses on Galileo and the Copernican Revolution and the replacement of Newtonian physics with Einsteinian relativity. His analysis of these historical episodes leads him to conclude:

> The idea of a method that contains firm, unchanging, and absolutely binding principles for conducting the business of science gets into considerable difficulty when confronted with the results of historical research. We find, then, that there is not a single rule, however plausible, and however firmly grounded in epistemology, that is not violated at some time or other. It becomes evident that such violations are not

accidental events, they are not the results of insufficient knowledge or of inattention which might have been avoided. On the contrary, we see that they are necessary for progress. (Feyerabend 1970, p. 21–22)

As the preceding quotation makes abundantly clear, at this point in Feyerabend's writings, he still believes in a nontrivial view of the progressivity of science, and he contends that the violation of methodological rules is absolutely essential for such progressivity.

Given the subtitle of his 1970 work ("An Outline of an Anarchistic Theory of Knowledge") and given his expression "anything goes," Feyerabend has often been accused of being a "naive anarchist." Such an anarchist would observe that "both absolute rules and context dependent rules have their limits and infer that all rules and standards are worthless and should be given up" (Feyerabend 1978, p. 32). Feyerabend denies vigorously such a characterization of his views, and assails those he refers to as "lazy anarchists" who "accept the slogan and interpret it as making research easier and success more accessible" (1987, p. 284). He states succinctly how "anything goes" should be interpreted:

> "Anything goes" does not express any conviction of mine, it is a jocular summary of the predicament of the rationalist: if you want universal standards, I say, if you cannot live without principles that hold independently of situation, shape of world, exigencies of research, temperamental peculiarities, then I can give you such a principle. It will be empty, useless, and pretty ridiculous—but it will be a "principle." It will be the "principle," "anything goes." (Feyerabend 1978, p. 188)

A similar elucidation of his use of "anything goes" is given in his later work (Feyerabend 1987, p. 284).

Now that we have an "official" interpretation of "anything goes," one might wonder what all the fuss was about. That is, Feyerabend originally attacked with logic, historical evidence, and substantial quantities of derision and scorn his fellow philosophers of science on the basis that they were proposing "universal" rules and "absolutely binding principles" for the conduct of science. To the charge that Feyerabend was claiming that rules and standards were "universally worthless," he states that this is a "misinterpretation," since his intention all along was "to convince the reader that all methodologies, even the most obvious ones, have their limits," and that "I do not argue that we should proceed without rules and standards" (Feyerabend 1978, p. 32). Stated succinctly, Feyerabend attacked other philosophers of science with vim, vigor, and invective on the charge of advocating "naive universalism" regarding rules and standards for conducting science, and his later work lashed out at those accusing him of "naive anarchism." However, a careful reading of the works of those philosophers that Feyerabend attacked will show that they were as guiltless of the charge of naive universalism as was Feyerabend of the charge of naive anarchism.

The "anything goes" controversy directly relates to our previous discussions on fallibilism, the "philosophers' fallacy," the search for certainty, and the K-K thesis. That is, not only are the knowledge-claims of science fallible, but so also are the procedures and processes (method) that *produce* those knowledge-claims. In Feyerabend's terms, there are no *universal* rules and standards. The preceding analysis demonstrates, in part, how Suppe arrives at the conclusion that the search for certainty and the K-K thesis underlie Feyerabend's "extreme view on scientific knowledge" (Suppe 1977a, p. 719). Thus, this part of Feyerabend's philosophy poses no problem at all for those advocating fallibilism with regard to science (as does this book and Hunt 2002a). We turn now to examining Feyerabend's views on the incommensurability of theories and scientific progress.

Incommensurability, Scientific Progress, and Reality Relativism. As discussed in section 3.5, the logical empiricists and critical rationalists believed that science progressed through four different means: (1) the development of new theories for phenomena not previously explained, (2) the falsification of existing theories and their replacement with new theories, (3) the expansion of the scope of a theory to include new phenomena, and (4) the reduction of specific theories into more general theories. With respect to the fourth way that science progresses, the logical empiricists claimed that science made genuine progress (we *knew* more) both when Galileo discovered that the distance an object falls toward the earth is directly related to the square of the elapsed time, and that science made further progress (we knew more) when Newton proposed that the gravitational attractive force of two bodies increases as the distance between the two bodies decreases (implying that their mutual acceleration will increase). Finally, the logical empiricists held that science made genuine progress with the general theory of relativity of Einstein and its proposal that (among other things) space, time, and mass (which were considered to be absolutes in Newtonian mechanics) were relative to the observer. The standard treatment of the logical empiricist view is given by Nagel (1960), and contends that these are genuine instances of scientific progress because the physics of Galileo can be "reduced" to Newton, and the physics of Newton can be "reduced" to Einsteinian relativity.

In a series of articles and books (Feyerabend 1962, 1965a, b, 1970,1975, 1978, 1987), Feyerabend attacked the conception that science progresses through reduction. Basically, Feyerabend's early attempt (1962) to show that science is not progressive proceeds by demonstrating that Galileo's "law of descent" cannot be mathematically *derived* from Newtonian mechanics. That is, since Galileo's law of descent assumes that the acceleration of the falling body is constant and Newtonian theory proposes that the acceleration increases as the falling body approaches the earth, Galileo's formula, formally speaking, cannot be derived from Newton's laws. Simply put, if d is the distance of a body from the surface of the earth and D is the radius of the earth, Galileo's law of descent holds only if the ratio d / D equals zero. (The reason why Galileo's law predicts very well in most cases is that the ratio for most situations is "close" to zero). Thus, Galileo's law does not reduce to Newton's because (unlike most mathematicians) Feyerabend does not consider derivations "in the limit" as legitimate derivations. Therefore, Feyerabend concludes, science does not progress through reduction.

Because the preceding argument lacks persuasiveness for most observers of science, Feyerabend's later attempts to demonstrate that science does not progress through reduction focused on "meaning-change" in theory. For example, he claims that in relativity theory the concepts of "length" and "mass" change radically in their meaning from the same terms in Newtonian mechanics, and, therefore, Newtonian mechanics does not "reduce" to quantum mechanics. This is the meaning-variance thesis regarding incommensurability discussed in section 4.2.

Many writers have pointed out the severe deficiencies in the meaning-variance thesis (see the references in section 4.2 for sources). Specifically with respect to the derivation thesis and its relationship to reduction, writers have pointed out that Galilean mechanics reduces to Newtonian mechanics in the limit. That is, the ratio d / D will approach zero (and thus approach Newtonian mechanics) as either d gets very small or D gets very large. Furthermore, in the limit the concepts of "relativistic length" and "relativistic mass" approach their Newtonian equivalents. Thus, Einsteinian mass (M) is related to Newtonian "rest mass" (m_0) by $M = m_0 \div \sqrt{(1 - v^2/c^2)}$ (Levin 1979). Thus, it is the case that most philosophers of science (and practicing scientists) continue to claim (1) that the transitions from Galileo to Newton to Einstein represent genuine instances of scientific progress; (2) that we are warranted in claiming that we know more about the physical world now than we did in 1500; (3) that the best interpretation of Galilean mechanics is that it is a limiting case of Newtonian mechanics, and, thus, we are warranted as referring to it as approximately true, in many situations; and (4) that Newtonian mechanics is best interpreted as a limiting case of Einsteinian relativity, and, thus, we are warranted in claiming that it is in some meaningful sense approximately true, especially in cases where velocities are low. Feyerabend's analysis was (1) that Galilean mechanics is *incommensurable* with Newtonian mechanics; (2) that Newtonian mechanics is *incommensurable* with Einsteinian relativity; (3) that no warranted claim to progress can be made in science; which, therefore, implies the nihilistic conclusion (4) that we cannot claim to know more about the physical world now than we did in A.D. 1500.

How can Feyerabend continue to reject the claim of scientific progress in general, and, more specifically, the claim of "reduction"? The answer, in part, lies in Feyerabend's specific characterization of "incommensurability." Feyerabend (like Kuhn) complains bitterly that his version of incommensurability has been misinterpreted by many writers as claiming that theories cannot be *compared*. Thus, for him, theories or paradigms are to be considered incommensurable only when they "use concepts that cannot be brought into the usual logical relations of inclusion, exclusion, and overlap," and that "when using the term 'incommensurable' I always meant deductive disjointedness, *and nothing else*" (Feyerabend 1977, pp. 363, 365). Moreover, Feyerabend states: "mere *difference* of concepts does not suffice to make theories incommensurable in my sense. The situation must be rigged in such a way that the conditions of concept formation in one theory forbid the formation of the basic concepts of the other" (Feyerabend 1978, p. 68). Consistent with these views, he acknowledges that "incommensurability as understood by me is a rare event. It occurs only when the conditions of meaningfulness for the descriptive terms of one language (theory, point of view) do not permit the use of the descriptive terms of another language (theory, point of view); mere difference of meanings does not lead to incommensurability in my sense" (Feyerabend 1987b, p. 81).

On Feyerabend's Incommensurability: For Reason. Given Feyerabend's clarification of his version of incommensurability, we are now in a better position to evaluate the basis for his claim that science does not and cannot make progress through "reduction." The reader should note carefully the words "logical relations of inclusion, exclusion, and overlap" in the preceding paragraph. Basically, what Feyerabend is using as a standard is that (he claims) the examples of theory reduction cannot be shown using the tool of formal logic, and, therefore, such theories have "deductive disjointedness." In short, Feyerabend sets up the following standard: The progressivity of scientific knowledge can be asserted warrantedly only if we know with the certainty of formal logic that theories can be "reduced," (the K-K thesis once again). He then purports to show that several examples of supposed theory-reduction cannot be shown with the conclusiveness of formal logic and proceeds to claim that this "incommensurability" dooms the claim of progress in science. Thus he commits the philosophers' fallacy.

There are at least three responses to Feyerabend's claim that his version of incommensurability leads to the conclusion that science is not progressive. First, one can show that, contra Feyerabend, formal logic is capable of accommodating the changes in meaning associated with different theories. This has been shown by Hintikka (1988). Second, one can deny that theory reduction needs to be warranted with the conclusiveness of formal logic. That is, reject the K-K thesis and assert that we have good reasons to believe that the general theory of relativity better describes the characteristics of the world than does Newtonian mechanics, which itself better describes the world than Galilean mechanics, which itself better describes the world than Aristotelian mechanics. Such an approach implies that we are warranted in believing that not all theories are "equally false," or "equally true." Further, we are warranted in using phrases such as "true within certain boundary conditions" and "true in the limiting case." This, essentially, is the approach of Rohrlich and Hardin (1983).

A third approach is to deny the assertion that theory reduction is a necessary requirement for scientific progress. Many writers in the philosophy of science implicitly assume that highly general, hierarchical theories employing a few universal laws (such as those found in physics) are both necessary for, and the only constituent of, scientific progress. Yet, in many sciences such powerful, highly general, hierarchical theories are the exception, rather than the rule. Certainly, there exist no such powerful theories in any of the behavioral sciences at the present time, and the prospects for developing such powerful, hierarchical theories in the future are, to say the least, open to debate. (General theories in the behavioral sciences are more likely to be collections of subtheories (El-Ansary 1979). Thus, to require as a condition for scientific progress that a discipline be able to reduce all its knowledge claims to highly general and very powerful theories (like Newtonian mechanics) would seem to necessarily establish *in advance* that there has never been any progress in many sciences, including *all* of the behavioral sciences (for now at least and possibly forever). On the other hand, if we broaden the concept of scientific progress to include lower-level theories, propositions, and empirical findings, the claim of scientific progress could be warranted (and in my judgment *is warranted*) without the claim of "theory reduction." Siegel makes a point similar to this when he suggests that we should distinguish between what he calls "theoretical cummulativity" and "low-level empirical or experimental cummulativity" (Siegel 1983, p. 66).

Feyerabend is well aware of the many weaknesses of his views on incommensurability, theory reduction, and scientific progress. Nevertheless, he advocates these positions because, in part, they are absolutely necessary for his version of reality relativism:

> [W]e certainly cannot assume that two incommensurable theories deal with one and the same objective state of affairs (to make the assumption we would have to assume that both at least *refer* to the same objective situation) . . . we must admit that they deal with different worlds and that the change (from one world to another) has been brought about by a switch from one theory to another. . . . We concede that our

epistemic activities may have a decisive influence even upon the most solid piece of cosmological furniture—they may make gods disappear and replace them by heaps of atoms in empty space. (Feyerabend 1978, p. 70)

Another reason for Feyerabend maintaining his discredited views about incommensurability, theory-reduction, and scientific progress is that they are necessary to buttress his case that "Western science has now infected the whole world like a contagious disease" (Feyerabend 1987a, p. 297). We must recall that many of Feyerabend's early works were, essentially, polemical attacks on his fellow colleagues in the philosophy of science (the "illiterates" and "academic rodents"). However, these attacks formed the foundation for his assault on science itself, and to admit the deficiencies of his attacks on his philosophical colleagues would destroy the foundations for his claim that science is a "disease." To understand how Feyerabend arrives at the conclusion that science is a "disease," we need to trace the development of his own version of conceptual-framework relativism.

Feyerabend's Conceptual-Framework Relativism. In his 1978 and 1987 books, Feyerabend recounts the experiences that influenced the development of his thoughts. In both books, he identifies the "turning point" in his career as occurring in the turbulent 1960s when he was a professor at the University of California at Berkeley and had to teach courses having numerous "Mexicans, blacks and Indians" (Feyerabend 1987a, p. 317). These students "wanted to know, they wanted to learn, they wanted to understand the strange world around them—did they not deserve better nourishment? Their ancestors had developed cultures of their own, colorful languages, harmonious views of the relation between man and man, and man and nature, whose remnants are a living criticism of the tendencies of separation, analysis, self-centeredness inherent in Western thought" (Feyerabend 1987a, p. 317, reprinted from 1978, p. 118). Feyerabend believed that Western science and culture was destroying other cultures, or, in his words, "traditions." The Western "tradition" had its origins in the triumph of "rationalism" in seventh-century Greece (Feyerabend 1978, p. 120). Now, the Western tradition, a descendant of Greek "rationalism," was asking him to teach those whose traditions had been destroyed:

> I looked at my audience and they made me recoil in revulsion and terror from the task I was suppose to perform. For the task—this now became clear to me—was that of a very refined, very sophisticated slave driver. And a slave driver I did not want to be. (Feyerabend 1987a, p. 317, reprinted from 1978, p. 118)

Thus began Feyerabend's assault on "rationalism," Western science, and (ultimately) Western civilization.

Central to understanding Feyerabend's assault on Western science is his construct of a "tradition." As Feyerabend (1978, p. 66) relates, this construct comes directly from Wittgenstein's "forms of life," discussed in section 4.1.3. Of the many different kinds of traditions in life, some are given the designation of "knowledge-creating traditions." Science, Feyerabend contends, is but one of many knowledge-creating traditions. Throughout his 1978 book, Feyerabend discusses and defends examples of other such traditions: mysticism (Feyerabend 1978, p. 31), magic (p. 74), astrology (p. 74), rain dances (p. 78), religion (p. 78), mythical world views (p. 78), tribal medicine (p. 96), parapsychology (p. 103), all non-Western belief traditions (p. 102), and witchcraft (p. 191). One might suppose that some of these traditions may be better "ways of knowing" than others, but for Feyerabend they are all equally valid. Feyerabend, like Winch before him, relies heavily on the work of Evans-Pritchard concerning the primitive society of the Azande and its reliance on witchcraft. Science and witchcraft are equal, claims Feyerabend, because any argument of science that would tend to refute witchcraft, when "translated into Zande modes of thought would serve to support their entire structure of belief. For their mystical notions are eminently coherent, being interrelated by a network of logical ties and are so ordered that they never too crudely contradict sensory experience but, instead, experience seems to justify them" (Feyerabend 1987a, p. 74). Feyerabend approvingly quotes Evans-Pritchard on the "rationality" of using the oracles of witchcraft for making day-to-day decisions: "I found this as satisfactory a way of running my home and affairs as any other I know of" (1987a, p. 74). Feyerabend then compares the Zande beliefs in witchcraft and the processes of justifying those beliefs as being no different from the processes used to settle disputes in science. In particular, he cites the dispute between Einstein and other physicists over the nature of quantum theory. He, therefore, justifies his all-encompassing relativism:

> For every statement, theory, point of view believed to be true (with good reasons) *there exists* [sic] arguments showing a conflicting alternative to be at least as good, or even better. (Feyerabend 1987a, p. 76; italics in original)

Feyerabend's all-encompassing relativism includes (among others) all the versions we have discussed so far, that is, cultural, moral, rationality, reality, and conceptual framework. Note that Feyerabend does *not* say there "may" exist, he states *there exists*. Note also that he does *not* say an alternative "may" be as good, but will be "at least as good, or even better." The reader may think that Feyerabend is simply engaging in sophistry to "make a point." One might suppose that Feyerabend's works are just academic gamesmanship and that he did not intend for his readers to take his views seriously. Brodbeck notes that relativists believe "science is in effect a game" (Brodbeck 1982, p. 3), which is consistent with the view in marketing that "the important question that we must ask is how I can convince my colleagues in the scientific community that my theory is correct"? (Anderson 1982, p. 15) As noted in section 2.1.3, the sophists in ancient Greece were among the first relativists in Western intellectual history. One test for the presence of sophistry is whether people behave consistently with their stated beliefs. On this criterion, Feyerabend is clearly no sophist. (We defer our discussion of this issue to section 6.1.)

Feyerabend's Attack on Science. The preceding discussion about the irrationalism implied by relativism becomes even clearer by examining precisely how Feyerabend uses relativism to attack science. Recall that Feyerabend believes science is but one knowledge-creating tradition among many and that "traditions are neither good nor bad, they simply are" (Feyerabend 1978, p. 27). Feyerabend notes that in the seventeenth, eighteenth, and nineteenth centuries the scientific tradition was but one of the many competing ideologies and was in fact a "liberating force" because it "restricted the influence of other ideologies and thus gave the individual room for thought" (1978, p. 75). However, he believes science today does not have a liberating effect, because it has turned into a "dogmatic religion." He believes "the very same enterprise that once gave man the ideas and the strength to free himself from the fears and prejudices of a tyrannical religion now turns him into a slave of its interests" (1978, p. 75). How did the consensus emerge that the knowledge-claims of science were preferred by society over the knowledge-claims of competing traditions? Is it not because society determined rationally and reasonably that scientific knowledge-claims had more epistemological warrant, and were more likely to be true? Is not the "societal consensus" backed by good reasons? Emphatically not, asserts Feyerabend:

> It reigns supreme because some past successes have led to institutional measures (education; role of experts; role of power groups such as the AMA) that prevent a comeback of the rivals. Briefly, but not incorrectly: Today science prevails not because of its comparative merits, but because the show has been rigged in its favor. (Feyerabend 1978, p. 102)

Specifically, for Feyerabend, how did other knowledge-creating traditions lose out? "These myths, these religions, these procedures have disappeared or deteriorated not because science was better, but because the *apostles of science were the more determined conquerors*, because they materially suppressed the bearers of alternative cultures" (Feyerabend 1978, p. 102; italics in original). How was the material suppression of rival traditions and the triumph of the "apostles of science" accomplished? The suppression of rival traditions was accomplished, he contends, through the actions of scientists, both individually and through their collective associations, aided and abetted by such diverse groups as "liberal intellectuals, white missionaries, adventurers, and anthropologists" (1978, p. 77).

As examples of suppressive tactics, Feyerabend notes that anthropologists "collected and systematized" knowledge about non-Western traditions and developed "interpretations" that "were simply a consequence of popular antimetaphysical tendencies combined with a firm belief in the excellence first, of Christianity, and then of science" (Feyerabend 1978, p. 77). Liberal intellectuals aided the suppression by first: "loudly and persistently" proclaiming that they defend freedom of thought, while at the same time not recognizing that this freedom of thought "is granted [only] to those who have already accepted part of the rationalist (i.e., scientific) ideology" (1978, p. 76). Feyerabend, himself, even contributed to the suppression while teaching at the University of California at Berkeley: "My function was to carry out the educational policies of the State of California, which means I had to teach people what a small group of white intellectuals had decided was knowledge" (1978, p. 118).

Feyerabend concludes that "the prevalence of science is a threat to democracy" (Feyerabend 1978, p. 76) and proposes his "solution" to the problem of science in society. He addresses this issue by, first, proposing the following rhetorical questions:

> But—so the impatient believer in rationalism and science is liable to exclaim—is this procedure not justified? Is there not a tremendous difference between science on the one side, religion, magic, myth on the other? Is this difference not so large and so obvious that it is unnecessary to point it out and silly to deny it? (Feyerabend 1978, p. 78)

Feyerabend answers his rhetorical questions concerning the differences between science and other "traditions" with: "Rationalists and scientists cannot rationally (scientifically) argue for the unique position of their favorite ideology" (Feyerabend 1978, p. 79). Therefore, he proposes, in order to have a free society, "is it not rather the case that traditions [mysticism, magic, astrology, rain dances, religion, mythical worldviews, tribal medicine, parapsychology, all non-Western belief traditions, and witchcraft] that give substance to the lives of people must be given equal rights and *equal access to key positions in society* no matter what other traditions think about them"? (1978, p. 79; italics added)

So Feyerabend's relativism began in the 1960s by attacking the philosophy of science and then progressed in the 1970s to attack science itself. Feyerabend's 1980s efforts, like *Farewell to Réason*, continued by attacking all elements of Western culture and civilization. Briefly, *Farewell to Reason* states the case for relativism again and claims: "Western forms of life are found in the most remote corners of the world and have changed the habits of people who only a few decades ago were unaware of their existence. Cultural differences disappear, indigenous crafts, customs, and institutions are being replaced by Western objects, customs, and organizational forms" (Feyerabend 1987a, p. 2). He notes that the spread of Western culture has not been beneficial: "Many so-called

'Third World problems' such as hunger, illness and poverty seem to have been caused rather than alleviated by the steady advance of Western Civilization" (1987, p. 4). He identifies the "two ideas that have often been used to make Western expansion intellectually respectable—the idea of Reason and the idea of Objectivity" (1987, p. 5). These ideas, which he identifies as coming down to Western Civilization from the ancient Greeks, are fallacious and should be discarded in favor of accepting relativism because "there exist no 'objective' reasons for preferring science and Western rationalism to other traditions" (1987, p. 297). Given that (1) "western science has now infected the whole world like a contagious disease"; and that (2) "western Civilization was either imposed by force, . . . or accepted because it produced better weapons"; and that (3) "its advance, while doing some good, also caused enormous damage" (1987, p. 297), what recourse is there left for the relativist Feyerabend? He contends that the concepts of Reason and Objectivity must be abandoned and, thus, he concludes with: "FAREWELL TO REASON" (Feyerabend 1987, p. 319).

Given the extreme nature of Feyerabend's philosophy, it is easy to understand and sympathize with Suppe's characterization of it as "hopeless" (Suppe 1977a, p. 648). Nevertheless, Feyerabend's relativistic philosophy, though now thoroughly discredited in the philosophy of science, has had a warm and welcome reception throughout much of marketing and the social sciences. It has left a legacy for society in general. To coopt Feyerabend's metaphor, many scholars believe relativism has "infected" Western society.[4] Our next section explores why the relativism and irrationalism of Kuhn and Feyerabend were so influential in the 1960s.

4.3   THE RISE AND FALL OF HISTORICAL RELATIVISM

Kuhnian relativism totally dominated philosophical thought on science in the 1960s (Laudan et al. 1986). In fact, a good case can be made that Thomas Kuhn dominated the philosophy of science in the 1960s in a manner unparalleled in the entire twentieth century. Given that many of its deficiencies seem painfully obvious today, how and why was Kuhnian relativism accepted so swiftly and passionately in the 1960s? One answer is that the seeds of relativism found fertile soil in the irrationalistic environment of that troubled and turbulent decade. As just one of the more sorrowful legacies of the 1960s, the irrationalistic manifesto "turn on, tune in, drop out" left behind many in Western societies dangerously dependent on drugs. Most shamefully, many university faculty preached that the "establishment" had lied to its young about the dangers of drugs. Hallucinogenic drugs in particular were touted by prominent faculty as being safe, "mind expanding," and opening up "new ways of knowing." Alas, the education efforts of public and private health authorities have had only limited success in reestablishing the pre-1960s societal consensus that drugs, far from "expanding minds," destroy them. In Pogo's famous words, "We have met the enemy and he is us."

Although all institutions of American society (representing the "received views" of the "establishment") came under vigorous attack in the 1960s, universities may have suffered the greatest damage. Bloom chronicled the revolutionary violence, both verbal and physical, that engulfed American universities in that decade: "Enlightenment in America came close to breathing its last during the 1960s. The fact that the universities are no longer in convulsions does not mean that they have regained their health" (Bloom 1987, p. 314). All the fundamental values underlying Western universities (academic freedom, rational discourse, tolerance for the views of others, the importance of objectivity, and the search for truth) came tumbling down when "students discovered that pompous teachers who catechized them about academic freedom could, with a little shove, be made into dancing bears" (Bloom 1987, p. 315).

In a section of his book titled "The Decomposition of the University," Bloom recounts the behaviors of the faculties in the various departments in response to the siege of their universities. Unfortunately, "there was no solidarity in defense of the pursuit of truth" (Bloom 1987, p. 347). Distressingly, "the professional schools—engineering, home economics, industrial-labor relations and agriculture—simply went home and closed the shutters." Likewise, the natural scientists, believing themselves "not threatened," refused to speak out: "Only one natural scientist at Cornell spoke out against the presence of guns or the bullying of professors" (Bloom 1987, p. 347). This is because "the natural sciences were not a target, as they had once been in high-grade fascism and communism. There were no Lenins thundering against positivism, relativity or genetics, no Goebbels alert to the falseness of Jewish science" (1987, p. 348). The humanities' faculty, on the other hand, not only capitulated to the revolutionary radicals, but warmly embraced them:

> To find hysterical supporters of the revolution one had, not surprisingly, to go to the humanities. Passion and commitment, as opposed to coolness, reason and objectivity, found their home there. The drama included a proclamation from a group of humanities teachers threatening to take over a building if the university did not capitulate forthwith. A student told me that one of his humanities professors, himself a Jew, had said to him that Jews deserved to be put in concentration camps because of what they had done to blacks. (Bloom 1987, p. 352)

Why were the faculty in the humanities such easy targets for the revolutionaries? Because, Bloom observes, of the overwhelming influence of relativism and such kindred as deconstructionism: "On the portal of the humanities is written in many ways and many tongues, 'There is no truth—at least here'" (Bloom 1987, p. 372). He writes:

> The reasons for this behavior [embracing the irrationalism of the student revolution-
> aries] on the part of many humanists are obvious and constitute the theme of this
> book. Cornell was in the forefront of certain trends in the humanities as well as
> politics. It had for years been a laundering operation for radical Left French ideas in
> comparative literature. From Sartre, through Goldmann, to Foucault and Derrida,
> each successive wave washed over the Cornell shores. These ideas were intended to
> give life to old books . . . and make them a part of revolutionary conscience. At last
> there was an active, progressive role [i.e., overthrowing the "Establishment"] for the
> humanists. (Bloom 1987, p. 352)

Given that the professional schools "closed their shutters," the natural scientists stood mute, and the humanities were coopted, the social sciences re-
mained "the only place where any kind of stand was made" (Bloom 1987, p.
353). Bloom recounts that, when (1) "historians were being asked to rewrite
the history of the world, and of the United States in particular, to show that
nations were always conspiratorial systems of domination and exploitation";
when (2) "psychologists were being pestered to prove the psychological damage done by inequality and the existence of nuclear weapons, and to show that
American statesmen were paranoid about the Soviet Union"; when (3) "political scientists were urged to interpret the North Vietnamese as nationalists
and to remove the stigma of totalitarianism from the Soviet Union"; and when
(4) the "major student activity in social science was to identify heretics" who
questioned the truth of these positions, it was then that many social scientists
fought back (Bloom 1987, pp. 354, 355). Seeing that "objectivity was threatened, and without respect and protection for scholarly inquiry anyone of them
might be put at risk . . . social scientists of the Left, Right and Center . . .
joined together to protest the outrage against academic freedom and against
their colleagues that took place there and continues in more or less subtle
forms everywhere" (1987, p. 355).

Against the backdrop of the tidal wave of irrationalism sweeping across
the universities in the 1960s, the swift and passionate (some have called it
"mindless") acceptance of Kuhnian relativism was virtually ensured. It provided another superficially plausible (yet, due to Kuhn's stature, formidable)
intellectual arrow in the revolutionary's quiver. Against attempts to defend
university values, Kuhnian relativism gave the revolutionary an arsenal of
epithets: "Does not the eminent historian Kuhn show that all *genuine* progress
comes about only through revolutionary activity"? "Doesn't Kuhn clearly show
that everything, even physics, is inherently just persuasion and politics"? "Is
not everything either the *irrelevant* puzzle-solving of the received view of the
Establishment, or *relevant* revolutionary change"? "Is it not the case that there
is no such thing as the rational pursuit of truth, only the pursuit of power"?

Fortunately, tidal waves recede. The revolutionary irrationalism of the 1960s
gradually gave way to the more sober reflection and rational discourse of the
1970s, both in universities in general and the philosophy of science in par-

ticular. As detailed in the previous sections, Kuhnian relativism began to crumble under the carefully reasoned analyses of Shapere, Scheffler, and Suppe (among many others). Many writers believe the turning point was the often-cited symposium on the structure of scientific theories held at the University of Illinois in 1969. Believing, in Suppe's words, that the philosophy of science was being "castigated for irrelevance," ("irrelevant" was a 1960s epithet) and that the entire discipline was in "an acute state of disarray," the symposium brought together many of the discipline's most prominent members, including: Peter Achinstein, Robert L. Causey, Bernard Cohen, Bas C. van Fraassen, Carl Hempel, Thomas Kuhn, Hillary Putnam, Dudley Shapere, Frederick Suppe, Patrick Suppes, and Stephen Toulmin (Suppe 1977b). Attesting to the importance of the symposium, many of the sessions drew audiences exceeding a thousand people, most of whom represented disciplines other than philosophy (Suppe 1977b, p. viii). It was at this symposium that the deficiencies of the "received view" of the logical empiricists (the "establishment") concerning the nature of scientific theories were detailed. Also, the alternative *Weltanschauungen* theories of Hanson, Kuhn, and Feyerabend were explicated and evaluated. Thus, it was at this symposium that Kuhn began his steady retreat from relativism, noting that *incommensurability* "is a term I have used, although it is not one I have been very fond of" (Kuhn, in Suppe 1977b, p. 409). The proceedings of the symposium and the 240-page critical introduction written by Frederick Suppe provided significant input into the research agenda of the philosophy of science in the early 1970s.

By the late 1970s, the verdict was in on the historical relativism of Kuhn and Feyerabend. As Causey, one of the participants in the 1969 symposium, cogently observes: "In the Sixties it appeared that there was a crisis in the foundations of science. Recent work indicates there was not really a crisis; instead the Sixties were a transitional period leading to significant modifications of earlier views" (Causey 1979, p. 199). In 1977, Suppe prepared his "Afterword" to summarize the results of the research on Kuhn's and Feyerabend's theories of science conducted since the 1969 symposium. In a section titled "The Waning of the *Weltanschauungen* Views," Suppe reviews a long list of "weighty objections" that had been brought to bear on Feyerabend's version of relativism. He concludes: "Collectively, these objections are weighty indeed, displaying how bizarre, implausible, and unattractive is Feyerabend's view of science" (Suppe 1977a, p. 641). Suppe notes that Feyerabend's *Against Method* had moved toward a "subjective idealism," and other "than perhaps to the most fanatical Hegelian, Feyerabend's philosophy of science has little to recommend itself and is losing whatever importance and influence it once had within philosophy of science" (Suppe 1977a , p. 643). As noted in the previous section, since Suppe's 1977 conclusion on Feyerabend's philosophy, Feyerabend took his relativism to its logical conclusion, that is, there is no reason to prefer the knowledge-claims of science over mysticism, magic, astrology, rain dances, and, furthermore, Western civilization is a "disease."

Unlike Feyerabend, Suppe points out that Kuhn took the views of the other participants in the 1969 symposium quite seriously and in the ensuing years made numerous modifications and clarifications of his theory of science. In particular, as we have noted previously, he emphatically rejected relativism and irrationalism by attempting to redefine his concept of incommensurability. He concluded by defining two theories as being incommensurable when there is no procedure (like a mathematical algorithm) to compare rival theories on a "point by point" basis and know-with-certainty (the "philosophers' fallacy" again) which theory to choose. Readers will note that this is a far cry from his previous "Gestalt-shift" view and its radical implications.

Suppe reviews the work on Kuhn's relativism that had been conducted since the 1969 symposium and concludes that "since the symposium, Kuhn's views have undergone a sharply declining influence on contemporary philosophy of science," because (1) "as Kuhn has modified and attenuated his views, it has seemed to many that he was retreating toward a neo-positivistic view"; (2) "Kuhn's account unnecessarily but essentially shortchanges the role of rationality in the growth of scientific knowledge"; (3) "There is a growing skepticism over Kuhn's claims that the history of science exemplifies his views on how science oscillates between normal and revolutionary science"; and (4) "Kuhn's position commits him to a metaphysical and epistemological view of science which is fundamentally defective since it makes discovering how the world really is irrelevant to scientific knowledge." Therefore, "collectively, these factors have led increasing numbers of philosophers of science to reject Kuhn's approach as irredeemably flawed, although not as hopeless as Feyerabend's" (Suppe 1977a, p. 648).

Since the rejection of relativism in the late 1970s, the trend in the philosophy of science has been toward *historical empiricism* and *scientific realism*:

> The directions in which contemporary philosophy of science is heading are profoundly influenced by the repudiated *Weltanschauungen* analyses: Like the *Weltanschauungen* analyses, they view the history of science, as well as contemporary scientific practice, as providing important evidence to be used in developing and evaluating their philosophical analyses . . . further, contemporary work in philosophy of science increasingly subscribes to the position that it is a central aim of science to come to knowledge of how the world *really* is, that correspondence between theories and reality is a central aim of science as an epistemic enterprise and crucial to whatever objectivity scientific knowledge enjoys—in sharp repudiation of the "sociological" views of knowledge found in the more extreme *Weltanschauungen* [Kuhn and Feyerabend] analyses, while acknowledging the defects of positivistic and earlier empiricist treatments. (Suppe 1977a, p. 649)

In the next chapter, we investigate the views of the two most prominent advocates of historical empiricism: Imre Lakatos and Larry Laudan. We then explore scientific realism.

QUESTIONS FOR ANALYSIS AND DISCUSSION

1.   The epigraph to this chapter states "the cruelest fate which can overtake *enfants-terribles* is to awake and find that their avowed opinions have swept the suburbs." When Stove made his comment, he was referring to the philosophy of Thomas Kuhn. Why would Stove suggest that it would be a "cruel fate" for Kuhn if, in fact, "the suburbs" truly accepted all of Kuhn's philosophy? There is an old expression that goes: "Sophistry is the most dangerous game you can play." What does this have to do with the epigraph?

2.   Rachels points out that "if we took cultural relativism seriously, we would have to admit that these social practices are also immune from criticism." What does he mean "if we took cultural relativism seriously"? Under what circumstances will individuals propose philosophies that are "not to be taken seriously"? How do we *know* when a philosophy is to be "taken seriously"? Is it *ever* appropriate to propose philosophies that one does not "take seriously"?

3.   What is absolutism with respect to ethics? Critics of absolutism often spell it "Absolutism." What is the implication of capitalizing the "A"? Likewise, critics of truth often spell it "Truth," or even "TRUTH!" Evaluate the thesis that such critics fall prey to the "philosophers' fallacy."

4.   Section 4.1.2 points out that the "strong thesis" is often used synonymously with "relativism" in sociology. What is "strong" about the "strong thesis"? In what way does the fear of ethnocentrism result in the "strong thesis"? One writer has claimed that it is actually ethnocentrism of the most vicious and condescending kind to claim that other people have "reasoning processes" that are radically different from so-called Western reasoning processes. How could it be "ethnocentric" *not* to believe in rationality relativism and "viciously ethnocentric" to believe in rationality relativism?

5.   As pointed out in section 4.1.3, reality relativism has its historical origins, in part, in Winch's monograph entitled *The Idea of a Social Science and Its Relation to Philosophy*. In this monograph Winch analyzed the primitive society of the Azande and its reliance on witchcraft. Curiously, many modern advocates of relativism wish to deny their historical heritage: "Siegel dredges up the hackneyed example

of witchcraft practices among the Zande people as Evans-Pritchard found them in the late 1920s and early 1930s. Ever since Winch's misreading of Wittgenstein sparked the so-called 'rationality debates,' philosophers have imagined that important epistemological issues were at stake in Azande ethnography" (Anderson 1988, p. 134). Why is it important for relativists to (now) deny their historical heritage? Under what circumstances is it appropriate (inappropriate) to deny the historical heritage of one's philosophy?

6. Section 4.1.3 contends that reality relativism is "morally impotent." What would be the difference between a philosophy being, simply, "morally impotent" and one being "morally outrageous"? The statement was made that the distinction between moral relativism and cognitive relativism is often "difficult to make." Why should this be the case? Why should, or should not, the morality of cognitive relativism be an issue?

7. Discuss the various usages of the term "paradigm." How does a "paradigm" differ from a "Weltanschauung"? What difference does it make if everyone uses the term "paradigm" in his or her own way? (Hint: Reflect on the purpose of language.)

8. Thomas Kuhn believed that his theory of science did not apply to the social sciences because they were in the "pre-paradigm stage." Many writers, however, have pointed out that Kuhn's theory has been actually *applied* most often in the social sciences. Why has this been the case? Should it be the case?

9. Discuss the three major interpretations of the word "incommensurable." What does "rival" mean? Why is it important to recognize that it is only "rival" theories or paradigms for which the concept of "incommensurability" poses a potential problem for science? Why is it important to distinguish between theories and paradigms being "incommensurable" and being, simply, "different"?

10. What are the "Orwellian implications" of reality relativism? Why does the book claim that it is "surprising and sorrowful" that Kuhn did not repudiate reality relativism earlier? To what extent do you believe that current advocates of reality relativism have recognized its "Orwellian implications"? Should they so recognize?

11. What does it mean and why is it important to recognize that "what is required for objectivity in science is not an observation-language that is neutral to all potential theories; rather, what is required is an observation-language that is neutral with respect to the theories in question." How have many philosophers erred by claiming that objectivity requires an observation-language that is "neutral" with respect to

all theories? What does it mean to claim that an observation-language is "neutral" with respect to a *particular* theory? (Hint: What does "question begging" mean?)

12. Define the terms "objective" and "subjective" as they might apply to any method or procedure for justifying knowledge-claims. Draw a continuum with your definition of objective at the left end of the continuum and your definition of subjective at the right. Now, place an *x* on the line where you believe "science" should go. Continue by positioning other societal institutions on the line, such as religion and politics. Use the continuum and your definitions to evaluate the thesis: "Science is subjective." It is often claimed that "relativism destroys language." What does this mean with reference to the objectivity/subjectivity issue? Is science subjective? Should it be?

13. Why do you believe that Kuhn stated that it was "obscene" for Feyerabend to claim that their views were advocating the same thing? Why is Kuhn referred to as a "reluctant relativist" and Feyerabend an "exuberant relativist"?

14. After the publication of Feyerabend's *Science in a Free Society*, Tibor Machan wrote a review for the *Philosophy of Social Science* (Machan 1982b). Feyerabend then commented on the review of Machan, referring to Machan's views as "academic ratiofascism" (Feyerabend 1982a, p. 191). Machan then replied:

> Oh my, what have I unleashed with my humble little review! A veritable Don Rickles of the journal circuit, only without the fun. But let me try, as hard as I can, to keep away from derision, not without saying first, however, that it does hurt. (Machan 1982, p. 197)

Machan then proceeds to respond to the charges that he is a "ratiofascist" and concludes his response with:

> Feyerabend may wish to have us think that all he, but no one else, asks for is a tolerance for different lifestyles. But there is plenty of room in my own standard-ridden outlook . . . for enormous varieties of lifestyles within societies with the very same legal framework—the U.S. liberal melting pot is really far richer, though getting less so, than Feyerabend allows. What with his calling me a fascist for thinking and publishing my libertarian notions, I doubt that a polity of his conception would be anywhere near so open and pluralistic as one I have in mind. . . . It really makes me doubt that Feyerabend is a man with whom any kind of conversation that does not begin with total submission to his views could be carried out in a civilized fashion. (Machan 1982a, p. 199)

How does Machan's comment relate to the epigraph of this chapter? Some writers have pointed out that many advocates of relativism, like Feyerabend, seem totally intolerant of others whose views may differ with their own. How does this relate to the acceptance of relativism in the 1960s? How does it relate today?

15. Suppe points out the distressing tendency for the behavioral sciences to uncritically accept many theories of science from the philosophy of science, even after those philosophies have been long repudiated: "Increasingly, behavioral and social sciences are reading and being influenced by Thomas Kuhn's *Structure of Scientific Revolutions.* Within anthropology, economics, political science, psychology, and sociology there has been a spate of publications attempting to view these disciplines from a 'Kuhnian' perspective, either in an attempt to discern the current state of the field or in an attempt to resolve various methodological disputes within the discipline" (Suppe 1984, p. 89). He goes on to relate that "I am dismayed and worried by the burgeoning influence Kuhn is having on behavioral and social scientists. My fears here rest not on the fact that Kuhn's structure of scientific revolutions is bad history of science and fundamentally defective philosophy of science, but rather on the way in which behavioral and social scientists are resorting to and relying on Kuhn's work" (Suppe 1984, p. 69). Suppe concludes that "science must approach philosophy of science with a critical eye" and:

> In short, scientific methodologies are strategies for ascertaining the likelihood that accepted theories or hypotheses are correct, and to the extent that science has been progressive it has involved the development of increasingly more sophisticated strategies or cannons of rationality for deciding which theories to accept or reject on the basis of increasingly smaller data bases, in such a way that such strategies lead to increasingly higher success rates in the acceptance of true theories or hypotheses and the rejection of false ones. The methodologies codified by philosophers of science or methodologically-concerned scientists are codifications of such strategies, often coupled with assessments of the relative merits of these strategies compared to other available ones. (Suppe 1984, p. 102)

To what extent are Suppe's comments relevant to marketing and social science today? To what extent is Suppe arguing that scientific *methodology* is progressive? Would it be possible to know with certainty that scientific methodology is progressive? Why is the issue of the progressivity of scientific methodology important, or not important?

16. Why is it a fallacy to restrict discussions of scientific progress to only hierarchical, general theories, such as Newtonian mechanics? To what extent has marketing science made progress? To what extent would it be *possible* for marketing science to exhibit progress if one adopts relativism?

17. Evaluate Peter and Olson's position that "truth is a subjective evaluation that cannot be properly inferred outside of the context provided by the theory" (Peter and Olson 1983, p. 119).

18. Peter and Olson argue, following the lead of Feyerabend, that "'anything goes'—that is, any methodology or theory, no matter how unconventional, *can contribute* to scientific progress" (Peter and Olson 1983, p. 121, italics added). What is the difference between "can contribute," and "may contribute," or "is likely to contribute," or "is likely not to contribute"? Does the phrase "can contribute" make the statement trivially true? Demonstrably false?

19. Peter and Olson state "alternatively, researchers with an R/C orientation conceive of many possible realities, each of which is relative to a specific context or frame of reference. According to this view, scientists construct 'realities' by developing a degree of social agreement about the meanings of their theories and empirical observations" (Peter and Olson, 1983, p. 120). Evaluate this position. How does it relate to the "consensus theory of truth"?

NOTES

1. The term "received view" was originally coined by Putnam (1962) and referred to certain tenets of logical empiricism about the nature of theories in science. However, the meaning of the term became extremely pejorative in the 1960s, used by many to refer to *all* views on science other than the "new orthodoxy" of historical relativism.

2. The issue of whether "feminist epistemology" is meant to be "taken seriously" is examined by Pinnick (1994).

3. Slezak examines the "social construction of social constructionism" and finds that "the new sociology of science is perhaps the only confirming instance of its own thesis that science is not founded on considerations of evidence, logic or rationality" (Slezak 1994, p. 336). For other evaluations of the "strong thesis" in sociology, see Bunge (1991, 1992, 1998, 1999).

4. For a discussion by physicists of how the acceptance of relativism has severely damaged British science, see Theocharis and Psimopoulos (1987). See Gross and Levitt (1994) for a review of the impact on science education of "cultural studies," including postmodernism, feminism, radical environmentalism, and multiculturalism.

5   POST-RELATIVISTIC PHILOSOPHY OF SCIENCE

To say that truth is no part of the aim of science is on a par with saying that curing is no part of the aim of medicine or that profit is no part of the aim of commerce.

—John W.N. Watkins

In the 1980s and thereafter, philosophy of science turned sharply toward historical empiricism and scientific realism. Advocates of historical empiricism share with Kuhn and Feyerabend a belief that philosophy of science should reflect and explain the actual history of science, but they reject Kuhn and Feyerabend's relativism/irrationalism. Advocates of scientific realism, though sensitive to the history of science, often place more emphasis on understanding science as it is currently practiced. As Suppes points out: "[A]bout ninety percent of all scientists who have ever lived are now alive, and the development of science since World War II is the most smashing success story in the history of thought. To be concerned only with the long historical perspective and not to understand the systematic details of modern science is as mistaken as the pursuit of empty formal methods that make no contact with developed scientific theories and their supporting experiments" (Suppes, in Asquith and Kyburg 1979, p. 25). Kuhn himself lamented the growing trend of historical critics of science (in his terms, "external studies") to be ill-informed about actual scientific practice (his "internal studies"):

> [A] phenomenon which alarms me sometimes accompanies the increasing trend toward external studies. It is here and there possible these days to enter graduate school in the history of science without significant scientific training and to complete a degree without ever having to analyze a technical document in depth. That is a bit like studying the history of music without ever having heard a concert or examined a score. (Kuhn, in Asquith and Kyburg 1979, p. 124)

We now turn to the historical empiricism of both Imre Lakatos and Larry Laudan. The chapter concludes with an introduction to scientific realism.

5.1   IMRE LAKATOS'S HISTORICAL EMPIRICISM

Imre Lakatos (1922–1974) was a Hungarian philosopher of science and mathematics who changed his name from Imre Lipschitz to escape the Nazis during World War II. After the war, he was appointed Secretary, Hungarian Ministry of Education (1947–49), was imprisoned as a dissident (1950–53), and was able to flee from his homeland during the 1956 Hungarian uprising. He received his Ph.D. at Cambridge University in England in 1958, and he taught at the London School of Economics, as a professor of logic, from 1960 to 1974. At the London School of Economics, he worked closely with Popper, and "His philosophy helped me to make a final break with the Hegelian outlook which I had held for nearly twenty years. . . . Since Hegel, each generation has unfortunately needed— and has fortunately had—philosophers to break Hegel's spell on young think- ers who so frequently fall into the trap of impressive and all-explanatory theories . . . which act upon weak minds like revelations" (Lakatos 1978, p. 139).

Having seen the consequences of totalitarian regimes of both the left and the right, Lakatos was a determined opponent of authoritarianism. Sampson points out that Lakatos saw "the 'barren skepticism' that results from strict application of Popper's principle and the immature frivolity of Paul Feyerabend's intellectual anarchism (which, like the anarchism of the 1960s political movements, Lakatos saw as a front for a particularly intransigent form of authoritarianism)" (Sampson 1987, p. 313). Lakatos recognized that the falsificationism of his mentor Popper was not in accord with much of the actual history of science, and, also, was inadvertently fostering skepticism and irrationalism. At the same time, he abhorred the position of "some soci- ologists of knowledge" that science is just "truth by (changing) consensus" (Lakatos 1970, p. 92). Noting that Kuhn's historical theory of science pro- moted "truth by consensus" and had "authoritarian overtones," Lakatos states: "My concern is that Kuhn, having recognized the failure of both justificationism [foundationalism] and falsificationism in providing rational accounts of sci- entific growth, seems now to fall back on to irrationalism" (Lakatos 1970, p. 93). Therefore, Lakatos adopted for himself the problem of developing a gen- eral theory of science that would be faithful to the actual history of scientific progress, and, at the same time, would avoid the irrationalism implicit in Kuhnian relativism. He titled his theory "The Methodology of Scientific Re- search Programmes," and it drew heavily from Popperian falsificationism. We shall now develop and evaluate his general theory of science. We begin by examining what Lakatos considered to be its rivals.

5.1.1 Justificationism, Dogmatic Falsificationism, and Naïve Falsificationism

"The Methodology of Scientific Research Programmes" relies heavily on the concept of "sophisticated methodological falsificationism." But to understand how Lakatos defends this concept as central to understanding science, he first discusses and evaluates what he considers to be its major rivals: justificationism, dogmatic falsificationism, and naïve methodological falsificationism. First, Lakatos points out that "for centuries knowledge meant proven knowledge—proven either by the power of the intellect [classical rationalism] or by the evidence of the senses [classical empiricism]" (Lakatos 1970, p. 8). Therefore, like religious knowledge that was guaranteed to be certain by the Church, scientific knowledge must be justified (hence "justificationism") by methods that will guarantee with certainty its truth. Justificationism (or, alternatively, "foundationalism") was entirely credible for several hundred years because of the spectacular success of Newtonian mechanics. However, Lakatos observes, the downfall of the Newtonian empire showed that science cannot yield truth with certainty. Justificationism is, therefore, untenable, and the Humean "problem of induction" shows precisely *why* justification is untenable. However, "one cannot simply water down the ideal of proven truth—as some logical empiricists do—to the ideal of 'probable truth'" (Lakatos 1970, p. 92). What is the answer to the problem of induction? For Lakatos, scientific knowledge could be guaranteed with the certainty of the *modus tollens* of deductive logic by adopting a sophisticated form of Popperian falsificationism.

Lakatos differentiates dogmatic falsificationism from both naïve falsificationism and his own, "sophisticated" falsificationism. Dogmatic falsificationism demands that, for a theory to be scientific, it must forbid the occurrence of certain events and scientists must stipulate in advance of some test what kind of events in an experiment would constitute a "falsifier," and, therefore, would permit the theory to be refuted. There are three problems with dogmatic falsificationism. First, "there are and can be no sensations unimpregnated by expectations and therefore there is not a natural (i.e., psychological) demarcation between observational and theoretical propositions" (Lakatos 1970, p. 99). That is, Lakatos (correctly) observes that there is no "observation language" that is neutral to all theories and (mistakenly) concludes that this poses an insurmountable problem for maintaining objectivity in science. (As discussed in section 4.2.1, what is required to maintain objectivity in science is an observational language that is neutral to genuinely rival theories, not to all potential theories.) A second problem for dogmatic falsificationism is that "the truth-value of the 'observational' propositions cannot be indubitably cited: no factual proposition can ever be proved from an experiment" (Lakatos

1970, p. 99). That is, formally speaking, deductive logic applies only to the relationships among sentences or propositions. Only a sentence can "disprove" another sentence; observing some real world event may in some sense be inconsistent with a sentence but it does not "refute" or "disprove" the sentence. Here, we see the impact of formal logic and mathematics on Lakatos's analysis.

The third problem with dogmatic falsificationism is that "exactly the most admired scientific theories simply fail to forbid any observable state of affairs" (Lakatos 1970, p. 100). Here, Lakatos is referring to what is normally called the "Quine-Duhem thesis." Named after the philosophers W.V.O. Quine and Pierre Duhem, this thesis holds that, when one conducts a test of a theory, one is actually testing a host of initial conditions, measuring instruments, and auxiliary hypotheses that together form the *ceteris paribus* conditions. If a particular experiment yields results inconsistent with the theory, the researcher cannot know with certainty whether it is the theory, measures, procedures, or some auxiliary hypotheses that are at fault. Therefore, no theory can be disproved conclusively in the same sense as a mathematical proof/disproof. Again, we see Lakatos setting the standard for acceptability in science as that of the certainty of a mathematical proof.

Lakatos considers the three problems of dogmatic falsificationism to be conclusive, points out that many writers have falsely charged Popper with advocating such a falsificationist theory of science, and then discusses the actual version of falsificationism advocated by Popper, that is, "naïve methodological falsificationism." Naïve falsificationism addresses the first problem of dogmatic falsificationism by having scientists make a methodological decision that some terms will be called "observation terms" and some sentences "observation sentences" or "basic sentences." These "basic sentences" are then accepted "by convention" (i.e., without proof) by the scientists as potential falsifiers of the theory in question. As a response to the second problem, "the methodological falsificationists separate action and disproof, which the dogmatic falsificationists had conflated" (Lakatos 1970, p. 109). Therefore, scientific theories are not "disproved" with the certainty of mathematics. Rather they are *rejected* or *refuted*.

The third problem of dogmatic falsificationism is addressed by, first, subjecting all aspects of the *ceteris paribus* clause to "severe tests." That is, the scientist must delineate carefully all of the specific assumptions and auxiliary hypotheses associated with the theory in question, and subject these assumptions and auxiliary hypotheses to empirical testing. The scientist then must devise an experiment to control for these assumptions and auxiliary hypotheses, and stipulate in advance of conducting the experiment that certain events would constitute a conclusive falsification of the theory. Such an experiment would constitute a "crucial experiment," and the researcher is committed to rejecting the theory. What does "rejecting" mean? Lakatos contends: "Since, for our savage falsificationist, falsifications are methodologically conclusive, the fateful decision amounts to the methodological elimination of [a] theory, making further work on it irrational" (Lakatos 1970, p. 111).

Being a firm believer in the historical approach to the philosophy of science, Lakatos compared the theory of science according to naïve falsificationism with the actual behaviors of scientists in significant historical episodes. He found that when naïve falsificationism was "tested" by comparing it with the history of science, the theory fared poorly. Many of the "most celebrated crucial experiments" were "accepted as crucial for no rational reason or their acceptance rested on rationality principles radically different from the ones we have just discussed" (Lakatos 1970, p. 114). Second, many "stubborn theoreticians" in the history of science seemed to refuse to accept the "experimental verdicts" of crucial tests, and continued to work on their theories. Third, many prominent scientists in history seemed to have been "irrationally slow" in accepting the falsification of a theory: "For instance, eighty-five years elapsed between the acceptance of the Perihelion of Mercury as an anomaly and its acceptance as a falsification of Newton's theory" (Lakatos 1970, p. 114). Fourth, scientists seem often to be "irrationally rash" in accepting a theory, despite apparent falsifications. For example, "Galileo and his disciples accepted Copernican heliocentric celestial mechanics in spite of the abundant evidence against the rotation of the earth" (Lakatos 1970, p. 115). Fifth, on many occasions the history of science indicates that a single theory is not tested by some crucial experiment; rather, rival theories are tested against each other. Sixth, "some of the most interesting experiments result, *prima facie*, in confirmation rather than falsification" (Lakatos 1970, p. 115).

Lakatos viewed the problems of naïve methodological falsificationism as devastating to the notion of scientific rationality, and he saw only two alternatives: "One alternative is to abandon efforts to give a rational explanation of the success of science" (Lakatos 1970, p. 115). This alternative was "Kuhn's way," where the idea of scientific *progress* vanishes and is replaced by a series of changes in paradigms, brought about by Gestalt shifts and religious conversions. But this alternative inexorably leads to relativism, irrationalism, "mob rule," and "authoritarianism." Therefore, Lakatos opted for a *sophisticated* version of methodological falsificationism that would "rescue methodology and the idea of scientific *progress*" (Lakatos 1970, p. 116). Lakatos called his general theory of science the "methodology of scientific research programmes."

5.1.2   Acceptance, Pursuit, and Rationality in Science

Before discussing Lakatos's general theory of science, we should point out a fundamental confusion in Lakatos's analysis of the problems of naïve falsificationism and its lack of consistency with the history of science. As pointed out by his friend and colleague, John W.N. Watkins, all of Lakatos's writings contain a confusion between a researcher "accepting" a theory and "working on" a theory (Watkins 1984, p. 156). That is, it is one thing for a researcher to accept a theory as being the best theory of the day to explain truly some set of phenomena, or, alternatively, to be the best theory to guide decision making. It is another thing for a researcher to select a theory to *work* on. Furthermore, the decision to work on a theory may be rational (i.e., guided by good reasons) *even though* it is not the best theory of the day in the sense of explaining phenomena and/or guiding decision making. Laudan refers to this fundamental confusion as the difference between the "context of acceptance" and the "context of pursuit" (Laudan 1977, p. 108). In this regard, the context of acceptance is very similar to what is normally referred to as the "context of justification," and the context of pursuit is analogous to, but not identical to, the "context of discovery." (See Hunt 2002a, section 1.5.1.) In any respect, just like Kuhn and Feyerabend, Lakatos confuses continually and consistently "acceptance" with "working on," as in the following: "Since, for our savage falsificationists, falsifications are methodologically conclusive, the fateful decision amounts to the methodological elimination of [a] theory, *making further work on it irrational*" (Lakatos 1970, p. 111; italics added).

Lakatos interpreted naïve falsificationism as a *logic of pursuit,* and, when he found that the history of science was inconsistent with his logic of pursuit, he was faced with adopting Feyerabend's solution ("anything goes") or developing a logic of pursuit that would not (he thought) imply that science was irrational. Four observations are in order here. First, the logical empiricists, but not necessarily Popper, believed that there was no "logic of discovery," for they believed that discovery was an inherently untidy process. Therefore, though they never wrote about the "context of pursuit," we may infer that they would have viewed it as being, similarly, untidy. Second, many writers, such as Laudan, do not believe that "anything goes" in the context of pursuit (see section 5.2.1). Third, the fact that scientists often choose to "work on" theories that are not the best, as far as explanatory and predictive power, in their day, does not imply that science is irrational. Even if "anything goes" in the context of pursuit and/or discovery, such a conclusion does not imply that "anything goes" in the context of acceptance and/or justification. Fourth, as Toulmin points out, in the final analysis it is the rationality of the scientific community that counts (Toulmin, in Suppe 1977, p. 672). That is, even if individual scientists are demonstrably irrational in their acceptance of the best theory of the day with regard to a set of phenomena, this would not imply that the *community* of scientists is (or, most assuredly, ought to be) *collectively* irrational. We turn now to a discussion of Lakatos's general theory of science.

5.1.3 The Methodology of Scientific Research Programmes

Just as the key concept in Kuhn's general theory of science is the paradigm, the key concept in Lakatos's theory is the "research programme." A research program (American spelling) is a sequence of related theories: *T1, T2, T3,* etc. In one sense, a research program is similar to Kuhnian "normal science," because this is what the researchers "work on" or "pursue." Also like Kuhn, the existence of a research program (paradigm) separates *mature* science from *immature* science. Lakatos considers the latter to be "a mere patched up pattern of trial and error" (Lakatos 1970, p. 175). However, unlike Kuhn, Lakatos believed that "one must never allow a research program to become a *Weltanschauung,*" because "normal science is nothing other than a research program that has achieved monopoly," and "the history of science has been and should be a history of competing research programs (or, if you wish, paradigms), but it has not been and must not become a succession of periods of normal science: the sooner competition starts, *the better for progress*" (Lakatos 1970, p. 661, italics added).

Every research program has a "positive heuristic" that contains a set of methodological rules that guide the development of the research program and a "negative heuristic" that suggests paths of research to avoid. Lakatos notes that a research program "at any stage of its development, has unsolved problems and undigested anomalies. All theories, in this sense, are born refuted and die refuted." He continues by asking the following question: "But are they equally good"? (Lakatos 1978, p. 5). Lakatos believed (unlike Kuhn) that rival, or alternative, research programs could be evaluated in terms of their progressivity: Some research programs are *progressive*; others are *degenerating*. Thus, Lakatos's theory differs sharply from Kuhnian relativism and its Gestalt shifts. However, Lakatos's theory also diverges from the naïve falsificationism attributed to Popper: "Contrary to Popper, the difference [between rival research programs] cannot be that some are still unrefuted, while others are already refuted. When Newton published his *Principia,* it was common knowledge that it could not properly explain even the motion of the moon; in fact, lunar motion refuted Newton" (Lakatos 1978, p. 5). But if Newton's theory was "refuted when it was born," why was Newton's theory *progressive*? For Lakatos, Newton's theory was progressive because it predicted "novel facts." In general, research programs that are *theoretically progressive* "predict novel facts, facts which had been either undreamt of, or have indeed been contradicted by previous or rival programs" (Lakatos 1978, p. 5). For example, Lakatos notes that Newton's theory predicted the existence and exact motion of small planets that had not even been observed.

How do theories change within a Lakatos research program? Successor theories in a research program are formed with the aid of the positive heuristic by adding additional clauses to predecessor theories, with the proviso that each successor theory must have more "empirical content" than its predecessor. That is, a successor theory must predict everything that its predecessor predicted, and, in addition, some novel, hitherto unexpected, facts. However, each research program has a "hard core" of assumptions and clauses that are not to be subjected to refutation. In fact "we must use our own ingenuity to articulate or even invent auxiliary hypotheses which form a *protective belt* around this core" (Lakatos 1970, p. 133).

If each new theory in a research program eliminates its predecessor by virtue of having greater empirical content (and, thus, is progressive), how are entire research programs eliminated? For Lakatos, a research program can be eliminated "only if there is a better one to replace it" (Lakatos 1978, p. 150). Thus:

> The idea of competing scientific research programs leads us to the problem: *how are research programs eliminated?* It has transpired from our previous considerations that a degenerating problem shift is no more a sufficient reason to eliminate a research program than some old-fashioned "refutation" or a Kuhnian "crisis." Can there be any objective (as opposed to socio-psychological) reason to reject a program, that is, to eliminate its hard core and its program for constructing protective belts? Our answer, in outline, is that such an objective reason is provided by a rival research program which explains the previous success of its rival and supersedes it by a further display of *heuristic power*. . . . I use "heuristic power" here as a technical term to characterize the power of a research program to anticipate theoretically novel facts in its growth. I could of course use "explanatory power." (Lakatos 1970, p. 155)

Given that Lakatos uses "eliminate" to mean "cease working on," the preceding would seem to imply that Lakatos is counseling scientists that they should cease pursuing, or working on, a degenerating research program that has been "overtaken" by some rival. However, Lakatos claims such is not the case:

> One may rationally stick to a degenerating program until it is overtaken by a rival *and even after*. What one must *not* do is to deny its poor public record. Both Feyerabend and Kuhn conflate *methodological* appraisal of a program with firm heuristic advice about what to do. It is perfectly rational to play a risky game: what is irrational is to deceive oneself about the risk. (Lakatos 1978, p. 117)

Why should it be rational to stick to a degenerating research program even after it has been overtaken by a rival? Because Lakatos's reading of the history of science led him to conclude that many research programs that had been overtaken had subsequently "staged a comeback" (Lakatos 1978, p. 113). Once again, we see Lakatos getting into serious difficulty because he confuses "working on" with "acceptance." Therefore, he conflates the following two questions: (1) When is it rational for a scientist to work on, or cease working on, a research program? (2) When is it rational for a scientist, or a community of scientists, to accept a theory or research program as the best explanation for a set of phenomena? Given that Feyerabend's writings share the same confusion as Lakatos, it is no wonder that Feyerabend could claim that Lakatos's theory was "anarchism in disguise" (Feyerabend 1975, p. 181). Thus, Feyerabend endorsed Lakatos: "I also agree with two suggestions which form an essential part of Lakatos's theory of science. . . . Neither blatant internal inconsistencies, . . . nor massive conflict with experimental results should prevent us from retaining and elaborating a point of view that pleases us for some reason or other" (Feyerabend 1975, p. 183). Note that Feyerabend uses "retaining and elaborating" in his agreement with Lakatos.

There are numerous critiques of Lakatos's general theory of science, including: Suppe (1977, pp. 659–70), Laudan (1977, pp. 76–78), Hausman (1992), Levey (1996), Rosenberg (1992), and the articles by Kuhn, Feigl, Hall, and Koertge in Buck and Cohen (1971). Many of the criticisms seem particularly devastating, which is not surprising given his confusion of "working on" with "accepting." Consider first, for example, that a Lakatosian research program exists only when there is a succession of theories in which later theories entail earlier theories: every successor theory must explain *everything* that a predecessor theory explained and "more." However, what most scientific disciplines would call "research programs" often contain successor theories that do not have this characteristic. Furthermore, Lakatos endorses three progressively weaker senses of what constitutes a novel prediction: (a) predictions of phenomena not yet known, (b) implications that were not considered when the theory was generated, and (c) new interpretations of known phenomena (Hausman 1992, pp. 193, 197). Second, Lakatos claims that "immature" disciplines do not have research programs and are nothing more than "patched up trial and error." Yet, many of the disciplines that Lakatos would characterize as "immature" seem to have research programs that exhibit a high degree of systematic inquiry, rather than "patched up" work. Third, the claim that research programs have a "hard core" that cannot be changed or modified seems inconsistent with actual practice in many sciences, and, furthermore, would not seem to be a characteristic of "ideal" science. For example, Leong (1985) claims that the "hard core" of marketing science are the "four fundamental explananda" identified in Hunt (1983a). However, I never intended the four explananda to be "hard core" in a Lakatosian sense. Rather, I advanced the four explananda as suitable candidates for organizing the structure of marketing science and specifically urged readers to attempt to find counter-instances.

Laudan reviewed Lakatos's general theory of science and concluded that it was "a decided improvement on Kuhn's" because it "stresses the historical importance of the co-existence of several alternative programs at the same time, within the same domain." Furthermore, "unlike Kuhn, who often takes the view that paradigms are incommensurable and thus not open to rational comparison, Lakatos insists that we can objectively compare the relative progress of competing research traditions" (Laudan 1977, p. 76). However, Laudan found that "Lakatos' model of research programs shares many of the flaws of Kuhn's paradigms, and introduces some new ones as well" (1977, p. 77). Therefore, Laudan developed his "theory of research traditions," while acknowledging his "great debt" to the "pioneering work" of Kuhn and Lakatos (1977, p. 78).

5.2 LAUDAN'S HISTORICAL EMPIRICISM

Larry Laudan was born in Austin, Texas, in 1941; received his Ph.D. from Princeton University in the history and philosophy of science in 1965; and has taught at Cambridge University, the University of London, the University of Pittsburgh, the Virginia Polytechnic Institute and State University, and the University of Hawaii. A prominent advocate of the historical approach to the study of science, Laudan's major publications include: "Theories of Scientific Method from Plato to Mach" (1968), "Two Dogmas of Methodology" (1976), *Science and Hypothesis* (1981), "A Confutation of Convergent Realism" (1981a), and "Relativism, Naturalism and Reticulation" (1987). Drawing upon these works (among others), Laudan develops his general theory of science in *Progress and Its Problems* (1977) and *Science and Values* (1984).

Laudan developed his general theory of science to satisfy five objectives. First, a satisfactory theory of science should be consistent with the actual history of the development of science. In this regard, Laudan has been critical of Kuhn for developing a theory of science that was radically at odds with actual historical episodes in science, and critical of Lakatos for using a "rational reconstruction" approach to the history of science (Laudan 1977, pp. 74–77). Second, an adequate theory of science must reveal that science is progressive in some meaningful sense, but such progressivity *cannot* involve the acceptance of the "cumulativity postulate." That is, Laudan holds that science is progressive, but that changes from one theory to another are seldom, if ever, *strictly* cumulative in the sense of the successor theory being able to explain everything that its predecessor did and *more*. The cumulativity postulate, Laudan contends, is one of the (false) "two dogmas" of methodology (Laudan 1976). Third, Laudan proposed that a satisfactory theory of science must show that progress in science is *rational*, in sharp contrast to the irrationalist, "Gestalt shift," and "incommensurable" versions of Kuhn and Feyerabend. Laudan held that a second of the "two dogmas" of methodology is that rival theories would be incommensurable because of the absence of an observation language that was neutral to all theories. Rather, he noted, all that was required for objectivity was an observation language that was neutral between the two rival theories (i.e., the observation language itself did not *presume* that one or the other of the two theories was true) (Laudan 1976). Fourth, an acceptable general theory of science must be non-relativistic because, he contends, there are a wide range of evaluative criteria that can be applied within science to rationally adjudicate disputes within science. Fifth, we should approach scientific progress and rationality "without presupposing anything about the veracity or verisimilitude of the theories we judge to be rational or irrational" (Laudan 1977, p. 125). Laudan insists that, though there may be many appropriate goals for science, such goals must not be "utopian," because, "to adopt a goal with the feature that we can conceive of no actions that would be apt to promote it, or a goal whose realization we could not recognize even if we had achieved it, is surely a mark of unreasonableness and irrationality" (Laudan 1984, p. 51). How does Laudan come to the conclusion that veracity, verisimilitude, and truth are utopian? Because, he claims:

> Philosophers and scientists since the time of Parmenides and Plato have been seeking to justify science as a truth-seeking enterprise. Without exception, these efforts have foundered because no one has been able to demonstrate that a system like science, with the methods it has at its disposal, can be *guaranteed* to reach the "Truth," either in the short or the long run. . . . Realizing this dilemma, some philosophers (notably Peirce, Popper, and Reichenbach) have sought to link scientific rationality and proof in a different way, by suggesting that although our present theories are neither true nor probable, they are closer approximations to the truth than their predecessors. Such an approach offers few consolations, however, since no one has been able even to say what it would mean to be "closer to the truth," let alone to offer criteria for determining how we could assess such proximity. (Laudan 1977, pp.125–26; italics added)

We shall return to the issue of truth and its role in science later. For now, the reader should carefully note Laudan's word "guaranteed."

In effect, Laudan has produced *two* general theories of science, because the theory in *Science and Values* repudiates several of the major positions taken in *Progress and Its Problems*. However, the five considerations developed in the preceding paragraph remain constant throughout both theories. We shall first develop the "early Laudan" theory and examine its strengths and weaknesses, before developing the "later Laudan" theory and evaluating it.

5.2.1   The "Early Laudan" Theory of Science

The central theme of *Progress and Its Problems* is that there is one overriding goal, or aim, for science: the solution of problems. Thus, the very first sentence of the first chapter is "Science is essentially a problem-solving activity" (Laudan 1977, p. 11). Similarly, "it is the purpose of this short book to sketch what seem to be the implications, for both the history of science and its philosophy, of a view of scientific inquiry which perceives science as being— *above all else*—a problem-solving activity" (1977, p. 12; italics added). Likewise, "it has often been suggested in this essay that the solution of a maximum number of empirical problems, and the generation of [a] minimum number of conceptual problems and anomalies is the *central aim* of science" (1977, p. 111; italics added).

Laudan differentiates between two major kinds of problems: empirical problems and conceptual problems. Empirical problems are "anything about the natural world which strikes us as odd, or otherwise in need of explanation," and scientists recognize empirical problems as such because "our theoretical presuppositions about the natural order tell us what to expect and what seems peculiar or 'problematic' or questionable (in the literal sense of that term)" (Laudan 1977, p. 15). On the other hand, conceptual problems are "higher-order questions about the well-foundedness of the conceptual structures (e.g., theories) which have been devised to answer the first-order [empirical] questions" (1977, p. 48). Conceptual problems spring from diverse sources. For example, some conceptual problems are "internal" problems, as when an individual theory is logically inconsistent or unclear. "External" problems come about when a theory is inconsistent with another theory or "worldview," or "areas as diverse as metaphysics, logic, ethics and theology" (1977, p. 61).

If the "central aim" of science is problem solving and empirical problems are those things about the world that strike us as "peculiar," how does science know when it has solved a problem? Laudan states that "generally, any theory, *T*, can be regarded as having solved an empirical problem, if *T* functions (significantly) in any schema of inference whose conclusion is a statement of the problem" (Laudan 1977, p. 25).

Four preliminary observations can immediately be made about Laudan's problem-solving theory. First, his concept of "problem solving" does not imply necessarily that science seeks solutions to practical problems of society. That is, Laudan is not *justifying* science and scientific activity on the basis that it is useful for solving significant social problems. Rather, a "problem" is something that seems "peculiar" or unexpected as a result of some theory held (explicitly or implicitly) by the scientist. Although the solution of the problem may have some practical applications, it need not. Second, Laudan's conceptualization as to what is to count as a "solution" to a problem is indistinguishable from what traditional philosophy of science has characterized as an "explanation" of some phenomenon. Therefore, Laudan's conceptualization that science is essentially "problem solving" differs little from the traditional view that science is essentially "explanation giving." Third, given that Laudan's "empirical problem" does not mean a practical problem of society, his theory is consistent with the view that science (at least "basic" science) is concerned with "knowledge for knowledge's sake." Finally, because Laudan specifically disavows truth and approximate truth as goals or aims for science (on the basis that such goals would be utopian), his view implies *necessarily* that theories and explanations in science should be viewed instrumentally, rather than realistically.

Continuing with our development of Laudan's theory, solving conceptual problems is "at least as important in the development of science as empirical problem solving" (Laudan 1977, p. 45). Conceptual problems arise from some inconsistency or incompatibility of a theory within itself ("internal"), or, more frequently, with some other theory. These other kinds of theories may be: (1) scientific theories, (2) theories of methodology, or (3) "worldview" theories, such as those in politics, theology, logic, or metaphysics. Inconsistencies between theories produce a "tension" that demands resolution, but not all conceptual problems are equally important. Indeed, a specific weight can be given to the relative importance of each conceptual problem: "Other things being equal, the greater the tension between two theories, the weightier the problem will be" (1977, p. 65) The conceptual problems are solved by modifying one or more of the theories. He notes: "[T]he *fact* [is] that a tension often exists between our 'scientific' beliefs and our 'nonscientific' ones, and that such a tension does pose a problem for *both* sets of beliefs. How that tension is to be resolved depends on the particularities of the case" (1977, p. 64).

As will be recalled, Laudan wanted his theory of science to demonstrate that science was indeed progressive and rational, but that such progressivity and rationality could not depend on truth. How is theory appraisal to be accomplished so that theory-change in science will be progressive? For Laudan, "the solved problem—empirical or conceptual—is the basic unit of scientific progress" (Laudan 1977, p. 66). Therefore, we should evaluate theories on the basis of their problem-solving effectiveness, where "overall problem-solving effectiveness of a theory is determined by assessing the number and importance of the empirical problems which the theory solves and deducting therefrom the number and importance of the anomalies and conceptual problems which the theory generates" (1977, p. 68). Thus, scientific progress inherently involves comparing theories through time: "Progress can occur if and only if the succession of scientific theories in any domain shows an increasing degree of problem-solving effectiveness" (1977, p. 68). Such a criterion gives specific guidance to practicing scientists, because "anytime we modify a theory or replace it by another theory, that change is progressive if and only if the later version is a more effective problem-solver (in the sense just defined) than its predecessor" (1977, p. 68).

But Laudan is not interested in explicating just the concept of scientific progress as it relates to a succession of individual theories. Like Kuhn before him, he is interested in the progress of some larger conceptual structure. For Kuhn, it was the paradigm; for Laudan, it is the "research tradition," which "is a set of assumptions: assumptions about the basic kinds of entities in the world, assumptions about how those entities interact, assumptions about the proper methods to use for constructing and testing theories about those entities" (Laudan 1977, p. 97). In other words, a specific theory within a research tradition "articulates a very specific ontology and a number of specific and testable laws about nature," and a research tradition "specifies [for each of its theories] a general ontology for nature, and a general method for solving natural problems within a given natural domain" (1977, p. 84).

Laudan's "research tradition" differs from the "research programme" of Lakatos because, unlike Lakatos, the "core assumptions" of research traditions are in fact testable and can be modified through time, although enough core assumptions remain relatively constant through time to give the research tradition continuity (Laudan 1977, p. 98). Furthermore, while the collected theories in a research tradition are related to each other, each theory does not specifically *entail* some predecessor theory, as with Lakatos.

How should research traditions be appraised? Laudan splits the appraisal process into two different contexts: the context of acceptance and the context of pursuit. He affirms that there are many circumstances, such as when one is conducting an experiment or when one is going to take some "practical action," where it is absolutely necessary to *accept* a theory or research tradition, meaning "*to treat it as if it were true*" (Laudan 1977, p. 108; italics in original). Under such circumstances, his recommendation is to "choose the theory (or research tradition) with the highest problem-solving adequacy" (1977, p. 109). Therefore, "the choice of one tradition over its rivals is progressive (and thus a rational) choice precisely to the extent that the chosen tradition is a better problem solver than its rivals." This choice criterion is better than other models of evaluation because "it is *workable*: unlike both inductivist and falsificationist models, the basic evaluation measures seem (at least in principle) to pose fewer difficulties" (1977, p. 109). At first glance, Laudan's criterion for "acceptance" would seem to be largely tautological, that is, if you want to adopt a theory for the solution of a problem of "practical action," then choose the theory that is the best problem solver. However, we must keep in mind that Laudan's "problem solving" relates not to practical problems, but rather to the problems that a theory has in explaining phenomena (in addition to conceptual problems).

Laudan relates that both Kuhn and Feyerabend had pointed out numerous occasions in the history of science where scientists chose to work on or pursue theories or research traditions that were not the best confirmed or most acceptable: "Indeed the emergence of virtually every new research tradition occurs under just such circumstances" (Laudan 1977, p. 110). Both Kuhn and Feyerabend concluded that these instances made the history of science seem to be largely irrational. For example, Kuhn claims that the decision to pursue a new theory or paradigm at an early stage of development is a decision that "can only be made on faith" (Kuhn 1962, p. 157). However, Laudan claims that "scientists can have good reasons for working on theories that they would not accept" (Laudan 1977, p. 110). What are these good reasons? He claims that "it is always rational to pursue any research tradition which has a higher rate of progress than its rivals (even if the former has a lower problem-solving effectiveness)" (1977, p. 111). That is, the scientist should calculate the *rate* at which a research tradition is progressing through time and pursue that tradition that has the highest rate because "the rationality of pursuit is based on relative progress rather than overall success" (1977, p. 112).

On Progress and Its Problems: For Reason. Many aspects of Laudan's general theory of science have significant merit. Most assuredly, much of science has to do with problem solving (both "practical" and empirical), and many of the activities of scientists involve the search for problem solutions. Distinguishing the empirical problems that confront a theory from its conceptual problems is a useful step forward in our understanding of theories. Distinguishing clearly between the context of acceptance and the context of pursuit clarifies much of the confusion in the theories of Lakatos, Kuhn, and Feyerabend. That is, even if it should be the case that "anything goes" in the context of pursuit (or discovery), this most assuredly does not imply that "anything goes" in the context of acceptance (or justification). Laudan's contention that both acceptance and pursuit can be viewed as having a significant rational component also seems meritorious, especially in light of the implicit irrationalism of Kuhn and the explicit irrationalism of Feyerabend. Finally, Laudan's refutation of the view that rival theories are incommensurable, and, hence, incapable of being objectively compared (a key assumption of relativism) is both convincing and consistent with other modern writers. Nevertheless, there are some major shortcomings in Laudan's theory, some of which are devastating. Many of these have been pointed out by McMullin (1979), Musgrave (1979), Kordig (1980), Krips (1980), Sarkar (1981), and Leplin (1981). Given that Laudan, in his *Science and Values* (1984), altered his theory of science in many important respects as a result of these criticisms, we shall briefly review only the major "problems" of *Progress and Its Problems.*

Recall that Laudan attacked all those "philosophers and scientists since the time of Parmenides and Plato" who had been "seeking to justify science as a truth-seeking enterprise" on the basis that such an aim is "utopian," because "we apparently do not have any way of knowing for sure (or even with some confidence) that science is true, or probable, or that it is getting closer to the truth" (Laudan 1977, pp. 125, 126, and 127). Therefore, he defends his model of scientific progress on the following basis: "The workability of the problem-solving model is its greatest virtue" (1977, p. 127). It is important to note that Laudan is not claiming just that science is involved in problem solving, nor that in some intuitive sense modern science solves "more problems" than the science of the seventeenth century. Rather, he claims his model is "workable" and that his system of "counting and weighting of problems" will yield a "calculus of problem weights" that can be objectively used to appraise theories and research traditions for both the context of acceptance and pursuit (1977, p. 32). But, is such a procedure of counting and weighting really "workable"? The reader should consider the following (very partial) list of activities that such a procedure would necessarily entail:

1. Determine in an unambiguous fashion what situation constitutes a problem.
2. Determine what shall constitute the solving of a problem by a theory.
3. Separate the individual problems sufficiently sharply to enable one to count them.
4. Unambiguously assign relative weights to both empirical problem solutions and conceptual problems.
5. Develop a measuring procedure with metrical properties powerful enough to be able to subtract the negative weight of conceptual problems from the positive weight of the solved empirical problems.
6. Unambiguously add up the problem-solving adequacy of all the theories in an entire research tradition to measure the problem-solving adequacy of the larger structure.
7. Identify over appropriate time periods the rate of change in the problem-solving adequacy of rival research traditions.

Contrary to the claims of Laudan, the commentators on Laudan's theory have pointed out that his problem-solving model of "counting and weighting" is patently *unworkable*. Furthermore, the claim that scientists in the past have actually *used* such a procedure to guide their decisions in the contexts of acceptance and pursuit borders on fantasy. Most tellingly for a historian of science, in Laudan's entire book he gives not a single case history where he actually applies his "counting and weighting" procedure. One might choose to defend the problem-solving model on the basis that it is a "rational reconstruction" of historical episodes. For example, Lakatos always claimed that his theory represented a "rational reconstruction" of science and that his model of rationality could be used to appraise historical episodes as to "what actually happened in the light of the rational reconstruction, pointing out the discrepancies between them" (Musgrave 1979, p. 457). However, Laudan rejects specifically the rational reconstruction procedure of Lakatos as being an inappropriate use of historical data (Laudan 1977, pp. 168–70). (It should be pointed out that, according to Musgrave, Laudan's discussion of Lakatos's method of "rational reconstruction" is grossly inaccurate and a "caricature" (Musgrave 1979, p. 457.)

Laudan's theory of science fails conclusively its own criteria of adequacy: (1) His theory is not in accord with the history of science, and (2) it provides no "workable" procedure for "acceptance" or "pursuit," for, in Laudan's own pejorative terms, his theory is "utopian." In fact, we can substitute "maximum problem solving" for the word "truth" in Laudan's own criteria: "No one has been able to demonstrate that a system like science, with the methods it has at its disposal, can be guaranteed to reach [maximum problem solving], either in the short or in the long run." Furthermore, "no one has been able even to say what it would mean to be 'closer to' [maximum problem solving], let alone to offer criteria for determining how we could assess such proximity."

Why has Laudan's theory of science foundered? In part because he attempted to develop a general theory of science that would be nonrelativistic and rational, while at the same time being truth-independent. First of all, though Laudan attempts to avoid the words "true" and "false," Musgrave (1979) shows that on numerous occasions throughout *Progress and Its Problems* Laudan implicitly appeals to truth. For example, a research tradition's problem-solving effectiveness, for Laudan, relies in part on recognizing and solving genuine (true) empirical problems, rather than pseudo (false) problems. Also in Laudan's "context of acceptance" the scientist is to "treat the theory as if it were true" (Laudan 1977, p. 108). More generally, and much more important, there are good grounds for believing that any theory of science that ignores truth is unlikely to escape sophistry, relativism, and irrationalism.

As will be discussed further in Chapter 7, on at least two separate occasions Laudan commits the "philosophers' fallacy of high redefinition." Laudan claims that before we may distinguish science from nonscience, or pseudoscience, we must provide a "universal" demarcation criterion that will "guarantee" that we can unambiguously separate disciplines or research traditions into various categories. Finding no such universal, completely unambiguous criterion, he proposes that we discard the concept of "science vs. nonscience" altogether. Likewise, Laudan claims that before we may believe warrantedly that a theory is true or false, or is approximately true, or has more truth-content than a rival theory, or is closer to the truth than a rival theory, we must demonstrate that we have a methodology that will *guarantee* our ability to know with certainty that a theory or knowledge-claim will be as described. Finding no such methodology to guarantee such results, Laudan claims (with unrecognized ironic certainty) that the concepts "truth" and "falsity" are "irrelevant" to science. Having already succumbed to the philosophers' fallacy (see section 3.6.2) on these two important questions, it is no wonder that Laudan's general theory of science fails—as did Kuhn's and Feyerabend's—to produce intelligible discourse about its subject. We turn now to a discussion of "the later Laudan," that is, to his general theory of science proposed in *Science and Values*.

5.2.2 Laudan's Science and Values

Whereas problem solving was the focal construct in Laudan's first general theory of science, the central construct in *Science and Values* (1984) is his research tradition. All research traditions contain three major domains: (1) theories, (2) methods, and (3) aims (Laudan 1984, p. 63). A Laudan "research tradition" is similar to a Kuhnian "paradigm," except that a research tradition does not have a *Weltanschauung*.

To understand *Science and Values*, we need to recapitulate how relativism was "moderated" in the 1970s and 1980s. As will be recalled, the "early" Kuhn implied that each scientist had a *Weltanschauung* that completely determined the scientist's theories, methods, and aims. Therefore, changes in theories and paradigms had to come about by way of *Gestalt* shifts and religious conversions, because the theories and paradigms were incommensurable. The "later" Kuhn both recognized and rejected the reality relativism and conceptual-framework relativism implicit in his earlier work. Even strong advocates of relativism such as Gerald Doppelt began to recognize that Kuhn's reality relativism and conceptual-framework relativism were, simply, untenable:

> If rival scientific paradigms are as insular, self-enclosed, and imprisoned within their own language as Kuhn maintains, in what sense can they be rivals or compete? If they cannot communicate or argue, how and on what can they disagree? If each is necessarily focused on its own data and problems, in what sense do they offer incompatible accounts of the same subject-matter or domain? The clear implication is that Kuhn's incommensurability cannot account for the evident facts of theoretical conflict in scientific development . . . if rival paradigms can thus speak to the same empirical situation, they must share *some* common concepts, data and problems. How is this possible, given Kuhnian incommensurability? *The implication is clearly*

that Kuhn is inconsistent and must violate his own relativism in developing a half-way plausible account of scientific development. (Doppelt, in Krausz and Meiland 1982, p. 117; italics added)

Given the nonviability of both reality and conceptual-framework relativism, Doppelt advocates a cognitive value relativism that he calls "moderate relativism." Basically, his moderate relativism is a relativism with respect to the aims, values, and goals of science. Thus, his version of cognitive-value relativism holds the following:

1. The aims, goals, or values in science are relative to a paradigm, research program, or research tradition.
2. The aims, goals, or values cannot be objectively, impartially, or nonarbitrarily evaluated across different paradigms, research programs, or research traditions.

Doppelt maintains that this version of relativism was implicit in Kuhn's work and, though a much more "moderate" form of relativism than its reality and conceptual-framework predecessors, it still justifies that science is irrational, and there has been no progress in scientific knowledge. One of the major aims of Laudan's *Science and Values* (1984) was to address the issue of cognitive value relativism: "Indeed, when I set out to write *Science and Values*, I had the Doppelt-ized version of Kuhn's position very much in mind." That is, Laudan sought to "explore the question whether—once we factor scientists' aims and methods into a description of their work—it follows that, as Kuhn and Doppelt maintained, there could never be rationally compelling grounds for preferring one tradition of research to another" (Laudan 1987, p. 223).

How do scientists choose between genuinely rival theories? Laudan argues that relativists such as Hesse, Bloor, Kuhn, and Collins have argued fallaciously the "underdetermination thesis" that:

> Since theory choice is undetermined by methodological rules, it follows that no rational preference is possible among rival theories, which entails, in turn, that every theory is as well supported as any other, and that every party to a scientific debate is thus as rational as every other. . . . [Therefore, advocates of the underdetermination thesis] confusedly take the fact that our rules fail to pick out a unique theory that satisfies them as a warrant for asserting the inability of the rules to make any discriminations whatever with respect to which theories are or are not in compliance with them. (Laudan 1984, p. 30)

Therefore, Laudan takes the position that, in general, theory choice among genuinely rival theories is normally made by scientists in precisely the manner historically advocated. That is, from among the rival theories, the scientists determine which is best supported by the evidence by using methodological rules.

Suppose there is a dispute concerning the most appropriate methodological rules? That is, how do methodological rules change in science? Laudan contends that methodological rules sometimes change as a result of the changing aims and goals of scientific communities and sometimes as a result of changes in our theories about the world. For example, Laudan recounts that the discovery of the so-called "placebo effect" brought about a change in a methodological rule in medical science. Medical researchers discovered that "many patients report an improvement upon being given an apparent medication, even if (unbeknownst to the patient) it is pharmacologically inert" (Laudan 1984, p. 38). Therefore, medical researchers adopted methodological rules to guide inquiry and went from simple, controlled experiments to single-blind and double-blind tests. Thus, Laudan claims that changes in methodological rules are not "underdetermined" in any strong sense but are the results of rational debate and "good reasons" (1984, p. 38).

Do different research traditions entail different cognitive values? That is, do different research traditions have different aims, objectives, and goals? Laudan contends they do. Moreover, he contends that these cognitive aims change through time within each research tradition. For example, at one point in time, a particular research tradition may have the aim of simplicity, and, at a later point in time, the aim of mathematical elegance may become much more important. Unlike Kuhn, Laudan contends that these changes in cognitive values can be rationally explained and disputes rationally adjudicated. He believes that several mechanisms are readily available and used by scientists to resolve disputes about goals and aims. If it were otherwise, the specter of relativism would emerge again: "In short, radical relativism about science seems to be an inevitable corollary of accepting (a) that different scientists have different goals, (b) that there is no rational deliberation possible about the suitability of different goals, and (c) that goals, methods, and factual claims invariably come in covariate clusters" (Laudan 1984, p. 50).

What are the mechanisms or criteria that Laudan suggests can be used (and are used) to evaluate cognitive values in science? First, he claims (consistent with his previous work) the cognitive values in science must not be "utopian." Goals are "demonstrably utopian" when "a certain cognitive goal cannot possibly be achieved, given our understanding of logic or the laws of nature" (Laudan 1984, p. 52). Laudan gives, as an example, the goal of "infallible knowledge." On the other hand, a goal suffers from "semantic utopianism" when a goal cannot be characterized in a "succinct and cogent way." Therefore, goals may not be imprecise, or ambiguous. As examples, he notes that "such familiarly cited cognitive goals as simplicity and elegance often have this weakness, because most advocates of these goals can offer no coherent definition or characterization of them" (1984, p. 52). Third, a goal may suffer from "epistemic utopianism." That is, "it sometimes happens that an agent can give a perfectly clear definition of his goal state and that the goal is not demonstrably utopian, but that nonetheless its advocates cannot specify (and seem to be working with no implicit form of) a criterion for determining when the value is present or satisfied and when it is not" (1984, p. 53). As previously discussed, Laudan gave the goal of "truth" as an example of a utopian goal in *Progress and Its Problems* on the basis that we "do not have any way of knowing for sure (or even with some confidence) that science is true, or probable, or that it is getting closer to the truth" (Laudan 1977, p. 127). Laudan again claims truth as a goal "cannot be rationally propounded" (Laudan 1984, p. 53).

Finally, Laudan suggests that the cognitive values in science can be evaluated on the basis of "reconciling theory and practice." That is, there should be a congruence between "explicit" and "implicit" goals (Laudan 1984, p. 53). We can criticize a scientist or a scientific community that claims to be pursuing one goal, but whose actions and behaviors imply the pursuit of some other goal, or set of goals. Sophistry would seem to be an obvious example of a lack of congruence.

Given that Laudan specifically states that the goals of truth, simplicity, and elegance will fail on utopian grounds, what goal or set of goals does Laudan recommend for science? Given Laudan's previous general theory of science, one might suspect that "problem solving" would be recommended as a central, or overriding goal. However, such is not the case: Problem solving does not even appear in the subject index of *Science and Values*. Whereas the "early Laudan" general theory of science confidently proposed and persuasively (to some people) argued that problem solving was the major aim of science, the "later Laudan," with equal confidence and great rhetorical skill, argues that there is *no* basic aim to science. Moreover, *Science and Values* contains not a single example of an aim or goal that Laudan argues would pass his own criteria for evaluating cognitive values. This should disturb those readers who recall the "early Laudan" theory proposing a "counting and weighting" procedure, but never giving a single example using such a procedure.

If "maximal problem solving" is no longer the goal toward which science is progressing, and if developing theories, lawlike statements, and other knowledge-claims that represent truly the external world is utopian, then how does science progress, if it progresses at all? Laudan's later view on progress is:

> Does a certain sequence of theories move scientists closer to realizing or achieving a certain goal state than they were before? Then progress (relative to that goal state) has occurred. If not, then not. The matter really is as simple as that. (Laudan 1984, p. 65)

We should note just how much Laudan has changed his position. Laudan's earlier theory claimed that any scientific community or research tradition was rational and making progress if it was progressing toward the overriding goal of maximal problem solving. Laudan's later view is that any scientific community or research tradition is rational and making progress if it has achieved or is making progress toward achieving any (nonutopian) goal or set of goals that it self-selects. Laudan's later view will strike many readers as surely more irrational than even Kuhn, who (ironically) is Laudan's chief foil. Although Kuhn rejected the concept that "changes of paradigm carry scientists and those who learn from them closer and closer to the truth," he did claim that science makes progress in its problem-solving capabilities: "Yet despite these and other losses to the individual communities, the nature of such communities provides a *virtual guarantee* that both the list of problems solved by science and the precision of individual problem solutions will grow and grow" (Kuhn 1970, p. 170; italics added). (Many commentators in marketing and the social sciences have misinterpreted Kuhn on this point. For example, "[f]or Kuhn, science progresses through revolutions, but there is no guarantee that it progresses *toward* anything" (Anderson 1983, p. 22; italics added).) Laudan closes his discussion on scientific progress with: "There is simply no escape from the fact that determinations of progress must be relativized to a certain set of ends, and that there is no uniquely appropriate set of those ends" (Laudan 1984, p. 66).

On Science and Values: **For Reason.** How well does *Science and Values* (*S&V*) achieve its stated objectives of being historically accurate, exhibiting the rationality of science, and being nonrelativistic, while at the same time avoiding having truth as an overriding value in science? Several critical analyses answer: "not well at all" Lugg (1986), Suppes (1986), Doppelt (1986), Brown (1987), and Siegel (1987). Briefly, these writers point out that *S&V*'s (1) historical examples often do not support its substantive positions, (2) analysis fails on numerous occasions to adequately differentiate between what constitutes a goal of science versus a methodological rule, (3) approach confuses the pragmatics of theory choice with cognitive values related to theory choice, and (4) theory may actually embrace relativism rather than avoid it (read carefully the quote in the last sentence of the preceding paragraph). Readers are urged to consult the above citations for elaborations on these views. Here, we shall focus exclusively on *S&V*'s view of the aims of science.

S&V claims that there are many aims in science, but no overriding aim or unique set of aims. Nevertheless, some aims are appropriate and others inappropriate, the latter, having failed his criteria of realizability (being nonutopian) and/or congruency. The aims of truth, simplicity, and elegance, he contends, fail these criteria. Laudan makes the task of evaluating his position difficult because he nowhere gives us a list of aims that he shows might pass his criteria of adequacy. Nevertheless, we must start somewhere, and perhaps using "maximum problem-solving" as a goal to evaluate would shed light on the issues involved. Such a goal would seem to serve as a useful example because Laudan held it in high regard in his earlier work and Kuhn believed that increasing problem solving was, most assuredly, an *outcome* of science, if not its goal.

Is maximum problem solving an appropriate goal for science? Does it pass the realizability and congruency criteria? First, just like the goal of truth, no one could ever claim that any particular theory has achieved the goal of solving the *maximum* number of problems. There could always exist some (unknown) theory that solves more problems, just like there could always exist some (unknown) theory that corresponds more truly with the external world. However, this is a much too quick and facile refutation. Is it not possible that we can give an explicit and rigorous explication of what it would mean for our theories to be progressing in the direction of solving the maximum number of problems? Could we not show we are coming "closer to" our goal? To answer this question, one might think that we could turn to Laudan's own "counting and weighting" methodology discussed in *Progress and Its Problems*. However, as has been demonstrated by numerous commentators on *Progress and Its Problems* (as previously discussed), any attempt to apply Laudan's "counting and weighting" methodology runs into the insurmountable difficulties of unambiguously identifying "problems," "problem solutions," and differential weights on a common metric. These difficulties seem to doom the task of unambiguously identifying when one is "coming closer to" the goal of maximum problem solving. In fact, the difficulties seem no less than those that Laudan attributes to the task of determining when one is "coming closer to" a theory that explains truly some aspect of reality. In short, a strong case can be made that "maximum problem solving" fails Laudan's criteria for a goal to be appropriate for science. Thus, we have the highly curious situation where maximum problem solving has gone from being the central, overriding aim of science in Laudan's earlier work to its being an *impermissible* aim of science in his later theory of science. Should this give readers grounds to question what is going on here? Indeed it should.

A fundamental flaw in *S&V*'s general theory of science is that it confuses (in Rokeach's [1986] terms) "terminal values" and "instrumental values." That is, it confuses enduring, end-state values that are prized in and of themselves, with instrumental values that are short range and valued because they tend to promote, or lead toward, terminal values. Examples abound of objectives in science that are demonstrably realizable, for example, developing a computer program to shorten the time required to do a particular multiple regression from 3 seconds to 2 seconds, completing a research report within the minimum number of pages required by a scholarly journal, cleaning the laboratory before leaving for home, and so on. Nevertheless, no one would suggest that these "realizable" objectives warrant consideration for the *goals* of science. Rather, they may or may not be instrumentally efficacious objectives leading toward more enduring, more important goals. Furthermore, self-serving, sociological goals, such as "to advance our own status within the field" (Anderson 1982, p. 15), hardly warrant consideration as goals worthy of scientific communities. Given Laudan's well-known objections to the "strong thesis" in the sociology of scientific knowledge (see Laudan 1977, pp. 196–222), he would be (rightly) loath to give serious consideration to institutionalizing self-serving, sociological goals. In short, Laudan conflates the long-range *mission* of science with its short-range, realizable, nonutopian, *objectives*.

The points made in the preceding paragraph may be generalized even further. There is a strong *prima facie* case that any cognitive value or goal for individual scientific communities, or science in general, that would be considered *worthy* of pursuit would most likely fail Laudan's utopian criterion. And this is as it should be. The terminal values of all societal institutions are, and ought to be, "utopian." When Laudan claims that "determinations of truth and falsity are irrelevant to the acceptability or the pursuitability of theories and research traditions," he is making a claim analogous to "determinations of *justice* are irrelevant to the legal system." Both are "utopian" (and appropriately so). As Watkins has stated most succinctly: "[T]o say that truth is no part of the aim of science is on a par with saying that curing is no part of the aim of medicine or that profit is no part of the aim of commerce" (Watkins 1984, p. 126).

Many exasperated readers may by now be crying "Enough!" and asking: Is all philosophy of science either incoherent or useless to practicing researchers, or both? Is there not a view of science that is intelligible, nonsophist, takes both science and truth seriously, and, at the same time, addresses some of the obvious deficiencies in the logical empiricists' research program? Many philosophers and practicing scientists believe that the "ism" coming closest is what is often referred to as "modern realism" or "scientific realism."[1]

5.3 SCIENTIFIC REALISM: AN INTRODUCTION

After the repudiation of Kuhnian relativism in the 1970s, the philosophy of science turned sharply toward a *realist* orientation: "Contemporary work in philosophy of science increasingly subscribes to the position that it is a central aim of science to come to knowledge of how the world *really* is, that correspondence between theories and reality is a central aim of science" (Suppe 1977, p. 649). Just as modern relativism and constructivism have their roots in Hegelian idealism, modern versions of realism stem from the classical realism of Russell, Moore, and (the early) Wittgenstein (see section 3.1). Whereas relativism-constructivism either explicitly or implicitly accepts the Hegelian, idealist view that the world does not exist independently of its being perceived, modern realists accept the classical realist position that the world exists independently of its being perceived. Modern realists reject Hegelian idealism on many of the same grounds as did their classical predecessors. That is, idealism is self-refuting; it represents sophistry, rather than genuine belief; it confuses the act of perceiving an object with the object so perceived; and it violates fundamental principles of intelligible discourse (see section 3.1.1). Modern realism, or "scientific realism," is usually associated with authors such as Bhaskar (1979), Boyd (1984), Harré (1986), Hendry (1995, 2001), Levin (1984), Leplin (1984), MacKinnon (1979), Maxwell (1962), McMullin (1984), Niiniluoto (1999), Putnam (1975), Sayer (1992), and Sellars (1963). By the late 1970s, "the majority of philosophers of science now profess to be scientific realists" (Causey 1979, p. 192). Nevertheless, Leplin observes, "[S]cientific realism is a majority position whose advocates are so divided as to appear a minority" (Leplin 1984, p. 1).

In short, there is no standard "general theory of science" according to scientific realism. Although most philosophers of science adopt some kind of realist orientation to science, scientific realism does not constitute a "school" developed around a general theory of science, such as the provocative theories offered by Kuhn, Feyerabend, Lakatos, and Laudan. This situation has led to a proliferation of "mini-theories," representing *versions* of scientific realism: transcendental realism (Bhaskar 1979, 1986, 1993, 1998), critical realism (Sayer 1992), measured realism (Trout 1998, 1999), ontic realism (MacKinnon 1979), critical scientific realism (Niiniluoto 1999), methodological realism (Leplin 1986), evolutionary naturalistic realism (Hooker 1985), referential realism (Harré 1986), experimental realism (Hacking 1983), constructive realism (Giere 1985, 1988), and internal realism (Putnam 1981), among others.

Aside from a rejection of idealism, relativism, and constructivism, is there any common denominator for the many versions of scientific realism? Even given the radical heterogeneity of the various versions of realism, McMullin suggests the following statement as a consensus fundamental tenet: "*The basic claim made by scientific realism . . . is that the long-term success of a scientific theory gives reason to believe that something like the entities and structure postulated by the theory actually exists*" (McMullin 1984, p. 26; italics in original). McMullin points out that there are four important qualifications built into the fundamental thesis of scientific realism. First, a theory must be successful over a significant period of time in order to give good reason for believing in the entities and structure implied by the theory. Second, the success of a theory gives "reason" to believe and not conclusive warrant to believe in the entities and structure. That is, McMullin wishes to avoid the philosophers' fallacy of providing that success warrants knowledge-with-certainty and the problems of the K-K thesis. Third, the success of a theory provides good reason to believe that "something like" the entities and structure postulated by the theory actually exists. Again, in order to avoid the philosophers' fallacy, the entities and structure believed to exist in the real world need not be *exactly* like the ones postulated by the theory. Fourth, the postulated entities do not have a special, privileged form of existence. That is, the entities are not like the "essences" of Aristotle.

To some, the fundamental thesis of scientific realism may seem rather innocuous. However, this thesis is totally at odds with the views of the logical positivists, is significantly different from the perspective of the logical empiricists, is *anathema* to the relativists and constructivists, and has been rejected by historical empiricists, such as Laudan. To understand why, we need to develop the implications of the fundamental thesis of scientific realism in more detail. We start with the relationship between the success of science and scientific realism.

5.3.1   Realism and the Success of Science

McMullin uses examples from geology and chemistry to examine the relationship between scientific realism and success in science. We shall use an example from medical science: the eradication of smallpox. Such an example would seem particularly pertinent for marketing, since both marketing and medicine have "basic" and "applied" dimensions, and the claim is often made that marketing (and the marketing academic discipline) should be "more like" medicine. (See Hunt 2002a, ch. 2.)

The disease called smallpox plagued the human community for thousands of years.[2] There are numerous references to a disease with symptoms like smallpox in the records of ancient India and Africa. For example, an analysis of the remains of several Egyptian mummies shows evidence of smallpox. In any respect, by the Middle Ages, smallpox was a scourge in most of Asia, Africa, and Europe: three million people died of smallpox in India's 1769 epidemic; by the end of the eighteenth century, Europe was losing over 400,000 people each year to smallpox; and it was responsible for over one-third of all the blindness in eighteenth-century Europe.

By the early part of the eighteenth century, it was widely recognized that people who once had smallpox seemed never to get the disease again. Furthermore, several European countries began adopting inoculation (as distinguished from "vaccination") procedures to prevent people from acquiring the disease during an epidemic. (Inoculation procedures had been used in Asia for several hundred years.) With the inoculation procedure, a subject was injected with material from a smallpox lesion obtained from an infected person. Inoculation became commonplace in England after a publication of the Royal Society, authored by James Jurian, showed that the risk of dying from smallpox from the inoculation was about 1 percent; whereas the overall risk of dying from smallpox was about 12 percent, and in times of epidemics the risk rose to about 20 percent. However, in addition to the risk of death, the inoculation procedure also had the disadvantage of the inoculated person spreading the disease to others. Furthermore, many religious groups were vigorously opposed to inoculation procedures on the basis that diseases were a result of God being angry, and, therefore, inoculations were "thwarting God's will."

Edward Jenner (1749–1823) was a physician who lived in Berkeley, England. For years, he had heard rumors to the effect that, in his words, "country girls" who had been infected by the mild disease called "cowpox" never contracted smallpox. Intrigued, Jenner began gathering data systematically on those who claimed to be immune to smallpox on the basis of having already had cowpox. The data seemed to confirm the claims of the "country girls." However, would someone *inoculated* with cowpox be immune from smallpox? On May 14, 1796, Jenner inoculated one James Phipps with cowpox taken from a sore on the hand of a milkmaid who had recently become infected. The child developed a mild reaction similar to that of a favorable smallpox inoculation. On July 1, Jenner inoculated the boy with smallpox taken from another patient, and the inoculation produced no significant reaction. Elated with the results of his experiment, Jenner repeated his experiment on five more children in 1798, when a fresh outbreak of cowpox next made the virus available to him. After the experiments yielded the same positive results, Jenner triumphantly announced his findings in a small pamphlet. Within a few short years, Jenner's experiments were repeated on much larger samples, and "vaccination" procedures with cowpox virus became commonplace. Even so, smallpox continued to kill thousands of people over the next 200 years.

It should be pointed out that, of course, Jenner never *saw* a virus in his entire life. Although the "germ" theory of contagious diseases was actively being promulgated during his time, it was not widely accepted. In 1836, using the recently invented achromatic microscope, Agostino Bassi (1773–1856) was the first person to isolate a specific microscopic organism that causes a disease. In this case, he isolated a parasitic fungus that causes a disease common in silkworms. In 1898, Loeffler and Frosch demonstrated that some diseases were caused by microorganisms so small that they would pass through a very fine filter. Such microorganisms came to be known as "filterable viruses," and the organism causing smallpox soon came to be known as one of these, as did the organism causing poliomyelitis. In fact, viruses are so small that it was not until the invention of the electron microscope in 1947 that anyone saw a virus. The advent of the electron microscope brought about rapid advances in our knowledge of the characteristics and properties of the smallpox virus, including its internal chemistry and how it is able to attack human cells and force them to reproduce the virus.

It was already well known by the time of the electron microscope that the smallpox virus could not reproduce itself outside a human host. Therefore, if there ever came a time when no one in the world had smallpox, the disease—according to theory—should be completely eradicated. This was the program adopted by the World Health Organization (WHO) at its 1966 meeting in Geneva. At that time, forty-four countries were still reporting smallpox and the disease was endemic in thirty-three of them. The WHO set a deadline of ten years for the eradication of the disease through massive vaccination programs. The last known case of smallpox—as of this writing—was in 1978, when the virus escaped from a laboratory in Birmingham, England. In 1980, the thirty-third World Health Assembly accepted the Final Report of the Global Commission for the Certification of Smallpox Eradication.

Most people would consider the eradication of smallpox to be a significant "success story" for science. How can this success story be explained? Scientific realism posits the following theory to explain the success of the smallpox eradication program. If it is true that:

1.   something like the phenomenon denoted by "smallpox disease" exists; and
2.   something like the entity denoted by "smallpox virus" exists; and
3.   the smallpox virus cannot exist outside human subjects; and
4.   something like the "cowpox virus" exists; and
5.   vaccinating people with cowpox virus will cause the body to produce antibodies that can successfully attack the smallpox virus; then
6.   vaccinating people with cowpox virus will prevent them from contracting smallpox; and, therefore,
7.   instituting a massive vaccination program throughout all parts of the world where smallpox currently exists can eradicate smallpox.

The preceding argument shows (in highly summarized form) how scientific realism can explain the millions of "micro" success stories making up the "macro" success story of smallpox eradication by science. Note the crucial role that "entities" play, for example, "something like the smallpox virus exists." Furthermore, "structures" of entities play a key role, for example, "if injections of cowpox virus cause the body to produce antibodies." Now, though the smallpox eradication is a highly visible "macro" success story, over the past 400 years science has produced, literally, countless such episodes where the knowledge obtained through science has been (1) pragmatically successful in solving real-world problems and (2) empirically successful in explaining and predicting phenomena. What else, other than some form of scientific realism, can explain the pragmatic and empirical success of science? That is, explaining the *failure* of a program like the smallpox eradication program would be easy. For example, if the injections of cowpox virus *do not* cause the body to produce antibodies, then the eradication program would likely fail. But, what other viable theory is there, except scientific realism, to explain the success of the smallpox eradication program in particular and the overall pragmatic success of science in general? Aside from divine intervention, there currently exists no rival theory. Indeed, "The positive argument for realism is that it is the only philosophy that doesn't make the success of science a miracle" (Putnam 1975, p. 69).

How does science progress? As will be recalled, most theories of science fail miserably in enabling us to understand both the nature and the mechanisms of scientific progress. First of all, scientific realism holds that science does progress by means of the four procedures discussed in section 3.5, that is, by the development of new theories, the falsification of existing theories, the expansion of the scope of a theory, and the reduction of specific theories into more general theories. However, scientific realism goes much further. In particular, scientific realism maintains that science progresses by (1) discovering new entities, (2) describing better the attributes and characteristics of entities, (3) measuring entities better, and (4) discovering the structures of the relationships among entities, including, most important, the structures of *causal* relationships.

Given that the long-term success of a scientific theory gives scientists reason to believe that something like the entities postulated by the theory actually exists, scientific realism holds that science progresses when researchers explore for the existence of new entities. For example, the belief in the "germ" theory of disease warranted researchers to search for other entities that may cause other diseases. Thus, as mentioned, by 1909, medical science had isolated the causal agent of poliomyelitis as a "filterable virus." Likewise, the warranted belief that entities exist prompted researchers to explore (and find) the virus resulting in the AIDS (Acquired Immunity Deficiency Syndrome) disease. If one does not have good reason to believe that the entities in one's theory exist, why engage in a search for them?

Scientific realism also holds that science progresses by better descriptions and better measures of the entities postulated by its theories. For example, how large is the viral entity? What is its shape? What is its chemical composition? By what means does it penetrate the cells of humans? Only scientific realism warrants the exploration of these kinds of questions. To work toward better descriptions and better measures of *nonexisting* entities is irrational. Absent the belief in scientific realism, the questions could be explored by the researcher only in doing the following: "Even though viruses do not exist, I shall attempt to explore precisely how large these nonexisting entities are." Scientific realism holds that researchers do not in fact engage in such elaborate rituals of self-deception.

Given that scientific realism holds that the long-term success of a theory is reason to believe that something like the *structure* postulated by the theory exists, scientific realism warrants the search for how the entities postulated by the theories interact with other entities. For example, how do viruses cause human cells to propagate the production of copies of the original virus? By what means does the viral entity produce the negative complications of the disease, that is, high temperature, rash, and so forth? By what mechanism and through what route does the cowpox virus cause the human body to produce antibodies? By what mechanism do the antibodies protect the human body against the smallpox virus?

As can be seen, scientific realism dramatically expands the concept of scientific progress to include many of the "lower-level" aspects of science. But "lower-level" does not mean unimportant. On the contrary, by focusing exclusively on "grand theories," many commentators on science have missed much of the real progress in the development of science.

In summary, scientific realism recognizes that science has been enormously successful over the past 400 years. This success, particularly the pragmatic and empirical aspects of this success, warrants the belief that "something like" the entities and structures postulated by scientific theories actually exist. Perhaps the easiest way to understand scientific realism is to start with "belief," rather than "success." Scientific realism holds that the *belief* that "something like" the entities and the structure postulated by a scientific theory exists provides *warrant* for using the theory to take action. For example, the belief that the cowpox virus exists and that vaccinating people with cowpox virus will protect them from smallpox *warrants* the action of vaccinating people. The action of vaccinating people results in certain consequences. These consequences may be favorable (success) or unfavorable (failure). This pragmatic success (failure) involved in the use of a scientific theory warrants the belief (disbelief) in the truth of the theory. By "truth of the theory" we mean that "something like" the entities and structure postulated by the theory exists. The "something like" becomes synonymous with the notion of "approximate truth." The reader should recognize that the preceding does *not* imply the acceptance of the much-maligned "pragmatic theory of truth." Scientific realism does not contend that the *meaning* of the statement "theory *X* is true" is the same as accepting the pragmatic consequences of "theory *X*." Rather, scientific realism holds that the pragmatic and empirical consequences of a theory (its "success") give *warrant* (good reason) for believing the theory to be true, that is, the world is "something like" the theory.

5.3.2   Scientific Realism and Logical Empiricism

Although scientific realism and logical empiricism share a common belief that science does in fact make progress, scientific realism differs sharply from logical empiricism on several issues, two of which I discuss here. First, most scientific realists do not share the logical empiricists' confidence in formal logic. As will be recalled, the logical empiricists and logical positivists were enamored with the formal logic developed by Russell and Frege (see sections 2.5.2 and 3.1.2). They believed that most philosophical problems could be solved (or at least can and should be addressed) through the application of formal logic. Furthermore, they believed that science could be reconstructed using formal logic. Although some scientific realists, such as Niiniluoto (1999), make use of the tool of formal logic, most realists have less confidence than did the logical empiricists that reconstructing science using this tool can solve important issues in philosophy of science. The second, and more important, difference between scientific realism and logical empiricism is the issue of the "theoretical term/observation term" dichotomy.

Following their logical positivist predecessors, the logical empiricists believed in a sharp distinction between "observation terms" and "theoretical terms" in a scientific theory. Adopting, essentially, the "early" Wittgenstein "picture theory" of meaning, observation terms referred in a nonproblematical manner to entities in the real world. Thus, the logical empiricists adopted a kind of "empirical realism" with respect to observation terms in a theory (see section 3.2.3). However, some terms in some theories did not *refer* in the direct manner of the observation terms. The logical empiricists labeled all terms that did not directly refer to some aspect of the observable world as "theoretical terms." In order for scientific theories to be "meaningful" (as opposed to meaningless metaphysics), theoretical terms would have to be given meaning by being defined through "correspondence rules" with observation terms. However, this posed an enormous problem for the logical empiricists: the problem of theoretical dispensability. As discussed in Hempel's famous article, "The Theoretician's Dilemma" (Hempel 1958, reprinted in

1965), if all theoretical terms can be defined through correspondence with observation terms and if the purpose of science is to determine relationships among observation terms, then theoretical terms are "unnecessary" in science. (See section 3.3.3 for a discussion of the "Theoretician's Dilemma.")

For scientific realism, the "theoretician's dilemma" is no dilemma at all. Scientific realism dismisses the theoretical term/observational term dichotomy as a false dichotomy. That is, scientific realism acknowledges that all the terms in a theory are, properly speaking, "theoretical terms." The phrase "theoretical term" means nothing more than "a term in a theory." For scientific realism, some terms in a theory may denote something more observable, more detectable, more easily measurable than other terms. In fact, some terms may denote nothing, in principle, observable at all. However, all the terms in a theory (excepting, of course, mathematical and logical terms) can lay a legitimate claim to denote the existence of some entity based on the senses (classical realism) and/or the success of the theory.

Consider, for example, the concept of "intelligence." For the logical positivists and empiricists, "intelligence" would always be a theoretical concept whose *meaning* was totally contained within its measure ("when I say 'intelligence,' this is to be interpreted as a 'shorthand' way of saying 'the results that a person has obtained on the Stanford-Binet intelligence quotient test'"). From the perspective of a scientific realist, the concept of "intelligence" *may* refer to a real, existing, nontangible entity, whose characteristics can be measured or indicated through a variety of measuring devices. Stated in modern measurement terms, scientific realism acknowledges the possibility of both a *reflective* measurement model and a formative measurement model being appropriate, depending on the particular circumstances. In contrast, logical empiricism assumes a (kind of) *formative* measurement model as being the only appropriate tool (Diamantopoulos and Winklhofer 2001; Howell 1987; Fornell and Bookstein 1982).

Why could not the logical empiricists adopt the position that theoretical terms could be real, yet nonobservable? Several factors made it impossible for them to adopt a realistic interpretation of theoretical terms. First, like Popper and many other philosophers, the logical empiricists were firmly convinced that Hume was correct: It is impermissible to go from observables to unobservables (like "cause"), because only deductive logic is an acceptable method of reasoning. Therefore, no nonobservable entity may be *inferred* from the conjoining of experience and observation. Second, the logical empiricists implicitly accepted foundationalism and the K-K thesis. That is, in order for science to be secure, it must rest on incorrigible foundations (the certainty of observation), and it must proceed by infallible methods. Third, the "lesson" that the logical empiricists had learned from the downfall of

Newtonian mechanics was that never again should science allow itself to believe it had found genuine knowledge about nonobservable entities existing in the world. Fourth, and finally, the "lesson" of quantum mechanics was that, because no one knew how to interpret quantum mechanics realistically, *all* theories should be interpreted instrumentally. That is, theories are calculation devices for making predictions about observable phenomena, and do not refer or represent any underlying reality. In fact, the impact of quantum mechanics on all the debates about the nature of science in the philosophy of science has been enormous, but underappreciated. Therefore, the issue of quantum mechanics and its "lessons" deserves more attention.

5.3.3   Scientific Realism and Quantum Mechanics

Many of the major participants in the debate about the nature of science have had strong backgrounds in physics. For example, Thomas Kuhn's formal training was in physics and Feyerabend's background leaned heavily toward physics. Indeed, Feyerabend acknowledges that it was a discussion with Professor C.F. von Weizsäcker on the foundations of quantum mechanics that played a decisive role in his turn toward relativism and irrationalism (Feyerabend 1978, p. 117). To illustrate the impact of quantum mechanics, consider the philosophy of Bas C. van Fraassen (1980).

Van Fraassen's (1980) "constructive empiricism" shares many of the same tenets of the logical positivists and logical empiricists, since constructive empiricism is decidedly antirealist. Ever since the famous paper by Maxwell (1962), philosophy has recognized that the concept of "observation" should be interpreted as a continuum. On this view, we have a large number of sense-extending instruments that enable us to "see," for example, microscopes and telescopes of varying powers. Actually, "observable" is often used, and most appropriately so, as roughly synonymous with "detectable" or "measurable" in modern philosophy of science literature. Van Fraassen's theory of science rejects totally the notion of observation being a continuum and contends that we do not "see" through a microscope. For van Fraassen, only those entities exist that can be, in principle, observed by the unaided human eye. Therefore, genes, bacteria, and viruses do not exist (but the "backsides" of the moon and stars do) (Hacking 1985, p. 135). Van Fraassen proposes: "That the observable phenomena exhibit these regularities, because of which they fit the theory, is merely a brute fact, and may or may not have an explanation in terms of unobservable facts 'behind the phenomena'—it really does not matter to the goodness of the theory, nor to our understanding of the world" (Van Fraassen 1980, p. 54).

What is the aim of science? For van Fraassen's constructive empiricism, "science aims to give us theories which are empirically adequate; and acceptance of a theory involves a belief only that it is empirically adequate" (Van Fraassen 1980, p. 12). How does van Fraassen reach his conclusion that "empirical adequacy" is the only appropriate aim for science? Because he interprets this to be the "lesson" of quantum mechanics: "He [van Fraassen] takes it that the realist is committed to finding hidden variables in quantum mechanics" (McMullin 1984, p. 34). As with most versions of antirealism, van Fraassen's philosophy is an impoverished one. He would have us believe, for example, that the Nobel Prize committee was somehow totally confused about the nature of science when they awarded the Nobel Prize in medicine in 1962 to James D. Watson for his discovery that DNA had the structure of a double helix. How can nonexisting entities have any structure, let alone, a double helix? (See also Alspector-Kelly (2001) on van Fraassen's constructive empiricism.)

The "lesson" of quantum mechanics has also been highly influential in convincing many behavioral scientists to adopt reality relativism and constructivism. Because of the indeterministic nature of measurement in quantum mechanics, as postulated by the Heisenberg uncertainty principle, both the position and momentum of a subatomic particle cannot be known at the same time. As discussed previously, quantum mechanics is *just* a series of equations. Although the equations, within probability limits, predict well, no one understands the *meaning* of the equations. This has led to what the physicist Polkinghorne refers to as numerous cases of "quantum mechanical folklore" (Polkinghorne 1984, p. 61). One such example of folklore is "Schrödinger's cat":

> The unfortunate animal in question is incarcerated in a closed box which also contains a radioactive atom with a 50–50 chance of decaying in the next hour, emitting a gamma-ray in the process. If this emission takes place it triggers the breaking of a vial of poison gas which instantaneously kills the cat. At the end of the hour, before I lift off the lid of the box, the orthodox principles of quantum theory bid me consider the cat to be in a state which is an even-handed superposition of the states "alive" and "dead." On opening the box the wave packet collapses and I find either a cooling corpse or a frisking feline. (Polkinghorne 1984, pp. 61–62)

Many advocates of reality relativism cite such treatments of quantum mechanics as that found in Zukav's *The Dancing Wu-Li Masters* (1979). Such treatments emphasize one interpretation of "Schrödinger's Cat": By opening the box, the "reality" (either a dead or live cat) has been "created." For example, Lincoln and Guba are prominent proponents of reality relativism-constructivism. They propose that "it is dubious whether there is a reality. If there is, we can never know it" (Lincoln and Guba 1985, p. 83). On what do they base their position? Their conclusion rests almost exclusively on citing examples such as "Schrödinger's Cat" drawn from interpretations of quantum mechanics by authors such as Zukav.

Now, if there is one thing we can say for sure about quantum mechanics, it is that there are *many* interpretations of what quantum mechanics means. In fact, there appear to be as many interpretations of quantum mechanics as there are quantum "mechanicians." J.C. Polkinghorne reviews many of the possible interpretations in his book, *The Quantum World*. With respect to Schrödinger's Cat, he notes: "It is scarcely necessary to emphasize *the absurdity* of the proposition that this state of affairs, whichever it is, has been brought about by my action in lifting the lid. It must surely be the case that the cat is competent to act as observer of its own survival or demise and does not need me to settle the issue for it" (Polkinghorne 1984, p. 62). In fact, Polkinghorne points out that there is absolutely nothing in quantum mechanics that compels us to abandon realism. "It is astonishingly anthropocentric . . . to suppose that in the thousands of millions of years before conscious life emerged in the world—and still today in those extensive parts of the universe where no conscious life has yet developed—no wave packet has ever collapsed, no atom for certain decayed . . . that quantum mechanics as we know it is a biologically induced phenomenon" (1984, p. 66). Thus, he concludes: "If in the end science is just about the harmonious reconciliation of the behavior of laboratory apparatus, it is hard to see why it is worth the expenditure of effort involved. *I have never known anyone working in fundamental science who was not motivated by the desire to understand the way the world is*" (1984, p. 79). Again, as MacKinnon (1979) has noted, are we to assume that the Nobel Prize committee was hopelessly confused for awarding Nobel Prizes to the physicists who discovered such subatomic particles as the pi-meson and anti-proton?

Quantum mechanics has also strongly influenced the "relativist/constructionist" perspective of Peter and Olson (1983), and the "critical relativism" of Anderson in marketing. For example, Anderson (in his critique of Cooper (1987) claims to have "demonstrated that 'truth' is an inappropriate objective for science, and that consumer research will do well to abandon such a quixotic ideal" (Anderson 1988b, p. 405). Anderson justifies his conclusion concerning truth in sections attacking what he calls (following Laudan) "convergent realism" and "motivational realism." His section attacking "motivational realism" is based *exclusively* on the "lesson" of quantum mechanics as interpreted by the well-known, antirealist philosopher, Arthur Fine. However, the very same Fine who pronounces emphatically that "Realism is dead" (Fine 1984, p. 83) (relying on quantum mechanics), in the very same article confidently asserts: "I certainly trust my senses, on the whole, with regard to the existence and features of everyday objects," and he continues by stating that he has no problem believing that "there really are molecules and atoms" (Fine 1984, p. 95). Thus, Fine's *antirealism* looks similar to the *realism* espoused here and by others elsewhere. Moreover, Fine's version of anti-realism, far from disparaging the role of truth in science, leads him to conclude that "truth is the fundamental semantical concept" (Fine 1986a, p. 149). Truth is fundamental because "there is no form of life [using Wittgenstein's terms, see section 4.1.3], however stripped down, which does not trade in truth," and this "redundancy property of truth makes truth a part of any discourse that merits the name" (Fine 1986b, p. 170).

5.3.4 Scientific Realism: Conclusion

What can we conclude about scientific realism? First of all, the thesis that "the long-term success of a scientific theory gives reason to believe that something like the entities and structure postulated by the theory actually exists" does not imply that in actual practice all the sciences and all individual scientists are committed to realism. Nevertheless, the "conventional wisdom" is that most sciences and most scientists embrace some version of it. As noted by Suppe, "Science is overwhelmingly committed to metaphysical and epistemological realism" (1977, p. 716). Also, as Meehl states:

> As to realism, I have never met any scientist who, when doing science, held to a phenomenalist or idealist view; and I cannot force myself to take a nonrealist view seriously even when I work at it. So I begin with the presupposition that the external world is really there, there is a difference between the world and my view of it, and the business of science is to get my view in harmony with the way the world really is to the extent that is possible. There is no reason for us to have a phobia about the word "truth." The idea that you shouldn't ask whether a scientific statement is true, separate from the anthropologists or the Hogo Bogos' belief in it, *because you can't be absolutely certain*, is a dumb argument . . . (Meehl 1986, p. 322; italics added)

What does scientific realism imply? First, some parts of the actual workings of science are totally incomprehensible and irrational if not viewed from a realist prospective. Indeed, many research programs require scientific realism (Leplin 1986, p. 38). If a scientist does not believe that viruses exist, then such activities as engaging in experiments to determine the size, shape, and structure of "nonexisting viruses" is irrational. Second, realism gives the practicing scientist prescriptive warrant for engaging in certain kinds of research activities. For example, the belief that viruses exist (ontological realism) and that they have caused smallpox and polio (epistemological realism) gives warrant for the practicing scientist to attempt to discover if there is a virus that may cause another disease (such as AIDS).

Third, many of the attacks on scientific realism seem to be attacks on strawmen caricatures of scientific realism, or unintelligibly incoherent, or fundamentally misguided. It is very curious and highly suspect that antirealists rely so heavily on the difficulty of interpreting realistically one scientific theory (i.e., quantum mechanics) and then generalize (in a monumental act of inductive *hubris*) that the entire universe of scientific theories should, therefore, be treated in a nonrealist fashion. To consider the absurdity of this situation, how about if the facts of the matter were in reverse? Suppose that quantum mechanics were the only theory that could be interpreted realistically, and that it was very difficult, if not impossible, to interpret all other theories in a realist manner? Are we to believe that those who currently adopt the antirealist position would suddenly argue powerfully in favor of realism? My strong suspicion is that they would not. Although the "lesson" of quantum mechanics may truly motivate some antirealists, there is good reason to believe that many others have radically different agendas.

Fourth, as discussed in section 7.6, scientific realism occupies a kind of "middle ground" among varying philosophical systems (see Table 7.1). At one extreme is the "naïve realism" (Siegel refers to it as "vulgar absolutism" (1987) characteristic of the Newtonians of the nineteenth century. This realism held (1) that science had at its disposal methods that, when followed rigorously, would inevitably lead to the objective of truth with certainty, and (2) that the existing scientific theories had (essentially) achieved this objective. At the other extreme lie the various versions of relativism/constructivism and their attendants: nihilism and skepticism. Between these two positions lie scientific realism and logical empiricism. Because of its acceptance of Humean skepticism, logical empiricism lies "closer" to relativism and constructivism. Given its rejection of Humean skepticism and its optimistic (basically Enlightenment) outlook with respect to the possibility of obtaining genuine knowledge about the world, scientific realism lies "closer" to naïve realism. Although scientific realism adopts a thoroughgoing fallibilist orientation toward both the methods and products of science, its fallibilism differs dramatically from the skepticism of relativism. Most unfortunately, as pointed out by Harré, relativism conflates the logical possibility of error with the real chance of being wrong: to abandon all claims to know because of the possibility of error is "absurd" (Harré 1986, p. 62).

5.4 PHILOSOPHY OF SCIENCE AND MARKETING

Some readers, having followed our narrative from its beginnings in Platonism, classical empiricism, and classical rationalism through to its conclusion with historical relativism, historical empiricism, and scientific realism, may feel a sense of disappointment. In particular, those readers expecting a set of truths with certainty at the end of our discussion may feel let down. Hopefully, however, most readers will by now have a greater appreciation and understanding of the fundamental differences among various philosophical perspectives and will, at least, no longer be bewildered about many of the issues in the philosophy debates. If so, perhaps the level of debate on philosophical issues in marketing may rise to a more productive level.

The philosophy of science plays a significant role in marketing science because (if for no other reason) of the fact that all research activity implies *necessarily* some underlying "philosophy." When a scholar engages in a research project, there are always underlying assumptions about the goal or goals of the project, the nature of reality relative to the project, the appropriateness of the underlying methodology, the role of theory, and so forth. Therefore, the philosophy of science literature can help practicing researchers be aware of the underlying assumptions of the project. This *explicit* awareness and acknowledgment of the oftentimes *implicit* assumptions of research, in my judgment, is likely to lead to better, more effective research.

We turn now to using the preceding chapters on the philosophy of science to analyze several issues in the philosophy debates in marketing. We begin in Chapter 6 with an analysis of the sciences vs. nonsciences controversy, before exploring the "positivism is dead" argument advanced by those advocating qualitative methods in marketing. Chapter 7 focuses on the role of truth in marketing research. Chapter 8 argues for objectivity in marketing research. Chapter 9 concludes by arguing for scientific realism.

QUESTIONS FOR ANALYSIS AND DISCUSSION

1. An article in the *Journal of Marketing* by Siew Meng Leong (1985) has attempted to apply a Lakatosian reconstruction to marketing science. This reconstruction proposes that there are four levels to any science: (1) the hard core, (2) the protective belt, (3) middle-range theories, and (4) working hypotheses. Leong proposes that the four fundamental explananda and four guiding research questions proposed by Hunt form the "hard core" of marketing science. Accordingly, the "protective belt" is comprised of research programs in buyer behavior, seller and competitive behavior, institutional behavior, and environmental behavior.

    Suppose marketing science were to be composed *exclusively* of marketing management. That is, suppose marketing were to be a completely (micro) normative discipline, rather than a discipline having both positive and normative dimensions. How could a Lakatosian reconstruction of marketing science be accomplished under these as-

sumptions? What would be the implications for marketing researchers if these assumptions were true? In your judgment, is the marketing discipline moving closer to the acceptance of these assumptions?
Should it?

2. Define the concept of "research programme" as the term is used by
    Lakatos. How does it differ from a "research tradition" for Laudan
    and a "paradigm" for Kuhn? Choose several of the "schools of
    thought" identified by Sheth, Gardner, and Garrett (1988). To what
    extent are there one, or more, "research programs," "research tradi-
    tions," and "paradigms" in each "school of thought"? Discuss the
    overall usefulness of these concepts for marketing.

3. Define and differentiate among "dogmatic falsificationism," "naïve
    falsificationism," and "sophisticated methodological falsificationism."
    To what extent has marketing been characterized by these "isms"?
    How does the "context of acceptance" versus the "context of pursuit"
    distinction severely limit the ability of Lakatos's theory of science to
    adequately describe the process of scientific change?

4. What is the "historical approach" to the philosophy of science? How
    does the "historical approach" differ from the approaches used by
    the logical positivists and logical empiricists? Suppose that the meth-
    odology of science has truly been progressing over the past 400 years.
    That is, suppose that we have, in fact, developed better measurement
    procedures, better scientific instruments, better statistical methods,
    and more powerful mathematics. Under what circumstances could
    the "historical approach" explain this progressivity? Suppose, now,
    that there has been *no* progressivity in the methodology of science.
    That is, electron microscopes are not "better" than the human eye,
    and the mathematics of today, though different, is not more power-
    ful. How could the "historical method" explain this circumstance?
    Which circumstance do you believe better describes reality?

5. How does the "context of pursuit" versus the "context of acceptance"
    relate to the issue of the rationality of science? Create a set of stan-
    dards that would lead someone to conclude that "scientific commu-
    nities are collectively irrational." Using the same set of standards,
    would *any* institution in society be rational? If there remain any ra-
    tional institutions in your analysis, justify that these institutions are,
    indeed, rational. If there do not remain rational institutions in your
    analysis, justify having a term, that is, "rational," for which nothing
    applies. That is, does not the term "irrational" imply that you should
    be able to find something that is rational?

6. Discuss how it could be the case that Feyerabend could claim that

Lakatos and he were in agreement on essential issues. How do both fall prey to the "philosophers' fallacy"?

7. What are the major differences between Laudan's "early" theory of science and his "later" theory? How does each of these two theories differ from the theory of science proposed by Kuhn?

8. What is the difference between "problem solving" in the sense that Laudan uses the term and "problem solving" as the term is used pragmatically in society? Why is the issue of the differing uses of the term "problem solving" important?

9. How did science progress according to the "early" Laudan? How does science progress according to the "later" Laudan? Which of these two notions of progress is superior? Why? If, science does make progress by "solving problems better," is it important to *explain* how this progressivity comes about? Why? What are the rival hypotheses as to the reasons for science making progress in the sense of solving problems better?

10. Kuhn later retreated to the point where "incommensurability" means simply that we do not have a procedure like a mathematical proof for deciding among various theories. Show how this is another example of the "philosophers' fallacy." Doppelt advocates "moderate relativism." His moderate relativism is virtually indistinguishable from "the underdetermination thesis." That is, since we have nothing like a mathematical proof for choosing among theories, such choice is "underdetermined." To what extent does the "underdetermination thesis" pose some significant problem for science? If you believe that it does not, why do so many writers believe they are saying something terribly provocative when they, in solemn tones, claim that theories are "underdetermined by the data"? If you believe that the "underdetermination thesis" poses significant problems for science, what are these problems and why are they important?

11. Laudan desires that his theory of science should speak meaningfully about science, and, at the same time, avoid the concept of truth, and be nonrelativistic. Evaluate the inherent difficulties in attempting to achieve these objectives simultaneously.

12. What is scientific realism? How does it differ from logical positivism and logical empiricism? Many people believe that when the critics of science attack the logical positivists/empiricists, such critics are actually attacking scientific realism (but they do not realize it). Evaluate this thesis.

13. How does scientific realism explain the success of science? In this respect, what does "success" mean? What is the "miracle theory" of

scientific success? Evaluate it as a genuine rival for scientific realism. Is it true that the "miracle theory" is the only genuine rival to scientific realism for explaining the success of science? Philosophers like to hypothesize a world where we are all "brains floating in a vat." In such a world, everything is "illusion." Is this a genuine rival for scientific realism?

14. Scientific realism expands the concept of scientific progress to include many of the "lower-level" aspects of science. What does "lower level" mean? How have philosophers erred by focusing exclusively on "grand theories"? Is marketing making progress at the "lower-level"? Give examples.

15. What is the difference between a correspondence rule *defining* a "theoretical term" and *measuring* a "theoretical term"? To what extent does marketing rely on "correspondence rules" versus "measures"? To what extent should it?

NOTES

1. Our discussion of scientific realism here and in Chapters 6, 7, 8, and 9 draws on that in "Truth in Marketing Theory and Research" (Hunt 1990b). See also Bagozzi (1980, 1984), Blair and Zinkham (1984), and Easton (2002).

2. The information on smallpox in this section (and much more) can be found in Hopkins (1983) and Fenner and White (1976).

6 ON SCIENCE, QUALITATIVE METHODS, AND MARKETING RESEARCH

This chapter is the first of four that use the historical material developed in Chapters 2 through 5 as a foundation for analyzing controversies that have been prominent in the philosophy debates in marketing. First, this chapter investigates the sciences versus nonsciences controversy. Then, the chapter analyzes the often-employed "positivism is dead" argument, and explores the controversy concerning positivism and qualitative methods.

6.1 THE SCIENCES VERSUS NONSCIENCES CONTROVERSY

What is the nature of science? Traditionally, marketing theory has viewed a science as having four characteristics: (1) a distinct subject matter, (2) the description and classification of the subject matter, (3) the presumption that underlying the subject matter are uniformities, regularities, and causal structures that sciences seeks to discover, and (4) the adoption of the scientific method (Hunt 1976a, b).[1] The first criterion distinguishes the sciences in general from instances of science in particular. In marketing, for example, it has been argued that the transaction is the distinct subject matter (Bagozzi 1974; Hunt 1976a, b; Kotler 1972). The second and third criteria, jointly, differentiate the sciences (such as psychology and chemistry) from the arts and humanities (such as music and English). The fourth criterion, scientific method, distinguishes the sciences (such as astronomy and medicine) from the nonsciences and pseudosciences (such as astrology and palmistry). As discussed in section 2.2, the scientific method, called by many "the most significant contribution of Western civilization" (Morris 1955, p. 63), traces to the seventeenth-century natural philosophers who conjoined (1) the emphasis on logic and speculation implicit in Plato's method of critical discussion, (2) the powerful tool of mathematics, as proposed by Pythagoras, (3) the belief in systematic observation and the syllogistic logic of Aristotle, and, very important, (4) the reliance, when possible, on experimentation, as advocated by Galileo (and subsequently articulated by Sir Francis Bacon).

The traditional view in marketing theory, as well as the mainstream view in philosophy of science, has been challenged by the relativist conception of the nature of science. Relativism maintains that there are no fundamental differences between the sciences and nonsciences (Anderson 1983, 1989; Peter and Olson 1983, 1989). This section reviews the relativist argument, before (1) evaluating the argument, (2) revisiting a partial formalization of the argument, (3) examining whether the argument is a straw man, and (4) evaluating the "weak form" version of the argument.

6.1.1 Relativism and the Nature of Science

Relativists point out that the search for criteria that would separate science from nonscience dates from the very beginnings of Western philosophy, and that Popper has labeled the question "the problem of demarcation" (Anderson 1983, p. 18). However, "philosophers have been signally unsuccessful in their search for such criteria" and many "consider the question to be a chimera" (Anderson 1983, p.18). After rejecting the notion that sciences differ from nonsciences in any fundamental respect, Anderson proposes that marketing science should adopt a relativistic stance, and he distinguishes between two different ways that the term "science" can be used. He designates them as science$_1$ and science$_2$:

> It is proposed that science$_1$ should refer to the idealized notion of science as an inquiry system which produces "objectively proven knowledge" (Chalmers 1976, p. 1). On this view, science seeks to discover "the truth" by the objective methods of observation, test, and experiment. Of course it should be clear that no such inquiry system has ever existed—nor is it very likely that such a system will ever exist. (Anderson 1983, p. 26)

Given his belief that science as a process that searches for truth by objective methods cannot exist, he proposes that marketing adopt the notion of science$_2$:

> The defining element here is that of societal consensus. On this view, science is whatever society chooses to call a science. In Western cultures this would include all of the recognized natural and social sciences. (Anderson 1983, p.26)

On Relativism and the Nature of Science: For Reason. Is there no fundamental difference between sciences and nonsciences? As a point of departure, we should note that Anderson cites Chalmers (1976) as supporting the view that "science$_1$" has never existed and is unlikely ever to exist in the future.

This is, I suggest, a fair reading of *What Is This Thing Called Science?* (Chalmers 1976). However, like Kuhn before him, Chalmers repudiated his 1976 views on objectivity, truth, and science$_1$ in his later work:

> This book is a sequel to *What Is This Thing Called Science?* In that earlier book I subjected some of the standard accounts of science and its methods to a critical scrutiny but did not elaborate on an alternative to them in any detail. I have become convinced that some such elaboration is necessary, especially given the extent to which, against my intentions, my position has been read as a radically skeptical one that denies any distinctive, objective status to scientific knowledge. This book contains an extension and elaboration of the argument of its predecessor. I persist in my rejection of orthodox philosophical construals of the so-called scientific method but show how a qualified defense of science as objective knowledge is possible nevertheless. Consequently, I will no doubt be scorned by many philosophers to my right and sociologists of science to my left. . . . I wish [in this book] to resist the subjectivist, relativist response to the critique of empiricism for which, it would appear, I am partly responsible. (Chalmers 1990, pp. xi, 41)

Even though Chalmers has repudiated the science$_1$ versus science$_2$ view, we may still inquire whether there are, indeed, differences between the sciences and nonsciences. Stated more precisely, do the knowledge-claims of the nonsciences have epistemological status equal to the knowledge-claims of the sciences? This is equivalent to asking whether there are good grounds for accepting the knowledge-claims of sciences in preference to the knowledge-claims of nonsciences. Perhaps an example from Hunt (1984) that uses medical science can provide a clearer perspective on the issue in question.

Suppose your father visited his family physician because he was feeling poorly. Suppose further that the physician conducted some tests and diagnosed your father's condition as a bone cancer that, if left unattended, would probably result in your father's death within a year. Upset with this diagnosis, your father visits his local palmist. The palmist reads your father's palm and tells him that he does not have bone cancer, and that he will live a long life without any medical treatment. The fundamental question here is whether there are good reasons for accepting the knowledge-claim (the diagnosis) of the physician (and acting accordingly) and for rejecting the knowledge-claim (the diagnosis) of the palmist? Do medical science and palmistry justify their claims about knowledge by equally acceptable methods?

When asked to justify his diagnosis of bone cancer, the family physician would refer to the results of experiments that have found that when the results of certain medical tests are "positive," then the patient usually has a kind of bone cancer. Furthermore, the physician would point out that over time medical scientists have observed that the average life expectancy of someone with this kind of bone cancer is approximately one year. When the palmist is asked to justify his diagnosis, he indicates that his knowledge is based on the "gift of reading." He was born with this "gift," and only others who have been similarly "blessed" with this gift can understand truly his knowledge or powers.

Modern empiricists, scientific realists, and practicing scientists would claim that the diagnosis of the physician is better justified than the knowledge-claim of the palmist. That is, mainstream philosophy of science maintains that open empirical testing of the knowledge-claims of medical science provides good reasons for accepting the diagnosis of the physician in preference to those of the palmist. This process is often referred to as simply "intersubjective certification" (Hunt 2002a).

Relativists reject the claim that empirical testing provides good reasons for preferring the knowledge-claims of medical science over palmistry. Relativists point out that there not only is no "unique scientific method," but also that science is "subjective" (Peter and Olson 1983, 1989). Furthermore, the observations used to test theory are "theory laden," which makes objective knowledge impossible (Sauer, Nighswonger, and Zaltman 1982, p. 380; Anderson 1983, pp. 20, 26; Peter and Olson 1983, pp. 121–22; Mick 1986, p. 207; Jaworski and MacInnis 1987, p. 164; Olson 1987, p. 388; Hudson and Ozanne 1988, pp. 515, 518; Holbrook and O'Shaughnessy 1988, p. 401; Firat 1989, p. 95; Peter and Olson 1989, p. 26; Thompson 1990, p. 29; Peter and Dacin 1991, p. 280). Indeed, relativists could point out that many times medical science conducts the same test and the patient turns out *not* to have bone cancer. Thus, the palmist's diagnosis will sometimes be correct, and the diagnosis of medical science will be incorrect. They could also point out that terms such as "disease" and even "death" are theory-laden. For example, perhaps what medical science calls a disease is in reality the normal state of affairs. Furthermore, what is to be our definition of "death?" Finally, relativists could contend that science is a "social process" and put forth Feyerabend's (1978b, 1987a) argument that the primary reason that many people often accept the diagnoses of physicians over the diagnoses of palmists is that people have been in essence "brainwashed" by the self-serving interests and propaganda of the members of the scientific community. After all, is science not "whatever society chooses to call as science" (Anderson 1983, p. 26)? It would seem that relativists must either (1) accept the view that medical science and palmistry have equal epistemological merit or (2) deny their relativism. Or do they?

6.1.2 Revisiting the Nature of Science Arguments

Anderson (1989) addresses the medical science versus palmistry example. He claims that "we currently have *no* universally applicable criterion by which we can demarcate scientific knowledge from any other kind of knowledge" (Anderson 1989, p. 1). He then cites Laudan (1980) as a reference and notes that "unfortunately this is often thought to imply that all knowledge-claims are on an equal epistemic footing" (Anderson 1989, p. 1). He claims that "very little follows from the fact that philosophers have been unable to come up with a *universal* demarcation criterion" (1989, p. 1), and speaks again in favor of what he calls "science$_2$—the definition of science by societal consensus" (1989, p. 2).

Is it the case that nothing of great importance follows from the demarcation issue? Stated more succinctly, is it the case that "societal consensus" alone constitutes the reason why there are astronomy departments in universities, but not astrology departments, that there are medical science departments, but not palmistry departments? The mainstream philosophy of science view is that it is not just "societal consensus," but rather that the societal consensus is backed by good reasons. Embedded within the medical science versus palmistry example in the preceding section is both an argument for relativism and one for mainstream philosophy of science. As discussed in Hunt (2002a, Chapter 7), it is often useful to reconstruct (or partially formalize) arguments for purposes of clarifying and evaluating issues.

The "nature of science argument" according to the relativist point of view of science may be summarized concisely (i.e., reconstructed) as follows:

R1.   *There are no fundamental differences separating the sciences and the nonsciences.* ("The search for [demarcation] criteria that separate science from nonscience." . . has been "signally unsuccessful" (Anderson 1983, p. 18). Since there are no objective criteria separating science from nonscience, "science is whatever society chooses to call science" (Anderson 1983, p. 26).)

R2.   *The knowledge-claims of the nonsciences have as much epistemological warrant as the sciences.* (That is, we have no good reason to believe and act on the knowledge-claims of the sciences in preference to the nonsciences. Statement R2 is *logically implied* by R1 because, if we had good reasons to believe and act on the knowledge-claims of the sciences, such reasons would constitute "fundamental differences" that could be used to separate science from nonscience.)

R3.   Therefore, statement R2 implies that if a palmist should diagnose a person as *not* having bone cancer (an example of a nonscience knowledge-claim), such a diagnosis would have equal warrant as the diagnosis of a medical doctor that the person *did* have bone cancer (an example of a science knowledge-claim).

A reconstruction of the nature of science argument according to mainstream philosophy of science would be:

M1.   *There are fundamental differences separating the sciences and nonsciences.* (Sciences differ from nonsciences in their method of verifying knowledge-claims.)

M2.   *The knowledge-claims of sciences have greater epistemological warrant than the knowledge-claims of the nonsciences.* (Because the knowledge-claims of the sciences are intersubjectively certifiable through open empirical testing, people have good reasons for accepting such claims and acting upon them in preference to the knowledge-claims of nonsciences.)

M3.   Therefore, M2 implies that if a palmist should diagnose a person as *not* having bone cancer and a medical doctor should diagnose that same person as *having* bone cancer, the person has good reasons for believing the diagnosis of the medical doctor and acting accordingly. (Palmistry has not adopted the verification system of open empirical testing, and, therefore, is not a science.)

Anderson reviewed the narrative versions (as detailed in Hunt 1984) of the two nature of science arguments and lamented that empiricists often cast "proffered alternatives" as "relativistic flights of fancy that lead to epistemological anarchy and the abandonment of rationality and objectivity" (Anderson 1986, p. 156). He did not deny that the second version accurately reflected the views of mainstream philosophy of science. Nor did he do a detailed analysis of the relativist version, pointing out logical flaws or empirical inadequacies. Rather, he dismissed the argument as a "straw man." To avoid the impression of possibly mischaracterizing Anderson's reasons for dismissing the argument, he is quoted at length:

> The type of relativism attacked by Hunt (1984) has *never* been advocated by any of the participants in the current debate. The object of Hunt's critique is a straw man known as judgmental (Knorr-Cetina and Mulkay 1983) or "nihilistic" relativism. In this view, all knowledge claims are equally valid and there is no basis on which to make judgments among the various contenders. (*Indeed, a careful reading of even the most radical of contemporary relativists will reveal that this does not even approximate their views*, e.g., Collins 1975, 1981; Feyerabend 1975, 1978a). (Anderson 1986, p. 156; italics added)

Is it true that the above argument (indicating that relativism inexorably leads one to be indifferent between the claims of palmistry and medical science) is a "straw man?" Is it truly the case that "a careful reading of *even the most radical* of contemporary relativists will reveal that this does not even *approximate* their views?"

6.1.3   Is the Relativist Nature of Science Argument a Straw Man?

Because Anderson (1986) uses Feyerabend as an example of a relativist who would not subscribe to the so-called "nihilistic" relativism presented in the relativist argument, we shall examine Feyerabend's views on the subject. As discussed in section 4.2.2, Feyerabend is one of the most prominent and widely cited supporters of a relativist view of science (Suppe 1977a). Indeed, all of the relativist writers in marketing and consumer research draw heavily from his works for intellectual sustenance, reference him liberally, and even refer to him as a relativist "hero" (Olson 1987). In *Science in a Free Society* (Feyerabend 1978b), he addresses and answers many of the criticisms of his work from other philosophers of science. He is quoted here at length (to avoid the possibility of a paraphrase mischaracterization) concerning his answer to a critique by a philosopher named Tibbets:

> [Tibbets] also asks: "If *he* had a child diagnosed with Leukemia would he look to his witchdoctor friends or to the Sloan Kettering Institute?" I can assure him that I would look to my "witchdoctor friends" to use his somewhat imprecise terminology *and so would many other people in California* whose experience with scientific medicine has been anything but encouraging. The fact that scientific medicine is the only existing form of medicine in many places does not mean that it is the best and the fact that alternative forms of medicine succeed where scientific medicine has to resort to surgery shows that it has serious lacunae: numerous women, reluctant to have their breasts amputated as their doctors advised them, went to acupuncturists, faithhealers, herbalists and got cured. Parents of small children with allegedly incurable diseases, leukemia among them, did not give up, they consulted 'witchdoctors' and their children got cured. How do I know? Because I advised some of these men and women and I followed the fate of others. (Feyerabend 1978b, pp. 205–6; italics in original)

Recall that Anderson dismissed the relativist nature of science argument on the basis that "a careful reading of even the most radical of contemporary relativists will reveal that this does not even approximate their views" (Anderson 1986, p. 156). The above quote shows clearly that, to the contrary, careful observers of relativists' writings know that the relativist nature of science argument closely reflects the logical implications of their views. How do relativists (such as Feyerabend) reach such extreme positions that even their followers (such as Anderson and others) dismiss relativist views as "nihilistic" nonsense? The answer lies precisely in Feyerabend's fundamental beliefs— as detailed in section 4.2.2—about the existence of many, equally viable "ways of knowing" that he calls research "traditions." These fundamental beliefs are strikingly similar to, if not precisely the same as, those (supposedly) championed by relativist marketing and consumer researchers.

The discussion in section 4.2.2 of Feyerabend's relativist views on research traditions shows clearly how he arrives at conclusions so extreme as to be labeled "nihilistic" and "a straw man" by Anderson. One might suppose that Feyerabend is simply engaging in academic gamesmanship or sophistry, and that he did not intend for readers to take his views seriously. Brodbeck notes that relativists believe "science is in effect a game" (Brodbeck 1982, p. 3), which is consistent with the view that "the important question we must ask is how can I convince my colleagues in the scientific community that my theory is correct?" (Anderson 1982, p. 15). As Krausz and Meiland (1982, p. 6) have pointed out, the sophists in ancient Greece were among the first relativists in Western intellectual history. From whom we get the term "sophistry," these philosophers delighted in weaving incredibly convoluted arguments that *they* knew to be false, but that the *less sophisticated* would (or could) not know.

Clearly, however, Feyerabend is not a sophist. The preceding long quote demonstrates that he recognizes how extreme his premises are concerning the nature of the scientific "tradition" (the knowledge-claims of the sciences are no better than the knowledge-claims of the nonsciences), and he is willing to accept their logical consequences (palmistry and medical science should have "equal rights" and "equal access to key positions"), no matter how extreme those consequences may appear to others. Most important, he not only accepts intellectually these extreme consequences, but (unlike a sophist) he also acts upon them (referring now to the long quote of Feyerabend in which he indicates that he has both used and referred others to "witchdoctor friends").

Unfortunately, many relativists are not as consistent as Feyerabend. The issue is never whether relativists embrace nihilistic conclusions (like R3), but whether relativist beliefs (like R1) *imply* nihilism. Relativist advocates wish to emphatically proclaim Feyerabend's extreme premises concerning the nature of science. Yet, unlike him, they wish to deny (indeed, pejoratively dismiss) the logical consequences of those premises. Neo-Marxist, "critical theory" relativists have also been forced to address the nihilism/sophistry dilemma:

> Political radicals are quite as dedicated to the concept of privilege as their opponents: they believe, for example, that the level of food supplies in Mozambique is a weightier issue than the love life of Mickey Mouse. The claim that one kind of conflict is more important than another involves, of course, *arguing* for this priority and being open to disproval; but nobody actually believes that "power is everywhere" in the sense that any manifestation of it is as significant as any other. On this issue, as perhaps on all others, nobody is in fact a relativist, whatever they may rhetorically assert. (Eagleton 1991, pp. 8–9)

For the purposes of present discussion, let us try to salvage a view that might be called "weak-form" relativism (consistent with Anderson's [1986, p. 164] "weak-form incommensurability"). In this view, one wants to avoid the charges of nihilism, sophistry, and/or the pain of logical inconsistency, yet still embrace a relativistic position concerning science.

6.1.4   Weak-Form Relativism

Most (but not necessarily all) marketing and consumer behavior relativists do not agree with the extreme conclusions on the nature of science held by writers like Feyerabend (such as statement R3 in section 6.1.2). Yet, they wish to embrace Feyerabend-like premises on science (such as statement R1). Is it possible, therefore, to salvage the weak-form relativism championed by them? A satisfactory answer to this question lies not in simply denying that they agree with the extreme conclusions of the relativist argument on the nature of science (that the diagnoses of palmists should be given equal epistemological status to the diagnoses of medical science). To do so is much like killing the messenger who brings bad news. Rather, because the conclusions of any argument are entailed in its premises, advocates of weak-form relativism must reexamine their premises in order to salvage their position, for extreme premises must yield extreme conclusions.

Modifying statement R1 to make it less extreme might be a useful starting place for weak-form relativists. Such a modification might be as follows:

R1a.   Although in most cases it is impossible to find fundamental differences separating what society chooses to call "science" from "nonscience," there are isolated instances (like medical science versus palmistry) where such differences are obvious.

Weak-form relativists would then have to identify and state the characteristics that so obviously differentiate science from nonscience in each such isolated instance. Furthermore, they would have to show how these differentiating characteristics lack commonality (each "obvious" instance is totally idiosyncratic) and defend this lack of commonality as a reasonable position. Or, they would have to identify the *common* differentiating characteristics across the "isolated instances" and defend how these commonalities differ in some significant fashion from what practicing scientists and mainstream philosophers of science call the *scientific method* of verification through open empirical testing. Otherwise, weak-form relativists would be forced to deny one of their most cherished precepts: that science does not differ from nonscience through its method of verifying its knowledge-claims.

Clearly, the preceding procedure for salvaging weak-form relativism would seem to be an extraordinarily difficult task at best, or devastating to the relativist agenda at worst. Therefore, modifying statement R2 as a possibility to salvage weak-form relativism should be examined.

Statement R2 of the relativist argument indicates that the knowledge-claims of the nonsciences have as much epistemological warrant as the knowledge-claims of sciences. Anderson has already made a useful start in the direction of modifying R2 when he noted that "society bestows a high epistemological status on science because it believes that science generally functions in the best interests of society as a whole" (Anderson 1983, p. 26). Advocates of weak-form relativism could modify their position on R2 by *agreeing* with society:

> R2a.   Society does bestow and ought to bestow a higher epistemological status on the knowledge-claims of the sciences than on the knowledge-claims of the nonsciences.

Justifying statement R2a would pose a significant challenge for relativists. Although society may bestow a privileged epistemological position on science capriciously and arbitrarily (as Feyerabend states and Anderson implies in his science$_2$: "science is whatever society chooses to call a science"), weak-form relativists, as professed scholars of science, would have to explain exactly why society ought to bestow a superior position on the knowledge-claims of science. Precisely why is it reasonable to believe that science, in preference to nonscience, functions "in the best interests of society as a whole?" This would seem to imply necessarily that weak-form relativists would have to claim that the procedures that science uses to justify its knowledge-claims are somehow *better*. That is, its "way of knowing" or "tradition" is *superior* or should be *privileged*. But if the verification procedures for scientific knowledge-claims are better than the procedures used by nonsciences, then, on pain of continuing inconsistency, weak-form relativists would again have to give up their belief that there are no fundamental differences separating the sciences from the nonsciences. And therein lies the rub. In order to "save" relativism, weak-form relativists have to destroy it.

Contrary to the verdict of Anderson (relying on Laudan's views), many philosophers of science continue to believe that there are fundamental differences separating science from nonscience, and these differences provide good reasons the for societal consensus (Grove 1985). For example, in an article in *Philosophy of Science*, Siegel reviewed the demarcation debate and notes that "Laudan's rejection of a unique SM [scientific method] depends on a failure to distinguish between general principles of appraisal and specific instantiations of such principles" [or "techniques"] (Siegel 1985, p. 528). He goes on to note that the methodological criteria of science that constitute collectively the scientific method can best be expressed as a "commitment to evidence," as exemplified by "a concern for explanatory adequacy, however that adequacy is conceived; and insistence on testing, however testing is thought to be best done; and a commitment to inductive support, however inductive inference is thought to be best made" (Siegel 1985, p. 528). Thus, "science's commitment to evidence, by way of SM, is what justifies its claim to respect—science is to be taken seriously precisely because of its commitment to evidence" (1985, p. 530). However, the preceding conclusions by Siegel about scientific method do not imply that he claims that science is the *only* domain in which the epistemic worthiness of beliefs, hypotheses, or claims may be putatively established on the basis of evidence. Rather, "SM extends far beyond the realm of science proper. But this is only to say that SM can be utilized widely. It is still properly labeled *scientific* method" (Siegel 1985, p. 530).

One of the problems with the entire demarcation issue in the philosophy of science is the word "demarcation," itself. This unfortunate choice of words (by Popper) tends to suggest (connote) that an *unequivocal* judgment can be made in all cases using a single, simple criterion (like "falsifiability"). Borderline cases, such as parapsychology, are then brought forth by relativists as examples that purportedly demonstrate the science/nonscience distinction to be just a societal convention, rather than a societal consensus based on good reasons. The fallacy of such a ploy is pointed out by Grove (1985): most, if not all, genuine and useful categorizational schemata have borderline cases. Should biology dispense with the male/female distinction because some entities share characteristics of both sexes? Should marketing research dispense with consumer goods/industrial goods because some goods at some times can be either? Should advocates of qualitative methods dispense with the trustworthy research/nontrustworthy research distinction just because the truth-content of knowledge-claims cannot be known with certainty? How about rational/irrational? Objective/subjective? Or, as I shall discuss in Chapter 7, truth/falsity?

Should marketing adopt relativism? The preceding analysis should at the very least sound a cautionary note: *Any* philosophy whose underlying premises lead to conclusions so extreme that they are dismissed as "nihilistic" nonsense by the philosophy's own advocates must be considered highly suspect, if not intellectually impoverished. Such a philosophy would seem to poorly serve the needs of researchers of any kind. Nevertheless, Hudson and Ozanne (1988, p. 520) imply that consumer research should strongly consider relativism since it is "based on the premise that every approach to consumer research may have something to offer." Hudson and Ozanne (mistakenly, as Muncy and

Fisk [1987], Vallicella [1984], Margolis [1983], and Hacking [1982] point out) equate the premises of relativism with diversity, tolerance, and pluralism. But relativism, as Feyerabend has so forcefully argued, implies epistemological anarchy, not a tolerant epistemological pluralism. And just as ethical relativism does not imply the tolerance of ethical diversity (Harrison 1982), and just as political anarchy does not imply a tolerant, pluralistic democracy, epistemological anarchy does not imply a tolerant, pluralistic science.

6.2   THE POSITIVISM VERSUS QUALITATIVE METHODS CONTROVERSY

Studies in the social sciences, marketing, management, and consumer research are increasingly using qualitative methods or "interpretivism" as alternative "ways of knowing" (Hudson and Ozanne 1988, Ozanne and Hudson 1989). Examples include naturalistic inquiry (Belk, Wallendorf, and Sherry 1989), humanistic inquiry (Heath 1992; Hirschman 1986), ethnographic methods (Arnould and Wallendorf 1994; Daft and Lewin 1990; Sherry 1983; Van Maanen 1993), historical methods (Fullerton 1987), "enchanted inquiry" (Monieson 1988), critical theory (Denzin 2001; Dholakia 1988; Murray and Ozanne 1991), semiotics (Holbrook and Grayson 1986; Mick 1986), feminism (Bristor and Fischer 1993; Hirschman 1993; Stern 1993), literary explication (Stern 1989a, b), deconstructionism (Stern 1996), existential-phenomenological methods (Thompson, Locander, and Polio 1989), and postmodernism (Firat and Vankatesh 1995; Sherry 1991).

Many, if not most, of the advocates of the various qualitative methods argue for their own preferred qualitative approach by noting that it represents an alternative to the "positivist research" that supposedly dominates marketing, management, and consumer research.[2] Thus, Van Maanen (1993, p. 224) maintains that "Ethnographers are learning to overcome . . . the conceits of positivism" and Putnam (1993, p. 233) states that both "ethnography and critical theory stand in opposition to positivism." Similarly, Daft and Lewin (1990, p. 2) decry the "normal science" paradigm in organizational studies, which they equate with "positivism," and liken to a "straitjacket" that restricts theory and research. More specifically, most advocates of qualitative methods use some version of the "positivism is dead" argument:[3]

1.   Positivist research (i.e., research guided by the tenets of logical positivism) dominates marketing, management, and consumer research.
2.   Positivist research is the same thing as "quantitative research," and is causality seeking, adopts determinism and the machine metaphor, is realist, reifies unobservables, and is functionalist.

3. Positivism has been shown to be dead (or thoroughly discredited) in the philosophy of science.
4. Therefore, all research that is quantitative, causality seeking, and so forth, is also discredited.
5. Therefore, researchers should adopt some form of qualitative or "interpretivist" method.

As to the "positivism is dead argument," not only do some participants contend that their opponents' "criticisms largely reflect misrepresentations and misunderstandings" (Calder and Tybout 1989, p. 205), "misconceptions" (Peter and Olson 1989, p. 25), and "honest misunderstandings" (Anderson 1989, p. 11), but others contend more strongly that the debate is full of "mischaracterizations and caricaturizations" (Hunt 1989a, p. 185) or, even worse, "nastiness and purposeful distortions" (Hirschman 1989, p. 209) and "ridicule" (Pechmann 1990, p. 7). This section's underlying thesis is that these "misses" (misconceptions, misunderstandings, misrepresentations, and mischaracterizations) stem, at least in part, from the fact that much of the debate has been historically ill informed about the origins and fundamental beliefs of a group of philosophers called logical positivists. Therefore, this section shows that the first two premises of the "positivism is dead" argument are false. To show this, I use historical method to illuminate and clarify not only what logical positivism was, but what it was not. The purpose here is not to attack qualitative methods, for I believe such methods have much to offer. (Indeed, this section adopts a qualitative method, that is, historical method.) Rather, my purpose is to use historical method to expose the intellectually impoverished state of the now ritualistic "bashing of positivism" rhetoric and to encourage all qualitative researchers to move beyond (rise above?) such historically uninformed—and, when done knowingly, downright shameful—argumentation. I begin by detailing the misconceptions about logical positivism.[4]

6.2.1   Misconceptions About Positivism

As discussed in detail in Chapter 3, in the 1920s and 1930s, a group of German philosophers in Vienna (hence, Vienna Circle) developed a philosophy—later given the label "logical positivism"—that relied heavily on Machian neopositivism, Humean skepticism, Wittgenstein's *Tractatus Logico-Philosophicus*, and Russell's *Principia Mathematica*. From Mach, the positivists drew their conviction that science should avoid metaphysical concepts and rely exclusively on observables. From Hume, they derived their belief that inductive reasoning is impermissible. For Hume, only the conclusions of deductive logic and the beliefs derived from direct observational experience could be known with certainty. Because, according to "foundationalism," science should restrict itself to knowledge with certainty, inductive reasoning is therefore impermissible. From Wittgenstein, the positivists developed both their famous "verifiability principle" (only statements that can be shown conclusively to be true or false are "cognitively meaningful") and the belief that the objective of philosophical inquiry should be the "critique of language" or "meaning analysis." From Russell, they adopted formal (symbolic) logic as an analytical tool for their meaning analyses.

The objectives of the logical positivists were to (1) help science make sense of the indeterministic nature of quantum mechanics, (2) help science avoid another Newtonian debacle, (3) help draw together or "unify" the various scientific disciplines, and (4) effect a rapprochement between science and the discipline of philosophy. (Under Hegelian idealism in the preceding half-century, philosophy had been, at best, irrelevant to modern science, and, at worst, openly hostile to it.) The positivists were successful in effecting a rapprochement between large portions of the philosophical and scientific communities, and they did explicate and emphasize the commonalities of apparently diverse scientific disciplines. They did, indeed, develop a philosophy that could accommodate a major interpretation of the indeterminism of quantum mechanics (the "Copenhagen view"), and, at least to the present, there has been nothing in science comparable to the Newtonian debacle (Stove 1982, p. 51). However, misconceptions about the logical positivists and their philosophy abound in the current literature. Here, I focus on five major ones: (1) quantitative methods, (2) causality, (3) determinism and the machine metaphor, (4) reality and reification, and (5) functionalism.

Quantitative Methods. Many writers equate "positivism" with "quantitative." For example, "very simply, the logical positivist view of the world is synonymous with the quantitative paradigm" (Deshpandé 1983, p. 102). In like manner, others claim the "opposing research camps" to be the "relevant" researchers versus the "rigorous" researchers, and contend that the latter value the "quantifiable results" of "positive empiricism" (Dholakia 1985, p. 3). Similarly, Belk, Wallendorf, and Sherry (1989, p. 13) state that "we have not called for the development of quantitative measures because the nature and experience of the sacred may be antithetical to such measurement. The ontological and epistemological assumptions of positivist methods are not sympathetic to the mystical and experiential nature of sacredness." Even Wilk (2001, p. 310), who maintains: "There is no particular reason why a positvist or a humanist cannot use any of the whole range of methodologies available," equates "quantitative" with "positivist."

Is the use of quantitative methods the same thing as adopting positivism? The logical positivists and logical empiricists did hold mathematics and statistics in high regard. Given the positivists' view that quantum mechanics is *just* mathematics, they were sympathetic to quantification in science. (In contrast, at least some advocates of qualitative methods not only avoid the use of mathematics and statistics, but, consistent with Hegelian idealism [see section 2.4], at times seem hostile to these tools.) Nonetheless, equating positivism with quantitative methods is ahistorical: "A positivist, *qua* positivist, is not committed to any particular research design. There is nothing in the doctrine of positivism that necessitates a love of statistics or a distaste for case studies" (Phillips 1987, p. 96). The distinctive features of positivism, such as the verifiability principle (see section 3.2), do not mandate quantitative research.

August Comte (1798–1857) and his colleague Saint-Simon (1760–1825), the nineteenth-century originators of the word "positivism" to describe a philosophical position, actually opposed the use of statistics in sociology. For this reason, Comte coined a new word, "sociology," to distance his "positivism" from the statistical emphasis of what was then called "social physics." Moreover, contemporary qualitative researchers could draw upon such positivist writings as those of Brodbeck to buttress their case for qualitative methods: "The qualitative-quantitative dichotomy is spurious. . . . Although quantification has considerable merit, it is neither a necessary not a sufficient condition for science" (Brodbeck 1968, pp. 573–74). In short, one can be a very good positivist and not engage in quantitative research, and one can be a very good quantitative researcher and not be a positivist.

Causality. The marketing, management, and consumer research literatures claim that the search for causal relations or causal explanations figures prominently in "positivistic social science." For example, in delineating "alternative ways of seeking knowledge in consumer research," Hudson and Ozanne (1988, p. 512) state: "The positivists, with their goal of explanation and prediction, place a high priority on identifying causal linkages." Hirschman (1986, pp. 239, 241) contrasts the "positivistic metaphysic" with the "humanistic metaphysic" and claims that the former implies that "elements of reality can be segregated into causes and effects," "first stage causes," "second stage causes," and "third stage causes." Thompson et al. (1989, p. 134) believe that a broad "set of assumptions underlies the use of positivist methods" and that "these assumptions are manifested in many normative methodological prescriptions," including the prescription that "science should uncover causal laws that explain the functioning of phenomena." Ryan and Bristor (1987, p. 193) claim that the "positivistic approach" emphasizes "causal explanation," and Lutz (1989, pp. 4, 7) asserts that "whereas, the Positivist aspires to causal explanation, the Naturalist eschews notions of linear causality." He further notes that "positivist consumer research" will seek "causal explanation" because the assumption of "real causes" is an "axiom" of the "Positivist paradigm." Ozanne and Hudson (1989, p. 3) claim that a "basic assumption" of positivism is that "real causes exist." Anderson (1989, p. 17), in discussing the "implications for positivism and interpretivism" of Wittgenstein's philosophy, asserts that "perhaps the most damaging implication for positivistic psychology is Wittgenstein's acausalism." He then maintains that positivistic research is discredited because, "on a Wittgensteinian construal, there can be no question of invoking a memory as a cause of behavior" (1989, p. 18). Finally, Wallendorf and Belk (1989, p. 74), in developing criteria for assessing trustworthiness in naturalistic consumer research, point out that "triangulation does not always mean that only one interpretation will emerge," and note that, "given the post-Positivist rejection of the assumption of a single causal reality, this is entirely appropriate."

Statements in the marketing, management, and consumer research literatures notwithstanding, it is historically false that research guided by a positivistic philosophy would seek causal explanations or linkages. It is also false that such research would assume that "real" causes or a "single causal reality" exist. Any research guided by positivism would necessarily avoid both the assumption of causality and the search for "real causes." For example, Brodbeck (1962, p. 250) defended Hempel's "thesis of structural symmetry in explanation" (which states that explanation equals prediction and nothing *more*) by derisively noting that Hempel's critics had adopted the "causal idiom" and that the truth content of "statements like 'C is the cause of E' is problematic." Kyburg (1968, p. 236) claimed that causality is in the "realm of metaphysics" and stated that "it is questionable to what extent causality is of scientific interest." Braithwaite (1968, p. 308) asserted that attempting to identify causal laws would be a "thankless task." Finally, in discussing the concept of causal explanations, Hempel (1965b, pp. 353–54) concluded, "It is not clear what precise construal could be given to the notion of factors 'bringing about' a given event, and what reason there would be for denying the status of explanation to all accounts invoking occurrences that temporally succeed the event to be explained."

The positivists rejected causality because they viewed "cause" as an unobservable, metaphysical concept that violated their Humean skepticism. As noted by Ayer (1959, p. 4), "It is indeed remarkable how much of the doctrine that is now thought to be especially characteristic of logical positivism was already stated, or at least foreshadowed, by Hume." For the positivists, following Hume, if a scientist observes that phenomena A and B occur with uniform regularity, there is no way to show deductively anything other than a regularity relationship. In particular, one cannot (and should not) conclude that A *causes* B. Positivism, despite claims to the contrary, does not imply the search for causation.

Determinism and the Machine Metaphor. A third major misconception about "positivistic social science" is that such a science would necessarily be deterministic, machine-like, or mechanistic. Thus, Ozanne and Hudson (1989, pp. 3, 7) contend that a "basic assumption" of the "positivist approach" is that the "nature of social beings" is "deterministic," or, even more strongly, "entirely deterministic." Similarly, Thompson et al. (1989, pp. 134, 137) believe that one of the assumptions that "underlies the use of positivist methods" is the "machine metaphor": "Cartesianism's world view is a mechanistic view in which reality is perceived as a machine-like event determined by forces and constraints." Like the view that positivism implies causality, these views also are ahistorical.

"Determinism" is "the view that every event has a cause. . . . All things in the universe are 'governed' by, or operate in accordance with, causal laws" (Angeles 1981, p. 60). Because of the success of Newtonian mechanics, the philosophy of mechanistic materialism, with its Laplacian, deterministic "machine metaphor," was prominent at the close of the nineteenth century. In tracing the historical origins of logical positivism, Suppe (1977, p. 10) notes that "by the turn of the century, the three main philosophic positions held in the German scientific community were mechanistic materialism, neo-Kantianism, and Machian neo-Positivism. . . . [However,] relativity theory and quantum theory were thought to be incompatible with all three of these philosophies of science." Because the logical positivists were all German-speaking scientists, primarily mathematicians and physicists, they were well aware that quantum mechanics was incompatible with mechanistic materialism, the machine metaphor, and Laplacian determinism. They were well aware of the "breathtaking revolutionary developments simultaneously taking place in mathematical physics and the foundations of mathematics" (Friedman 1999, p. xiii). Indeed, a primary objective of the Vienna Circle was to develop an alternative to such a view. They did so by creating one that replaced the Newtonian machine metaphor with the view that indeterministic, probabilistic prediction was appropriate for science (Carnap 1966).

In short, in light of the fact that the best that could be accomplished with quantum mechanics is probabilistic prediction (the positivist "Copenhagen view"), such an accomplishment must be acceptable for all science. Again, it should be emphasized that only prediction is sought, not "deeper" or causal explanations. Theories and laws, therefore, must be treated solely as calculation instruments for making predictions. Any research motivated by the "positivistic metaphysic" would view as naïvely misguided the belief that ultimate reality, either physical or social, follows the Newtonian/Laplacian "machine metaphor." Stephen Hawking, the prominent physicist and originator of the big-bang theory, specifically acknowledges the debt that his (nonmachine metaphor) position owes to the positivists.

You can say that the use of imaginary time [to explain the origins of the universe] is just a mathematical trick that doesn't tell us anything about reality. . . . But if you take a *positivist* position, as I do, questions about reality don't have any meaning. All one can ask is whether imaginary time is useful in formulating mathematical models that describe what we observe. (Hawking, as quoted in Strong 1990, p. 71; italics added)

Positivism, despite claims to the contrary, does not imply determinism or the machine metaphor.

Reality and Reification. How the positivists viewed the nature of reality (their "ontology") is a fourth confused area in the debate. Hirschman (1986, p. 239) contends that the "humanistic metaphysic" proposes that "human beings construct multiple realities," while the "positivistic metaphysic" believes that "there is a single reality composed of discrete elements." Similarly, Hudson and Ozanne (1988, p. 509; italics added) claim, "The positivists tend to take a *realist* position and assume that a single, objective reality exists independently of what individuals perceive. . . . In contrast, the interpretivists deny that one real world exists; that is, reality is essentially mental and perceived." The concept "reification" also figures prominently in the debate on reality: "Positivists reify subjective states and treat them like objects," according to Hudson and Ozanne (1988, p. 515). In much stronger terms, Monieson (1988, p. 7) claims that "positivistic social science" is pernicious because it "reifies social relations so that they . . . are forged into marketable traits, into commodities." Again, these claims are ahistorical.

In philosophy, the study of ontology asks, "What does 'to be,' 'to exist' mean?" (Angeles 1981, p. 198). Although ontology has been perhaps the most prominent area of philosophical inquiry for millennia, space limitations dictate that the analysis here be restricted to certain fundamental issues regarding idealism, realism, and reification.

As discussed in section 2.4, the philosophical view labeled idealism holds that the material world of tangible objects, such as trees and rocks, does not exist unperceived: "All reality is mental (spiritual, psychical). Matter, the physical, does not exist" (Angeles 1981, p. 120). In direct contrast, realism holds that the world of tangible objects exists unperceived: "Philosophical idealism is . . . opposed to realism and is thus the denial of the common-sense realist view that material things exist independently of being perceived" (Acton 1967, p. 110). "Reification" is inextricably associated with the concept "reality." (Both words have the common Latin root *res*, meaning "thing.") Reification implies treating an abstract concept as having a real existence in the same sense that a thing exists: It is "the fallacy of taking abstractions and regarding them as actual existing entities that are causally efficacious and ontologically prior and superior to their referents" (Angeles 1981, p. 243).

Given that it is a fallacy by definition, "reification" is, customarily, used pejoratively in philosophy to indicate that one has somehow improperly treated an abstraction as having a "thing-like" reality. With the preceding distinctions in mind, we can now investigate the ontology of logical positivism.

Were the positivists realists? If, by "realist," we mean only the minimal position that tangible objects, such as what we call "trees" and "rocks," exist independently of our perception and labeling (i.e., they exist "out there"), then the logical positivists were realists. Recognizing that idealism always degenerates into nihilism, sophistry, and/or solipsism,[5] the positivists embraced a minimal realism called "empirical realism" (Manicas 1987, p. 247). But, when philosophers today refer to their own positions or to science as "realist," they customarily mean something much stronger than the minimal belief that the existence of trees and rocks is independent of human thought.

As discussed in Chapter 5, although operating under the common rubric of "scientific realism," there are almost as many versions of realism today as there are realist philosophers. Nevertheless, all realists, either explicitly or implicitly, reject Humean skepticism with respect to the ontology of scientific theories: "The basic claim made by scientific realism . . . is that the long-term success of a scientific theory gives reason to believe that something like the entities and structure postulated by the theory actually exists" (McMullin 1984, p. 26). Thus, scientific realism contends that the explanatory, predictive, and pragmatic success of a theory provides evidence for the existence of its associated entities, be they observable or unobservable, tangible or intangible, "thing-like" or "nonthing-like." The evidence is not presumed conclusive, in that "success" does not enable us to know with certainty that the entities and structure exist. For example, as discussed in section 5.3.1, the long-term success of viral theory in explaining, predicting, and solving pragmatic problems with respect to diseases provides evidence warranting our belief in the existence of the entity labeled "virus" (a tangible unobservable). Similarly, to the extent that theories in marketing, management, and consumer research incorporating latent constructs, such as "attitude," "intentions," and "beliefs" (intangible unobservables), have been successful in explaining, predicting, and solving pragmatic problems, such evidence provides warrant for believing that these psychological states of consumers and others exist independently of researchers' labeling of them. That is, the psychological states are real.

Did the positivists adopt a realist ontological view? According to how "realism" is most commonly used today in the philosophy of science (i.e., unobservables can exist and are appropriate for theory construction), the positivists were, most definitely, not realists. The positivists, guided by the views of Mach and Hume, viewed unobservables as metaphysical concepts to be strictly avoided. In fact, many philosophers of science actually use positivism's opposition to realism as its major defining characteristic: "A philosophy (of science) [is] positivist if it holds that a scientific explanation must thoroughly eschew appeal to what is in principle beyond experience. . . . By contrast, a realist holds that a valid scientific explanation can appeal to the in principle non-observable" (Manicas 1987, pp. 9–10).

Did the positivists engage in reification? That is, did the positivists improperly treat abstract concepts as having a real existence in the sense that a "thing" has existence? Most assuredly, they did not. Their Humean skepticism and revulsion toward metaphysics led them to insist that theories must contain only observables, that is, labels for "things."[6] In contrast, those scientists and philosophers of science guided by scientific realism, because they contend (on the basis of "success") that some unobservables may actually exist, could, at least *potentially*, be faulted for reification. Therefore, the claim that positivist researchers engage in reification—in the philosophy of science sense of reification—is historically false. Exactly the opposite is true: Researchers adhering strictly to positivism cannot engage in reification.

A second use of "reification" draws on Marxist social philosophy.[7] Marxist philosophers (e.g., Berger and Luckman 1967; Lukacs 1971) castigate contemporary social science on the basis of charges of "reification" and "commoditization." As Belk et al. (1989, p. 24) point out, Marxist philosophers see "a general 'drive to commoditization' in capitalist society." This "commodity fetishism" is uniquely associated with capitalism, Marxists contend, because only in capitalism does the production of commodities dominate society. Such societies necessarily, then, reify social relations. For example, the relationship between two people called "love" becomes nothing more than a commodity, a "thing" to be bought and sold. This reification extends to Western science, particularly sociology, which reifies societal institutions so that they are taken to have the causal power to determine how humans behave. Thus, Western science and Western, democratic societies assume that societal institutions (e.g., corporations, the Roman Catholic Church, and "bourgeois science") have an existence separate from the people that produce them. Futhermore, and important for Marxist theory, individual human beings are assumed in Western science and societies to be powerless to change these "immutable" institutions.

From the Marxist view, then, "positivistic social science" just means "Western science" or "bourgeois science" in toto, and, therefore, it must engage in reification because this is an underlying characteristic of all aspects of Western, democratic societies. Because the objective of Marxist social philosophy is to "liberate the proletariat," from the "false consciousness" that a market economy serves their interests, Marxist philosophers offer the following argument: (1) social science is dominated by positivism, a "dead" philosophy; (2) positivism implies reification; (3) reification is pernicious; therefore, (4) contemporary (bourgeois) social science is not only fundamentally misguided (in adopting a "dead" philosophy), but its reification of social relations is pernicious as well. In marketing, this appears to be Monieson's (1988) argument in favor of his "enchanted inquiry."

Did the positivists engage in reification in its Marxist sense? This seems implausible because, as historians of logical positivism point out, the rhetoric of the positivists had "explicitly Marxist overtones" (Friedman 1999, p. xiii). Indeed, Levin examines this issue and concludes:

> Whether or not positivism contributed to reification in its Marxist sense—which seems doubtful, if only because many positivists were socialists in their political moments—this sense has little to do with any position taken by positivists in the philosophy of science. (Levin 1991, p. 59)

Whether or not contemporary marketing, management, and consumer researchers engage in reification in either its philosophy of science or its Marxist sense is an issue that could be addressed only by a detailed examination of extant research. We can say, however, that any research guided by positivism, because of its focus on "observables," *cannot* engage in reification.

Functionalism. Is functionalist research positivist? Functionalism as a distinctive research method has its origins in cultural anthropology. Although "function" and "functional analysis" are used in a variety of ways (see Hunt 2002a, Chapter 3), functionalism generally seeks to understand a behavior pattern or a sociocultural institution by determining the role it plays in keeping a given system in proper working order or maintaining it as a going concern. Thus, Radcliffe-Brown (1952, p. 179) states that "the *function* of any recurrent activity, such as the punishment of a crime, or a funeral ceremony is the part it plays in the social life as a whole and therefore the contribution it makes to the maintenance of the structural continuity." And Malinowski (1954, p. 132) maintains that "the functional view of culture insists therefore upon the principle that in every type of civilization, every custom, material object, idea, and belief fulfills some vital function, has some task to accomplish, represents an indispensable part within a working whole."

Not only should functionalism not be *equated* with positivist research, but the positivists were sharply critical of functional analysis and the claim that functional explanations constituted a distinctive method. For example, Nagel (1961, p. 527) points out that, although functional or "teleological" analyses are appropriate under certain circumstances in biology, such analyses do not transfer to social systems because "there is nothing comparable in this domain [i.e., society] to the generally acknowledged 'vital functions' of biology as defining attributes of living organisms." Furthermore, "proposed explanations aiming to exhibit the functions of various items in a social system in either maintaining or altering the system have no substantive content, unless the *state* that is allegedly maintained or altered is formulated more precisely than has been customary" (Nagel 1961, p. 530). Therefore, concludes Nagel, "the cognitive worth of functional explanations modeled on teleological explanations in physiology is . . . very dubious" (1961, p. 535).

Similarly, Hempel (1965b, p. 319) analyzes functional explanations and finds them often to be "covert tautologies" because "the vagueness of the qualifying clauses . . . deprives them of the status of definite empirical hypotheses that might be used for explanation or prediction." Hempel analyzes the "law of adaptation to an obvious end" as an example of functionalist laws and concludes that "the 'law' asserts nothing whatever, therefore, and cannot possibly explain any social (or other) phenomena" (1965b, p. 328). More generally, Hempel concludes that "for most of the self-regulatory phenomena that come within the purview of functional analysis, the attribution of purposes is an illegitimate transfer of the concept of purpose from its domain of significant accessibility [in physiology] to a much wider domain, where it is devoid of objective empirical import" (1965b, p. 327). In like manner, Rudner (1966, p. 88) evaluates teleological explanations and concedes that "the term 'purpose' *may* come to figure essentially in some scientific theories and explanations." Nevertheless, when he analyzes actual functionalist explanations in anthropology, he concludes:

> However, not a single one of the myriad claims in the anthropological literature can be accepted without serious qualification. . . . All too frequently these claims [of functional explanations] may be counted as at most containing some more or less accurate *descriptions*, rather than explanations of specific phenomena, couched in or accompanied by a rhetoric that may be mistaken for explanations by the unwary. (Rudner 1966, p. 108)

Even though the positivists did not believe that functional explanations constituted a distinctive type of scientific explanation, and even though they were sharply critical of the actual output of functionalist research, they did not claim that functionalism was devoid of merit. Rather, the positivists believed that whatever merit functionalism had was to be found in the "context of discovery" (see Hunt 2002a, section 1.5). That is, adopting a "functionalist orientation" or "functionalist set" in approaching a research project might have heuristic value in suggesting either relationships among social phenomena or hypotheses to be tested. On the subject of scientific explanation, however, which falls into the context of justification, the positivists believed that functionalism had nothing of value to contribute. Indeed, as previously noted, they believed it was just "rhetoric that may be mistaken for explanations by the unwary" (Rudner 1966, p. 108). Functionalism, therefore, is not positivistic. If marketing, management, and consumer research are dominated by functionalism—a big if, if "functionalism" is construed in its anthropological sense (see Nagel 1961, pp. 522–34)—such inquiry isn't positivist.

6.2.2   On Antipositivism: For Reason

In a section entitled "Rampant Antipositivism," Phillips (1987, p. 94) reviews the social science literature and concludes that "there have been many exaggerated claims about the evils of positivism . . . [and] many factual errors are made when researchers refer to [it]." As we have seen, there have been similar errors in the marketing, management, and consumer-research literatures. Antipositivist claims to the contrary, "positivism" does not equal "quantitative." Furthermore, the positivists did not search for causal explanations or causal linkages; they did not adopt, nor hold that science should adopt, determinism or the machine metaphor; they did not have a realist view with respect to scientific theories; they could not possibly have been guilty of reification; and they did not argue for functionalist explanations. Phillips (1987, p. 44) also compares the views of social science antipositivists with the actual positions of the positivists and concludes that "some of the most boisterous celebrants at positivism's wake are actually more positivistic than they realize, or have more in common with the positivists than they would care to admit." As we shall see, a similar situation prevails in the marketing, management, and consumer-research literatures.

Positivism Versus Contemporary Antipositivism.[8] Although often reaching their positions by different routes, those who advocate alternatives to "positivistic social science" actually share many views with their supposed antagonists. First, the positivists explicitly embraced Humean skepticism, and, similarly, many antipositivists are strongly influenced by it (see, e.g., Anderson 1983, p. 19; Anderson 1989, p. 11; Hudson and Ozanne 1988, p. 515). Even those who (quite correctly) believe that "the term positivist is used much too loosely to be descriptive of any approach" (Calder and Tybout 1989, p. 200) embrace Humean skepticism. For example, in explaining why the "comparative" approach is superior to the "confirmatory" approach in testing theories, Sternthal, Tybout, and Calder (1987, p. 124) put forth the standard Humean position that it is impermissible to reason inductively from the successful predictions of a theory to its truth-content: "The goal of the confirmatory approach cannot be realized because theories cannot be proven." Similarly, Calder and Tybout (1987, p. 137) argue in favor of "sophisticated falsificationist methodology" by contrasting their view with the "common view of science . . . that empirical data are used to accumulate evidence for a theory until it is proven. This view of science is, of course, unacceptable . . . [because, in part] inductive proof is logically impossible."[9]

Second, antipositivist methodology shares a striking similarity with that of the positivists in the use of meaning analysis. The positivists adopted the tool of formal logic and the goal of meaning analysis to clarify the language employed in the scientific community. Contemporary antipositivists, often under the rubric of "interpretivism," explore how the language of consumers consists of "shared meanings" (Ozanne and Hudson 1989, p. 2). As Hirschman (1989, p. ix) puts it, "The best definition I have encountered of interpretive consumer research is that presented recently by Holbrook and O'Shaughnessey (1988). They view interpretation as 'the critical analysis of a text for the purpose of determining its single or multiple meaning(s).'"

The similarities notwithstanding, contemporary antipositivists diverge from positivism on several issues. Because the positivists were sympathetic toward both philosophy and science as institutions, a major part of their program was to effect a rapprochement between them. In contrast, some contemporary antipositivists are openly hostile to the institution of science, relying on—as detailed in Chapter 4—the views of such bitterly antiscience authors as Feyerabend, who, as will be recalled, contends that "Western science has now infected the whole world like a contagious disease" (Feyerabend 1987, p. 297). In discussing the history of science, Firat (1989, pp. 95–96) asks, "Is science an institution we want to preserve?" He concludes that it may be desirable to "erase the accumulation of scientific knowledge" because "science is a political institution [that] has lost its relevance for the solution of present human problems. Thus, the scientific establishment has become antichange and reactionary."[10] Not only would Firat's assessment of science differ from that of the positivists, the "book burning" implicit in "erasing the accumulation of scientific knowledge" would have been repugnant to them (as well as to most scholars).

A final difference between positivism and contemporary antipositivism centers on two different meanings of "meaning analysis." The English word "meaning" (and, therefore, "meaning analysis") suffers from systematic ambiguity. It can refer to the *communicative* characteristics of a word, phrase, or "text," and, thus "meaning analysis" can imply the exploration of how such expressions serve this communicative role. However, "meaning" is also used in an evaluative sense, referring to something's importance, value, or significance. The positivists recognized this systematic ambiguity and restricted their meaning analyses to communicative meaning (Rudner 1966, pp. 75–83). Similarly, as previously mentioned, those referring to their research as "interpretivist" often define their area of inquiry as exploring communicative meaning, as do those using the label "semiotics": "[Semioticians] investigate the sign systems or codes essential to all types of communication for the latent rules that facilitate sign production and interpretive responses" (Mick 1986, p. 197). However, contemporary antipositivists, in contrast to the positivists, have not, in general, focused their meaning analyses on communicative meaning. In fact, most of their published works have actually focused on *evaluational* meaning. The most obvious example is the extensive work of Belk et al., which explores how things become either "sacred" or "profane," and they, thereby, acquire "personal meaningfulness" (Beck et al. 1989, p. 31), "transcendent meaning in their lives" (p. 32), or "significance" (p. 32) through a "process of meaning investment and divestment" (p. 2).

6.2.3   Paradigm Dominance in Marketing, Management, and Consumer Research

The preceding enables us to reexamine premises 1 and 2 in the "positivism is dead" argument. To this point, our analysis reveals not only that "positivism" does not imply "quantitative," but also: (1) Mesmerized as they were by Humean skepticism, the positivists considered the concept "cause" to be metaphysical and (at best) superfluous to science. (2) Absorbed as they were with quantum mechanics, they did not contend that science should be deterministic or adopt the machine metaphor. (3) Obsessed as they were with restricting scientific theories to nonmetaphysical observables, the positivists did not adopt a "realist view" with respect to scientific theories, and (4) could not possibly have been guilty of reification. Therefore, premise 2 is false. Furthermore, if antipositivist writers are correct that *marketing*, *management*, and *consumer research* are dominated by the search for causality, by the machine metaphor, by reification, and by the realist view with respect to unobservables, then such research is "antipositivist," or, more accurately, "nonpositivist."[11] Thus, premise 1 is also false. In conclusion, the argument underlying much of the debate has been woefully uninformed: Contemporary marketing, management, social science, and consumer research are neither motivated by the "positivistic metaphysic" nor, most assuredly, "dominated by logical positivism."

6.2.4   The Dominance of Positivism: A Postmodern View

Firat discusses the major themes of "postmodern culture," and, drawing on the Marxist social philosophy of Baudrillard, advocates adopting "hyperreality":

> A second major reason for the attacks on science is clarified in the postmodernist critique and analysis of culture. . . . Currently, the most powerful articulator of this recognition [that social reality is produced or constructed] in the postmodernist lit-

> erature seems to be Baudrillard. . . . His theory articulates the creation of the culture of "hyperreality," a reality that is constructed based on signifiers that become separated from their original referents and "free floating," [to] which, then, are attached new meanings. Thus, new symbols are created as well as a new reality independent of the original referents or foundations. Hyperreality is produced when these new symbols are accepted as real and so acted upon by the social actors. (Firat 1989, p. 94)

On the basis of postmodernism, then, one might attempt to sanction the use of the term "positivism" stripped from its "original referents" (what the positivists actually believed in and advocated) and use it to refer to any set of beliefs or methods one chooses. The only restraint is rhetorical success, that is, whether this new "constructed reality" is "accepted as real and so acted upon by the social actors." Thus construed, "positivism" becomes a pejorative term of rhetorical abuse that can effectively stifle discussion and critique. If one's work is subjected to critical evaluation, rather than defending the research on its merits, one can shut down all discussion by retorting: "You're just using outmoded positivistic criteria to evaluate my post-positivistic, postmodern study." Phillips (1987, p. 94) reviews the debate in the social sciences and concludes that many writers do appear to be socially constructing a hyperreality: "Without suggesting that those who make the errors are deliberately dishonest, it seems as if the word 'positivism' arouses such negative feelings that it is often used in a blanket way to condemn any position at all that the writer disagrees with, irrespective of how positivistic that position really is." Likewise, Friedman (1999, p. xiii) finds logical positivism to be, essentially, an "intellectual scapegoat" for uninformed scholars.

A major problem with the use of "positivism" as a socially constructed hyperreality dominating marketing, management, social science, and consumer research is that it violates the integrity of history. Lavin and Archdeacon (1989, p. 62) review the advantages of historical method and discuss its two "central imperatives": "Respect the integrity of the past and call attention to what was unique about it." No one disputes that the positivists were real people in an identifiable historical period and that they shared some common views. One may argue that some of their views were correct and others incorrect, or some well reasoned and others poorly thought out. One may further argue that some of the consequences of positivism were good for science and society and others were bad for both. Nevertheless, historical integrity and respect for those who can no longer speak for themselves obligate us (at the very least) to criticize the positivists for the beliefs they actually held and the views they actually espoused.

The article by Van Eijkelenburg (1995) represents an example of the contemporary postmodernist approach. He reviews the version of the "positivism is dead" argument in Hunt (1994c) and concludes that he sees "no reason to accept this criticism" (Van Eijkelenburg 1995, p. 209) of the argument because "it does not make sense . . . to condemn a specific usage of words by arguing that it does not conform to the meaning originally attached to the term" (1995, p. 209). As I replied in Hunt (1995a), I regret that Van Eijkelenburg "sees no reason" to maintain the integrity of history with respect to "positivism." Indeed, I see at least three reasons.

First, the purpose of using language is to communicate with others. Although "positive" is a common English word, the word "positivism" is a term of art from philosophy, just as "Marxism" and "Nazism" are terms of art from political economy. If scholars use the term positivism in methodological discussions with the idiosyncratic disclaimer, "of course, when I use 'positivism' I do not refer at all to the positions of the logical positivists or logical empiricists," they jeopardize communication—just as would discussions that use the terms Marxism or Nazism followed by "of course by 'Marxism' I do not refer to its traditional sense related to a certain nineteenth-century economist" or "by 'Nazism' I do not refer to its traditional sense related to certain Germans during the 1920s, 1930s, and 1940s." Communication, I argue, is important in academic discourse. Is it, or should it not be, in postmodernist discourse?

Second, if one chooses to use the term positivist idiosyncratically and then alerts readers that one is doing so with a disclaimer, then readers will know that the "positivism is dead" argument for qualitative methods has lost all probative force. Note carefully that the persuasiveness of the argument depends crucially on Premise 3 (i.e., positivism in its traditional, philosophical sense is dead or discredited). Probative force, I argue, is important in academic discourse. Is it, or should it not be, in postmodernist discourse?

Third, if writers know that Premise 2 is false in the argument (i.e., that positivism is not the same thing as quantitative methods, and so forth), and if at the same time they know that their readers will *not* know this fact, then it is sophistry—if not prevarication—to use the "positivism is dead" argument without the idiosyncratic disclaimer. Although sophistry and prevarication are widely practiced in many areas of human interaction, I argue that they are inappropriate in academic discourse. Are they not, or should they not be, unacceptable in postmodernist discourse?

6.2.5   Logical Empiricism as the Dominant Paradigm

If logical positivism is not the dominant paradigm in marketing, management, social science, and consumer research, what is? Some might be tempted to conclude that, if not logical positivism, then surely logical empiricism must dominate such research. However, there is as much confusion in the philosophy debates about logical empiricism as there is about logical positivism.

Confusions About Logical Empiricism. Arndt (1985, p. 199) claims that, in logical empiricism, "marketing systems are viewed as being equilibrium-seeking," and that "the real world is considered essentially as harmonious and conflict-free in the long run." As is abundantly clear from section 3.3, there is nothing in logical empiricism that implies that marketing systems are necessarily "equilibrium-seeking." Similarly, there is nothing in logical empiricism that implies that the world must be considered "essentially as harmonious and conflict-free." It is true that some researchers choose to treat marketing systems as equilibrium-seeking, and it is true that some researchers either choose to treat the world as conflict-free or choose not to have conflict as a central theme of their research. (Indeed, relationship marketing focuses on cooperation, rather than conflict [Berry and Parasuraman 1991; Hunt and Morgan 1994; Morgan and Hunt 1994; Sheth and Parvatiyar 1995].) However, there is nothing in the nature of logical empiricism that suggests, implies, demands, or impels researchers to deemphasize conflict.

Arndt (1985, p. 203) also claims that the influence of logical empiricism has resulted in marketing being an "applied discipline concerned with the improvement of management practice and research methodology." However logical empiricism's emphasis was on the positive, that is, "what is." In contrast, marketing management's emphasis is on the normative, that is, what one "ought to do." Therefore, it is uninformed, if not absurd, to claim that logical empiricism leads to an emphasis on the "improvement of management practice."

Contrasted with Arndt (1985), consider Dholakia's (1988, p. 13) claim that the emphasis on marketing management has actually *prevented* the discipline from being dominated by logical empiricism. As to this claim, readers should note that it is obviously the case that the marketing discipline has historically been interested in problems concerning the improvement of marketing management. Furthermore, a good case can be made that the marketing discipline should be more concerned with societal, or "macro" issues concerning marketing. Moreover, as discussed in Hunt (2002a, Chapter 1), an exclusive focus on marketing management (the profit/micro/normative dimensions in the "three dichotomies model") may retard the development of theories that explain and predict marketing phenomena (the profit/micro/positive dimensions). Thus, to focus exclusively on marketing *management* may retard the growth of marketing *science*. Therefore, Dholakia's claim that marketing's emphasis on managerial issues has thwarted the dominance of logical empiricism makes sense *only* if one equates "logical empiricism" with "science." However, such an equating is not just false, but it is also an equating that is specifically denied by Dholakia and other antipositivists, relativists, and postmodernists. Such arguments, therefore, are incoherent.

As another example of a common error concerning logical empiricism, Anderson (1983, p. 19) states: "logical empiricism is characterized by the inductive statistical method. On this view, science begins with observation, and its theories are ultimately justified by the accumulation of further observations." As an illustration, Anderson cites and discusses the well-known PIMS studies. Although it is true that empirical testing and observation play significant roles in logical empiricism, it is not true that logical empiricism implies "the inductive statistical method," where "science begins with observation." That is, whereas the classical empiricism of Bacon (see section 2.3.1) viewed science as inducing generalizations from observations, logical empiricism (because it separated the context of discovery from the context of justification) did not propose a method for generating hypotheses, laws, and theories. Rather, it focused exclusively on the justification of hypotheses, laws, and theories.

Does Logical Empiricism Dominate? As discussed in section 3.3, logical empiricism was a research program that emerged directly from the logical positivist movement. Indeed, prominent logical empiricists, such as Carnap and Feigl, had themselves been logical positivists. The major characteristic distinguishing logical empiricism from logical positivism was the substitution of the "testability principle" for the "verifiability principle." Because they accepted Humean skepticism with respect to induction, the positivists came to realize that the generalized nature of scientific laws rendered them "unverifiable," that is, incapable of being proved conclusively true. Therefore, Carnap (1936) replaced the verifiability principle with the "testability principle," which requires that all statements must be observationally "testable" to be "cognitively meaningful" (for them to have done otherwise would have implied the absurd claim that scientific laws were meaningless). However, what is most important for our purposes here is that the logical empiricists continued to embrace Humean skepticism, continued to reject "realism" with regard to theories, laws, and explanations, and continued to consider "causality" to be a metaphysical concept that (at best) was superfluous to science. Therefore, on the very same grounds as for logical positivism, we may conclude with great assurance that logical empiricism does not dominate marketing, management, social science, and consumer research.

The issue of the dominant paradigm in marketing, management, and consumer research can be addressed best by first returning to the work of Kuhn (see section 4.2.1), whose *Structure of Scientific Revolutions* (1962) originated the view that each mature science has a dominant paradigm, which consists of (1) a knowledge content (i.e., theories, laws, concepts, symbolic generalizations, and "exemplars"), (2) a methodology (i.e., procedures by which knowledge is to be generated), and (3) an epistemology (i.e., criteria for evaluating knowledge-claims). The construct "dominant paradigm" assisted Kuhn in his efforts to explain, among other things, why "mature" sciences progressed and others (e.g., the social sciences) did not. For Kuhn, each "mature" science has a dominant paradigm, and, rather than engage in endless, unproductive disputation on methodological and epistemological issues, researchers spend their time making progress by fleshing the dominant paradigm out through "puzzle solving."

Like almost all the major views in *Structure*, that of the "dominant paradigm" or *Weltanschauung* has been totally discredited. For example, Laudan (1977, pp. 74, 151) reviews the history of science and concludes, "Virtually every major period in the history of science is characterized both by the coexistence of numerous competing paradigms, with none exerting hegemony over the field, and by the persistent and continuous manner in which the foundational assumptions of every paradigm are debated within the scientific community. . . . Kuhn can point to no major science in which paradigm monopoly has been the rule, nor in which foundational debate has been absent."

If paradigm dominance has been found to be absent in the historical development of even mature sciences, one would hardly expect to find a dominant paradigm in marketing, management, and consumer research, areas of inquiry whose systematic study is only several decades old. Indeed, as pointed out by numerous observers, the history of marketing, management, and consumer research is best characterized by the open, often indiscriminate, borrowing of disparate methods and theories from everywhere.

6.2.6   Conclusion: For Reason

Because premises 1 and 2 in the "positivism is dead" argument are false, the "standard argument" (Hunt 2002a) for qualitative methods is false. It is no wonder, then, that participants in the philosophy debates have complained of "misses" (i.e., misconceptions, misunderstandings, misrepresentations, and mischaracterizations). The rhetoric of positivism bashing, so common in discussions justifying qualitative studies, actually degenerates into nothing more than simply the bashing of contemporary marketing, management, and consumer research. Indeed, the term "positivism" in the social science literature has become just a convenient term of abuse. As philosophers of science have noted, this way of using "positivism":

> is not a mere terminological confusion. It is so tendentiously inaccurate that *positivist* . . . becomes a term of abuse. . . . In reality, logical positivism was the most self-critical movement in the history of philosophy. Every major objection to positivism was proposed by positivists themselves or associates at work on problems set by positivism, all in the scientific spirit of seeking truth. It is particularly unfortunate

> that the technical failure of particular positivist doctrines is so often used . . . to cover an attack on clarity and science itself. (Levin 1991, p. 63–64)

Because it is so well known that positivism's technical failures have resulted in its being discredited or even "dead" in the philosophy of science, attacking contemporary marketing, management, and consumer research by labeling it "positivist" has, no doubt, been rhetorically successful in gaining converts to qualitative research. But there is a price to pay when academic communities justify historically false argumentation on the grounds of rhetorical success.

If qualitative researchers knowingly (and *knowingly* is key here) justify their methods by using rhetoric that violates the integrity of the past and constitutes sophistry or prevarication, this prompts *users* of qualitative research to wonder: Are the results reported in qualitative studies *also* untrustworthy? Academic integrity is worth safeguarding. Words have meaning. Rhetoric has consequences. Communities of academic researchers have fiduciary responsibilities to their colleagues, to other academics, to students, and to society at large. The price paid for historically false rhetoric is the potential destruction of trust, both (1) among academics and (2) between academics and each of their client publics. This price, I suggest, is too high—it is also a price that it is unnecessary to pay.

The rhetoric of positivism bashing is, I argue, unnecessary for justifying qualitative methods. That is, it is unnecessary for qualitative researchers to discredit quantitative research in order to justify their own studies. Disciplinary change does not require the kinds of techniques associated with Kuhnian revolutions, that is, destroying one's (perceived) adversary. Qualitative research can "stand on its own two feet." Furthermore, we should recall that a Kuhnian *rival* paradigm is one—like Copernicus vs. Ptolemy—that makes conflicting knowledge-claims, and, therefore, requires *choice*. In this philosophy of science sense of "rival," qualitative and quantitative methods are not even rivals. They are not, or at least should not be, *adversaries*. Rather, sometimes qualitative studies add to what we know from quantitative research and sometimes it is just the reverse. Therefore, rather than *rivals*, qualitative studies *complement* quantitative research.

Is it not time for recognizing the complementarity of qualitative and quantitative methods? Is it not time for recognizing our responsibility for producing trustworthy knowledge, whether it be from qualitative *or* qualitative methods? Is it not time for advocates of both qualitative and quantitative methods to move on? Is it not time for a truce between qualitative and quantitative researchers, or, at the minimum, a rhetorical "cease fire?" I argue for a "yes" on all these questions.

QUESTIONS FOR ANALYSIS AND DISCUSSION

1. In contrast to Anderson (1983), who holds that logical empiricism is characterized by the "inductive statistical method," Arndt (1985) contended that the opposite was true: "A corollary of this view [empiricism] is that the hypothetico-deductive method of the unified science is elevated into being the only acceptable scientific approach" (1985, p. 9). Arndt also stated that logical empiricism assumes: "Marketing relations have a concrete, real existence and systemic character producing regularities in marketing behavior." Furthermore, "marketing systems are viewed as being equilibrium-seeking," and "the real world is considered essentially as conflict-free" (1985, p. 12). Evaluate these descriptions of logical empiricism. If you conclude that Arndt is not talking about logical empiricism, then what is he talking about? What set of circumstances has resulted in Arndt making these kinds of assertions?

2. "Many critics claim to attack positivistic science. However, because most of science is not 'positivistic' in any true sense of the term, such critics are actually attacking science itself." Evaluate this thesis.

3. Paul Meehl, at a conference on social science, states the following:

    > It was agreed that logical positivism and strict operationism won't wash . . . the last remaining defender of anything like logical positivism was Gustav Bergman, who ceased to do so by the late 1940s. Why, then the continued attack on logical positivism and its American behaviorists' near-synonym 'operationalism'? My answer to this is unsettling but, I think, correct. Our conference on social science came about partly because of widespread dissatisfaction about the state of the art, and we have always been more introspective methodologically than the physicists and biologists, who engage in this kind of thing only under revolutionary circumstances. My perhaps cynical diagnosis is that one reason the conference members spent needless time repeating that logical positivism and simplistic operationalism are incorrect views of scientific knowledge is that this relieves scientific guilt feelings or inferiority feelings about our disciplines. It is as if somebody said, 'Well, maybe clinical psychology isn't up to the standards of historical geology or medical genetics, let alone theoretical physics; but we need not be so fussy about our concepts and empirical support for them because logical positivism, which was so stringent on that score, is a nefarious doctrine and we are no longer bound by it.' (Meehl, in Shweder and Fiske 1986, pp. 315–16)

    Evaluate the thesis of Meehl. To what extent does it, or does it not apply to marketing?

4. What is the most appropriate philosophy to guide marketing? Marketing science? Why?

5. J. Paul Peter contends: "While logical positivism is the dominant

philosophical force in consumer research, it has been eschewed by philosophers since the late 1960's. Evaluate. In what way or ways has it been eschewed?

NOTES

1. Hunt (1976a, b) assumed that "causal structures" was implied by "uniformities and regularities." I now make "causal structures" explicit, to avoid ambiguity.

2. The belief that contemporary social science, marketing, and consumer research are dominated by positivism is a consensus position (Anderson 1986, p. 155; Arndt 1985, p. 11; Belk, Sherry, and Wallendorf 1988, p. 467; Deshpandé 1983, p. 101; Firat 1989, p. 93; Hirschman 1986, p. 237; Hirschman 1989, p. 209; Holbrook, Bell, and Grayson 1989, p. 35; Holbrook and O'Shaughnessy 1988, p. 402; Hudson and Ozanne 1988, p. 508; Lavin and Archdeacon 1989, p. 60; Lutz 1989, p. 3; Mick 1986, p. 207; Ozanne and Hudson 1989, p. 1; Peter and Olson 1983, pp. 1, 18; Thompson et al. 1989, p. 134; Venkatesh 1989, p. 101).

3. See also the "standard argument" discussion in Hunt (1994b, 2002a, section 2.3.3).

4. The arguments in this section follow those developed in Hunt (1989a, b, 1991a, b, 1994b, c, 1995a).

5. Nihilism is "the theory that nothing is knowable. All knowledge is illusory, worthless, meaningless, relative, and insignificant." Sophistry holds that "victory in argumentation at whatever cost, outwitting opponents, is the sole aim of disputation, no matter how bad the argument." Solipsism is "the theory that no reality exists other than one's self" (Angeles 1981, pp. 188, 265, 266).

6. For the positivists, as discussed in sections 3.2 and 3.3, theories could also contain "theoretical terms," but all such terms must be explicitly and completely definable through "correspondence rules" to "observables." Therefore, a "theoretical term" is a shorthand way of talking about a collection of observable terms and *nothing more*. Most especially, a theoretical term does not refer to anything unobservable.

7. I am indebted to Michael E. Levin of the Department of Philosophy, City College, City University of New York, for pointing out the Marxist view of reification. I hasten to add, however, that Levin does not subscribe to this view.

8. For the limited purpose of this section, "antipositivist" seems a more appropriate label than either "qualitative" or "interpretivist." For example, many writers believe that "interpretivism" does not properly characterize their views. They rightly point out that all research necessarily involves interpretation. The fundamental issue is whether all research is *just* interpretation. Those (mis)labeled as "positivist" insist that their inquiry touches base with a reality that is outside their paradigm or theory. Antipositivists at times seem to claim that all research, including by implication their own, is linguistically encapsulated and paradigm bounded. That is, it is *just* interpretation, nothing else.

9. For a discussion of the implications using "proof" as a criterion for "acceptable" science, see sections 3.4 and 5.1.

10. Here, Firat is clearly referring to all science, not just social science, or, even more narrowly, "positivistic" social science.

11. For the record, I believe that causality and the realist view with respect to unobservables are prominent—but not dominant—in social science research. I reject the charges of determinism, the adoption of the machine metaphor, and reification.

7 ON TRUTH AND MARKETING RESEARCH

A general respect for truth is all that is needed for society to be free.

—Michael Polanyi

Consistent with the views of the sixteenth- and seventeenth-century founders of modern science, all the major schools of thought in philosophy of science in the first six decades of the twentieth century held the pursuit of truth in high regard, including the classical realism of Moore and Russell, the pragmaticism of Peirce, the logical positivism of Schlick and Neurath, the logical empiricism of Hempel and Nagel, and the critical rationalism (falsificationism) of Popper. Though differing greatly in numerous respects, all these philosophical "isms" held that it is possible for science to develop genuine knowledge, or truth, about the world. As detailed in Chapter 4, this "traditional image of science" was challenged dramatically in 1962 by Kuhn's *Structure of Scientific Revolutions*. In *Structure*, Kuhn came to the same conclusion about truth as did Protagoras in his debate with Socrates (see section 2.1.3) some twenty-five centuries earlier:

> One often hears that successive theories grow ever closer to, or approximate more and more closely to, the truth. . . . There is, I think, no theory-independent way to reconstruct phrases like "really there"; the notion of a match between the ontology of a theory and its "real" counterpart in nature seems to me illusive in principle. (Kuhn 1970b, p. 206)

Relying heavily on the works of Kuhn and Feyerabend, advocates of relativism and postmodernism in marketing, management, social science, and consumer research have raised significant issues regarding the role of truth as either an objective or a regulative ideal in marketing research. This chapter analyzes the "truth controversy." It argues *against* the view that truth should be abandoned. It argues *for* the view that truth is an important objective and/ or regulative ideal.

Prior to the advent of relativism (and approaches such as postmodernism), truth was considered to be an overriding, central goal of marketing theory and research. For example:

> When confronted with any theory, ask the basic question: *Is the theory true?* Less succinctly, to what extent is the theory isomorphic with reality? Is the real world actually constructed as the theory suggests, or is it not? (Hunt 1976a, p. 130; italics in original)

The traditional view has been derided as a "fairytale" version of research that is "outdated" (Peter and Olson 1983, pp. 122–23). The fairytale version, it is argued, should be replaced by relativistic/constructionist truth, in which, "Truth is a subjective evaluation that cannot be properly inferred outside of the context provided by the theory" (Peter and Olson 1983, p. 119). In contrast, rather than arguing that relativistic truth should just replace the traditional view, advocates of "critical relativism" disdain any role at all for truth. Indeed, they urge its abandonment: "I have made it quite clear that 'truth' plays no role in the ontology of critical relativism" (Anderson 1988a, p. 134). Therefore, "the foregoing has demonstrated that 'truth' is an inappropriate objective for science, and that consumer research will do well to abandon such a quixotic idea" (Anderson 1988b, p. 405).

Should "relativistic truth" be accepted? Is the pursuit of truth an inappropriate goal for marketing theory and research? Does critical relativism, with its abandonment of truth, provide the most appropriate philosophical foundations for marketing theory and research? This chapter explores these questions by (1) examining the nature of truth, (2) discussing the scientific realist approach to truth, (3) evaluating the argument for relativistic truth, (4) exploring whether truth should be abandoned in marketing theory and research, (5) showing how those opposing truth in marketing commit the "philosophers' fallacy," (6) discussing the implications of the differences between TRUTH and truth, (7) exploring the relationships among truth, reality relativism, and idealism, and (8) arguing for truth on the basis of trust.[1]

7.1 THE NATURE OF TRUTH

In viewing marketing science as a truth-seeking enterprise, we conceptualize *truth* as not an entity, but an *attribute*. It is an attribute of both beliefs and linguistic expressions. For example, it is an attribute of such linguistic expressions as those denoted by the labels "theories," "laws," "hypotheses," and "propositions." As introduced in section 3.6.1, the correspondence theory of truth provides that the truth-content of an expression is the extent to which *what* the expression refers *to* does, in fact, correspond with reality. Although versions of the correspondence theory of truth can be traced to Aristotle (Agazzi 1989), the defense of correspondence theory has come to be associated closely with its articulation in formal logic by Tarski (1956). Using Tarski's famous example, the sentence "snow is white" is true iff (if and only if) *snow is white*. In this Tarskian "biconditional," what is within quotes refers to a linguistic expression, and what is italicized refers to an aspect of reality that is independent of the language used to form the linguistic expression. That is, "A statement (proposition, belief, . . .) is true if and only if what the statement says to be the case actually is the case" (Alston 1996, p. 6).

Briefly, as interpreted by scientific realism, the correspondence theory of truth holds that an assertion such as "gas flames are hot" is true if there is in fact something like a real entity corresponding to "gas flames" that has the corresponding attribute, "hot." In contrast, the coherence theory of truth holds that an assertion is true if it follows from, is consistent with, or coheres with another statement or system of statements that is believed to be true. That is, because "all flames are hot" is true, so is "gas flames are hot." Many relativist and postmodernist writers adopt what is called the "consensus theory of truth" (e.g., Lincoln and Guba 1985), which holds that there can be no objective criterion of truth. If the consensus of a group of people is that an assertion is true, then it is true. For example, if a group believes that gas flames are not hot, then it is true that they are not hot, and nothing more can be said on the subject. That is, there is no objective truth to any assertion independent of group beliefs.

A marketing example from Hunt (1992a) illustrates the correspondence theory of truth. Suppose a marketer wants to test two, genuinely rival, explanatory theories (i.e., two theories having conflicting knowledge claims). Suppose further that both theories entail the concept "intentions to buy," which is measured on a scale from "1" equals "definitely will not purchase" to "10" equals "definitely will purchase." After being asked to mark the box that "best describes your beliefs," a subject puts a checkmark on the questionnaire. The coder of the questionnaire then reports, "The subject checked the ninth box." For the correspondence theory of truth, "The subject checked the ninth box" linguistic expression is true if and only if the subject actually checked the ninth box. Furthermore, when the example is interpreted by scientific realism, the subject checking box 9 may (if our measurement theory is good) be an indicator (albeit, a fallible indicator) of the subject's actual intentions to buy.

7.2 TRUTH AND SCIENTIFIC REALISM

Scientific realism maintains that the long-run success of a theory gives reason to believe that something like the entities and structure postulated by the theory

Figure 7.1   **Truth and Scientific Realism: Successes, Failures, and the External World**

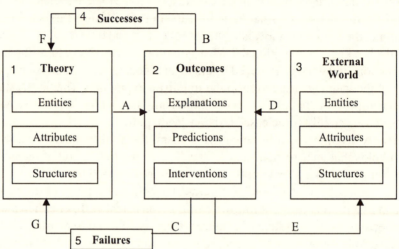

Source: Hunt (2002b). Reprinted by permission of the author.

actually exists (see section 5.3.1). Figure 7.1 is a model that explicates the meaning of "theory *X* is true" in the scientific realist approach to science. As an example of how to apply the model, we use the smallpox theory developed in some detail in section 5.3.1.

Assume that box 1 in Figure 7.1 contains the linguistic expression denoted by "smallpox theory." The theory posits entities (e.g., the smallpox and cowpox viruses), attributes of entities (e.g., the smallpox virus requires human hosts), and structures (e.g., the disease called "cowpox" results from the cowpox virus and having cowpox causes the body to produce antibodies that can successfully attack the smallpox virus). The theory posits that the entities, attributes, and structures in box 1 exist in the world external to the theory (i.e., box 3). That is, the theory in box 1 is *about* the world in box 3.

Path A, from box 1 to 2, shows that the theory has certain implications. That is, the theory can be used to explain some phenomena (e.g., "country girls" tend not to get smallpox), predict some phenomena (e.g., vaccinating people with the cowpox virus will produce antibodies that can attack the smallpox virus and prevent smallpox), and interventions (e.g., a massive vaccination program can eradicate smallpox).

Paths B and C show that the theory's outcomes are sometimes successful (box 4) and sometimes not (box 5). For example, as to explanations, often the "country girls" did not get smallpox, but sometimes they did. As to predictions, often vaccinated people did not get smallpox, but sometimes they did.

As to interventions, the massive vaccination program (appears to have) eradicated the (naturally occurring) disease of smallpox. Both the successes and failures are impacted by the entities, attributes, and structures existing in the external world (box 3), as shown by path D. In turn, the outcomes in box 2 impact (by way of path E) the entities, attributes, and structures in box 3 (e.g., humans no longer are hosts for the smallpox virus).

What, then, is the import of a high or low proportion of successes (box 4), and a low or high proportion of failures (box 5)? Paths F and G represent inferences from a theory's successes and failures to the truth-content and falsity-content of a theory. For scientific realism, a high proportion of successes, relative to failures, gives reason to believe that something like the entities, attributes, and structures posited by the theory in box 1 (e.g., smallpox theory) actually exist in the world external to the theory (i.e., they exist in box 3). That is, we infer that something like the theory posited in box 1 is likely true. From a high proportion of failures, relative to successes, we infer that something like the theory is likely false. In a sense, paths F and G depict a "weighing" of evidence, as Bunge (1967, p. 319) puts it.

7.2.1   Not an Entity

Note that truth is an attribute of beliefs and linguistic expressions, it is not an entity in the external world (i.e., truth is not in box 3 in Figure 7.1). Therefore, *truth* is not an entity that researchers do (or can) study. To treat truth as an entity in box 3 is to engage in reification, that is (as discussed in section 6.2.1), it is "to postulate as an entity fallaciously" (Levin 1991, p. 57). For example, with regard to truth, Anderson (1988b, p. 404) asks, "Indeed, how would we know truth even if we held it in our hands"? His query is (one suspects) meant to be taken as just an instance of colorful, relativist rhetoric. Nevertheless, his reification of truth vividly illustrates the conceptual danger of treating an unobservable, intangible concept, such as truth, as if it referred to an observable, tangible object, such as an apple. By wrongly leading us to believe that truth could be held in our hands, the reification of truth, absurdly, leads us to inquire how we could recognize it with our eyes.[2]

A common accusation by relativists is that those holding that marketing science should seek true theories must also reify truth. For example, Zinkhan and Hirscheim (1992, p. 83) maintain that those in marketing who hold truth in high regard must assume that "there is an immutable truth out there which scientists can study." However, they provide no quotations of realists or any other evidence of instances of reification—and for good reason: It is likely that no such evidence exists. Truth is not an entity for study, let alone, an "immutable" entity.

7.2.2   Not with Certainty

Neither the correspondence theory of truth nor the realist interpretation of correspondence theory equates "truth" with "truth with certainty." As the realist Siegel (1983, p. 82) puts it, "To claim that a scientific proposition is true is not to claim that it is certain; rather, it is to claim that the world is as the proposition says it is." And the realist Groff argues:

> The conclusion that truth cannot be known with certainty to have been achieved . . . follows from an appreciation of the reality that there is no extracognitive standpoint from which to assess the relationship between scientific propositions and that to which they refer. . . . The metatheoretical implications of this situation, however, should not be thought to be terribly grave. Indeed, the metatheory of truth that I have proposed is nothing other than a statement of what it means to be a fallibilist about knowledge. For how are we to understand fallibilism, except as the belief that the norm of truth may never be conclusively determined to have been met? (Groff 2000, pp. 428–29)

In the philosophy of social science, Fox (1994) evaluates the confusions in the relativist writings of a philosopher named Raven:

> It seems to be from the *fallibility* of theories that Raven infers we cannot say what the world is really like; for if our accounts were mediated through a theory that was *certainly true*, they would surely be of what the world is really like. Here again, an anti-realist argument seems to depend on a demand for certainty. If this is the reason, it is confused. That something is infallibly known implies that it is true, but not vice versa; that our descriptions are fallible . . . does not imply that they are not what the world is really like. (Fox 1994, p. 507)

There is a confusion similar to Raven's in the marketing literature. Thus, Peter maintains:

> Unless science can know with certainty what truly is the real world, it is impossible to judge *the extent to which* knowledge claims truly represent or correspond to that world. In other words, without independent knowledge of a standard (i.e., what reality truly is), how can scientists know how close they are to reaching the standard? (Peter 1992, p. 73)

Peter's argument, however, represents an example of the "philosophers' fallacy" (see section 3.6.2): If we cannot know with certainty, we cannot know anything. How, we might ask, could Peter *know* that we can never know anything?

The traditional view in marketing theory is that the search for true theories must be distinguished from knowing truth with certainty. As Hunt (1983b, p. 372) put it, "The concept 'certainty' belongs to theology, not science." There is no reason either to (1) abandon the traditional view of truth or (2) equate truth with certainty.

7.2.3 Not Equal to Pragmatic Success

Critics of scientific realism often maintain that, for realism, truth and pragmatic success are equated. As an example from postmodern marketing:

> The issues of "truth" and pragmatic success, however, are neither mutually implicative nor inexorably intertwined. . . . The [scientific realism] narrative equation of truth = pragmatic success is one that focuses attention only on the technocratic dimensions of science: that is, the power of science to provide technologies for "controlling" natural and/or social phenomena. (Thompson 1993, p. 331)

However, scientific realism does not maintain that truth and pragmatic success are (a) mutually implicative, (b) inexorably intertwined, or (c) equated. Indeed, Thompson's postmodernism is wrong on four counts. First, note that scientific realism maintains that the long run success (in terms of explanations, predictions, and interventions) of a theory gives reason to believe that something like the entities and structure posited by the theory actually exists. Therefore, scientific realism, which stresses the fallibility of science, maintains that success *gives reason* for believing a theory has truth-content; it does not claim that success and truth-content are "mutually implicative." Second, *gives reason that something like* implies the fallibility of the existence inference; it does not make the claim of "inexorably intertwined." Third, scientific realism infers truth content, that is, *something like*, from success; it does *equate* the two in the manner of "truth = pragmatic success." (Equating truth with pragmatic success is—see section 3.6.1—a characteristic of the pragmatic theory of truth, not the correspondence theory.) Fourth, for scientific realism, success has three dimensions, successful (1) explanations, (2) predictions, and (3) interventions; it does not "focus attention *only* on the technocratic dimensions of science" (Thompson 1993, p. 331; italics added).

In conclusion, scientific realism does not equate truth with pragmatic success. The cause of postmodern marketing, it would seem, is served poorly by such, obviously erroneous, analyses. Griffin (1988) demonstrates that it is possible for postmodern discourse on philosophy of science to be informed by reason. What is lacking in marketing's postmodernism is the will to do so, not the way to do so.

7.3 RELATIVISTIC TRUTH

Several writers argue for a relativistic view of truth to be accepted. The various arguments for relativistic truth may be reconstructed or partially formalized as follows:

The Relativistic Truth ("RT") Argument

RT1. All research takes place within paradigms (or conceptual frameworks, research traditions, and so forth).

RT2. Paradigms are "highly encapsulated" (Anderson 1986, p. 158) and "context dependent" (Peter and Olson 1983, p. 119).

RT3. Rational choices across rival paradigms, as Kuhn and Feyerabend have shown, are impossible due to their "incommensurability" (Anderson 1989, p. 19; Ozanne and Hudson 1989, p. 1; Peter 1992, p. 76).

RT4. Therefore, "Truth is a subjective evaluation that cannot be inferred outside of the context [e.g., paradigm or research tradition] provided by the theory" (Peter and Olson 1983, p. 119).

Note that the RT argument draws heavily on the concept of incommensurability in the works of Kuhn and Feyerabend. As discussed in section 4.2, Kuhn and Feyerabend (at various times) offered three different interpretations of what it meant for paradigms to be incommensurable: (1) the *meaning-variance* view that scientific terms change meaning between paradigms, (2) the *radical translation* view that in some meaningful way the terms in one paradigm cannot be translated into the language of its rivals, and (3) the *incomparability* view that rival paradigms cannot be meaningfully compared. Which interpretation(s) do marketing's relativists adopt? Here, two examples illuminate this question.

Ozanne and Hudson (1989, p. 1) compare "interpretivist" research with what they (misleadingly, see Chapter 6) call "positivist" research and conclude that "the knowledge outputs of these two approaches are incommensurable." The evidence for their conclusion comes from their examination of Bower's approach to studying emotion, which he defines as "a physiological, internal state that is not dependent on the surrounding context," and comparing it with Denzin's "interpretivist approach," in which "emotions are defined as self-feelings, they are feelings of and for one's self" (Ozanne and Hudson 1989, p. 4). Thus, their claim of incommensurability is based on the assertion (which for the present purposes we shall assume to be true) that, for the two researchers, "it was clear that what was perceived to be the phenomenon of emotion changed when investigated" (1989, p. 14). Ozanne and Hudson then buttress their incommensurability claim by citing Shapiro's (1973) work. They report that Shapiro had attempted to integrate "the data of a more interpretive methodology and the data of a more positivist methodology," and she had concluded that her problems "were the result of her measuring different things" (Ozanne and Hudson 1989, p. 6).

As a second marketing example of incommensurability, Anderson (1989) compares the work of Tybout, Sternthal, and Calder (1983) on "multiple request effectiveness" with that of ethnomethodologists, such as Heritage (1984). Anderson argues that the approach of Tybout, Sternthal, and Calder is a kind of "psychological instrumentalism," in which "man is often a psychological dope whose verbal and motor behavior result from the operation of an autonomous central nervous system" (Anderson 1989, p. 21). In contrast, "while ethnomethodologists see man performing his mundane everyday activities in a largely unreflective fashion, there is always the possibility of choice" (1989, p. 21). More important for our purposes, however, he concludes that the " 'psychological' and ethnomethodological approaches to this phenomenon are largely incommensurable [because,] while it can be seen that both perspectives 'cover' or 'save' multiple requests, it should also be clear that they do so by completely redefining the subject matter of the problem" (Anderson 1989, p. 21).

It is clear that both the works of Ozanne and Hudson (1989) and Anderson (1989) are using the meaning-variance interpretation of incommensurability. That is, for Ozanne and Hudson, though Bower and Denzin were using the same term (i.e., emotion), they were not referring to, or measuring, the same phenomenon. Similarly, for Anderson, though Tybout, Sternthal, and Calder and the ethnomethodologists would discuss "multiple requests," the topic would be redefined when investigated. Do the examples of Anderson, Ozanne, and Hudson constitute a nontrivial, interesting, or meaningful kind of incommensurability? Obviously, the (presumed) fact that Bower and Denzin mean very different things when using the same term poses significant problems for them in communicating with each other. Also obviously, Tybout, Sternthal, and Calder might have difficulty communicating with ethnomethodologists. But, in what meaningful way does this communication problem imply that the knowledge outputs of these approaches are *incommensurable*?

As noted in Chapter 4, the concept of incommensurability comes from the classic examples of Kuhn, such as the rival knowledge-claims of Ptolemy and Copernicus: One paradigm claimed that the Sun revolved around the Earth, and its rival claimed that the Earth revolved around the Sun. Clearly, these are two *rival*, or competing, claims. Choice is required. If Ptolemy is right, Copernicus is wrong, and vice versa. The problems between Ptolemy and Copernicus were not, simply, as a result of them using common terms (e.g., "Earth," "Sun," and "revolve") in different ways. In the examples of Anderson and of Ozanne and Hudson, however, the researchers are using the same labels (i.e., "emotion" and "multiple requests") to mean very different things. Therefore, the knowledge-claims of Bower and Denzin, as well as those of Tybout, Sternthal, Calder, and the ethnomethodologists, though *different*, cannot be considered *rival*, or *competing*. No choice is required. Therefore, their claims are not *incommensurable* in any meaningful epistemic sense.[3]

In conclusion, the argument for relativistic truth fails because a key premise (RT3) is false. We turn now to the argument advanced by critical relativists that truth should be abandoned.

7.4   TRUTH SHOULD BE ABANDONED

Doppelt's (1978) "moderate" relativism and Laudan's (1987) reticulated model of scientific rationality—see section 5.2—form the philosophical foundations for marketing's "critical relativism" (Anderson 1986, 1988a, 1988b), with its requirement that truth is inappropriate and should be abandoned. Critical relativists point out that many different cognitive aims have "figured prominently in the history of natural and social science" (Anderson 1986, p. 159). Critical relativism entails "axiological relativism" (cognitive value relativism) because: "Whether those aims are themselves worthy of pursuit will be judged differently by various research programs. However, no 'independent arbiter' of the merits of an axiology can exist as long as the axiology is neither utopian nor inconsistent with the practices of the program" (Anderson 1988a, p. 134).

Critical relativism never attempts "to discriminate genuine from nongenuine knowledge. The bottom-line claim of critical relativism is that some programs deliver on certain axiologies, and others deliver on different aims and objectives" (Anderson 1988a, p. 134). Truth ("genuine knowledge") and falsity ("nongenuine knowledge") are thus absent from the lexicon of critical relativism. Not only is truth absent in critical relativism, it "is an inappropriate objective for science," and marketing and consumer behavior researchers would "do well to abandon" it (Anderson 1988b, p. 405). Critical relativism's case against truth stems from two arguments, the argument from the falsity of realism and the argument from utopianism.

7.4.1   The Falsity of Realism

The claim that realism is false is based on an analysis of "convergent" realism and "motivational" realism. Because the arguments are similar, we focus here on convergent realism. As Anderson explains it:

> In a nutshell, the main tenets of convergent realism would include the following assertions: 1) "mature" scientific theories are approximately true, 2) the concepts in these theories "genuinely refer" (that is, there really are things in the world that correspond to these concepts), 3) successive theories in a domain will retain the ontology of their predecessors; 4) truly referential theories will be successful; and, conversely, 5) "successful" theories will contain central terms that genuinely refer. (Anderson 1988b, p. 403)

Critical relativists conclude that the theory of convergent realism is false because "we can easily produce historical evidence from the so-called 'hard-sciences' that demonstrates that the fourth and fifth assertions are false" (Anderson 1988b, pp. 403–4). The empirical evidence includes the fact that the atomic theory of the eighteenth century was "singularly unsuccessful" but we now believe it to be genuinely referential. In contrast, such theories as the phlogistic theory of chemistry were "successful in their day" but are now "thought by scientists to be non-referring" (1988b, p. 404). Therefore, critical relativists maintain, because assertions 4 and 5 of the theory of convergent realism "are false," and because "the cognitive aim of 'truth' is linked ineluctably with realism" (1988b, p. 403), truth is an "inappropriate objective for science" and we should abandon it (1988b, p. 405).

On the Falsity of Realism: For Reason. Our analysis of the argument from the falsity of realism does not examine the historical episodes used as evidence for the falsity of convergent realism.[4] Instead, it focuses on the structure of the argument itself. Skipper and Hyman (1987, p. 60) point out that many of the scholarly works in marketing are "argument-centered," containing "nothing resembling a rigorous proof, yet the conclusion apparently 'stands to reason' or 'is intuitively obvious' given the premises." Our question here is: Does it stand to reason that marketing should abandon truth because convergent realism is false? Clearly, the answer must be "no."

First, note that scientific realism is a theory of science. It is totally incoherent to claim that truth should be abandoned as a goal for all theories because a particular theory of science (i.e., convergent realism) is false. The claim that the assertions of realism are "false" is unintelligible without the presumption that, under different circumstances, the assertions could have been true. Thus, critical relativism uses the concepts "truth" and "falsity" in the very argument that purportedly demonstrates that truth is inappropriate for science. Such an argument fails even minimal standards for coherence.

Second, if it is true that the assertions of realism are *false*, as critical relativism maintains, then truth plays a very definite role in critical relativism, which (ironically) constitutes evidence for truth having a role in both critical relativism and science. Another way of stating the preceding analysis is that critical relativism is self-refuting: The argument for critical relativism contains its own refutation. As discussed in section 4.1, for more than 2000 years, relativists have been attempting to develop a nontrivial, interesting version of relativism that would not be self-refuting. Starting with Socrates versus Protagoras, all attempts have failed (Siegel 1986, 1988). Given two millennia of repeated failures, the fact that marketing's version of relativism is also self-refuting is not surprising.

Demonstrations that relativism is self-refuting are often counterargued on the basis that relativists "simply argue for their positions by employing the intellectual resources that are sanctioned by the 'scientific culture' of the present age and/or by attempting to change the evaluative criteria, aims, or methods of contemporary intellectual discourse" (Anderson 1986, p. 157). Applying this line of reasoning here would mean the following: Though critical relativism contends that truth should be abandoned in science, because most marketing researchers are "country bumpkins" (Calder and Tybout 1989, p. 203), who believe in the value of truth, it is appropriate to rely on truth to demonstrate that truth is inappropriate.[5] Not only is this standard counterargument of relativism an example of disingenuous argumentation, it is also unavailable here on other grounds. In particular, critical relativism explicitly adopts the norm of "reflexivity" (Anderson 1986, p. 157), which implies that the criteria proposed by critical relativists to explain and understand science must also be applied to critical relativism itself. Therefore, if critical relativism claims that truth is inappropriate for science, reflexivity requires that truth must be inappropriate for critical relativism. Consequently, critical relativism cannot *coherently* claim that any analysis demonstrates a theory to be *false*.

The issue here is not simply a "slip of the pen." It is not that critical relativism uses the words "true" and/or "false." Everyone acknowledges that by a suitable selection of euphemisms and surrogates (e.g., "consistent/inconsistent," "accords with/does not accord with"), careful relativists can avoid the use of the words "true" and "false." It would be insulting to critical relativists for marketing to interpret critical relativism's total cognitive content to be such trivial semantics. Rather, critical relativism is obviously making a substantive claim that the meanings that "stand behind" the terms "truth" and "falsity" are inappropriate for science and should be abandoned. And that claim, as has been shown, is incoherent—it makes no sense.

7.4.2   Reticulational Philosophy and Truth

Critical relativism is grounded primarily in Laudan's work, particularly his reticulated model of scientific rationality (see section 5.2). Therefore, further light can be shed on the argument from the falsity of realism by examining Laudan's philosophy, which, for convenience, we refer to as "reticulational philosophy."

Although reticulational philosophy's perspective on truth has its origin in Laudan's (1973) article on the "self-corrective" thesis of Charles Sanders Peirce, Laudan's 1977 book, *Progress and Its Problems* (hereafter *P&P*) has an attack on truth as its major focus. *P&P* attempts to replace the search for truth with the search for maximum problem solving as the overriding goal of science: "It has often been suggested in this essay that the solution of a maximum number of empirical problems, and the generation of a minimum number of conceptual problems and anomalies is the central aim of science"

(Laudan 1977, p. 111). The history of science and of the philosophy of science reveal, for reticulational philosophy, the hopelessness of the search for truth: "Attempts to show that the methods of science guarantee it is true, probable, progressive, or highly confirmed knowledge—attempts which have an almost continuous ancestry from Aristotle to our own time—have generally failed, raising a distinct presumption that scientific theories are neither true, nor probable, nor progressive, nor highly confirmed" (Laudan 1977, p. 2).[6] Furthermore, the search for truth is utopian and utopian goals are undesirable: "We apparently do not have any way of knowing for sure (or even with some confidence) that science is true, or probable, or that it is getting closer to the truth. Such aims are *utopian* in the literal sense that we can never know whether they are being achieved" (1977, p. 127). Thus, "determinations of truth and falsity are irrelevant to the acceptability or the pursuitability of theories and research traditions" (1977, p. 120).

In the article, "A Confutation of Convergent Realism," reticulational philosophy links modern versions of realism with the search for truth: "If the realist is going to make his case for CER (Convergent Epistemological Realism), it seems that it will have to hinge on approximate truth" (Laudan 1981, p. 29). The article argues that history shows the theory of convergent realism to be false: "The realist's claim that we should expect referring theories to be empirically successful is simply false" (Laudan 1981, p. 24). Furthermore, "S2 [a thesis of convergent realism] is so patently false that it is difficult to imagine that the realists need to be committed to it" (1981, p. 25). And, "I shall assume that [the two realist philosophers] Putnam and Watkins mean that 'most of the time (or perhaps in most of the important cases) successor theories contain predecessor theories as limiting cases.' So construed, the claim is patently false" (1981, p. 39). Finally, "the realist's strictures on cummulativity are as ill-advised normatively as they are false historically" (1981, p. 43).

The case against truth as a goal for science comes to full flower in *Science and Values* (Laudan 1984). Whereas *P&P* argued that maximum problem solving was the "central aim" of science (Laudan 1977, p. 111), *Science and Values* maintains that there is no overriding goal for science: "There is simply no escape from the fact that determinations of progress must be relativized to a certain set of ends, and that there is no uniquely appropriate set of those ends" (Laudan 1984, p. 66). However, not all goals are appropriate for scientific communities. First, the goals or "cognitive values" must not be "utopian" (1984, p. 52). As in *P&P*, Laudan claims that truth is utopian, and, therefore, truth as a goal " cannot be rationally propounded" (1984, p. 53). Second, goals can be evaluated on the basis of "reconciling theory and practice." This congruency criterion allows us to criticize a scientist or a scientific community that claims to be pursuing one goal, their explicit goal, but whose actions and actual choices imply the pursuit of some other implicit goal. Scientific rationality, honesty, and the justified fear of the reprobation of one's peers require goal congruency:

> When we find ourselves in a situation where there is a tension between our explicit aims and those implicit in our actions and judgments, we are naturally under significant pressure to change one or the other, or both. On pain of being charged with inconsistency (not to mention hypocrisy, dishonesty, etc.), the rational person, confronted with a conflict between the goals he professes and the goals that appear to inform his actions, will attempt to bring the two into line with each other. (Laudan 1984, p. 55)

On Reticulational Philosophy: For Reason. Like all of Laudan's writings, his arguments against truth are meticulously crafted, engagingly written, and "come alive" with their many historical examples and anecdotes. Unlike the writings of many contemporary philosophers of science, even those who have not mastered modern logic (which would include most of us in marketing) can follow his arguments. Unfortunately, though his case against truth is brilliantly developed, it is fundamentally flawed.

The works of many philosophers suggest that any philosophy abandoning the goal of truth must choose ultimately between incoherence and irrelevance (e.g., Newton-Smith 1981; Watkins 1984). Consider, for example, the societal debate on whether the theory of scientific creationism should be taught in public schools. Defenders of scientific creationism claim that it is a genuine scientific theory and should (at least) be taught in addition to evolutionary theory. Others claim that scientific creationism is basically a religious theory and (at the minimum) oppose laws that would require it to be taught in public schools. In 1982, a U.S. District Court struck down the Arkansas law requiring scientific creationism to be taught in public schools.[7] The court concluded that scientific creationism was principally a religious theory and not science, which agreed with the many traditional, realist philosophers of science who testified at the trial.

A philosophy relevant to the scientific creationism debate might take the traditional view of pointing out some significant differences among science, nonscience, and religion, and on those grounds argue for or against scientific creationism (see section 6.1). Alternatively, a relevant philosophy might opt for a second traditional view that the empirical evidence is strongly in favor of the truth or falsity of either evolutionary theory or scientific creationism (see Figure 7.1). However, as just discussed, the truth-falsity option is closed to reticulational philosophy. As for the first option, "it is probably fair to say that there is no demarcation line between science and nonscience, or between science and pseudoscience, which would win assent from a majority of philosophers. Nor is there one which should win acceptance from philosophers or anyone else" (Laudan 1983, p. 112). Thus, reticulational philosophy seems to be faced with the choice of incoherence or irrelevance on this societal issue. And it chose incoherence.

In a widely discussed article, Laudan (1982) applied reticulational philosophy to the societal issue of scientific creationism. Though he concluded, "the verdict itself is probably to be commended," it was "reached for all the wrong reasons and by a chain of argument which is hopelessly suspect" (Laudan 1982, p. 16). How should the federal court have justified its ruling? Laudan argues that "to make the inter-linked claims that Creationism is neither falsifiable nor testable is to assert that creationism makes no empirical assertions whatever. That is surely *false*" (1982, p. 16; italics added). He then details many of the assertions and claims of Creationism and states, "In brief these claims are testable, they have been tested and they have failed those tests" (1982, p. 16). He concludes: "Indeed, if any doctrine in the history of science *has ever been falsified*, it is the set of claims associated with 'creation-science'" (1982, p. 17; italics in original).[8]

As the preceding discussion demonstrates, reticulational philosophy is incoherent. To claim that "determinations of truth and falsity are irrelevant to science," and nevertheless claim that the theory of scientific creationism has "been falsified" by science is incoherent. Indeed reticulational philosophy violates, in the most egregious manner, its own "noncongruency" criterion. Hence, marketing's critical relativism and Laudan's reticulational philosophy (on which critical relativism is anchored) are both unintelligible. In fact, a strong, *prima facie* case can be made that all philosophies that seek to abandon the pursuit of truth in discussions about science will inexorably generate unintelligible, incoherent discourse, or face irrelevancy, or both.

7.4.3 Truth and "Utopianism"

Critical relativism (1) defines truth as "that which is unequivocally the case," (2) refers to truth as a "utopian" goal, (3) insists that utopian goals are "inappropriate" for science, and (4) concludes that truth should be "abandoned" (Anderson 1988b, pp. 404–5). One might ask: Why could science not choose to pursue a utopian goal? Because, critical relativism claims, "to adopt a goal with the feature that we can conceive of no actions that would be apt to promote it, or a goal whose realization we could not recognize even if we had achieved it, is surely a mark of unreasonableness and irrationality" (Anderson 1988b, p. 404). Setting aside the philosophers' fallacy involved in defining "true" as "unequivocally the case," we now address a second question: If truth is utopian and utopian goals are to be strictly avoided, what, then, might be an acceptable goal for marketing science? Unfortunately, the reticulational philosophy on which critical relativism is based provides no guidance as to which goals will pass the utopian criterion; *Science and Values* (Laudan 1984) provides not a single example of an acceptable goal for science (see section 5.2.2). However, as "early" reticulational philosophy argued powerfully that maximum problem solving was the *central* aim of science (Laudan 1977), it might serve as an example.

On Utopianism: For Reason. Basically, *P&P* (Laudan 1977) proposed a counting and weighting procedure to demonstrate the rationality of science and the fact that it was making progress toward the goal of maximum problem solving. *P&P* contended that "the workability of the problem-solving model is its greatest virtue" (Laudan 1977, p. 127). This counting and weighting procedure—as discussed in section 5.2.2—has been evaluated by Kordig (1980), Krips (1980), Leplin (1981), McMullin (1979), Musgrave (1979), and Sarkar (1981). They point out that applying the model in actual scientific practice would require an extraordinarily complex procedure. Neither Laudan in *P&P* nor anyone else since has actually employed this complex procedure; all commentators have concluded that it is manifestly unworkable. In fact, we can be stronger yet in our claim. The counting and weighting procedure that was claimed to be the central aim of science in 1977 is utopian by the very same criterion now employed to dismiss the aim of truth in science. So, we have the highly curious situation of a goal for science slipping from the central aim of all inquiry (according to 1977 reticulational philosophy) to an impermissible aim that would have to be abandoned on the basis of the utopian criterion (and 1984 reticulational philosophy).

How would other potential aims for science stand up to the utopian criterion? For example, how about falsifiability, parsimony, explanatory power, fruitfulness, mathematical elegance, and so forth? If each were defined in "high redefinition" fashion (we must know "unequivocally" that a theory is falsifiable, or has maximum explanatory power, or has the greatest fruitfulness), then all these aims would be utopian and impermissible. But this conclusion, again, is nihilism and would not be countenanced by anyone who wants to talk meaningfully about science. (And critical relativism has—most appropriately—expressly adopted the goal of being non-nihilistic (Anderson 1986).) Therefore, we should examine more closely why the utopian criterion fails.

First, Stern (1989) has suggested that in evaluating the rhetorical force of argumentation in marketing, both the denotative and connotative meanings of terms must be examined. Using this procedure enables us to recognize that the choice of the word "utopian" has "loaded the semantical dice." To see this, compare the meaning of "utopian goal" with that of "visionary goal." Both are denotative synonyms (Morehead 1985), implying an aim that is probably unrealizable, yet "utopian" connotes images such as impractical, hopeless, foolish, or quixotic, whereas "visionary" connotes lofty, exalted, or highly desirable. However, if critical relativists had advocated the abandonment of all *visionary* goals, a criterion that would have had the same denotative meaning as the abandonment of utopian goals, the proposal would, for most scholars, have lacked initial plausibility.

Second, critical relativism confuses the short-run, tangible, realizable objectives of a societal institution with its long-run aims, regulative ideals, or mission. Consider higher education as a societal institution. Though it has many "realizable" objectives (e.g., increasing the number of student credit hours, increasing the number of volumes in the library, decreasing the heating bill, and so forth), no one would claim that these realizable objectives constitute the mission of higher education. Or, consider "the law" as a societal institution. Historically, the pursuit of justice has served as a regulative ideal for our legal system. Obviously, a mission such as justice cannot always be "cashed out" in a set of completely unambiguous practices and procedures. Yet, does this imply that the visionary ideal of justice should be abandoned? How about "utopian" personal goals, such as honesty, fairness, ethics, and morality? Should all these, as Feyerabend (1975) implies, be abandoned as well? On the contrary, rather than advocating that utopian (visionary) goals should be abandoned, a better case can be made that the overriding goals worthy of pursuit, both in personal relations and in science, are likely to be utopian (visionary).

7.5   THE PHILOSOPHERS' FALLACY REVISITED

The works of Adler (1985) and Harré (1986) can help us understand how so many scholars, in both philosophy and marketing, generate philosophies that produce unintelligible discourse. Adler details ten key mistakes that have plagued philosophy for centuries, one of which is to define "knowledge" in such an exacting and circumscribed manner that knowledge becomes impossible for anyone to attain, and to conclude, therefore, that all knowledge claims are "mere opinion." As discussed in section 3.6.2, Harré (1986, p. 4) addresses the same fallacy, which he labels the "philosophers' fallacy": the "fallacy of high redefinition." Basically, the philosophers' fallacy is to take a perfectly good term (e.g., "truth," "knowledge," "progress," "objectivity," or "science") and subject it to such a "high redefinition" that the term no longer can be applied to anything. For example, if "knowledge" and "truth" must be known with certainty, it becomes easy to demonstrate that truth and knowledge do not exist. Harré shows that much of the irrationalism found in the works of Kuhn and Feyerabend (as detailed by Stove 1982) have their origins in the philosophers' fallacy.

To consider Kuhn and the philosophers' fallacy, recall that he "always meant" for "incommensurability" to be defined as equivalent to a logical or mathematical proof (Kuhn 1970a, p. 260). Finding no such *proofs* available to empirical science, his philosophy collapsed into relativism and irrationalism. Similarly, Feyerabend sought "absolutely binding principles" (Feyerabend 1970, p. 21) and "general rules that would cover all cases" in relation to the concepts "truth," "reason," and "morality" (Feyerabend 1978, p. 117). Finding no such universal principles for guaranteeing the accomplishment of these aims, he characterizes truth, reason, and even morality as "abstract monsters," and his relativism counsels us to allow them to "wither away" (Feyerabend 1975, p. 180). In short, if one cannot know with certainty (high redefinition) that one can apply a concept (truth, reason, morality), it should be abandoned. Such nihilism, Harré maintains, is "absurd" (Harré 1986, p. 62).

At least in part, critical relativism and the reticulational philosophy on which it is based produce unintelligible discourse on science because of the philosophers' fallacy. For example, "If 'truth' is properly defined as that which is unequivocally the case, then *there can be no criterion* for absolute truth. Indeed, how would we know truth even if we held it in our hands"? (Anderson 1988b, p. 404; italics in original). Note that truth should be "properly" defined as that which is "unequivocally the case." With such a high redefinition of truth, the slide into incoherence and irrationalism is to be expected. Similarly, critical relativism demands a "universal demarcation criterion" to justify distinguishing among science, nonscience, and pseudoscience (Anderson 1989). Then, if no *universal* criterion can be supplied, "science is whatever society chooses to call a science" (Anderson 1983, p. 26). But such a set of beliefs implies nihilism. That is, one cannot distinguish between astronomy and astrology (Feyerabend 1975), medical science and palmistry (see section 6.1), or, as shown here, science and religion.

7.6 TRUTH and truth

Scientific realism distinguishes between truth and TRUTH, that is, between "this proposition is true" and "I know with certainty this proposition is true." In like manner, it distinguishes between "science is objective" and "science has the objectivity of a god's eye view," that is, between "objectivity and OBJECTIVITY." The philosophy debates in marketing often fail to make these distinctions. For example, Peter sees no distinction between "to know" and "to know with certainty," because "Surely, 'to claim that the world *is* as the proposition says it *is*' appears to suggest that the world is *unequivocally* or *certainly* as the proposition says it is" (Peter 1992, p. 72). (With unintended irony, we should note, Peter begins his assertion with "Surely.") What, then, are the epistemological differences between "truth" and "TRUTH"?

Table 7.1

The Truth Continuum

Dogmatic skepticism (TRUTH)	Humean skepticism (truth)	Fallibilism (truth)	Dogmatism (TRUTH)
Academic skepticism	Logical positivism	Scientific realism	Vulgar absolutism
Solipsistic skepticism	Logical empiricism	Critical pluralism	Scientism
Relativism	Critical rationalism	Naturalism	Fundamentalism
Idealism	Falsificationism		Theocracy
Subjectivism	Instrumentalism		Marxism-Leninism
Constructionism			Nazism
Deconstructionism			Fascism
Deconstructive postmodernism			
Neo-Marxism			
Critical theory			
Radical feminism			

Source: Adapted from Hunt (1992a).

Table 7.1 displays a continuum of perspectives on truth, a label for the epistemological position underlying the perspective, and a series of exemplars.[9] For example, starting from the right, dogmatism claims to have found TRUTH. Dogmatists not only know that truth is findable but they have found the one and only truth, unequivocally, certainly, or surely. Furthermore, their TRUTH is not to be questioned. In the philosophy of science, both vulgar absolutism and scientism are exemplars, where the former refers to a set of beliefs and a set of principles for generating beliefs based on a unique privileged framework that produces incorrigible truth (Siegel 1987, p. 162), and the latter refers to "the unwarranted idolization of science as the sole authority of truth and source of knowledge" (Angeles 1981, p. 251). Exemplars of dogmatism in political philosophy include Nazism and Marxism-Leninism.

At the extreme left of Table 7.1, we find the TRUTH of dogmatic skepticism. "Skepticism" comes from the Greek *skeptesthai*, which means "to examine," "to look carefully about," and the Greek *skeptikos*, which means "thoughtful" and "curious." Therefore, skepticism can be a healthy attitude of suspending doubt, pending thoughtful, reflective examination. However, dogmatic skepticism claims to have incorrigibly, certainly, surely found the one and only TRUTH, that is, there is no truth to be found. Both academic skepticism, the belief that "there is but one thing one can know, namely that one can know nothing else" (Watkins 1984, p. 3), and solipsistic skepticism, the position that all one can know is "(a) that one exists and (b) that one is having certain ideas" (Angeles 1981, p. 262) are philosophy of science examples of dogmatic skepticism.

It seems that marketing versions of relativism have embraced academic and solipsistic skepticism, and their one TRUTH: Nothing is knowable (because of incommensurability, the theory-ladenness of observation, and so forth). Curiously, however, throughout marketing's philosophy debates we find assertions such as "objectivity is *impossible*," "scientists do not *discover* anything about the world," "intellectualization in marketing is *inexorable*," "the results of research based on hypothetico-deductive method are *illusory*," "reality is *all* mental and perceptual," and so on. Unlike the knowledge claims found in traditional marketing research (where, quite properly, cautions of the "do not overgeneralize" variety abound), the claims of relativists, postmodernists, and others are customarily put forth with bold certitude, great emphasis, and total lack of equivocation. As Calder and Tybout (1989, p. 203) question, how can relativist writers *know* such claims? If the absence of a "god's-eye view" supposedly defeats even highly qualified stochastic propositions or tendency laws (see Hunt 2002a, section 6.3, on tendency laws), what unique privileged position justifies the certitude of relativists' sweeping generalizations? The answer is, of course, there can be none: Relativism is best described as dogmatic skepticism.

Between the extremes in Table 7.1 lies the acceptance of "truth" by those embracing Humean skepticism and fallibilism. In the philosophy of science, both the logical positivists and logical empiricists embraced Humean skepticism, whereas scientific realists reject it. Although science can exist within a positivist framework (as the "Copenhagen" interpretation of quantum mechanics and behaviorist psychology attest), most scientific disciplines and their research programs require a much bolder ontology than positivist "observables" (Levin 1991; Manicas 1987). Indeed, many science scholars (e.g., Fay 1988) contend that, positivist rhetoric notwithstanding, even those researchers and research programs that *claim* to be "positivist" are mostly realist. One reason is that the ontology of scientific realism has heuristic value for generating new hypotheses and theories, whereas positivism and the "constructive empiricism" of Van Fraassen (1980) are heuristically impotent (Levin 1991). At any point in time science can be interpreted in a positivist manner. But, to move forward, science (at least most of science) seems to require realism.[10]

7.6.1   Postmodernism and Dogmatic Skepticism

It must be emphasized that, though radical feminism and postmodernism are grouped under dogmatic skepticism, not all researchers who refer to themselves as feminists and postmodernists embrace extreme skepticism.[11] For example, there are splinter groups within the postmodernist research tradition who neither disdain truth nor embrace postmodern "methodological babble" (Calder and Tybout 1989), or "epistobabble" (Coyne 1982).

Consider the "constructive postmodernism" of Griffin (1988). Griffin notes that "the term *postmodern* is used in a confusing variety of ways." For him, "deconstructive or eliminative postmodernist . . . thought issues [or results] in relativism, even nihilism" (Griffin 1988, p. x). In contrast, his "constructive postmodernism" endorses the "notion of truth as correspondence, . . . [in that] science can lead to ways of thinking about the world that can increasingly approximate to patterns and structures genuinely characteristic of nature" (Griffin 1988, p. 29).

Although Griffin rejects "scientism" as dogmatic (see Table 7.1), his "constructive or revisionary postmodernism involves a new unity of scientific, ethical, aesthetic, and religious institutions" (Griffin 1988, p. x). This new unity requires not just retaining "science's concern for truth," but also "the principle of noncontradiction" (1988, p. 30). Under this principle, incoherent arguments must be rejected:

> If two statements contradict each other, both cannot be true. . . . Accordingly, science must aim for coherence between all its propositions and between its propositions and all those that are inevitably presupposed in human practice and thought in general. (Obtaining such coherence is indeed the primary method of checking for correspondence.) (Griffin 1988, p. 30)

Constructive postmodernism, alas, is a minority view; deconstructive postmodernism (in marketing, management, social science, and consumer research) appears to be the majority view (e.g., Thompson 1993).

7.6.2 On Marketing and Noncontradiction: For Reason

In marketing's philosophy debates, the principle of noncontradiction is often held in low regard. Indeed, it is considered to be just a technical nicety. For example, Zinkhan and Hirschheim report that Hunt (1990b) "castigates critical relativism for using the very concepts that it purports to stand against, viz., truth and falsity . . . [and] showing that this latest version of relativism is still self-refuting and, moreover, incoherent and unintelligible" (Zinkhan and Hirschheim 1992, p. 81). For them, incoherence and unintelligibility are not problems. Rather:

> The problem seems to be with the notion of "truth." Any attempt to dispense with that notion typically incurs the wrath of the realist community. Hunt clearly cannot accept its abandonment . . . one must question whether, in the social domain, it makes sense to focus on the notion of truth as *it is essentially a social construction.* (Zinkhan and Hirschheim 1992, pp. 81–82; italics added)

In contrast, I argue, the problem is not anyone's "wrath," nor (as discussed in the next section) is the solution to regard truth as "essentially a social construction." The problem is that arguments for one's proposed philosophy, including arguments proposing relativism, should make sense. And *making sense*, being coherent and abiding by the principle of noncontradiction, is—as even the version of postmodernism argued for by Griffin (1988) agrees—a minimum desideratum for any academic discourse, including marketing. Similarly, the solution, I argue, is not to accept the reality relativism—see section 4.1.3—implicit in regarding truth as "essentially a social construction." Instead, the solution is to (1) develop coherent arguments and (2) adopt a philosophy that makes sense of (and for) science. One such philosophy is scientific realism. There may be others.

7.7   TRUTH, REALITY RELATIVISM, AND IDEALISM

Scientific realism embraces the classical realist view—see section 3.1—that the external world exists unperceived. Indeed, the reality of the external world, shown as box 3 in Figure 7.1, is posited to impact the outcomes (i.e., box 2) of theories (i.e., box 1) by path D. This section explores how marketing's relativism addresses the reality of the external world. Peter (1992) provides a detailed exposition of the relativist/constructionist view of reality. We shall review and then evaluate his exposition.

7.7.1   Relativistic Reality

Peter (1992) develops a model he calls the "Relativist/constructionist View of Reality" (see 1992, Figure 2, p. 74). In this model, "uninterpreted reality" is shown with a solid arrow as impacting on three constructs: (1) "scientist's worldview," (2) "research paradigm," and (3) "mental interpretation of reality." In turn, these three constructs influence science's "public construction of reality," which then provides feedback to "uninterpreted reality."

What is "uninterpreted reality," and to what extent is the solid arrow from this construct the same thing as path D in the realist model in our own Figure 7.1? Peter (1992, p. 73) answers: "the relativistic view has no problem with the possibility of an external world that is independent of the scientist." So far, so good. However, readers might wonder why the qualifier "possibility"? Elsewhere in the same article, Peter urges marketers to research problems like "starving third world countries, the delivery of a standard of living to the poor and homeless, the misuse of drugs, or the spread of AIDS" (1992, p. 78). So, why does Peter imply that it is only a "possibility" that third world countries, the poor and homeless, drugs, and AIDS exist "independent of the scientist"? Also in the same article, Peter confidently speculates that the motivations of those philosophers of science who have examined the concept of incommensurability (and found it wanting) resulted from them being "threatened." Indeed, the philosophers feared that incommensurability "then and now . . . drastically reduces the importance of philosophy of science in society" (1992, p. 77). Given such confidence, why is it only a "possibility" that, "then and now," such philosophers actually have motivations (fearful or not) that are independent of Peter?

Peter (1992) continues his exposition by arguing for relativistic reality. Compared with scientific realism, "the difference in the relativistic perspective [compared with the realist view] is that *no interpretation of that world can be made independently* of human sensations, perceptions, information processing, feelings, and actions" (Peter 1992, p. 74; italics in original). I quote at length how Peter argues for relativistic reality, that is, how science socially constructs reality:

> A construction of reality is not equivalent to uninterpreted reality. The reason is that the meanings given to phenomena are humanly constructed and bounded by cultural, historical, and theoretical limitations . . . there are clearly differences in the naming and meaning of even simple objects across languages and culture. The meanings of more complicated terms, such as "attitude," "brand loyalty," or "brand equity," differ across theories and research paradigms, even within the same culture and language. . . .

> An important point of this discussion is that, even for simple objects, the labels placed on them and the meanings given to them are human constructions in the form of language, mathematics, or other symbols; *they are not the objects themselves.* However, concepts are easily confused with the phenomena they are intended to represent. . . . In sum, there is no theory-independent way to know what an object is or, indeed, whether it is an object.

> Similarly, empirical data are not equivalent to uninterpreted reality. Empirical data are constructed by scientists through processes such as measurement and sampling; *they are not the phenomena themselves.* Measures cannot be constructed meaningfully unless one has at least an implicit theory of what is to be measured, that is, an interpretation to guide measure development. The meaning of data derived from measures also depends entirely on the interpretations scientists give to them concerning what was measured, how well, and from what theoretical perspective. . . . Hence, empirical data are not independent criteria for judging the closeness of a theory to reality because they are entirely dependent on theory for their meaning and interpretation. Without a theory that describes, among other things, what concepts are putatively measured, empirical data are merely numbers.

> Human constructions in the form of language, mathematics, and other symbols are the "reality" scientists analyze, evaluate, debate, and compare with their own beliefs. As stated previously, these constructions of reality are in no sense equivalent

to uninterpreted reality nor is there any method to evaluate whether they truly cap-
ture uninterpreted reality. (Peter 1992, p. 75; italics in original)

7.7.2   On Relativistic Reality: For Reason

Our evaluation begins with the claim that the labels we use to identify objects
"are not the objects themselves," though they "are easily confused with the
phenomena they are intended to represent." Furthermore, we evaluate the claim
that the meanings of labels such as "apples," "trees," "star," and "planet" depend on "theory," which implies: "In sum, there is no theory-independent
way to know what an object is or indeed, if it is an object."

While it is true that words, the labels we use to refer to objects, are not
themselves the objects we intend to represent, Peter presents no evidence of
any such confusion in the scientific realism he is attacking. Furthermore, while
the meanings of words often depend significantly on context, and sometimes
the context might legitimately be referred to as a "theory," it is a *non sequitur*
that "there is no theory-independent way to know what an object is or indeed,
if it is an object." First, it is incorrect that accurate human recognition (perception) of all objects depends on language. We may safely assume (since we
are here) that our ancestors, long before the development of language, recognized lions, tigers, and bears as (dangerous) objects. Second, when humans started communicating with each other through the use of language
(e.g., English), their use of "lions," "tigers," and "bears" to refer to lions,
tigers, and bears, required nothing that might be properly referred to as a
"theory." Third, even if we—sloppily and inappropriately—extend the word
"theory" to mean "a consensus as to the use of terms in a specific language
community," lions, and tigers, and bears would be unchanged. Indeed, they
would still be dangerous, even if we labeled them (for example) "bunnies,"
"fawns," and "kittens."

In conclusion, contra Peter, even in the absence of "theory" we can recognize many objects as objects and know what they are. Equally important,
"labels" and "theory" neither create genuine objects nor change their characteristics. Why does Peter feel the need to deny the preceding? As we shall see,
one possible reason was hinted at when he admitted that the world external to
the researcher is only a "possibility."

To evaluate relativistic reality, let us return to the example in section 7.1.
The example involved a marketer who wants to test two, genuinely rival, explanatory theories (i.e., two theories having conflicting knowledge-claims).
Recall that both theories entail the concept "intentions to buy," which is measured on a scale from "1" equals "definitely will not purchase" to "10" equals
"definitely will purchase." After being asked to mark the box that "best de-

scribes your beliefs," a subject puts a checkmark on the questionnaire. The coder of the questionnaire then reports, "The subject checked box 9." For the correspondence theory of truth, "The subject checked box 9" is true, if and only if, the subject actually checked box 9. Futhermore, when the example is interpreted by scientific realism, the subject checking box 9 may (if our measurement theory is good) be an indicator (albeit, a fallible indicator) of the subject's actual intentions to buy.

How does Peter's relativism, in his words, "account for" (Peter 1992, p. 97) the "9"? Peter states, "empirical data are not equivalent to uninterpreted reality" (1992, p. 75). Now, no one would deny that "9" is not the *same* as the reality to which it is intended to relate or refer, that is, the subjects' genuine intentions to buy. In short, we will all agree with Peter that "they are not the phenomena themselves" (1992, p. 75). However, Peter continues, because one needs "an interpretation to guide measure development," then "the meaning of data derived from measures also depends entirely on the interpretations scientists give to them concerning what was measured, how well, and from what theoretical perspective" (1992, p. 75). We should note carefully his words, "depends entirely." Later in the same paragraph he states that empirical data are "entirely dependent on theory," and empirical data are "merely numbers without a theory." In the next paragraph he states that data "are in no sense equivalent to uninterpreted reality."

Why does Peter say "depends entirely" and not "depends"? Why does he say "merely numbers" and not just "numbers"? Why does he say that data are "in no sense equivalent," rather than "are not equivalent"? Three possibilities are apparent. First, if he meant only "the same as," his view reduces to a banal triviality. Just as no physician believes that "106" on a fever thermometer is the *same as* a child's high fever, it would be the height of condescension for Peter to claim that his fellow marketers are such silly, confused, "country bumpkins" (Calder and Tybout 1989, p. 203) that they believe that "9" is the *same as* a high intention to buy. Second, he cannot mean that (just as "106" on a fever thermometer is associated with, is an indicant of, or corresponds to a child's high fever) the "9" (if our measurement theory is good, like that underlying a fever thermometer) is associated with, is an indicant of, or corresponds to a consumer's intentions to buy. In short, he cannot mean that the greater the subject's intentions to buy, the higher the number on our scale. He cannot mean that the sentence "the subject checked box 9" is true if the subject indeed checked box 9. Why "cannot"? Because this view is the realist view being argued against, an example of the very correspondence theory of truth implied to be a "fairytale" by Peter and Olson (1983, p. 122) and referred to as "naïve" by Zinkham and Hirschheim (1992, p. 81).

There appears to be one and only one interpretation left—and an unfortunate one it is. Peter must mean that the meaning of empirical data, for example, the "9," comes only from the researcher's theory and not at all from any "uninterpreted reality." For example, the meaning of "9," its information value, has nothing to do, *can* have nothing to do, with whatever prompted the subject to check "9." And, because Peter does not restrict his discussion to just the social sciences—indeed, he contends that the relativist view reflects that of modern physics (Peter and Olson 1983, p. 120)—the "106" on a fever thermometer is just a "created reality" and has nothing, can have nothing, to do with a child's fever (what he calls "uninterpreted reality" and realists call "the world external to the researcher"). The preceding appears to be the only nontrivial explanation available as to Peter's use of "entirely" with respect to interpretations of data, his use of "merely" with respect to numbers, and his use of "in no sense equivalent" with respect to the external world. In short, though Peter admits the "possibility" of an external world that is independent of the scientist on page 73, by page 75, even this slim, remote chance has vanished. Similarly, what Peter calls "uninterpreted reality" in his Figure 1 on page 74, and shows by means of an arrow as impacting on or influencing the process of science, is erased on page 75. Otherwise, Peter would state that the meaning of the data derived from measures depends in part on the researcher's theory and in part on something external to the theory, for example, the subjects. Why does Peter do this? Because relativism/constructionism requires it.

If relativists acknowledge that the meaning of data is influenced by *both* scientists' theories and a world external to their theories, then they would have to acknowledge that it is at least possible for scientists' theories to "touch base" with some reality external to the theorist. Furthermore, acknowledging that theories can touch base with some external reality would then imply that some theories might accomplish this task better, more accurately, more faithfully, more genuinely, than others. But this would imply that it is at least possible, just possible, that some of our theories may be false, and others may be true, or approximately true, or closer to the truth than others. And this, of course, is what relativism/constructionism denies. Therefore, the external world vanishes in Peter's relativism. All philosophies based on the idealist view (see section 2.4) that the external world does not exist unperceived degenerate into nihilism. And Peter's relativism, as acknowledged by Olson (1982, p. 14), embraces idealism. Thus, it degenerates to nihilism.

7.8   FOR TRUTH

The preceding shows that arguments *against* truth are uninformed by reason. We now turn to arguing *for* truth. Our argument is based on trust. What is trust? Trust exists when one has confidence in another's reliability and integrity (Morgan and Hunt 1994; Moorman, Deshpandé, and Zaltman 1993). In turn, the confidence of the trusting party in the trustworthy party's reliability and integrity is associated with the belief that the trustworthy party has attributes such as consistent, competent, honest, fair, responsible, helpful, and benevolent (Altman and Taylor 1973; Dwyer and LaGace 1986; Larzelere and Huston 1980; Rotter 1971). The importance of trust is recognized across disciplines and research traditions.

In organizational behavior, the study of "norms of trust" is considered a characteristic that distinguishes management theory from organizational economics (Barney 1990; Donaldson 1990). In communications, a key construct has been source credibility, originally defined by Hovland et al. (1953) as trust of the speaker by the listener. In social policy, Fukuyama (1995) argues that social trust positively affects the wealth of nations. In economics, Arrow (1972) stresses how trust increases productivity. In competition theory, Hunt (2000, pp. 235–37) explicates how resource-advantage theory can explain the relationships among trust, competitive advantage, and wealth.

In the marketing of services, Berry and Parasuraman (1991, p. 144) find: "Customer-company relationships require trust." Indeed, they contend, "Effective services marketing depends on the management of trust because the customer typically must buy a service before experiencing it" (1991, p. 107). In marketing education, Huff, Cooper, and Jones (2002) find that trust has consequences important to the success of student project groups. In strategic alliances, Sherman (1992, p. 78) concludes that "the biggest stumbling block to the success of alliances is the lack of trust." In retailing, Berry (1993, p. 1) stresses that "trust is the basis for loyalty," and Ganesan (1994) finds trust as influencing a retailer's long-term orientation. In relationship marketing, Morgan and Hunt (1994) find that trust promotes cooperation, increases the likelihood that conflict will be of the functional kind, and decreases uncertainty. In international marketing, Hewett and Bearden (2001) find that a multinational's subsidiary having trust in the headquarter's marketing function will increase the subsidiary's acquiescence to headquarter's direction. In the brand equity area, Chaudhuri and Holbrook (2001) find brand trust to impact purchase loyalty and attitudinal loyalty.

In short, trust is a key concept in many different literatures. What, then, are the relationships among trust, science, realism, and ethics?

7.8.1   Trust, Science, Realism, and Ethics

Zaltman and Moorman (1988) explore the factors determining whether marketing managers actually use the research generated by marketing research departments. The key factor, they find, is trust: "Perhaps the single most important factor affecting the use of research is the presence or absence of trust" (1988, p. 16). Indeed, a major requirement for developing and maintaining trust is "being a truth teller" (1988, p. 20). Thus, truth and trust are interrelated.

Mainstream philosophy of science views trust as a key construct for understanding the dynamics of scientific disciplines. Trust is essential in science (indeed, in all disciplines) because scientific knowledge is a shared form of knowledge; it is shared with its clients. The clients of commercial marketing researchers are limited in general to the organizations that purchase the research. However, the clients of academic marketing research include not only marketing practitioners, but also students, government officials, consumers, other academicians, and members of the general public (Hunt 2002a, ch. 2; Monroe et al. 1988). In essence, all researchers who share their research with clients state implicitly: "Trust me." Thus, science and trust are interrelated.

One consequence of the importance of trust in science is for those whose research projects are guided by philosophies maintaining that the research does not "touch base"—path D in Figure 7.1—with a reality external to the researcher's own linguistically encapsulated theory, or paradigm, or research tradition, or worldview. Such philosophies provide no grounds for the client trusting the knowledge claims of the researchers. Thus, philosophies such as reality relativism, constructionism, critical relativism, and deconstructive postmodernism that abandon truth are not only self-refuting for their philosophical advocates, but also self-defeating for practicing researchers who might adopt them at the "workbench" level.

Trust and Ethics. Studies indicate that a difficult ethical problem facing marketing researchers is "misinterpreting the results of a research project with the objective of supporting a predetermined personal or corporate point of view" (Hunt, Chonko, and Wilcox 1984, p. 312). Because such biases would destroy trust, marketing associations (e.g., the American Marketing Association, the Academy of Marketing Science, the European Marketing Academy, and the Society for Marketing Advances) are paying more attention to marketing's codes of ethics. It has been long-recognized that one of the major, distinguishing characteristics that separates professions from other vocations is that all true professions have a degree of self-control by means of formal and/or informal codes of ethics. An underlying tenet of all such codes is that the true professional, when interacting with clients of any kind, is not guided totally by self-interest. For example, when people go to physicians, they have a right to expect that their physicians will not adopt methods of treatment based solely on which method will best serve the physicians' interests. Because of the disparity in knowledge of diseases and their respective treatments, the social compact between laypeople and their physicians requires a significant element of *trust*. Many philosophers of science are coming to realize that both *trust* and *ethics* are interrelated keys to understanding scientific communities.

Rom Harré has been at the forefront of those philosophers advocating the importance of, in his terms, "moral order" in science. Avoiding the philosophers' fallacy, Harré (1986) defines scientific knowledge as "trustworthy knowledge," rather than truth with certainty: "Science is not a logically coherent body of knowledge in the strict, unforgiving sense of the philosophers' high redefinition, but a cluster of material and cognitive practices, carried on within a distinctive moral order, whose main characteristic is the trust that obtains among its members and [the trust that] should obtain between that community and the larger lay community with which it is interdependent" (1986, p. 6). What, for him, is trust? "To trust someone is to be able to rely on them in the matter in question. . . . Scientists believe that things personally unknown to them are as *another scientist* says they are." However, "trust is not maintained by telling each other only literal truths. Under that constraint the members of the community would perforce remain forever silent. It is enough that they tell each other what they honestly believe to be the truth" (1986, p. 12). In this regard, Harré is claiming that the moral order of science implies, among other things, the avoidance of sophistry and deception, as well as outright fraud.

Harré points out that trust in all societies is most often role-related: "it is because the trusted one is in the role of parent, guardian, policeman, research supervisor, and so on, that the trust is there until something happens to upset it" (Harré 1986, p. 21). Therefore, scientists in their role as researchers producing trustworthy belief are required by their peers and by the lay community to maintain a moral order. This moral order is necessary, Harré argues, because researchers are involved in producing "practically reliable scientific knowledge." This "reliance might be existential, concerning what there is or what might be, or it might be practical, concerning what can and cannot be done, or both. The moral quality of the product comes through clearly in the kind of outrage felt by the [scientific] community at the disclosure of scientific fraud" (Harré 1986, p. 13). Harré asks: "Is scientific method . . . and scientific morality, the fiduciary act of committing oneself to make one's scientific utterances fiduciary acts, the best way to discipline a community which exists to find out about the natural world"? (Harré 1986, p. 26). Harré answers this question affirmatively on the basis that science is committed to referential realism. This realism holds that "existence is prior to theory, and that while no ontologies for science could be absolute, nevertheless, ontologies (realized in referential practices) are always, at any moment, less revisable than their associated belief-systems. . . . On this view, truth and falsity migrate from the epistemology of science to the morality of its human community" (1986, p. 6). For Harré, any view of science that claims that scientific knowledge is "constructed" or "created" by the scientific community independent of some external reality is to be rejected on moral grounds. He summarizes his position as follows:

> Science has a special status, not because it is a sure way of producing truths and avoiding falsehood, but because it is a communal practice of a community with a remarkable and rigid morality at the heart of which is a commitment that the products of this community shall be trustworthy. . . . Science is not just a cluster of material and cognitive practices, but is a moral achievement as well. . . . Antirealism, which, like it or not, seeps out into the lay world as antiscience, is not only false, but morally obnoxious. (Harré 1986, p. 7)

As members of the marketing academic profession, we have numerous clients for marketing knowledge, our product. Concerning marketing knowledge, its development, and dissemination, does the *trust* that these constituencies have *in* us impose certain special responsibilities *on* us? If so, what is the nature of these responsibilities, and what does it imply about the most appropriate philosophy to guide marketing science? Philosophies based on reality relativism, constructionism, critical relativism, and deconstructive postmodernism would seem to be unlikely candidates for inspiring trust. Most assuredly, no philosophy of research can *guarantee* trustworthy knowledge. Nevertheless, researchers can find comfort in the fact that there exist philosophies of science—such as scientific realism—that, at the minimum, are not antithetical to truth and its surrogate, trustworthy knowledge, and, at the maximum, may (fallibly) yield knowledge that is truly worthy of others' trust.

QUESTIONS FOR ANALYSIS AND DISCUSSION

1. Define and differentiate among the following theories of truth: pragmatic, correspondence, coherence, and consensus. How does the consensus theory of truth fail to address the issue of the pragmatic success of science? What is the relationship between the consensus theory of truth and reality relativism? Should marketing adopt the consensus theory? Why, or why not?
2. Both boxes 1 and 3 in Figure 7.1 contain entities, attributes, and structures. Is Figure 7.1 not, therefore, a tautology or at least redundant? Does Figure 7.1 relate to empirical testing? If so, how? If not, why not?
3. If truth does not *equal* pragmatic success, how does (or does not) pragmatic success relate to truth? Could a theory be characterized as

having high explanatory and predictive success, yet have low pragmatic success?

4. In Orwell's *1984* (1949), the society of Big Brother maintained: "Reality is inside the skull . . . you must get rid of the 19th century ideas about the laws of nature. We make the laws of nature" (Orwell 1949, p. 168). Furthermore, the society exercised control of its citizens through "doublethink," which was the practice of holding "two contradictory beliefs in one's mind simultaneously, and accepting both of them" (Orwell 1949, p. 215). Doublethink was necessary in order "to deny the existence of objective reality and all the while to take account of the reality one desires" (1949, p. 216). Futhermore, it was necessary to destroy empirical science:

> The empirical method of thought, on which all of the scientific achievements of the past were founded, is opposed to [our] most fundamental principles. [Therefore,] in Newspeak there is no word for "science." (Orwell 1949, p. 194)

Are reality relativism and constructionism consistent or inconsistent with the society in *1984*? How? How does the principle of noncontradiction relate or not relate to *1984*? How does the issue of self-refutation relate or not relate? Find an example of "doublethink" in marketing and/or society. Analyze the example.

5. How does Laudan reach the conclusion that "truth" and "falsity" are "irrelevant" to science? Why has Laudan fallen victim to the "philosophers' fallacy" with respect to truth?

6. Evaluate the thesis of Laudan that "truth" is irrelevant to science, and, at the same time, science should "treat theories as if they were true" for purposes of "practical action" and "testing theories."

7. How does the dogmatic skepticism in Table 7.1 differ from dogmatism? How does each relate to trust? Which of the two, dogmatism and dogmatic skepticism, is more prevalent in marketing? Why?

8. How are trust, science, realism, and ethics related? How does truth relate to each?

NOTES

1. This chapter draws heavily on Hunt (1990b, 1992a).

2. Agazzi (1989, p. 95) claims that, in his elaboration of "verisimilitude," Popper reified truth.

3. Today, even Feyerabend, to whom Anderson (1986, p. 156) refers as "one of the most radical of contemporary relativists," concedes that incommensurability is a "rare event" and "is a difficulty for philosophers, not scientists" (Feyerabend 1987b, p. 81).

4. See, for example, McMullin (1984) for an evaluation of this issue and whether Laudan's "convergent realism" is a straw man.

5. Calder and Tybout (1989) in the passage quoted are complaining—quite appropriately, in my judgment—that relativist writers seem often to view nonrelativist scholars as "country bumpkins."

6. The quote of Laudan is sometimes referred to as the "pessimistic induction" thesis. See Psillos (1996).

7. The case is *McClean vs. Arkansas Board of Education*, 529 F. Supp. 1255 (E.D. Arkansas 1982).

8. See Reisch (1998) for a good discussion of the problems confronting those who wish to deny that science differs from nonscience in any substantive way, but who wish to deny the right of those advocating creation science to have their view taught in public schools.

9. Table 7.1 comes from Table 1 in Hunt (1992a). Since its original publication, numerous writers have suggested that feminism and postmodernism should be added to the table as examples of dogmatic skepticism. In contrast, the view here is that only radical feminism and deconstructive postmodernism embrace dogmatic skepticism.

10. The exception might be quantum mechanics.

11. In addition, not all ethnographic researchers are dogmatic skeptics. For example, Stewart, an ethnographic methodologist maintains: "Statistics-oriented researchers and ethnographers share an ultimate epistemic value. Whether or not they define themselves as 'scientists,' they both adhere to the fundamental purpose of science: to try to learn the truth about the world" (Stewart 1998, p. 12)

8   ON OBJECTIVITY AND MARKETING RESEARCH

The heart of the matter is that, while it is one thing to say that certain notions are "the socio-historical constructs of a particular time," it is quite another to add that they are no more than "the socio-historical constructs of a particular time." It cannot be right to proceed from a premise stating only that this is that, direct to the richer conclusion that this is merely that, that this is nothing but that, that this is that and nothing else.

—Antony Flew, "The Debunker's Fallacy" (1985)

Can marketing research be objective? Can any research be objective? As Rescher (1997, p. 25) has observed, "objectivity is not exactly popular in the present era." In the area of history, for example, Novick (1988, p. 6) reviews works (e.g., Kuhn 1962) in philosophy and concludes that "to say of a work of history that it is or isn't objective is to make an empty observation: to say something neither interesting nor useful." This chapter explores the objectivity question in marketing.[1] Specifically, this chapter evaluates the arguments that have led so many relativists, social constructionists, postmodernists, feminists, historicists, subjectivists, and humanists to deny the possibility of objectivity in marketing research. It then puts forth the "positive case" for pursuing objectivity. Like the case for truth, the positive case for objectivity focuses on trust.

8.1   THE NATURE OF OBJECTIVITY

The philosophy of science distinguishes ontological objectivity from epistemic objectivity. The former refers to whether the entities in a theory that are claimed to exist actually exist independent of someone's perception of them. The latter refers to certain aspects of how one justifies knowledge claims. Specifically, epistemic objectivity:

> relates to the appropriateness of *claims or contentions*, addressing the question of whether a claim is impersonally and generically cogent rather than personal and idiosyncratic—whether it holds not just for me (egocentric subjectivity) or for some of us (parochial subjectivity) but for all of us (impersonal or interpersonal objectivity). . . . Objectivity in this sense has to do not with the *subject matter* of a claim but with its *justification*. It pivots on the way the claim is substantiated and supported—namely without the introduction of any personal biases or otherwise distortive individual idiosyncrasies, preferences, predilections, etc. (Rescher 1997, p. 4; italics in original)

Thus, the *pursuit* of objectivity relates to efforts at minimizing bias of some kind (or kinds) in research findings. As to the objectivity of research methods, for example, bias is thought to be reduced in experiments and survey research by using control groups and placebos, by checking for nonresponse bias (Armstrong and Overton 1977; Hunt 1990a), by checking for same-source bias (Podsakoff and Organ 1986; Crampton and Wagner 1994), and by separating the measurement model analysis from the test of the structural model in structural equation modeling (Anderson and Gerbing 1988). As to the objectivity of ethnographic methods, Stewart (1998) argues for objectivity as a goal. For him, the specificity of the research circumstances of ethnographic research implies that strict replicability (i.e., the reproduction of identical results by other researchers) is not "humanly possible" (Stewart 1998, p. 30). Nevertheless, objectivity can (and should) be sought through bias minimization. The questions to ask of any ethnography include:

> To what extent, and in what ways, were the results affected by the peculiarities of researchers, insiders, or their interactions? How well were their biases, and the reactivity of insiders to researchers, minimized or offset by the use of research method? . . . Have the context and results been sufficiently specified that the findings could potentially be disconfirmed in a follow-up study? Replicability is not a precondition for scientific findings; intersubjective testability is. (Stewart 1998, pp. 30–31)

As to the objectivity of marketing research, for example, consider the issue of salesperson performance. Churchill et al. (1985, p. 117) conducted a meta-analysis of the determinants of salesperson performance and concluded: "Enduring personal characteristics such as aptitude variables and personal/physical traits do have some relationship to performance, but not as much as those characteristics which are 'influenceable' through increased training and experience or more effective company policies and procedures (e.g., skill levels, role perceptions, and motivation)." Is this knowledge-claim objective? In general, are any such knowledge-claims in marketing research objective? More generally yet, should the marketing research community even pursue the ideal of objectivity? Marketing's traditional view on these questions is summarized in the following statement:

Scientific knowledge, in which theories, laws, and explanations are primal, must be objective in the sense that its truth content must be intersubjectively certifiable. Requiring that theories, laws and explanations be empirically testable ensures that they will be intersubjectively certifiable since different (but reasonably competent) investigators with differing attitudes, opinions, and beliefs will be able to make observations and conduct experiments to ascertain their truth content. (Hunt 1976b, p. 27)

Participants in marketing's philosophy debates question or deny the possibility of objective marketing research. For example, some caution, "Scientific inquiry may not deserve the objectivity that we tend to assume to be true of it" (Sauer, Nighswanger, and Zaltman 1982, p. 19). Going much further, Peter and Olson (1983, pp. 119–20) not only caution that the "aura of objectivity has been steadily eroding for years across all sciences, including physics," but conclude that "science is subjective" and marketers, therefore, should adopt relativism and constructionism. Going further yet, Peter (1983, p. 385) examines the "received view on theories," contends that "leading philosophers no longer espouse this approach," puts forth what he calls "a more current understanding of the philosophy of science literature," and concludes, albeit incoherently, "objectivity is an illusion."[2] Even more strongly, Mick (1986, p. 207) advocates semiotics for marketing research because, among other reasons, "objectivity is impossible." Similarly, Fullerton (1986, p. 433) endorses historicism, claiming, "Researcher objectivity and intersubjective certifiability are chimeras—they cannot be achieved." Likewise, Hirschman (1986, p. 249) points out that "the humanist approach denies the possibility of discovering objective truth."

Therefore, in marketing's philosophy debates, the three questions posed concerning the possible objectivity of the claim of Churchill et al. (1985) and others in marketing are uninformed queries. If objectivity is a "chimera," an "illusion," or "impossible," its pursuit and all claims to its accomplishment are, to say the very least, naïve. If all inquiry is subjective, then so is the specific assertion of Churchill and his associates, as well as *all* marketing research.

At the outset of our analysis of objectivity, three preliminary issues warrant attention. First, many marketers believe that the relativist/subjectivist claims that objectivity in research is impossible and/or undesirable are so specious that they do not merit analysis. Some maintain, for example, that relativists and subjectivists do not intend for their views on objectivity to be taken seriously by anyone. Indeed, it is claimed, relativists *themselves* do not believe in their arguments. In contrast, I maintain that (1) the cogency of arguments against objectivity are such that they fully merit counterarguments, (2) it is patronizing to dismiss relativist/subjectivist arguments as being unbelieved by their proponents, (3) to be condescending toward relativist claims is to engage in impolite academic discourse, and (4) ideas (including, perhaps especially, wrong-headed ideas) have consequences. Therefore, relativist/subjectivist claims should be treated, not with condescending dismissal, but with both seriousness and civility.

Second, skillful rhetoricians recognize that many philosophies, when applied at the "workbench" level, are implausible or even bizarre. Nonetheless, these philosophies can be made to seem reasonable or commendable when argued in the abstract. Relativism, subjectivism, and constructionism, I maintain, are such philosophies (as well as Marxist utopianism—as the twentieth century reminds us). Therefore, each argument against objectivity is illustrated here by use of Churchill and his associates' claim (hereafter, simply "CW's claim") concerning salesperson performance as a continuing example at the "workbench" level. Lest there be any misunderstanding, however, this chapter is not critical of Churchill and his associates, their article, or their article's scholarship. CW's claim is used only to illustrate the implications of relativism/subjectivism at the level of actual marketing research practice.

The third preliminary issue is that many marketers confuse *objectivity* with *objectivism*. Because the confusion in marketing, management, social science, and philosophy, is so widespread, it is worth discussing in detail.

8.1.1   Objectivity and Objectivism

Many philosophers attack what they call "objectivism." For example, Bernstein contrasts relativism not with absolutism (its usual opposite) but with objectivism, which he defines as:

> the basic conviction that there is or must be some permanent, ahistorical matrix or framework to which we can ultimately appeal in determining the nature of rationality, knowledge, truth, reality, goodness, or rightness. . . . Objectivism is closely related to foundationalism and the search for an Archimedean point. (Bernstein 1983, p. 8)

Similarly, Lakoff and Johnson (1980, p. 187) argue against "objectivism," which they maintain is the belief that:

> There is an objective reality, and we can say things that are objectively, absolutely, and unconditionally true and false about it. . . . Science provides us with a methodology that allows us to rise above our subjective limitations and to achieve understanding from a universally valid and unbiased point of view. Science can ultimately give a correct, definitive, and general account of reality, and, through its methodology, it is constantly progressing toward that goal. (Lakoff and Johnson 1980, p. 187)

For anti-objectivists, seeking knowledge that is absolutely true, universally valid, absolutely correct, definitive, known with certainty, or known from a unique privileged position is not just impossible, it is also undesirable. Such objectivist views "inevitably turn into vulgar or sophisticated forms of ethnocentricism" (Bernstein 1983, p. 19).[3] Thus, Sapire (1988, p. 497) asks: "Is it possible to believe that science as it has developed mainly in the West reigns supreme among the systems intended to provide knowledge of the world, yet not be committed to derogatory views about other cultures and societies"? And he answers: "Orthodoxy . . . [holds that] all such comparisons are invidious and are to be avoided."

Stemming from the belief that objectivism is impossible (because knowledge with certainty is beyond human capability) and undesirable (because believing in the knowledge claims and method of science is necessarily ethnocentric), one might argue that objectivity is impossible and its pursuit undesirable. This appears to be Holt's (1991) argument. Wallendorf and Belk (1989) have argued that interpretivist researchers should use (and report the use of) checks, audits, triangulation, and purposive sampling as a means for minimizing bias. That is, these procedures, for Wallendorf and Belk, are meant to increase objectivity. Holt (1991, pp. 60–61) argues against these procedures on the grounds that they constitute adopting the "objectivist evaluative banner" of "positivist-inclined researchers" and "Western ways of thinking."[4] Similarly, Thompson (1991, pp. 63–64) cites Bernstein (1983) as showing that the pursuit of "objective knowledge" is misguided because it stems from "objectivism" and "foundationalism," which reflect a "Western view of knowledge."

On Objectivism: For Reason. Several observations illuminate the objectivism controversy and its implications for marketing and objectivity. First, though many philosophers in the past, and perhaps some in the present, subscribe to the foundationalist search for infallible knowledge and a "god's eye view" of absolute certainty, marketing's scientific realism advocates fallibilism. *Pursuing* objectivity (minimizing known sources of bias) differs from the claim that one has attained OBJECTIVITY (maintaining that one has eliminated *all* bias). Hence, to the extent that Bernstein's "objectivism" and "foundationalism" are problems at all, they seem (like paradigm incommensurability) to be problems for philosophy and some philosophers, not for science and most scientists.

Second, holding the claims and method of science in high regard is anything but ethnocentric. Without such Eastern contributions as the Arabic numeral system, science might never have arisen anywhere, let alone in the West.[5] Third, for Western humanists and intellectuals to denigrate science because it originated in their own cultures not only commits the genetic fallacy, but is perversely ethnophobic as well, for science, no matter where it originated, now belongs to all of humanity—just as does the Arabic numerical system.[6] Fourth, what Bernstein calls "objectivism"—because it is confused with *objectivity*—is better characterized as "vulgar absolutism" (Siegel 1987, p. 163). Using "objectivism" in the manner of Beach is recommended for marketing because it more accurately describes the practice of science and its goal of objectivity:

> Objectivism: The thesis that there exists a systematic method of reasoning and a coordinate set of beliefs embodying its principles, which, despite the vicissitudes of social psychological conditioning, are accessible to knowledge and are capable of sustaining a dynamic, self-correcting belief system. These principles may contain errors or half-truths, and they may never attain a fixed and final form. Yet insofar as (a) their consistency is publicly verifiable, (b) their development is rational, and (c) their truth-content is demonstrably greater than that of rival contenders, they do constitute reliable criteria by which to evaluate subsidiary beliefs and hypotheses. (Beach 1984, p. 14)

In conclusion, though objectivism in the sense of vulgar absolutism may be impossible, this does not imply that objectivity is impossible. Nor should a paranoid fear of ethnocentrism deter marketing from pursuing objectivity. Bernstein, on whom many writers in marketing's philosophy debates rely, was confused on both counts. As Schwandt explains:

> The confusion over the meaning of *objectivity* as a regulative ideal has arisen from [Bernstein's] confounding it with the notion of *objectivism* and juxtaposing the latter with *relativism*. Recognizing that [Bernstein's] objectivism is a bankrupt notion in no way entails rejecting the bid to be objective, neither does it follow that we must slide down the slippery slope of relativism. (Schwandt 1990, p. 270; italics in original)

The preceding sheds light on the claim by Zinkhan and Hirschheim (1992, p. 82)—who are professed *advocates* of scientific realism, no less—that "The realist position in the social domain is untenable." That is, after arguing that marketers "in the social domain" should adopt scientific realism because such concepts as "memory" and "desires" have "causal powers," Zinkhan and Hirschheim (hereafter ZH) claim that their own position is "untenable." ZH's position is, of course, incoherent.

To understand the source of the incoherency of ZH's position, we must first ask: What is the realist ontological position? Manicas (1987, pp. 9–10), the realist philosopher on whom ZH base their version of scientific realism, states: "A philosophy (of science) [is] positivist if it holds that a scientific explanation must eschew appeal to what is in principle beyond experience . . . by contrast, a realist holds that a valid scientific explanation can appeal to the in principle non-observable." It is the posited existence of unobservable, intangible entities in the "social domain" that ZH's realism claims will have "causal powers." For example, ZH use the Blair and Zinkhan (1984) study as a prototypical example of applying their realism to health-care marketing, and they claim that, in this study, "desire was the generative mechanism producing adherence" (Zinkhan and Hirscheim 1992, p. 86). As Manicas (1987) and Bhaskar (1979) point out, using concepts such as "desire" in scientific explanation is precisely what distinguishes the ontology of scientific realism from that of logical positivism.

ZH can maintain, like the logical positivists in the past and relativists (see Anderson 1989, p. 14) in the present, that "the realist ontological position, in the social domain, is untenable" (Zinkhan and Hirschheim 1992, p. 82). Alternatively, they can maintain that scientific realism, whether the realism of Manicas or some other version, is "more appropriate for describing marketing phenomena" (Zinkhan and Hirschheim 1992, p. 84). However, they cannot maintain coherently both positions simultaneously. Failing a test for coherence is not just some philosophical technicality, as ZH imply. Incoherent arguments make no sense, and *making sense* is a fundamental desideratum of academic discourse.

What led ZH to believe that their own realism's ontology was untenable? They cite Berger and Luckmann (1967) and Sayers (1987) as support for their claim that the "realist ontological position" requires the "certainty" of an "absolute viewpoint," or a "god's-eye or no-eye view." However, ZH are twice wrong. First, the realist ontological position does not require certainty. Indeed, it specifically adopts fallibilism. Neither realism, nor science, nor truth, nor objectivity requires the certainty of a god's-eye view. Only when truth (with a small "t") is turned into TRUTH, and objectivity (with a small "o") is turned into OBJECTIVITY, by the philosophers' fallacy of high redefinition (or by other means) do truth and objectivity imply the certainty of a god's-eye view.

Second, Sayers (1987), whom ZH cite for authority, was not even discussing the realist ontological position. Indeed, it is instructive to review what Sayers was actually discussing. Because Wittgenstein "seemed to advocate . . . what has been called cultural relativism . . . an often despised thesis . . . and justifiably so" (Sayers 1987, p. 134), what did this imply? Specifically, did it imply that Wittgenstein's views also supported the relativist "equivalence postulate" (Sayers 1987, p. 135). That is, does Wittengenstein support the view of Barnes and Bloor that "For the relativist there is no sense attached to the idea that some standards are really rational as distinct from merely accepted as such. . . . Hence the relativist conclusion that they are to be explained in the same way" (Barnes and Bloor 1982, pp. 27–28). Sayers argues that Wittgenstein, in fact, "does not grant equal status to other belief systems—he does not accept the equivalence postulate of the strong thesis" (Sayers 1987, p. 142). Wittgenstein's views actually imply that there is no *need* for a "god's-eye view," because "the lack of some ultimate standard of rationality . . . is a mere bogeyman" (1987, p. 142). Indeed, for Sayers:

> That we exempt some beliefs from doubt, that we ground our other beliefs on
> these, that we use them as the context in which we argue or disagree on other
> matters, and that they are products of a particular social environment which varies
> from group to group, is no reason to adopt relativism or seek to overcome it [by a
> futile search for god's-eye view]. This is the lesson to be learned from Wittgenstein.
> (Sayers 1987, p. 145)

In short, Sayers's work parallels the argument here: The absence of TRUTH
and OBJECTIVITY(a god's-eye view) constitutes a bogeyman and no grounds
for rejecting realism, adopting relativism, or abandoning the pursuit of truth
and objectivity. Though ZH embrace the very bogeyman that Sayers (and
Wittgenstein) warn against, marketing need not.

With the three preliminary issues out of the way, we begin our analysis of
objectivity with the work of the logical empiricists and falsificationists. These
philosophers addressed the issue of objectivity in the contexts of both the
natural and the social sciences.

8.2   LOGICAL EMPIRICISM, FALSIFICATIONISM,
AND OBJECTIVITY

As discussed in section 3.3, the logical empiricists, led by Carnap (e.g., 1956),
Hempel (e.g., 1965b), and Nagel (e.g., 1961), believed that all cognitively
meaningful statements must be either empirically testable (i.e., true or false
by observational tests) or else purely analytical (i.e., true or false by definition). For science, all other statements would be impermissible, metaphysical, "empty talk." Therefore, theories (i.e., *groups* of statements) would have
to be empirically testable, which could be guaranteed by segmenting unambiguously each theory's terms into (1) logical and mathematical terms, (2)
theoretical terms, and (3) observation terms. The theoretical (unobservable)
terms were not to be construed as genuinely *referring*. That is, every theoretical term was to be tied rigorously to a unique set of observation terms through
a series of definitions (i.e., correspondence rules). Contra scientific realism,
because the relationship between a theoretical term and its associated observable terms was purely analytical, a theoretical term was just a "shorthand"
way of referring to a unique collection of observation terms.

For the logical empiricists, objectivity in science presupposed the existence of a nonproblematical, theory-free, observation language. Just as a child
learns the meaning of the word "chair" ostensively—by adults pointing to
examples of objects to which "chair" refers—the observation language of
science, its observation terms, was thought to be purely observable,
presuppositionless, or theory-free. Thus, observation terms (measures and data)
would be a function only of the sensations that result from the retinal stimula-

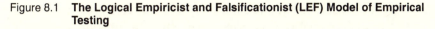

Figure 8.1 **The Logical Empiricist and Falsificationist (LEF) Model of Empirical Testing**

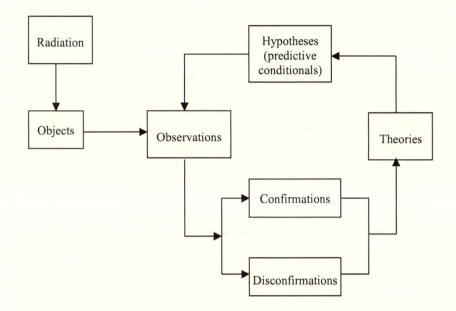

Source: Adapted from Hunt (1992a).

Note: Read—Radiation reflected from objects results in observations that are used to test our theories.

tion of the eye brought about by light reflecting from tangible objects. In short: observation terms $= f$ (sensations).

For the logical empiricists, "Science strives for objectivity in the sense that its statements are to be capable of public tests with results that do not vary essentially with the tester" (Hempel 1970, p. 695). For the falsificationists, "the objectivity of scientific statements lies in the fact that they can be intersubjectively tested" (Popper 1959, p. 44). These intersubjective, public tests, for both the logical empiricists and falsificationists, presumed a theory of the process of empirical testing. Figure 8.1 shows a path diagram of the process theory implicit in the logical empiricist and falsificationist view (hereafter, LEF view) of empirical testing. It should be stressed that Figure 8.1 is, intentionally, a parsimonious representation of the LEF view; only key concepts and their interrelationships are presented.

Starting from the right, the LEF view of empirical testing proposed that the scientist has a reasonably well-articulated theory (or theories) to be tested, and, from the theory, hypotheses (or predictive conditionals) are deduced. These hypotheses, roughly speaking, state: "If theory T is true, then, after

conducting this test procedure, we should expect to observe phenomenon *K*."
If the test procedure confirms the hypothesis, this confirmation or verification lends inductive empirical support to the truth of theory *T*. The LEF view
maintained that if phenomenon *K* is not observed, then the disconfirmed hypothesis would imply that at least some aspect of theory *T* is false. Popper's
(1959, 1963) falsificationism, relying on *modus tollens*, focused on the allegedly unique role of disconfirmations in the empirical testing process, in particular, and the development of science, in general (as in "bold conjectures
and refutations"). In contrast, the logical empiricists focused on (see section
3.3.4) the qualitative problem of when a positive instance of a generalization
counts as a confirmation (e.g., the "paradox of the ravens") and the quantitative problem of how much confirmation a confirming instance of observational evidence provides a theory (i.e., they focused on a theory of inductive
confirmation).

Starting from the left side of the model, the LEF view assumed that there
were both objects and radiation in the world that existed independent of human perception. When radiation in the visible spectrum is reflected from objects in the world, such objects are directly observable and describable in a
physicalistic language, in which each term directly refers to material things
and their observable properties (Suppe 1977b). Thus, according to the LEF
view, the objectivity of the empirical testing process relies on, among other
things, scientists having at their disposal a nonproblematic, physical-thing,
observation language. In this language, the meanings of the concepts were to
be determined ostensively, that is, by "pointing at." As originally conceived
by Schlick (1934, pp. 223, 226), such a foundation was intended to make
science "absolutely certain," with "absolute fixed points," and an "unshakable point of contact between knowledge and reality."

The LEF theory of the empirical testing process has much to recommend
it. By assuming that radiation and objects exist in the world independent of
perception, it denied—see section 2.4—idealism, which is "The theory that
(a) the knower and the thing known do not have independent existence; all
knowledge is knowledge of our conscious states and processes, and not of any
external world; (b) that which is known is created by the human mind; matter
is not real" (Angeles 1981, p. 121). Because idealism reduces empirical testing, and, indeed, all of science to a charade, denying idealism seems reasonable. Furthermore, observation, deduction, and induction play important roles
in empirical testing.

A major issue for the logical empiricists was whether their view of empirical testing and objectivity, as represented by the LEF model, precluded the
social sciences from being *science*. That is, is it the case that the social sciences are inherently subjective?

8.2.1   Are the Social Sciences Inherently Subjective?

Ever since the social science disciplines emerged in the latter half of the nineteenth century, a central concern has been whether social science, like natural science, could produce objective knowledge. In the 1940s and 1950s, the logical empiricists entered the debate over the alleged subjectivity of social science. The debate is summarized in Ernest Nagel's (1961, pp. 473–85) classic work, *The Structure of Science*. Nagel's analysis begins with a discussion of the "subjective categories" argument of Weber (1947) and others. According to this argument, social science cannot be objective because the subject matter of social science—in contrast to that of natural science—involves purposive human action directed at attaining various ends. Because the language used to explain these actions includes such terms as "motives" and "goals" that refer (if they refer to anything at all) to the private, unobservable, radically subjective experiences of individuals, social science must rely on such nonobjective techniques of inquiry as Weber's *Verstehen* (i.e., empathic understanding).

Nagel (1961) counterargues by first pointing out that many of the explanatory categories of the social sciences are objective—for example, the publicly observable environmental factors that influence human action. Therefore, knowledge claims relying on such factors are also objective. Second, concepts such as motives and goals can be accessed through subjects' introspective reports, and these verbal responses can be regarded as publicly observable, objective data for grounding objective knowledge. Third, though researchers' projecting themselves empathically into their subjects may be helpful in producing hypotheses in the context of discovery, such claims could rightfully constitute scientific knowledge only by later verification in the context of justification. Such verification must be on the basis of evidence obtained from observing physical phenomena, human behavior, or people's verbal responses.

Nagel (1961) next identifies three different versions of Weber's "value-bias" argument against objectivity. (1) Because researchers' selection of topics reflects their values, what constitutes a desirable social order will inevitably bias their claims as to what kind of social order currently exists. (2) Because fact and value are fused together in social language (e.g., "murder" not only describes a behavior, i.e., to kill, but also evaluates that behavior, i.e., to *wrongfully* kill), social science's value judgments cannot possibly be eliminated. (3) The time during which researchers lived (see this chapter's epigraph) and their social class, as argued in historical relativism and Marxism, bias social science.

Nagel (1961) counters by agreeing that the importance of a research topic is a value "bias," but then contends that this innocuous bias also occurs in natural science. He continues by agreeing that many, ostensibly objective, social science analyses are in fact disguised recommendations for social policy, but then urges social scientists to state their value assumptions fully, and he counsels their scholarly communities to adopt natural science's self-corrective mechanisms. These procedures, though neither infallible nor complete, he argues, can progressively diminish the effects of individual researchers' bias. Nagel then agrees that much social science discourse fuses fact and value, but maintains that careful scholarship can distinguish between statements that characterize states of affairs (i.e., positive) and those that appraise those states (i.e., normative)—see Hunt (2002a, section 1.7). Finally, Nagel argues that "social class determines knowledge" can be justified by Marxists only if they themselves have transcended their own social class. (How else could they know this?) But if Marxists can transcend their own social class and attain a "unique privileged position" to justify "social class determines knowledge," then why cannot other social scientists in a similar manner transcend their social class? Thus, Nagel argues that Marxism is self-refuting. As to whether the social sciences can be objective, Nagel concludes:

> it is not easy in most areas of inquiry to prevent our likes, aversions, hopes, and fears from coloring our conclusions. It has taken centuries of effort to develop habits and techniques of investigation which help safeguard inquiries in the natural sciences against the intrusion of irrelevant personal factors; and even in these disciplines the protection those procedures give is *neither infallible nor complete*. The problem is undoubtedly more acute in the study of human affairs, and the difficulties it creates for achieving reliable knowledge in the social sciences must be admitted. . . .
>
> In brief, the various reasons we have been examining for the intrinsic impossibility of securing objective (i.e., value-free and unbiased) conclusions in the social sciences do not establish what they purport to establish, even though in some instances they direct attention to undoubtedly important practical difficulties frequently encountered in these disciplines. (Nagel 1961, pp. 488, 502; italics added)

The preceding review prompts five observations. First, Nagel stresses the fallibility of science. He, a prominent logical empiricist, did not advocate the "god's-eye view" of Bernstein's *objectivism*. Second, all the debate's participants presumed that natural science was objective, which to them meant "value-free" and "unbiased," and that this objectivity resulted, at least in part, from theory-free observation. For example, Nagel locates the value neutrality that is "pervasive in the natural sciences" (Nagel 1961, p. 485) in its "purely observable data" and "publicly observable subject matter" (1961, p. 474). Similarly, his opponents ground the objectivity of natural science in its "presuppositionless investigation of empirical data" (Weber 1947, p. 76).

Third, some marketers ground their claim that objectivity is impossible by using arguments paralleling those in the Nagel-Weber debate. These include the discussions of "value-free" knowledge by Hirschman (1986), historicism by Fullerton (1986), and *Verstehen* by Hudson and Ozanne (1988) and Holbrook and O'Shaughnessy (1988). Fourth, these marketers do not provide, nor do they even attempt to provide, rebuttals to Nagel's well-known and forceful analysis. Fifth, most participants in marketing's philosophy debates reject a major underlying premise of the Nagel-Weber debate: the premise that natural science is objective. These writers claim, ostensibly "in line with modern philosophical positions" (Peter and Olson 1989, p. 26), that is, in line with historical relativism, that objectivity is impossible in *all* the sciences.

Before addressing the historical relativist view that objectivity is impossible in all science, we inquire: How would the logical empiricists have evaluated the objectivity of CW's knowledge claim? In reviewing CW's evidence, they would have paid special attention to the studies' measures, and, no doubt, would have criticized the measures of variables such as "aptitude," "motivation," and "role perceptions." These variables, which in the marketing literature are customarily presumed to be real, latent traits that imply "reflective" measures (Howell 1987), would have violated the logical empiricists' belief that all theoretical terms are only arbitrary labels given to "collections of observables." For the logical empiricists, only a kind of "formative" measure (Howell 1987; Diamantopoulos and Winklhofer 2001) is permissible. That is, even though Nagel accepted introspective reports from respondents as objective data, he admonished researchers never to consider such reports as "statements about private psychic states of the subjects" (Nagel 1961, p. 477). In our terms, such reports were never to be thought of as being reflective indicants of real, latent traits. Because CW's claim relies on studies employing reflective measures of hypothesized latent traits, its objectivity would have been questioned with much "clucking of tongues" by the logical empiricists.

How would the historical relativists and their "new image" view of science regard the objectivity of CW's claim? As we shall see, they would dismiss all claims to its objectivity as "impossible" (Peter and Olson 1989, p. 26).

8.3 HISTORICAL RELATIVISM AND OBJECTIVITY

Discussions of Kuhn's "new image of science" dominated philosophy in the 1960s (see section 4.2.1). Though all the major positions in *The Structure of Scientific Revolutions* were thoroughly discredited decades ago (Suppe 1977b), the book continues to be highly influential in marketing, management, social science, and consumer research. Much of *Structure* concerning the objectivity of science stems from Hanson's (1958) work on perceptual processes and scientific observation. Drawing on the psychology of perception, Hanson contended that the logical empiricists' assumption that science has access to theory-free data was false because experimental evidence from the psychology of illusions shows that what scientists "see" is determined by their theories and prior expectations. Indeed, a person:

> must learn some physics before he can see what the physicist sees . . . the infant and the layman can see: They are not blind. But they cannot see what the physicist sees; they are blind to what he sees . . . seeing is "a theory-laden" undertaking. (Hanson 1958, pp. 17, 19)

For Hanson, therefore, choices between rival theories cannot be made objectively because—in reference to whether the Sun revolves around the Earth (Ptolemy) or the Earth revolves around the Sun (Copernicus)—assuming that "Kepler and Tycho see the same thing at dawn just because their eyes are similarly affected is an elementary mistake" (Hanson 1958, p. 8). In this view, scientific observation = f(interpretation + sensations). However, anyone who thinks interpretation is anything other than *the* determining factor for scientific observation is making, for Hanson, an "elementary mistake."

Extending Hanson's work, Kuhn (1962)—see section 4.2.1—concluded that researchers' "paradigms" or "world views" guided the interpretive part of scientific observation and determined what researchers "saw." Therefore, collecting data for empirical testing could not adjudicate objectively any dispute among researchers who hold different paradigms or world views (because their respective paradigms would contaminate the data to guarantee each paradigm's truth). In short, paradigms determine observations (observations are theory-laden) and are incommensurable (there exists no theory-free means, no "privileged position," no "higher authority," no "god's-eye view," for adjudicating paradigm disputes). Therefore, objectivity in science is impossible. For example, even today we are not warranted in claiming that Ptolemy was wrong and Copernicus right; we can say only that current believers in the Copernican paradigm embrace the results of the most recent paradigm shift. Relying on the Gestalt theory of perception and laboratory experiments on reversible (duck/rabbit) figures, Kuhn (1962, p. 111) states, "What were ducks in the scientist's world before the revolution are rabbits afterwards." Scientific revolutions, like Gestalt shifts, cannot be accomplished by reasoned discourse about objective evidence (because data are theory-laden and paradigms are incommensurable), but must be produced by mass persuasion—much like religious conversions.

Kuhnian relativism dovetailed neatly with the Sapir-Whorf thesis of linguistic relativism. Sapir (1921; Mandelbaum 1949) and Whorf (1956), after studying American Indian languages and contrasting them with English, concluded that each language structures thought in such a manner that it determines the reality that speakers of that language perceive. One perceives only the reality that is permitted or required by one's language. Therefore, accord-

Figure 8.2 **The Historical Relativist Model of Empirical Testing**

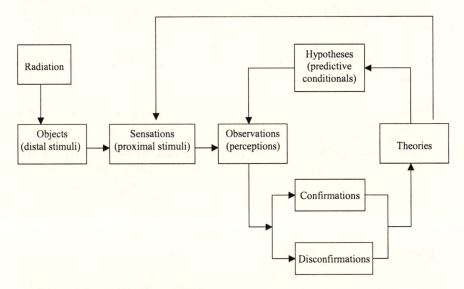

Source: Adapted from Hunt (1992a).

Note: Read—The observations used to test our theories are perceptions and result from sensations (proximal stimuli) informed by the theories being tested.

ing to linguistic relativism, the interpretation inherent in scientific observation is theory-laden by each scientist's language, which makes objectivity impossible across languages.

Figure 8.2 displays a model of the process theory implied by the historical relativist view. It differs from the LEF model by interpreting scientific "observations" to be equivalent to "perceptions" and by adding a new concept, "sensations" (or, in the terms of the psychology of perception, "proximal stimuli"), and a path from "theories" to "sensations." The theories to sensations path implies the cognitive process of interpreting sensations by means of theories. By acknowledging that the proximal stimuli of retinal images, "sensations," are always interpreted in the process of empirical testing, the model seems to fit what we know about perceptual processes better than the simpler, LEF model. Yet, it does so at a price. As the path from "theories" to "sensations" implies, because science's observations are not neutral to its theories, empirical testing, apparently, cannot adjudicate impartially disputes concerning rival theories. According to Churchland (1979, p. 41), "Perceptual judgments cannot provide a conceptually neutral level of factual information against which competing theories can always be effectively tested."

Embedded within the historical relativism of Kuhn and his followers are five intertwined arguments that purportedly defeat all claims to objectivity.

Table 8.1 presents the arguments, cites the works of philosophers of science that ground them, and identifies the marketing articles in which they are used to support the view that marketing research cannot be objective. For example, Peter and Olson (1983, p. 120) claim that "science is subjective" because researchers cannot provide "objective, unbiased representations of the real world" that are "independent of any theory." They claim:

> It is impossible to collect data that are "theory neutral," since at least some implicit theory is needed to create measures and attach a meaning to them. . . . [W]e know that well-trained researchers can construct empirical data and results to support or refute almost any theory without violating "accepted standards" of research in a field. In fact, we have pointed out that the creation of empirical data and empirical results is a process that is controlled by the researcher. . . . [E]mpirical data and research do not and cannot "test" hypotheses or theories. Rather they typically provide demonstrations of the researcher's predilections or skill at post hoc rationalization. (Peter and Olson 1989, pp. 26–27)

Similarly, for Hudson and Ozanne (1988, p. 515), "observations are value-laden, theory-laden and interpreted." Likewise, Mick (1986, pp. 198, 207), after favorably discussing the linguistic relativism of Sapir (1949) and Whorf (1956), asserts, "Objectivity is impossible: theories precede facts and interpretation precedes perception." Therefore, for Mick, researchers are misguided when they believe "what we are studying is 'out there' [in the real world] rather than 'in here' [in the mind]."

Relativism would hold that CW's knowledge claim cannot be objective because all the studies underlying the meta-analysis were theory-laden. That is, the findings were determined by the researchers' theories, perceptual processes, worldviews, paradigms, or language. In short, objectivity in marketing research is impossible because it is a "rigged game" (Olson 1987, p. 388). Greenwood (1990, p. 553) points out that relativist views on objectivity have become dogmas, for "many contemporary philosophers of science appear to accept them uncritically." Though the impossibility of objectivity is accepted uncritically by many philosophers of science, marketers, management scholars, consumer researchers, and social scientists, this uncritical acceptance is unwarranted—as we shall now argue.

8.4   FOR OBJECTIVITY: THE "NEGATIVE CASE"

Table 8.1 summarizes the five primary arguments that ostensibly imply the impossibility of objective marketing research. The counterarguments discussed here provide the "negative case" for objectivity. That is, they show that the arguments *against* objectivity fail. The "positive case" for objectivity is made in section 8.5. (How scientific realism addresses objectivity is shown in section 9.3, which develops a scientific realist theory of empirical testing.) Readers

Table 8.1

Objectivity and Marketing Research

Arguments against objectivity	Philosophy sources[a]	Marketing sources[b]
1. Objectivity is impossible because the language of a culture determines the reality that members of that culture see.	Sapir (1921), Whorf (1956)	Moorman (1984, p. 53), Rexeisen (1984, p. 329), Mick (1986, p. 198), Ozanne and Hudson (1989, p. 7)
2. Objectivity is impossible because the paradigms that researchers hold are incommensurable.	Kuhn (1962), Feyerabend (1975)	Anderson (1983, p. 22), Anderson (1986, p. 158), Hudson and Ozanne (1988, p. 508), Ozanne and Hudson (1989, p. 1)
3. Objectivity is impossible because theories are underdetermined by facts.	Kuhn (1962), Feyerabend (1975), Goodman (1973)	Sauer, Nighswonger, and Zaltman (1982, p. 19) Anderson (1983, pp. 22, 26), Rexeisen (1984, p. 330), Hudson and Ozanne (1988, p. 515), Anderson (1989, p. 11), Ozanne and Hudson (1989, p. 2), Peter (1991, p. 535)
4. Objectivity is impossible because the psychology of perception informs us that a theory-free observation language is impossible.	Hanson (1958), Kuhn (1962), Feyerabend (1975), Goodman (1978), Churchland (1988)	Anderson (1983, pp. 20, 26), Peter and Olson (1983, p. 188), Peter (1983, p. 385), Rexeisen (1984, p. 329), Mick (1986, p. 207), Holbrook (1986, p. 238), Jaworski and MacInnis (1987, p. 163), Peter and Dacin (1991, p. 279)
5. Objectivity is impossible because all epistemically significant observations are theory-laden.	Kuhn (1962), Feyerabend (1975), Brown (1977)	Sauer, Nighswonger, and Zaltman (1982, p. 380), Anderson (1983, pp. 20, 26), Peter and Olson (1983, pp. 121–22), Mick (1986, p. 207), Jaworski and MacInnis (1987, p. 164), Olson (1987, p. 388), Hudson and Ozanne (1988, pp. 515, 518), Holbrook and O'Shaughnessy (1988, p. 401), Firat (1989, p. 95), Peter and Olson (1989, p. 26), Thompson (1990, p. 29), Peter and Dacin (1991, p. 280)

Source: Hunt (1993). Reprinted by permission of the American Marketing Association.

[a]These philosophical and historical sources contain the foundational arguments that have led many writers to conclude that objectivity in science is impossible or problematic.

[b]These marketing sources either claim that objectivity is impossible on the basis of the arguments in the first column or imply that objectivity is impossible or problematic by citing and discussing the sources in the second column.

should note that Table 8.1 reveals that an impressively large number of distinguished scholars question (or deny) the possibility of objectivity in marketing research. Their views merit serious appraisal, not condescending dismissal.

8.4.1   Linguistic Relativism

The first argument maintains that the language of a culture determines the reality its members will see. For example, CW are members of the English language community, and, hence, the fact that they speak and think in English determines what they observe. Consequently, their knowledge claim cannot be objective, as it could not hold for other language communities. To think otherwise, so the argument goes, betrays simply the "ethnocentrism" of speakers of English in believing they have "privileged access" to the world.

If the thesis of linguistic relativism were true, objective inquiry across cultures (languages) would indeed be problematic. Fortunately, a host of studies on a large number of different languages strongly implies that language does not determine perceived reality. The works on perceptions of color are typical.

Heider and Oliver (1972) compared speakers of English with the Dani of West New Guinea in their ability to see different colors. After subjects had been exposed to a color chip for five seconds, the chip was removed and they were asked to pick out the color from an array of forty color chips. Because the Dani language divides the entire color spectrum into only two categories (roughly, "light" and "dark"), if the position that language determines reality were correct, the Dani should differ greatly from speakers of English in their ability to match color chips (in this case, the Dani language would *limit* their perception). Heider and Oliver found virtually no differences at all; the cognitive maps of the color spectrum of the Dani and Americans were almost identical.

Similarly, Berlin's and Kay's (1969) classic work on languages and human color perception, instead of finding evidence for linguistic relativism, actually found support for linguistic universalism. As just two of their many universals, Berlin and Kay found that languages having only three color terms always contain a term for red and those with four terms always contain a term for either green or yellow—but never both.[7] Steinfatt reviews the extensive literature on linguistic relativism and concludes, "The differences between languages are not to be found in what *can* be said, but in what it is *relatively easy to say*" (1989, p. 63; italics in original). Philosophers of science, using analytical (rather than empirical) methods, come to the same conclusion (Levin 1979).

A kind of linguistic relativism seems to underlie the proposed "rhetorical turn" in social science (Simons 1989), as advocated in economics by

McCloskey (1985) and in marketing by Sherry (1990). For example, Sherry (1990) cites current literature as showing that "objectivity is not generally possible in statistics" and concludes that the "rhetoric of inquiry replaces logic of inquiry in postmodern epistemology" because "the theory-ladenness of scientific observation ensures that all of consumer research is an interpretive task" (Sherry 1990, p. 551). However, Sherry's conclusion notwithstanding, a deeper interpretation of the philosophical foundations of the "rhetorical turn" is that rhetorical analysis *presupposes* objectivity. As pointed out by Keith and Cherwitz (1989), themselves scholars of rhetoric, if rhetorical analysis is anything, it is the exploration of persuasive communication among human beings. Communication may be either successful (persuasive) or unsuccessful (unpersuasive). Therefore:

> to deny objective status to the other person in a communicative situation . . . would amount to talking to oneself . . . [and] since it is clearly the case that the vast majority of the time we understand each other well enough to get along there must be something objective about language that permits it to be a medium of exchange. (Keith and Cherwitz 1989, p. 202)

Keith and Cherwitz show the clear implications of the objective status of language for both rhetoricians and other researchers. If successful communications, both rhetorical and nonrhetorical, "entail an objective status for language and its users, it makes little sense to deny an equivalent objective status to the objects . . . of scientific inquiry." Therefore, "not only do rhetorical views of language and communication not defeat objectivity, they actually entail it" (Keith and Cherwitz 1989, p. 203).[8]

In conclusion, the thesis of linguistic relativism (in any form that would pose a threat to the objectivity of science) is simply false. In fact, in a misguided effort to avoid "ethnocentricism," advocates of linguistic relativism actually embrace an extreme, if not bizarre, nihilism—for it is a truism that different language communities do, at least sometimes, successfully communicate. As put succinctly by Dennett (1981, p. 18), "the faculty of communication would not gain ground in evolution unless it was the faculty of transmitting true beliefs." Similarly, Jacobs (1989, pp. 79, 80) points out: "Awareness of propositions is not seen as a condition of their truth or validity. . . . Many people have never heard of botulinus or arsenic, while many others have; and the knowledge claim that botulinus and arsenic are lethal applies equally and indiscriminately to both groups."

So it is in marketing. Though knowing English is necessary for understanding CW's claim, thinking and communicating in English does not determine its truth or falsity for either speakers or nonspeakers of English. Language differences inhibit communications; they do not doom objectivity.

8.4.2   Paradigms Are Incommensurable

The second argument contends that objectivity is impossible because all knowledge claims are embedded in paradigms that are incommensurable. Of all the concepts that Kuhn introduced, none has been investigated more thoroughly than paradigm incommensurability, and no one has yet developed an interpretation of it that would pose a meaningful threat to the objectivity of science. Because the topic has been discussed in section 4.2.1, our treatment of the three interpretations of paradigm incommensurability (the meaning-variance, radical translation, and incomparability views) is brief.

The early meaning-variance view held that scientific terms change meaning from paradigm to paradigm—for example, Newtonian "mass" differs from Einsteinian "mass"—and was critiqued by Shapere (1964; 1966), Scheffler (1967), and Kordig (1971). The incomparability view that rival paradigms simply cannot be compared meaningfully was also critiqued by Scheffler, Shapere, and Kordig, and later by Laudan (1976) and Putnam (1981). When Kuhn, in his postscript to the 1970 edition of *Structure* (1970b, pp. 200–204), shifted to the radical translation interpretation, which suggested that the actual terms involved in one paradigm cannot be translated into the language of its rivals, it was analyzed by Kitcher (1978), Moberg (1979), and Levin (1979). Cumulatively, the critiques were so conclusive that Kuhn (1976) virtually abandoned the concept of paradigm incommensurability. His final position was that all he ever meant to say was that choices among rival theories could not be made on the basis of a mathematical algorithm or deductive proof—a view nonproblematical for objectivity. In his own work on the history of quantum mechanics, Kuhn (1978) uses neither the word "paradigm" nor the expression "paradigm incommensurability." (Kuhn ceased to be a "Kuhnian.") Similarly, Feyerabend (1987b, p. 81) concedes that incommensurability is not a problem for science but "is a difficulty for philosophers."

The key to understanding the incommensurability debate is to keep two points in mind. First, the very claim that two paradigms are incommensurable must imply that one can compare them—and, indeed, has compared them (Davidson 1973). (Otherwise, how could one know they are incommensurable?) Thus, it is simply incoherent—it makes no sense—to extensively discuss, compare, and contrast different so-called paradigms in marketing and then to claim that they are incommensurable because they are "noncomparable" (Anderson 1989, p. 21). Second, for incommensurability to thwart our ability to choose objectively between two paradigms implies that they are *rival*; they must make conflicting knowledge claims that require *choice* (as did Ptolemy and Copernicus). Most unfortunately, some marketers have blurred the distinction between *rival* paradigms and paradigms that are simply different (e.g., Ozanne and Hudson 1989).

As to the objectivity of CW's claim, for paradigm incommensurability to pose a threat, one would have to put forth a rival paradigm that not only resulted in a conflicting conclusion, but also resulted in a situation in which the choice could not be made on the basis of objective evidence. It is easy to find different paradigms in marketing if one uses a suitably loose interpretation of the word "paradigm," but no one has yet put forth different paradigms that (1) make conflicting knowledge-claims (and, thus, are rival) and (2) are in any meaningful sense incommensurable (objective choice is impossible). Until someone does so, we can only conclude that paradigm incommensurability poses no threat to the objectivity of CW's claim or to any others in marketing research.

8.4.3   Facts Underdetermine Theories

The third argument against objectivity contends that our theories about the world are underdetermined by our facts; no conceivable number of facts proves conclusively a theory's truth. Because theories contain lawlike generalizations (e.g., such generalizations as Newton's laws), even though the predictions of theories are validated every time they are tested empirically (the facts for 200 years supported Newton), new facts could invalidate the theory at some future time in some domain (e.g., tests on subatomic particles after 1900). Therefore, objectivity is impossible. In marketing, for example, there may well be other theories that could account for the same evidence (facts) marshalled by CW to support their claim, and the success of past empirical tests does not necessarily imply the success of future tests. Therefore, CW's claim, so the argument goes, cannot be objective.

Humean skepticism (see section 3.3.4), which underlies the "facts underdetermine theories" argument, maintains that, though genuine knowledge of the external world can be had through observation, only deductive logic is permissible (Watkins 1984). As Calder, Phillips, and Tybout (1983, p. 113) put it, "An inductive argument . . . has no basis in logic."[9] Therefore, we cannot know the truth-content of any of our theories about the world because any process that reasons to the truth of a theory from its successful predictions is inductive, and, therefore, improper.

Note that Hume's "problem of induction" presupposes the following standard for knowledge claims: One must not claim "I know" unless one knows with the certainty of deductive logic. The logical empiricists thought Humean skepticism was problematic for science, and tried to solve it by developing a system of inductive logic (Carnap 1950). Popper (1972, p. 88), claiming that induction is not "a justifiable way of reasoning," also accepted Humean skepticism as potentially defeating objectivity in science, and he attempted to locate the objectivity of science in its ability to falsify theories deductively, rather than confirm them inductively. Kuhn reveals the source of his own flirtation with relativism by explaining that "I make no claim to have solved the problem of induction" (1977, p. 332). Similarly, even some defenders of objectivity in marketing have (unfortunately) been influenced by Humean skepticism (e.g., Anderson and Gerbing 1988; Calder, Phillips, and Tybout 1983; Calder and Tybout 1989; Sternthal, Tybout, and Calder 1987).

Scientists and science differ from philosophers and philosophy in many ways. Since the Enlightenment, one striking difference has been that many philosophers have embraced "foundationalism" (see section 3.6.2), which holds that (1) all knowledge-claims have "foundations" and (2) the foundations of science must be known with certainty (McMullin 1985). Thus, Schlick (1934, pp. 223, 226), the founder of logical positivism, believed scientific knowledge must be "absolutely certain," with "absolute fixed points" and an "unshakable point of contact between knowledge and reality." For Hume and countless philosophers thereafter, "to know" meant to know with the certainty of the deductive logic in geometry and mathematics. However, Hume's "problem" of induction has seldom been viewed as serious by most practicing scientists. Most assuredly, all knowledge claims have foundations and some claims have firmer grounds than others. But restricting "knowing" to "knowing with certainty" is not just being prudently conservative or cautious. Rather, because it denies even the possibility that we can learn or *know* on the grounds of accumulated experience, such a restriction amounts to nothing less than nihilism.

The evolutionary success of humankind as perceiving and thinking beings implies the possibility of learning from experience (and strongly suggests its realization). Therefore, marketing science should reject foundationalism and Humean skepticism, while embracing fallibilism: "In science all knowledge claims are tentative, subject to revision on the basis of new evidence. The concept 'certainty' belongs to theology, not science" (Hunt 1983b, p. 372). Similarly, Suppe (1977b, p. 726) urges philosophers of science to adopt fallibilism, because it "appears to accord most closely with the actual means whereby science evaluates putative knowledge claims in the attempt to undergo the objective growth in scientific knowledge."

The preceding discussion warrants three conclusions. First, objectivity in marketing research is not doomed by Hume's problem of induction (the fact that facts underdetermine theories), except to those who insist misguidedly that one can never know without knowing with certainty. In marketing, though we do not know the truth of CW's claim with certainty, we nevertheless have good reasons for believing CW, and for acting on the basis of that belief. Second, because scientific realism specifically rejects Humean skepticism in its adoption of "inductive realism" (see Chapter 9), scientific realism provides grounds for objectivity in marketing research. Third, Bunge's (1967, p. 324) metaphor of "weighing the evidence" is most appropriate for marketing. Because empirical tests do not imply certainty, the community of marketing researchers can provide its clients with no more than a reasoned "weighing" of the evidence. As fiduciary agents, we should provide no less.

8.4.4   The Psychology of Perception

The fourth argument claims that, because the psychology of perception implies that our cognitively held theories determine what researchers perceive, theory-neutral observations in science are impossible. Because researchers see what their theories tell them is there, scientific observation is theory-laden. In short, as shown by the path from theories to sensations in Figure 8.2, scientific observation = perception = f(sensations interpreted by theories). In marketing, therefore, because the perceptions (observations) of the researchers on which CW's claim relied were "laden" by their theories (or world views, paradigms, etc.), CW's claim is not objective.

At the outset, note the implausibility on a priori grounds of the psychology of perception argument. If researchers' theories determined in any strong manner what they perceived, or *saw*, would they not always (as Peter and Olson [1989] maintain) find strong support for their theories? If so, why are most correlation coefficients so small in social science? Why do goodness-of-fit indexes in structural equation modeling usually reject the very models researchers are proposing? That is, if researchers' theories determine perception, why are there so many disappointing surprises. Indeed, why are there surprises at all? Scheffler (1982, p. 44) points out that to accept the "theories determine perceptions" view is "absurdly, to deny the common phenomena of surprise, shock, and astonishment, as well as the reorientations of belief consequent upon them." Nonetheless, the philosophy debates in marketing claim that the psychology of perception tells us just that.

Are researchers' perceptions "laden" with cognitively held theories? Fodor (1984, 1988), a philosopher of psychology, explores the psychological grounds for the argument, and he points out that all supporters of the theory-ladenness of observation rely on experiments from the psychology of perception, such as the Müller-Lyer figures (see Figure 8.3).

The Müller-Lyer illusion is, of course, that, though line *b* is perceived to be longer, it in fact is exactly the same length as line *a*. Thus, perception, it is argued, necessarily involves interpretation by our theories of the world. As Kuhn (1962, p. 113) put it, "The rich experimental literature [in psychology] . . . makes one suspect that something like a paradigm is prerequisite to per-

Figure 8.3   **The Müller-Lyer Illusion**

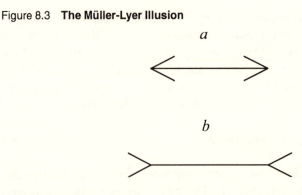

ception itself." However, Fodor points out that Kuhn and his legion of followers completely misinterpreted—and most continue to misinterpret—the findings of perceptual psychology.

Consider when students in a psychology course find out that the Müller-Lyer lines are an illusion or when others (the reader?) are told the truth about the lines' lengths. Even armed with this piece of knowledge, this background "theory" about the world, people (you?) still perceive line *b* to be longer than *a*. How can this be so if our cognitively held theories determine perception? As an everyday example, consider the little words on the bottom of the mirror on the passenger's side of our cars: "Objects in mirror are closer than they appear."[10] Even after we read (and believe) the cautionary message, the cars behind us still *look* deceptively distant. Fodor points out, "All the standard perceptual illusions exhibit this curiously refractory character: knowing that they are illusions doesn't make them go away" (1984, p. 34). Though perceptual psychology implies that perception = f (interpreted sensations), it manifestly does not imply that perception = f (sensations interpreted by cognitive theories):

> [The psychology of perception does not tell us that perception is] saturated with cognition through and through. On the contrary, it suggests just the reverse: that how the world looks can be peculiarly unaffected by how one knows it to be. . . . Because the way one sees the world is largely independent of one's theoretical attachments, it is possible to see that the predictions—even of theories that one likes a lot—aren't coming out. . . . [T]herefore belief in the best [of] science is rational because it is objective. (Fodor 1984, p. 34)

Not only does a proper reading of the implications of perceptual psychology for objectivity yield exactly the opposite of Kuhn's conclusion, but so do informed interpretations of Kuhn's duck/rabbit and "sunrise" examples. Ambiguous, "reversible figure" drawings from Gestalt psychology do not imply that theory determines perception. Theorizing that an ambiguous drawing can be seen as either a duck or a rabbit does not enable one to effect a Gestalt switch, nor does believing that the task can be accomplished so enable. Indeed, many subjects see only one figure, despite their firm convictions that it is possible to see two. Similarly, to Kuhn and Hanson's (now famous) question as to whether Kepler and Brahe "saw" the same thing at dawn, we should answer "yes." Both *saw*, or perceived, a "sunrise." Kepler perceived a "sunrise," and, on the basis of his cognitively held theory of the cosmos (Copernicus), believed correctly that it was an illusion. Brahe perceived a "sunrise," and, on the basis of his cognitively held theory of the cosmos (Ptolemy), believed incorrectly that it was true. Why do neither paradigms, nor theories, nor beliefs, nor even firm convictions determine or "laden" perception? It is because there is a "part of observation . . . [that is] bottom-up and in some important sense theory neutral" (Raftopoulos 2001, p. S188). That is, the human brain is not "programmed" for "ladening perception." Work in neurobiology on the brain's "wiring" reveals the absence of efferent nerves connecting higher brain centers (wherein reside our theories) with our perceptual mechanisms:

> We do not seem to understand any general and widespread class of cases in which higher brain centers appear to alter the character of empirical information. . . . As we know it, the wiring of the brain does not seem to suggest, either very strongly or otherwise, a role for beliefs or theories in perception. (Gilman 1991, p. 499)

The preceding discussion does not imply that the results of scientific observations—that is, "measures" or "data"—do not rely on human perception. Indeed, the accuracy or veridicality of perception is essential to science.[11] On a continuum from total veridicality to complete illusion, where does human perception lie? Evolutionary theory suggests that it is substantially veridical. The fact of human species survival implies that early humans were capable of distinguishing veridically (at least more often than not) alligators from logs, solid earth from quicksand, tigers from domestic cats, wolves from dogs, and human friend from human foe. In fact, the success of human evolution gives us confidence in the veridicality of perception unless our cognitively held theories of the world warn us of an illusion.[12]

As to marketing, the psychology of perception poses no threat to the objectivity of CW's claim. On the contrary, the psychology of perception explains how human perception enabled the researchers on whom CW relied to be objective, if in fact they were. The extraordinary recalcitrance of human perception to researchers' theories of the world enables them to strive for (and, thus, perhaps attain) objective knowledge about that world.

8.4.5   Epistemically Significant Observations

The fifth argument contends that all epistemically significant observation in science is theory-laden, which makes objectivity impossible. This fifth, much more sophisticated, argument must be distinguished carefully from the fourth.[13] Kuhn's mistake, so argument 5 goes, was to deny that researchers observe or see the same things. He erred by denying that human perception allows medical researchers to see the same nine inches of mercury in a cylindrical tube, physicists to see the same nine-degree deflection of a needle on a meter, social science researchers to see the same nine checkmarks on a questionnaire, or marketers to see the same box "9" (see section 7.7.2) checked on an intentions to buy scale. What Kuhn should have argued, so the argument goes, is that such observations are not epistemically significant in research. To be epistemically significant and play their designated role in empirical testing, such "percepts," or "raw" observations must be interpreted by cognitive theories. For example, nine inches of mercury means ninety degrees centigrade, a nine-degree needle deflection means ninety volts, nine checkmarks on a questionnaire mean a score of ninety on a brand attitude scale, and a checkmark in box "9" means a high inclination to buy. It is not perceptual psychology that informs us that observation ("measures" or "data") is theory-laden, it is the undisputed, actual practice of science itself. In brief, epistemically significant observation = f(observations or "percepts" interpreted by theory). Therefore, because all epistemically significant observation in research is theory-laden, objectivity is impossible.

As to marketing and CW's claim, advocates of the theory-ladenness of epistemically significant observation would point out that it was only through the application of theory that checkmarks on questionnaires became measures of "aptitude," "motivation," and "role perceptions." Therefore, all the studies on which CW relied were theory-laden, which defeats the objectivity of CW's claim.

Shapere (1982) and Greenwood (1990) point out two crucial mistakes in the theory-laden argument that prevent it from being compelling, or even moderately persuasive. First, advocates of the theory-laden argument fail to distinguish between two very different kinds of theories that are involved in empirical testing. On the one hand, there are theories that specify relationships among our concepts. These explanatory theories are the ones we test empirically. For example, CW compare the explanatory theory: salesperson performance = f(skills, role perceptions, and motivation) with its rival: salesperson performance = f (personal and physical traits). On the other hand, testing CW's explanatory theories required accessing a great amount of background information, or what we will call "measurement theory."[14] Just as studying cells in biology presumes measurement theory related to the use of a microscope, studying sales performance, motivation, and so on requires theories related to questionnaires, Likert scales, factor analysis, and so forth. Quite clearly, testing CW's explanatory theories presumed a great amount of measurement theory. Therefore, also unquestionably, epistemically significant observations ("data") in science are not theory-free.

However, the theory-informity of data by measurement theories does not doom objectivity. Advocates of theory-ladenness have failed to identify the characteristics of an observation language that are necessary for objectivity—their second critical error. Recall that empiricist philosophers of science (see section 8.2) thought that objectivity required a theory-free observation language. We now understand that objectivity requires a theory-neutral language, not a theory-free one. Our data, measures, or observations need not be theory-free, but only neutral. Neutral to what? Neutral to the theory or theories being tested. Our measurement theories must not presume the truth of our explanatory theories; they must not "beg the question." In multiple regression terms, one must not have the same "thing" on both sides of the equals sign. In structural equation modeling terms, our measurement model must not guarantee our structural model.

For CW's claim, do the measurement theories bias the analysis toward finding that aptitude, skills, and motivation are more important than personal characteristics in explaining sales performance? If so, such theory-informity compromises objectivity. If not, then objectivity is not threatened. Obviously, it is within our capabilities to examine CW's measures for such threats to objectivity. Furthermore, good researchers do precisely that.

The preceding discussion warrants not only that the theory-informity of epistemically significant observation does not make objective research impossible, but, much more strongly (surprisingly?), it implies that (measurement) theory-informity actually helps ensure objectivity:

> [Science] learns how to observe nature, and its ability to observe increases with increasing knowledge. . . . In the process of acquiring knowledge, we also learn how to learn about it, by learning (among other things) what constitutes information and how to obtain it—that is, how to observe the entities we have found to exist, and the processes we have found to occur. (Shapere 1982, pp. 513–14)

As our measurement theories progress, our epistemically significant observations improve and, thus, the theory-informity of observation helps ensure research objectivity. Kepler and Brahe's problem was that their measurement technology was primitive (in comparison with ours). Since then, fortunately, science has progressed in both its explanatory and measurement theories. Only after the development of X-ray diffraction techniques, a new "measurement theory," could researchers confirm the double helix structure of DNA by making epistemically significant observations (Greenwood 1990). In marketing, objectivity has been furthered by the introduction and development of multidimensional scaling (Green and Carmone 1969), conjoint analysis (Green and Rao 1971), true score measurement theory (Churchill 1979), causal modeling procedures (Bagozzi 1980), and item response theory (Singh, Howell, and Rhoads 1990). By such theories, marketing's "theory-laden" research becomes more objective, not less. As Trout (1998, p. 113) puts it, "at least some of the quantitative methods and practices of science reliably detect and identify some of the central posited entities, processes, states, properties, and events in the social and behavioral sciences." So it is in marketing.

8.5   FOR OBJECTIVITY: THE POSITIVE CASE

Should the marketing research community pursue the ideal of objectivity? The preceding discussion establishes the negative case that there is nothing in modern philosophy of science or perceptual psychology that makes objectivity either impossible or undesirable.[15] We conclude by exploring the positive case for objectivity. At the outset, we acknowledge that, because a community's regulative ideals are fundamental values, objectivity cannot be guaranteed or even known conclusively to be achieved. To restrict a community's goals, as discussed in section 7.4.3, only to those that can be conclusively achieved or guaranteed would be, misguidedly, to treat the regulative ideals of a community on a par with its tangible, short-run objectives.

When should any community of inquirers pursue the ideal of objectivity? Our argument here parallels our argument for truth in section 7.8. Both Scheffler (1982) and Harré (1986) maintain that the ideal of objectivity is related to the extent to which a community is relied on or trusted by others. Harré even develops his argument with the aid of marketing language. Almost as though he had read Levitt's (1960) "Marketing Myopia," Harré (1986, p. 12) contends that scientific communities are "in the business of producing practically reliable scientific knowledge." He asks, "Why are the products of the scientific community marketable"? (1986, p. 13) And he answers, "It can be nothing but the quality of the goods" (1986, p. 15). Indeed, "scientific knowledge, is itself defined in moral terms. It is that knowledge upon which one can rely" (1986, p. 20). Trust, the belief that one can rely confidently on others, sometimes arises out of direct personal experience. However, people often do not rely on others on the basis of direct knowledge, but because of others' roles in their communities (e.g., "professor" and "market researcher"). As to the marketing research community, the corporate clients of commercial marketing researchers, most assuredly, rely on them. Equally assuredly, students, academicians, practitioners, government agencies, and consumers at times rely on the output provided by academic marketing researchers (Hunt 2002a, Chapter 2; Monroe et al. 1988). Hence, the marketing research community, encompassing both commercial and academic researchers, has a moral, professional obligation to pursue objectivity.

What does the pursuit of objectivity imply? For Scheffler, objectivity requires the "commitment to fair controls over assertion" (1982, p. 2). For Harré, it requires the community to exercise "quality control over its products" (1986, p. 12). In short, communities producing knowledge that will be (and can be) relied on by others must have a set of norms to maintain quality control over assertion. Harré aptly points out a minimum norm: "For there to be public reliability, something must exist independently of whomsoever first found it" (1986, p. 12). The minimum norm, therefore, for a community's knowledge-claims to be relied on is for the community to reject reality relativism and constructionism. Because such doctrines specifically state that their knowledge-claims do not "touch base" with any reality other than that "constructed" by the researchers themselves, such doctrines self-defeat even the potential for being relied on by outside clients (see section 7.7.2).

It is important to recognize that the norms a community develops to control assertion in no way imply that such assertions are value-free or theory-free. Indeed, the clients of the marketing research community have the right to expect, nay insist, that our assertions be thoroughly "laden" with many values, one such being the ideal of objectivity. Similarly, clients have a right to expect our assertions to be informed, well-informed, by our theories—our very *best* theories. However, the norms that control assertion in the marketing research community must strike a reasoned and reasonable balance between being overly restrictive and overly permissive. For example, the norms, as implemented through such mechanisms as the peer review process, must not be so permissive that "anything goes" in assertion, for such a stance would be destructive of reliability and trust. (Indeed, if "anything goes," peer review is unnecessary.) If the norms are so restrictive that "nothing goes," the situation is equally undesirable. Avoiding error by remaining forever silent is not an acceptable option. What are the current norms that control assertion in marketing research? Where along the continuum between "anything goes" and "nothing goes" do these norms lie? Should these norms be modified? If so, how? These are questions worth investigating—objectively, that is.

QUESTIONS FOR ANALYSIS AND DISCUSSION

1.   What are the differences between objectivity and objectivism, between pursuing objectivity and attaining objectivity, and between "personal bias" and "methodological bias"? Is personal bias a more (or less) serious problem, compared with methodological bias, in marketing research?

2. What is sophistry? As pointed out in section 8.1, many marketers maintain that relativists and subjectivists do not intend for their views on objectivity to be taken seriously by anyone. Is it the case, therefore, that such marketers are accusing relativists and subjectivists of sophistry? What arguments could be put forth that defend the view that relativists and subjectivists are *not* engaging in sophistry?

3. Barnes and Bloor (1982, pp. 27–28) maintain that "for the relativists there is no sense attached to the idea that some standards are really rational as distinct from merely accepted as such . . . hence the relativists' conclusion that they are to be explained in the same way." What does it mean to say that "they are to be explained in the same way"? In what other way might they be "explained"?

4. What does it mean to state that "the absence of TRUTH and OBJECTIVITY constitutes a bogeyman"? How does the philosophers' fallacy of high redefinition relate to "bogeyman"? What is the difference between theory-free observation and theory-neutral observation? Why is this distinction important?

5. There are many ways to bias the results of a survey by choosing particular wordings of the questions. Develop three examples of questions that have biased wordings. Use the analysis of Nagel (1961) to discuss the different kinds of bias in the questions and how such bias could be minimized. Would it be the case that your revised wordings would be bias-free? What is the difference between *linguistic relativism* and the view that some languages are *more precise* than others?

6. There are several different uses for quotation marks. One use is to signify that a particular writer is being quoted. A second use is to signify that one is referring to a particular *word* and not to what the word refers to. Writers in marketing's philosophy debates, instead of writing truth, write "truth." Similarly, one often sees "objectivity," not objectivity. In these cases, what do the quotation marks signify? Do you agree with this use of quotation marks? When would such a use be appropriate? When would it be inappropriate? (Hint: See Stove 1982.)

7. Why does Greenwood (1990) use the phrase "theory-informity," rather than "theory-laden"? Should he?

8. Under what circumstances is quantitative research trustworthy? Under what circumstances is quantitative research not trustworthy? Is quantitative research inherently more or less trustworthy than qualitative research? If so, why? If not, why not?

NOTES

1. This chapter draws heavily on Hunt (1992a, 1993, 1994a).

2. "Incoherently," because the word "illusion" implies a false perception of reality. But to know that a particular perception of reality is false can be accomplished only by showing that it has been compared with a more veridical one. Therefore, the very claim "objectivity is an illusion" implies that which it rejects. That is, to be meaningful, "objectivity is an illusion" implies the existence of the very objective reality that it ostensibly contends is illusory. How else could one know that objectivity is an illusion?

3. Ethnocentrism, a major sin according to postmodernist social philosophy and a highly pejorative label in sociology, is "the belief that our ways, because they are ours, must be closer to the truth, goodness, and beauty than are the ways of others" (Shweder 1989, p. 99). Unfortunately, marketing's "consumer ethnocentrism" has been defined and measured as the belief that "purchasing imported products is wrong because . . . it hurts the domestic economy, causes loss of jobs, and is plainly unpatriotic" (Shimp and Sharma 1987, p. 280). Though ethnocentric consumers would support "buy American," those who "buy American" because of such factors as the fear of "loss of jobs" are not exhibiting ethnocentrism, for "loss of jobs" would be superfluous to ethnocentric consumers. (Such consumers would believe that domestic products are obviously superior to foreign-made ones.) Therefore, the CETSCALE seems closer to measuring a belief in "protectionism" than to measuring genuine "ethnocentrism." More generally, whenever marketing borrows concepts that have pejorative connotations, we have a *special* responsibility to exercise caution.

4. Holt (1991, p. 61) further argues that, because the use of audits, triangulation, and purposive sampling does "not necessarily lead to more trustworthy research" and does "not insure greater trustworthiness," researchers "should be discouraged from using them to gain added authority in the written representation of the research." Instead "interpretations should be judged on their insightfulness . . . and their ability to convince the reader, no more." Such an argument, however, self-destructs. If all procedures must necessarily lead to, or ensure, trustworthy findings before being in the written report of the research, then an article's method section in a research report should always be blank. On the contrary, why, except for the bogeyman fear of "objectivism" and "positivism," should researchers avoid conducting (and reporting) audits, triangulation, and purposive sampling? Such procedures may contribute to what Holt calls "insightfulness" or even to Holt's goal of "convince the reader."

5. Though no such monolithic entity as "Western culture" exists (for the individual cultures of Western nations, as well as Eastern ones, differ greatly), there is something that might be properly labeled "Western intellectual tradition," one of whose central tenets is openness to the ideas of outsiders (Barchas 1989, p. 27; Short 1988, p. 13; Silber 1990, p. 35). Thus, "Western ethnocentrism" (believing in and advocating Western ideas *because* they are Western) is oxymoronic.

6. As an example of the genetic fallacy, "The Nazis condemned the theory of relativity because Einstein, its originator, was a Jew" (Salmon 1963, p. 12). Ethnophobia, a peculiarly Western phenomenon, is the fear or hatred of one's own culture, as exemplified by the works of relativists such as Feyerabend (1987a) and many postmodernist writings (Barzun 1991, p. 34).

7. For other studies on the universality of color perception, see Brown and Lenneberg (1954), Lantz and Stefflre (1964), and Stefflre, Castillo-Vales, and Morley (1966).

8. Similarly, Maki (1988, p. 108) explores McCloskey's advocacy of rhetoric in economics and concludes that "the acceptance of realism does not depend on the rejection of any of the major insights of the rhetorical approach to studying economics, and vice versa . . . metatheoretical realism is subscribed to by the rhetorical approach as formulated by McCloskey and Klamer."

9. Calder, Phillips, and Tybout, though embracing Humean skepticism, do not conclude that objectivity is impossible. Rather, they conclude that falsificationism is required for objectivity.

10. I thank Roy Howell, Texas Tech University, for the example.

11. How human beings learn to apply language veridically (both verbal utterances and written words) to the world we see is complex. (Lenneberg's 1967 work is considered seminal. See also MacCormac 1985, especially pp. 80–85, for a useful introduction to the semantic marker theory.) One thing is clear, however, contra Kuhn and his followers, cognitively held theories about the world, that is, beliefs about how the world is structured, do not determine perceptual recognition. Such theories or beliefs are neither necessary nor sufficient for seeing. People can identify veridically and label as a "unicorn" a picture of a horse with a horn without believing in unicorns. (Theories about what exists in the world are not necessary for perception.) Likewise, in Kuhn's duck/rabbit example, people can believe in ducks, and, indeed, believe that others can see a duck in the duck/rabbit drawing, but may never be able recognize, see, or perceive the drawing as a duck. (Theories about what exists in the world are not sufficient for perception.) Finally, though one would need to know English to apply the label "duck" to what one perceives, one need not know English to *see* Kuhn's duck. (Linguistic relativism is false.) Even Whorf's (1956) famous example (supposedly illustrating linguistic relativism) was incorrect. Rather than the Eskimos having several words for the single English word "snow," they have several words that equate with several English words, such as "blizzard," "dusting," and "avalanche" (Martin and Pullman 1991).

12. See Giere (1988) and Harré (1986) for applications of evolutionary theory to science.

13. It is unsurprising that the marketing literature conflates arguments 4 and 5. As pointed out by Shapere (1982), they are seriously conflated throughout even the philosophy of science literature. For an example, see Churchland's (1988) discussion of "perceptual plasticity" and Fodor's (1988) reply, especially his pages 197–98.

14. Greenwood (1990) uses the term "exploratory theory." However, in marketing and other social sciences, "measurement theory" seems closer to describing what Greenwood is referring to. As Greenwood points out, the background information constituting a measurement theory in one context may be an explanatory theory one desires to test in another context.

15. Even philosophers strongly opposed to scientific realism agree (see Laudan 1990, especially pp. vii–x).

9 ON SCIENTIFIC REALISM AND MARKETING RESEARCH

The pluralist does not hold, with the relativist, that there is no possibility of nonneutral or non–question-begging evaluation of alternative claims, theories, schemes, versions, or the like. The pluralist subscribes, rather, to a willingness to tolerate and utilize a diversity of ideas and approaches, while at the same time acknowledging criteria which afford the possibility of objective comparison and evaluation of the diverse alternatives tolerated and utilized.

—Harvey Siegel

Chapter 5 introduced scientific realism, showed how it explained (indeed, discussed how it seemed to be the only philosophy that *could* explain) the success of science, contrasted scientific realism with logical empiricism, and discussed issues related to quantum mechanics and realism. This chapter extends our discussion of scientific realism and argues that it merits marketing's consideration as a foundation for research. Specifically, this chapter begins by articulating the fundamental tenets of scientific realism and their implications for research. It then explores versions of "critical realism," before developing a realist theory of empirical testing.

9.1 FOR REALISM

A major benefit of scientific realism is that, contrasted with many other philosophies, it produces intelligible, coherent discourse about science. With the exceptions of Bagozzi (1980, 1984), Blair and Zinkham (1984), Easton (1998, 2002), and my own works (Hunt 1989b, 1990, 1991a, 1991b, 1992a, 1992b, 1995, 1994a, 1994b), authors have given little attention to realist philosophy in marketing's philosophy debates. This omission is unfortunate, because not only do "the majority of philosophers of science profess to be scientific realists" (Causey 1979, p. 192), but much, if not most, marketing research seems implicitly to assume a realist perspective.

A major problem for realism is that there are so many different versions of it: "Scientific realism is a majority position whose advocates are so divided as to appear a minority" (Leplin 1984, p. 1). That is, there is no "grand theory" of science according to realism. Rather, there is (as the sample in section 5.3 shows) the transcendental realism of Bhaskar (1979. 1986, 1993, 1998), the ontic realism of MacKinnon (1979), the methodological realism of Leplin (1986, 1997), the critical realism of Sayer (1992), the evolutionary, naturalistic realism of Hooker (1985), the referential realism of Harré (1986), the critical scientific realism of Niiniluoto (1999), and the constructive realism of Giere (1985). Speaking somewhat loosely, we can lump together all the versions of realism and refer to them as "scientific realism." The approach in this section is not to advocate any particular version of scientific realism, but to examine the fundamental, unifying beliefs underlying all versions of scientific realism.

9.1.1   Fundamental Tenets of Scientific Realism

Scientific realism traces its heritage to the classical realism—see section 3.1—developed in the early part of the twentieth century. At that time, realist philosophers such as Moore (1903) and Russell (1929) debated advocates of Hegelian idealism. Briefly, Hegelian idealism's central tenet is that the world does not exist independently of its being perceived, and whatever is known is relative to the mind that knows it. Hegelian idealism provides the intellectual foundations for modern versions of relativism (Suppe 1977). Opposing idealism, Russell's and Moore's classical realism held that the world exists independently of its being perceived, and it argued that Hegelian idealism (1) confuses the mental act of perceiving with the object of that mental act, (2) produces unintelligible speech, and (3) appears to be sophistry rather than genuine belief. Note that these arguments parallel those in the philosophy debates in marketing about relativism.

A fundamental tenet of modern-day, scientific realism is the classical realist view that the world exists independently of its being perceived. That is, contra Olson's (1981, 1987) relativism, there really is something "out there" for science to theorize about. To hold otherwise makes nonsense of science. To hold that science does not "touch base" with some reality separate from its own theories is to make inexplicable the enormous success of science over the past 400 years (Stove 1982). However, scientific realism does not embrace "naïve" or "direct" realism.

"Naïve" or "direct" realism holds that our perceptual processes result in a direct awareness of, or straightforward confrontation with, objects in the external world. Thus, direct realism maintains that our perceptual processes always result in a veridical representation of external objects, which, in turn, results in knowledge about external objects that is known with certainty (Hooker 1985). Clearly, such a realism would warrant the pejorative adjective "naïve." Advocates of scientific realism, though agreeing that our perceptual processes can yield genuine knowledge about an external world, emphatically reject direct realism. They argue for a fallibilistic and critical realism. Believing that some of our perceptions may be illusions or even hallucinations, they argue that some of our perceptions may be true and others false or, alternatively, some of our perceptions are "more accurate" or "closer to the truth" than others. Hence scientific realism is a middle-ground position between direct realism and relativism. (Recall that reality relativism and constructivism—see section 4.1.3—hold that each perception constitutes one of many "multiple realities" and that all perceptions are equally valid.)

Scientific realism is also a critical realism, contending that the job of science is to use its method to improve our perceptual (i.e., measurement) processes, separate illusion from reality, and thereby generate the most accurate possible description and understanding of the world. For example, the practice of developing multiple measures of constructs and testing them in multiple contexts in social science stems from this critical orientation (Cook and Campbell 1986). As a second example, the critical orientation of science and science *education* serves as a foundation for arguing that the development of students' critical thinking should serve as a regulative ideal for *all* of education (Siegel 1989, 1997). In short, scientific realism proposes that (1) the world exists independently of its being perceived (classical realism), (2) the job of science is to develop genuine knowledge about that world, even though such knowledge will never be known with certainty (fallibilistic realism), and (3) all knowledge-claims must be critically evaluated and tested to determine the extent to which they do, or do not, truly represent or correspond to that world (critical realism).

McMullin (1984, p. 26)—see section 5.3.1—succinctly states the fourth and final tenet: "The basic claim made by scientific realism . . . is that the long-term success of a scientific theory gives reason to believe that something like the entities and structure postulated by the theory actually exists." Though this fourth tenet may appear rather obvious or innocuous, it runs directly counter not only to the relativism and irrationalism advocated by Kuhn and Feyerabend but also to the logical positivism of Schlick, the logical empiricism of Hempel, and the falsificationism of Popper. Put most simply, the "something like" tenet represents a rejection of Humean skepticism with respect to the development of knowledge. All the "isms" just mentioned, either explicitly or implicitly, accept Humean skepticism with respect to the "problem of induction" (McMullin 1984; Stove 1982; Suppe 1977a). Therefore, we label this fourth tenet "inductive realism," and, before examining its implications, must explicate it in more detail.

Theories can be successful in many ways. As Figure 7.1 shows, inductive realism focuses attention on the explanatory, predictive, and pragmatic success of a theory. Therefore, the phrase "long-term success" in the tenet identifies a theory that over some significant period of time has demonstrated its ability to explain phenomena, predict phenomena, or be useful in solving pragmatic problems. However, scientific realism does not equate pragmatic success with truth (see section 7.2.3). Likewise, for long-term success to "give reason" does not imply that one "knows with certainty." That is, the inductive realism tenet specifically adopts fallibilism and avoids the philosophers' fallacy (see section 7.2.2). At the same time, it avoids the skepticism of the Humean view that only deductive methods are appropriate for generating knowledge (see section 3.3.4). By "something like the entities," the tenet rejects the view of naïve or direct realism that the entities posited in the theory are (or must be) exactly as posited by the theory. Finally, by "something like the structure," the tenet claims that the success of a theory in explanation, prediction, and the solution of practical problems (usefulness) gives us reason to believe that the structure of relationships among the entities in the theory, both causal and otherwise, are as proposed in the theory. Again, however, this does not mean that the evidence will allow us to know with certainty that the structure of relationships is as posited. With the preceding clarifications in mind, we can examine how scientific realism approaches actual science.

9.1.2   Implications of the Fundamental Tenets of Scientific Realism

Scientific realism has implications for all branches of science. Here, I sketch some implications for physics, biology, and marketing and social science.

Physics. Consider the case of Newtonian mechanics. Is not Newtonian mechanics false? On the contrary, scientific realism contends that the 300-year story of Newtonian mechanics gives us reason to believe that something like the entities of Newtonian mechanics actually exists (i.e., apples, trees, planets, and stars actually exist). Equally important, scientific realism contends that the successes of Newtonian mechanics give us reason to believe that something like the structure of relationships, or "forces," postulated by Newtonian mechanics exists. That is, we are warranted in believing that Newtonian mechanics, within its validity limits, gives us significant truth about the world (Rohrlich and Hardin 1983). Scientific realism, therefore, joins theory acceptance and truth: "To rationally accept a theory as a basis for action is to accept it as telling us something or other about the world, and that is to accept the theory as being more or less true" (Newton-Smith 1981, p. 287). Therefore, for example, it was rational for NASA to accept and rely on the truth of Newtonian mechanics to put astronauts on the Moon.

How about quantum mechanics? The general acceptance of quantum mechanics in the early part of this century was the precipitative cause of the rejection of naïve realism with respect to science, and rightly so. The view that our perceptual processes always give a veridical representation of the world and that current science is known with certainty *ought* to be rejected. However, in part as a reaction to the excesses of naïve realism, many philosophies of science then went to the opposite extremes of relativism, subjectivism, constructionism, irrationalism, and nihilism. None of the extremes is satisfactory.

As discussed in section 5.3.3, though there are many interpretations of quantum mechanics, the "official" or "Copenhagen interpretation" suggests that quantum mechanics should be interpreted in a positivist, instrumental manner (Polkinghorne 1984). In this view, quantum mechanics is "just" a series of equations, albeit a series of equations that has been extraordinarily successful in predicting subatomic phenomena. Realism is often attacked for ostensibly being committed to finding "hidden variables" that will turn quantum mechanics from an indeterministic set of equations to a deterministic process (McMullin 1984). However, the scientific realism discussed here is not committed to the position that all theories must contain "entities," or "hidden variables that will turn all indeterministic theories into deterministic ones. Rather, scientific realism posits that the success of those theories that contain entities gives us reason to believe that something like the entities contained in the theories actually exists. Therefore, with respect to quantum mechanics, if the best interpretation of quantum mechanics is that it posits no "hidden variables," or "entities," so be it; no damage occurs to scientific realism. However, scientific realism is also relevant to quantum mechanics, because it maintains that the long-run predictive success of quantum mechanics gives reason to believe that it truly "says something" about the world. That is, quantum mechanics has truth-content (Dickson 1995).

The subject of the philosophical implications of quantum mechanics, like many other topics in the philosophy of science, has been misunderstood in marketing. For example, Marsden (2001) develops the "modern physics" argument that marketing should embrace postmodernism. The modern physics argument is that (1) marketing is positivist, (2) Newtonian mechanics was positivist, (3) modern physics (i.e., quantum mechanics) rejects positivism, (4) postmodernism rejects positivism, therefore, (5) "postmodern marketing is, paradoxically, more scientific than positivist marketing" (Marsden 2001, p. 75).

The modern physics argument is uninformed: (1) marketing is more realist than positivist (see section 6.2), (2) Newtonian physics was *not* positivist (see section 3.2), and (3) quantum mechanics does *not* reject positivism. Indeed, the dominant, "Copenhagen interpretation" of quantum mechanics is positivist, and logical positivism was actually developed *specifically* to accommodate the indeterminancy of quantum mechanics (see section 3.2.1). Therefore, postmodernism's rejection of positivism does not imply that postmodernism is "more scientific" (i.e., more consistent with the modern physics of quantum mechanics). Rather, postmodernism's rejection of positivism implies a rejection of the dominant (i.e., positivist) interpretation of quantum mechanics. Many scholars believe that postmodernism can be defended coherently. The modern physics argument is not such a defense.

Biology. The application of scientific realism to the biological sciences is straightforward. As the smallpox example in section 5.3.1 shows, the long-term success of theories such as the viral theory of diseases and the genetic theory of heredity provides reasons for believing that (1) something exists like the entities designated as "viruses," "genes," "AIDS virus," "chromosomes," and "DNA" (deoxyribonucleic acid), and (2) something exists like the structures postulated by the theories containing these entities. That is, the long-run success of the viral theory of diseases provides reason to believe that something like what we label a "virus" exists and that it does in fact cause illnesses, such as smallpox and polio. Similarly, the long-run success of genetic theory provides reason to believe that the DNA molecule exists and transmits heredity. Scientific realism helps us understand the actual workings of modern science without mocking it. The warranted belief that viruses exist and cause diseases provides justification for medical scientists, when confronted with a new disease (such as AIDS), to search for a new virus as its cause. Similarly, the warranted belief that the DNA molecule exists justifies the search for the description of the characteristics of that molecule, that is, the "double helix" (Watson 1968).

The preceding discussion of the DNA case history provides a striking illustration of why many philosophers of science, as well as most philosophically-oriented, practicing scientists, believe that only some version of realism can explain the actual workings of much of science without reducing it to a charade. (Because no rational person searches for the characteristics of a "nonexisting entity," what, other than the warranted belief that DNA *exists*, could motivate the search resulting in the "double helix"?) Even though both logical positivism and logical empiricism held truth in high regard, both were also under the spell of Humean induction (Stove 1982) and refused to countenance the real existence of "unobservable entities." Similarly, the acceptance of Humean induction was a cornerstone of Popper's falsificationism: "I regard Hume's formulation and treatment of the logical problem of induction . . . as a flawless gem . . . a gem of priceless value . . . a simple, straightforward, logical refutation of any claim that induction could be a valid argument, or a justifiable way of reasoning" (Popper 1972, pp. 86, 88; italics added). Thus Popper, by claiming that all positive results of a theory test are irrelevant to science (not a "justifiable way of reasoning"), fell into a form of irrationalism (Stove 1982).

Marketing and the Social Sciences. Applying scientific realism to marketing and the social sciences differs only in that most of the entities postulated in physical and biological theories are, at least in principle, tangible. In contrast, many, but not all, of the entities postulated by theories in marketing and the social sciences are intangible (i.e., unobservable in principle). The reason for the qualifying phrase "but not all" is that people occupy central positions in most social science theories, and people are, to say the least, *tangible*. Furthermore, most social science and marketing theories have manifestations or consequences that are tangible by any meaningful interpretation of that word. For scientific realism, intangible entities may be real in their consequences.

Applied to marketing and social science, scientific realism maintains that, to the extent that there are theories that have long-run success in explaining phenomena, predicting phenomena, or assisting in the solution of pragmatic problems in marketing and society, we are warranted in believing that something like the postulated entities and their structure of relationships exists. That is, the theories truly represent or correspond to some reality external to the theorist. In sociology, if a proposition such as "racist beliefs in a society generally result in the unfair treatment of a racial group" is successful, then we have reason to believe that something like "racist beliefs" exists, and they do result in the "unfair treatment of racial groups." In political science, if a proposition such as "totalitarian political regimes have a tendency to repress all human rights" is successful, then we are warranted in believing that something like the concept "totalitarian political regimes" actually exists, and that these regimes have their posited consequences—many of the manifestations of which will be, most assuredly, tangible.

Most research programs in marketing are at least consistent with scientific realism. For example, cognitive theories in consumer behavior, power and conflict theories in channels of distribution, and relationship marketing theories in strategy are consistent with realism. Indeed, the resource-advantage theory of competition adopts realism as its philosophical foundation (Hunt 2000; Hunt and Morgan 1995, 1996, 1997). Behavior modification theory in consumer behavior, a major exception, is positivistic in orientation because it admonishes the researcher to stay at the "observable" level of actual behaviors.

Because Bagozzi (1980, 1984) has been a prominent advocate of realism, many marketers seem to associate scientific realism only with his advocacy of structural equation modeling. But, though such modeling techniques *require* realism, scientific realism does not imply any specific mathematical or statistical technique. More strongly, scientific realism does not require any mathematical or statistical techniques at all. For example, Easton (2002) argues for case research based on critical realism. His approach centers on using cases to explore for entities that have causal powers and for the necessary and contingent relationships among the entities identified. As another example, the philosophical foundations of areas such as naturalistic, humanistic, and interpretive inquiry are unclear. Though these programs generally avoid mathematics and statistics, they need not avoid realism (Hunt 1989b). Similarly, at least some of their proponents seem to hold truth to be central in their research: "The humanities in general and artworks in particular contain truths that escape procedures of the hypothetical-deductive method" (Holbrook, Bell, and Grayson 1989, p. 40). Indeed, in ethnography, Stewart argues:

> Statistics-oriented researchers and ethnographers share an ultimate epistemic value. Whether or not they define themselves as "scientists," they both adhere to the fundamental purpose of science: to try to learn the truth about the world. . . . Certainly, it is difficult to see why people would put up with the tribulations of participant observation, would bother to *be there*, if they did not hope that their accounts would be more or less true. (Stewart 1998, p. 12; italics in original)

Scientific realism emphasizes the testing of marketing theories as a means for establishing their success. Therefore, theories comprising diverse concepts such as "attitudes," "intentions," "market segments," "purchase behavior," "channels of distribution," "retail store," "conflict," "brand awareness," "information search," "perceived risk," and so forth, warrant our believing (to the extent such theories are successful) that these entities have a real existence and the theories comprising these entities truly "say something"—and say something *objectively*—about the world.

9.2   CRITICAL REALISM

A fundamental tenet of scientific realism is that it is *critical*. That is, all knowledge claims must be critically evaluated and tested to determine the extent to which they do, or do not, truly represent or correspond to the world. Many philosophers of science use "critical realism" to designate their approaches to science. However, the word "critical" may be used differently in the different versions of critical realism. This section discusses the critical realisms of Niiniluoto (1999) and Sayer (1992). We select these two approaches for three reasons: First, they are widely cited and their proponents argue well for their respective positions. Second, though both are *critical*, their approaches differ in their implications for marketing research. Third, in marketing, Easton (2002) advocates the realism of Sayer, and Wensley criticizes the Niiniluoto approach as an "Alice in Wonderland" philosophy of science (Wensley 2002, p. 233). We begin with Niiniluoto.

9.2.1   The Critical Realism of Niiniluoto

For Niiniluoto, his "critical scientific realism" may be distinguished from its rivals on the following theses:

R0.   At least part of reality is ontologically independent of human minds.

R1.   Truth is a semantical relation between language and reality. Its meaning is given by a modern (Tarskian) version of the correspondence theory, and its best indicator is given by systematic enquiry using the methods of science.

R2.   The concepts of truth and falsity are in principle applicable to all linguistic products of scientific enquiry, including observation reports, laws, and theories. In particular, claims about the existence of theoretical entities have a truth value.

R3.   Truth (together with some other epistemic utilities) is an essential aim of science.

R4.   Truth is not easily accessible or recognizable, and even our best theories can fail to be true. Nevertheless, it is possible to approach the truth, and to make rational assessments of such cognitive progress.

R5.   The best explanation for the practical success of science is the assumption that scientific theories in fact are approximately true or sufficiently close to the truth in the relevant respects. Hence, it is rational to believe that the use of the self-corrective methods of science in the long run has been, and will be, progressive in the cognitive sense. (Niiniluoto 1999, p. 10)

Niiniluoto argues that the "ontological realism" of R0 (i.e. our classical realism) distinguishes his critical scientific realism (hereafter, CSR) from subjective idealism, solipsism, and phenomenalism. In turn, the "semantical realism" of R1 separates CSR from pragmatism (e.g., William James), neo-pragmatism (e.g., Richard Rorty), and relativism/constructivism (e.g., David Bloor and Bruno Latour). The "theoretical realism" of R2 (a variant of our inductive realism) and the "axiological realism" of R3 distinguish CSR from "half-realism" (e.g., Nancy Cartwright), methodological nonrealism (e.g., Larry Laudan), and constructive empiricism (e.g., Bas C. van Fraassen). The fallibilistic realism of R4 separates critical realism from both naïve realism and dogmatic skepticism (e.g., Paul Feyerabend). For Niiniluoto, this "fallibilist tradition in epistemology . . . has been advocated by such diverse thinkers as Friedrich Engels, Charles Peirce, Karl Popper, and Wilfrid Sellars" (1999, p. 13). Most of Niiniluoto's book represents a detailed exposition, often using the tool of formal logic, of his six theses. In doing so, he defends his critical scientific realism against critics, such as those advocating internal realism (Niiniluoto 1999, pp. 206–26), relativism (1999, pp. 227–41), feminism and postmodernism (1999, pp. 242–51), and social constructivism (1999, pp. 252–78.).

Readers should note that the word "critical" does not appear in any of Niiniluoto's six theses. How, then, is critical scientific realism *critical*? CSR is critical in two ways. First, note that "truth" appears in five of the six theses, and that "systematic inquiry using the methods of science" is in R1, and "the self-corrective methods of science" appears in R5. For Niiniluoto, therefore, CSR is critical in that it maintains that science uses systematic, self-corrective methods to seek, and in fact often achieve, linguistic products (e.g., observation reports, laws, and theories) that are "approximately true or close to the truth in relevant respects" (1999, p. 10). Indeed, for society, "trust in science depends on the fact that the community of its practitioners is employing the critical method of scientific inquiry" (1999, p. 299).

CSR earns the appellation "critical" in a second manner. Niiniluoto argues against "naturalism" in philosophy of science, which holds that "scientific rationality has to be grounded in the actual practice of science" (1999, p. 15). Pointing out that a normative *ought* cannot be derived from or rebutted by, a historical *is*, he maintains: "While it is important for the scientific realists to have a realistic picture of scientific activities, and therefore to pay serious attention to historical and sociological case studies, they should also maintain the possibility of *criticizing* the way science is actually done" (1999, p. 17; italics added). That is, CSR is critical in that it may criticize science, scientists, and scientific communities. Both of Niiniluoto's senses of "critical" are consistent with the critical realism of section 9.1.

9.2.2   The Critical Realism of Sayer

Sayer provides, as he puts it, eight "signposts" to identify the premises of his version of realism:

1. The world exists independently of our knowledge of it.
2. Our knowledge of that world is fallible and theory-laden. Concepts of truth and falsity fail to provide a coherent view of the relationship between knowledge and its object. Nevertheless knowledge is not immune to empirical check, and its effectiveness in informing and explaining successful material practice is not mere accident.
3. Knowledge develops neither wholly continuously, as the steady accumulation of facts within a stable conceptual framework, nor wholly discontinuously, through simultaneous and universal changes in concepts.
4. There is necessity in the world; objects—whether natural or social—necessarily have particular causal powers or ways of acting and particular susceptibilities.
5. The world is differentiated and stratified, consisting not only of events, but objects, including structures, which have powers and liabilities capable of generating events. These structures may be present even where, as in the social world and much of the natural world, they do not generate regular patterns of events.
6. Social phenomena such as actions, texts and institutions are concept-dependent. We therefore have not only to explain their production and material effects but to understand, read or interpret what they mean. Although they have to be interpreted by starting from the researcher's own frames of meaning, by and large they exist regardless of researchers' interpretations of them. A qualified version of 1 therefore still applies to the social world. In view of 4–6, the methods of social science and natural science have both differences and similarities.
7. Science or the production of any other kind of knowledge is a social practice. For better or worse (not just worse) the conditions and social relations of the production of knowledge influence its content. Knowledge is also largely—though not exclusively—linguistic, and the nature of language and the way we communicate are not incidental to what is known and communicated. Awareness of these relationships is vital in evaluating knowledge.
8. Social science must be critical of its object. In order to be able to explain and understand social phenomena we have to evaluate them critically. (Sayer 1992, pp. 5–6)

Sayer's purpose, he points out, is not to do a philosophical treatise. Rather, it is to discuss method in social science, in conjunction with considering social theory and philosophy of science. He wishes to counter two types of "imperialism": (1) the "scientism" that centers "around the search for regularities and hypothesis testing, to derogate or disqualify practices such as ethnography, historical narrative, or explorative research," and (2) the "kind of imperialism . . . which tries to reduce social science wholly to the interpretation of meaning" (Sayer 1992, p. 4). In this regard, he condemns how interpretivists use the terms "positivist" and "empiricist" as "purely pejorative" epithets (1992, p. 7).

As with Niiniluoto, we can make several observations concerning Sayer's eight premises. First, premise 1, in conjunction with 6, adopts classical realism. Second, premise 2 embraces fallibilistic realism. Third, unlike the realism of Niiniluoto, the word "truth" appears only once, in premise 2; and even on this occasion its purpose is not to put forth truth as a goal (as does Niiniluoto), but to claim that "truth and falsity fail to provide a coherent view of the relationship between knowledge and its object." Fourth, premise 3 rejects both the Kuhnian "revolution"—see section 4.2—and the Baconian "bricks in a pile"—see section 8.3.1—views of scientific progress. Fifth, premises 4 and 5 stress the importance of causal powers of objects, as emphasized and developed in marketing by Easton (2002).

Sixth, unlike Niiniluoto, the word "critical" appears in his premises—as number 5. However, again unlike Niiniluoto, by "social science must be critical of its subject," Sayer is using "critical" in the manner of the "critical theory" of the Frankfurt School. Whereas Niiniluoto advocated the criticism of *science*, Sayer advocates that social scientists should be social critics (i.e., criticize *society*) and social *activists*. That is, in their roles as social activists, social scientists "should develop a critical self-awareness in people and indeed assist in their emancipation" (Sayer 1992, p. 42). As pointed out (and advocated) in marketing by Hetrick and Lozada (1994, p. 549), "critical theory is a neo-Marxian critique of both capitalist societal arrangements and positivist science." Therefore, for critical theorists, the discussion of critical theory in, for example, Murray and Ozanne (1991) is a "sanitizing" of the very essence of critical theory, because it may "sustain social groups sympathetic to capitalism" (Hetrick and Lozada 1994, p. 549). Therefore, those marketers hostile to economic freedom may favor the "critical" in Sayer's critical realism; those sympathetic to economic freedom will not. Those marketers concerned that social activism may compromise objectivity will look "critically" at the "critical" in Sayer's realism; those marketers unconcerned will not. (See Nagel's arguments in section 8.2.1.)

Seventh, Sayer's premise 2 indicates that observational evidence is problematic because it is "theory-laden." Furthermore, contrasted with Niiniluoto, who maintains that "we choose the language L, and the world decides which sentences of L are true" (Niiniluoto 1999, p. 267), Sayer's premise 7 assumes that "the nature of language and the way we communicate are not incidental to what is known and communicated." Therefore, he suggests that "it may help to replace (or if you prefer, modify) the concept of truth with 'practical adequacy'" (Sayer 1992, p. 69). Indeed, he does so even though he maintains that observational evidence does provide an "external check" on the "objectivity of our knowledge" (1992, p. 65).

Clearly, the "critical" in different versions of critical realism means different things. Therefore, marketers are well advised to choose their critical realism carefully. Also clearly, even some realist philosophers of science, such as Sayer (1992), believe that both the "theory-ladenness" of observation and the "nature of language" pose difficulties for the pursuit of objectivity and truth in social science research. Therefore, it is time to make good on the promissory note of Chapter 8. That is, it is time to develop a realist theory of empirical testing.

9.3   A REALIST THEORY OF EMPIRICAL TESTING

Section 8.4 developed path diagrams of the process of empirical testing held by the logical empiricists and falsificationists (Figure 8.1) and historical relativists (Figure 8.2).[1] These models were used to analyze the five major arguments against objectivity: (1) linguistic relativism, (2) paradigms are incommensurable, (3) facts underdetermine theories, (4) the psychology of perception, and (5) epistemically significant observations. The positive case for objectivity was then advanced. This case, as is the case for truth, is grounded in trust.

It must be admitted, however, that the arguments in section 8.4 are unlikely to be probative for many researchers. Consider the views of Smith and Deemer:

> within Anglo-American philosophical circles, a good case can be made that it was Hanson (1958) and then, most definitely, Kuhn (1962) who brought the problematic associated with the dualism of subject and object to the forefront. . . . By the mid-to-late 1980s, the work of numerous people made it apparent that any claim of or hope for "theory-free knowledge" was untenable on all counts. . . . There is no possibility of theory-free observation and knowledge, the duality of subject and object is untenable, no special epistemic privilege can be attached to any particular method or set of methods, and we cannot have the kind of objective access to an external, extralinguistic referent that would allow us to adjudicate from among different knowledge claims. (Smith and Deemer (2000, p. 879)

Now, Smith and Deemer are respected, serious, education researchers, not members of some fringe minority. Furthermore, readers should note that their claims appear not in an obscure, ideological journal, but in the highly regarded *Handbook of Qualitative Research*, edited by Denzin and Lincoln (2000). Readers should also note that their position that "we *cannot* have . . . objective access to an extralinguistic referent" (2000, p. 879; italics added) is so obviously correct in mainstream qualitative research that no contrary view is even worth presenting in the over 1,000-page *Handbook*. However, Smith and Deemer's position that objectivity is impossible puts them in a quandary. They realize that "the charge of relativism as anything goes does not make sense, [and] if we no longer can speak of the absolute without embarrassment, then we must realize we cannot speak of 'anything goes' without embarrassment" (Smith and Deemer 2000, p. 895). Therefore, many mainstream qualitative researchers (and others) seek an alternative to the extremes of dogmatism and dogmatic skepticism shown in Table 7.1. The purpose of this section is to resolve Smith and Deemer's quandary by developing such an alternative. As with section 8.4, I use a path diagram of empirical testing to explicate the theory.

9.3.1   The Realist Model

Figure 9.1 displays the model of the proposed realist theory of empirical testing, which adopts and extends the insights of Fodor, Greenwood, and others, as discussed in section 8.4. At the same time, Figure 9.1 also retains the valuable aspects of the logical empiricist and falsificationist and historical relativist views. First, what was labeled "observations" in Figure 8.2 is split into (a) "percepts," the immediate results of visual processing, that is, the results of only perceptual discrimination and recognition, and (b) "data" or "measures," the results of percepts informed by theories, that is, epistemically significant observations. Second, what was lumped together under "theories" in Figure 8.2 is now split into "explanatory theories," "measurement theories," "perceptual mechanisms," and "natural language." Explanatory theories are the theories being tested by a process involving (among other things) observation reports, whereas measurement theories are the ontological and other theories that are assumed (explicitly or implicitly) in the process of testing the explanatory theories under investigation. Percepts, the immediate output of visual processing (e.g., the checkmarks on the Stanford-Binet test), become data (e.g., such epistemically significant observations as "IQ of 90") only after being interpreted with the aid of measurement theories.

A major deficiency of the historical relativist view is that it not only blurs the important distinction between explanatory and measurement theories, but it also confuses "sensations are theory-laden" with (1) sensations are informed by perceptual *mechanisms* and (2) patterns of sensations are labeled by natural language. Even Fodor (1984, p. 39) blurs important distinctions when he states that perceptual mechanisms must have access to "a grammar," which he refers to as a "background theory." Contrary to both Fodor and the historical relativist view, the proposed theory maintains that percepts do not result from sensations, or proximal stimuli, being informed by theory. Rather, they result from perceptual mechanisms interpreting proximal stimuli in conjunction with the interpreter's natural language. Percepts do not require theories, but (1) mechanisms that can perceptually discriminate among proximal stimuli (e.g., the proximal stimuli resulting from light reflected from such disparate distal stimuli as ducks and cyclotrons), (2) mechanisms that can recognize *patterns* of proximal stimuli associated with distal objects (this pattern re-

Figure 9.1   **The Scientific Realist Method of Empirical Testing**

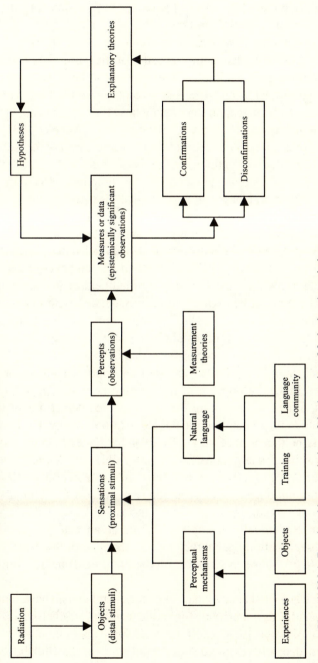

Source: Hunt (1992a). Reprinted by permission of the American Marketing Association.

Note: Read—From upper left, radiation reflected from objects (distal stimuli) results in sensations (the proximal stimuli of retinal images). From lower left, our experiences with objects in the world we inhabit contribute to developing our perceptual mechanisms' ability to recognize patterns of proximal stimuli, and our language community trains us to use our natural language to label the recognized patterns. Therefore, our percepts result from sensations or proximal stimuli being informed by our perceptual mechanisms and labeled by our natural language. Our data, measures, or epistemically significant observations result from percepts being informed by our measurement theories. These data can be used objectively to confirm or disconfirm hypotheses and, by implication, objectively test the explanatory theories, if the explanatory theories being tested do not prejudge the test by biasing the measurement theories.

sults from a duck, that from a cyclotron), and (3) a set of *conventions* for labeling the recognized patterns (my natural language community calls these patterns of proximal stimuli "ducks" and those "cyclotrons").

In contrast, at the minimum, *theories* of or about the world are cognitive constructions that purport to explain some aspect(s) of the world. Because no *mechanism* is a cognitive construction, no mechanism can be a theory of or about the world—a perceptual mechanism is no exception. Similarly, as a *convention* is "any commonly agreed upon statement whose truth is based not upon the way things are in nature but upon that agreement itself" (Angeles 1981, p. 49), no set of conventions (alone) can purport to explain any aspect of the world. Therefore, no set of labeling conventions is a theory of or about the world; the set of labels used to designate certain percepts (in, e.g., empirical tests of theories) by speakers of any natural language (e.g., English) is no exception.

Although the capability to process proximal stimuli is inborn universally to healthy humans, experience and training (as shown in Figure 9.1) play major roles in its development. We learn to recognize ducks and cyclotrons by *experiencing*, in the particular world we inhabit, ducks and cyclotrons (or representations thereof). We are then *trained* by members of our language community to label patterns of proximal stimuli associated with distal objects in our world, that is, ducks are "ducks," and cyclotrons are "cyclotrons." The perceptual recognition, *seeing*, of distal objects however does not imply understanding them. To see objects successfully, that is, to visually recognize cyclotrons and label them "cyclotrons," is often an important precursor to understanding them. Indeed, a premise of this section is precisely the view that path diagrams, a heuristic enabling the reader to see depictions of the views, can contribute to understanding the debate over objectivity. However, visual processing is neither a necessary precursor for understanding (consider the blind) nor is it sufficient (consider a small child). To accurately perceive, that is, see, recognize, and label the—in Greenwood's (1990) terminology—inten*tional* objects of observation (e.g., these are checkmarks) implies nothing about—again, in Greenwood's terms—the inten*sional* contents of observation. Specifically, it implies nothing about whether one understands the purpose, functioning, characteristics, or nature of the perceived intentional objects (e.g., "these checkmarks on the Stanford-Binet test imply an IQ of 90").

A major problem has been that advocates of historical relativism have indiscriminately used "seeing" as a metaphor for "understanding" (Scheffler 1986, p. 268). For example, Hanson (1958, p. 59) states: "A blind man cannot see how a timepiece is designed, or what distinguishes it from other clocks. Still, he may see that, if it is a clock at all, it will embody certain dynamical properties; and may explain the action to his young apprentice." Clearly, the second "see" in the quote is used completely as a metaphor for "understand." In most discourse, even scholarly discourse, using "see" metaphorically is nonproblematic. However, Hanson (1958) and others purport to establish that laboratory experiments from the psychology of perception (where "seeing" implies visual processing) inform us that scientific observation in empirical testing is laden with the explanatory theories being tested. Any such discourse must scrupulously preserve the distinction between "seeing" and "understanding."[2] Otherwise, as historical relativist discussions tellingly reveal, confusion reigns.

The proposed theory contends that, although percepts (the immediate output of perceptual processing) are formed from proximal stimuli, they are not proximal stimuli interpreted by our explanatory theories of the world. Contra Figure 8.2, it is simply not the case that small children do not or cannot see what the physicist sees. Indeed, small children with a modicum of worldly experience and language training, none of which involving what are (or ought to be) called "explanatory theories," can see (perceptually discriminate, recognize, and label) ducks as "ducks" and cyclotrons as "cyclotrons." What the small child cannot do, without extensive experience or training, is understand ducks and cyclotrons in the manner of the zoologist and physicist, respectively. Such accomplishments, the intensional contents of scientific observation, require percepts that have been informed, very well informed, by a host of complex theories about the world.

The distinction here between percepts and data differs from the position advocated by Greenwood (1991). Indeed even though he distinguishes between exploratory theories and explanatory theories, and between the intentional object of observation and the intensional contents of observation, he does not distinguish between percepts and epistemically significant observation. In advocating a realist approach to social psychology, Greenwood states:

> It is simply not true for example that our perception of trees and tables is unmediated by theoretical interpretation, any more than our perception of planets and anxiety. In order to observe that there are trees or pigeons present, we need to employ intersubjectively-agreed exploratory theories about how trees and pigeons manifest themselves to our "naked" eyes and ears. (Greenwood 1991, p. 109)

Contrary to Greenwood, psychologists do not perceive—see—anxiety, for it is precisely the kind of concept whose presence is suggested by perceiving checkmarks on questionnaires (or other behavioral or physiological indicators) and interpreting them by some measurement theory. The percept of a checkmark requires no measurement theory. Nor does perceiving tables and chairs. Recognizing that checkmarks, trees, and tables are checkmarks, trees, and tables and using the labels "checkmarks," "trees," and "tables" does not require—contra Greenwood—an "intersubjectively-agreed exploratory theory." What does it require? As shown in Figure 9.1, in addition to radiation, objects, proximal stimuli, perceptual mechanisms, and experiences with checkmarks, trees, and tables, the recognition process requires only the learning of an intersubjectively agreed-upon set of conventions for the application of one's natural language. This set of conventions does not constitute, and should not be confused with, an explanatory theory about the world. To repeat a prior point, no set of conventions, by themselves, can constitute a theory about the world. Because the truth content of a set of conventions is "based not upon the way things are in nature" (Angeles 1981, p. 49), a set of labeling conventions is not a theory about the world. This is not to say that one may not have theories about, as Greenwood puts it, "how trees and pigeons manifest themselves" to us. It is to say that such theories are not required to perceive trees and pigeons.

Why did Greenwood not distinguish between percepts and data? It appears that he associated any such distinction to be based on the foundationalist notion of direct perception, which implies for him that percepts would have to be "immune from error" (Greenwood 1991, p. 109). However, no such immunity is implied by the proposed theory, for our percepts may be nonveridical. But the absence of such immunity does not vitiate the important distinction between percepts and data.

9.3.2   Müller-Lyer Revisited

To illustrate how the proposed theory, modeled in Figure 9.1, can be employed, let us re-examine Fodor's (1984) analysis of the Müller-Lyer illusion. As discussed in section 8.4.4, the illusion results in the percept that line *b looks* longer than line *a*. Is this percept veridical? Fodor concludes it is not, but his contention is elliptical—it skips over the underlying rationale. By explicating Fodor's (implied) rationale, we can further explicate the proposed theory of empirical testing. The rationale may be framed as two, relatively trivial, rival theories: (1) All lines that look the same length *are* the same length, and (2) some lines that look longer than others are not so in fact, and line *b* in the figure labeled "Müller-Lyer" is such a case. What is required to test the rival explanatory theories are some measures, that is, epistemically significant observations. Here, the problem is easy. We place a tape measure or equivalent device first on line *a*, then on *b*, and observationally compare them. The resulting percepts are that both lines *a* and *b* extend to the identical hash mark on the tape. Therefore, relying on the measurement theory underlying our use of tape measures, these percepts become epistemically significant observations and we conclude that lines *a* and *b* are of equal lengths. This empirical test would tend to support theory 2 and undermine theory 1.

For most people, the preceding empirical test would be dispositive for the Müller-Lyer problem. But why is this the case? It is because we have confidence in our measures, that is, our percepts informed by our cognitively held measurement theories. In short, we have more confidence in the veracity of the measurement theory underlying the tape measure, and, thus, in our theoretically informed percepts (lines *a* and *b* are equally long when measured) than we do in the veridicality of our nontheoretically informed percept (line *b* looks longer than *a*). Therefore, we allow our percepts informed by our measurement theories (our "data") to overrule our nontheoretically informed percepts. Could we be wrong? Could the real illusion be that lines *a* and *b* in Müller-Lyer are equally long? It is (remotely) possible. Our tape measure theory could be faulty (as well as, of course, the procedures used in conducting the test). Empirical testing does not "buy us" certainty—as the experience of physics with Newtonian mechanics reminds us (or should remind us). Humility is a virtue everywhere. Science is no exception.

Is empirical testing objective? Do we believe *objectively* that lines *a* and *b* are the same length? There are several threats to objectivity implicit in the theory underlying Figure 9.1, and each will be addressed separately.

9.3.3   Threats to Objectivity

What is required for objectivity? Unfortunately, advocates of Figure 8.2 often confuse objectivity with omniscience. Agreeing with Shapere (1982), the proposed theory contends that what is required for objectivity in any particular empirical test is not an observation language that is omnisciently—"god's eye"—neutral to all theories. Rather what is required for objectivity is an observation language that is neutral to the theories being tested. Therefore, in terms of Figure 9.1, the first threat to objectivity would be the existence of a direct path from the explanatory theories being tested to the measurement theories informing our percepts. "Direct path" means that a particular explanatory theory informs our measurement theories in such a manner as to bias a test of it in its favor (over a rival). If such a path exists, the test is not objective. The existence of such a path in each case of empirical testing is a contingent issue.

In our Müller-Lyer empirical test, it seems obvious that our measurement theories do not prejudge the case; our tape measure and our procedure for applying it can be assumed to be unbiased. Clearly, other cases may not necessarily be so obvious. Also clear, however, is that *all* measurement theories in *all* cases of empirical testing do not necessarily prejudge the veracity of a particular theory over its rivals, as advocates of historical relativism contend. All empirical tests do not beg the question being investigated. Moreover, the potential biasing effects of explanatory theories on measurement theories is a contingent issue that can be addressed specifically by the researchers and those appraising their research. For example, the "two-step" procedure in structural equation modeling advocated by Anderson and Gerbing (1988) attempts to minimize the potential bias of explanatory theories on measurement theories.

A second threat to objectivity would be a direct path in Figure 9.1 from the explanatory theories to be tested to perceptual mechanisms, as advocates of historical relativism claim is implied by the psychology of perception. As discussed in section 8.4.4, the proposed theory claims that no path is there. That is, our percepts, what we literally see, are not determined by our explanatory theories of the world. To generate data, epistemically significant observations, our percepts must be informed by our theories. But, this does not mean our percepts are determined by our theories. Because Kuhn (1962), Churchland (1988), and others rely so heavily on the "inverting lenses" experiments in psychology to justify their opposing contention, reviewing these experiments is warranted.

Briefly, the inverting lenses experiments involve fitting normal humans with lenses that have the effect of inverting the orientation of all visual information accessible to the brain. The world, therefore, looks "upside down" (Kottenhoff 1957). However, when subjects fitted with the lenses are forced by practical necessity to interact with common objects, in about a week the subjects' perceptual mechanisms adjust to the lenses and the illusion of the world being upside down is claimed to fade away. The subjects now claim to see the world "right-side up."

Do the inverting lenses experiments not show that there is a path from our explanatory theories of the world to our perceptual mechanisms? No. As the proposed theory grants, our experiences with objects in our world (i.e., subjects with inverting lenses interacting with objects) unquestionably help develop our perceptual mechanisms (and, indirectly, help us form percepts from our proximal stimuli). However, the import of the inverting lenses experiments is not that our explanatory theories of the world shape our perceptual mechanisms. The import is that our perceptual mechanisms—marvelous as they are—are sufficiently adaptive that we could learn to function in other worlds by experiencing them, even worlds where we would have to reach down for objects that look up, and vice versa. What historical relativism advocates need to show, as Fodor's discussion of this issue reveals, is not that worldly experiences help shape our percepts, but "that you can somehow reshape the perceptual field by learning physics" (Fodor 1988, p. 194). He knows of no examples that have been shown of this kind of reshaping, and he "strongly suspect[s] that's because there aren't any" (1988, p. 194). I also strongly suspect this. An example from psychology will demonstrate explicitly why we are unlikely ever to be provided examples of the required kind of perceptual reshaping.

Consider two psychologists, *A* and *B*. Psychologist *A* strongly adheres to the theory that intelligence is determined primarily by heredity, and *B* believes, equally strongly, in the absolute primacy of the environment. In terms of the proposed theory, what would be required for there to be a path of influence from "theories" to "perceptual mechanisms"? What would be required for "reshaping the perceptual field" in a manner that *A*'s percepts would differ from *B*'s in potential empirical tests of their respective theories? We should recall that it is checkmarks on, say, the Stanford-Binet test form that constitute instances of percepts in the theory. Therefore, psychologist *A* would have to be so influenced by the genetic theory that, when compared with *B*, he/she would either not see the same checkmarks or see the checkmarks to be in different locations on the test. Even if *A* and *B* are ideologues of the most extreme kind, it is difficult to imagine them having percepts that will differ on account of paths from their explanatory theories to their perceptual mechanisms.

Therefore, it is no wonder that no examples of perceptual reshaping of the required kind have been offered, nor should we expect any. What have been offered, and in abundance, are such examples as "IQ tests do not measure intelligence," or "IQ tests are culturally biased," or "the study did not properly control for all environmental factors." But these are not examples of *theories* determining *percepts*. These are all examples of the potential biasing effects of (in the proposed theory's terms) different measurement theories in the formation of data from percepts. No one denies (or should deny) that measurement theories can potentially bias empirical tests and compromise objectivity. What is denied and should be denied is that (1) our measurement theories necessarily compromise objectivity by begging the question and (2) our explanatory theories of the world compromise objectivity by determining our percepts. Indeed, as our explanation of the Müller-Lyer illusion illustrates (i.e., arrowheads pointing inward or outward affect perceptions of distances and lengths), instead of our perceptual mechanisms employing explanatory theories, we employ explanatory theories to help us explain and understand our perceptual mechanisms.

Recall that, contrary to Greenwood (1990), the theory argues that applying natural language—an intersubjectively agreed upon set of conventions—to what our perceptual mechanisms recognize does not constitute applying an explanatory theory. Therefore, the conventions of natural language are not a direct threat to objectivity. Nevertheless, there could be a potential threat to objectivity if there were a direct path from the explanatory theories being tested to natural language and then a second path from natural language to perceptual mechanisms. In effect, these two paths would mean that the language within which the explanatory theories are stated (e.g., English) determines not just the labels that communities affix to the proximal stimuli that their perceptual mechanisms recognize, but that each language determines what members of a language community can or cannot see. If such were the case, then an objective choice between an explanatory theory stated in, say, English could not be made vis-à-vis a rival stated in French, because English determined what English speakers saw and French determined what French speakers saw. In essence, this is the Sapir-Whorf thesis of linguistic relativism. As discussed in section 8.4.1, however, the thesis of linguistic relativism is false: The evidence supports the view that the two paths do not exist, and, therefore, do not constitute a threat to objectivity.

9.3.4   Implications for Marketing and Social Science

The proposed theory provides practical guidance for marketers and social scientists in their appraisals of the objectivity of empirical research. In particular, the theory implies that the following question be explored: Do the measurement theories that inform the percepts, and, thereby, generate data in a particular empirical test bias the test for or against one theory over its rival? In contrast, the implication of the proposed realist theory of empirical testing is foundational for those marketers and social scientists using "theory-ladenness of observation" as a justification for their preferred research approach. They must abandon historical relativism or find alternative justificatory arguments—for the premise that no research can be objective is false.

The implications for the debates in marketing, social science, and philosophy of the proposed theory are also foundational. Consider Murphy's discussion of the ongoing debate pitting advocates of realism against those (she describes) as favoring "constructive empiricism," the "strong program" in sociology, "postmodernism," and Bernstein's (1983) "mitigated relativism."[3] She claims: "The debate over scientific or critical realism is characterized by confusion" (Murphy 1990, p. 291). Indeed, the participants "talk past one another" (p. 292). They do so even though "modern realists accept the same facts about science as do the sociologists," including "the underdetermination of theory by data; the theory-ladenness of data; [and] the effects upon perception of prior belief" (p. 299). What accounts for the confusion? It stems from, Murphy claims, the fact that the participants "operate with different 'paradigms' of rationality" (p. 299). Therefore, she recommends, "the best solution to the realist debate is to simply drop the issue" (p. 302).

We can agree with Murphy that a major factor contributing to the confused character of the debate in marketing, social science, and philosophy over realism has been the fact that both realists and antirealists have accepted the same (or at least similar) premises concerning the "problem" of theory-ladenness and perception. For example, Wylie argues for what she calls "mitigated objectivism" because, in part, it is "not the case that data are entirely plastic, that they are so theory-permeated that facts can be constituted at will in whatever form a contextually appealing theory requires" (Wylie 1989, p. 16). However, in the same paragraph Wylie agrees that "the vagaries of research practice make us aware that we very largely see or understand what our background knowledge and theoretical commitments prepare us to see—and that we can see things differently or even *see different things* when these presuppositions change" (1990, p. 16; italics added). By "see different things" because of "theoretical commitments," Wylie accepts one of the major premises that led Bernstein (1983) to his "mitigated relativism." That Wylie accepts Bernstein's foundational premise on perception is implied when she specifically distinguishes between "see things differently" and "see different things." Once one agrees that theories make us "see different things," the realist theory of empirical testing argues, one abandons a powerful resource for arguing against relativism, both "mitigated" and otherwise.

In conclusion, contra Murphy (1990), the proposed theory of empirical testing implies that the "best solution" to the "realist debate" in marketing, social science, and philosophy is not to drop the issue. Rather, realists should stop accepting the same foundational premises or "facts about science" as the antirealists. First, realists should reject the "fact" that "believing is seeing" and start from the premise that the theory-independence of percepts enables science to test objectively its theories. Second, realists should reject the "fact" that the theory-ladenness of data based on observation is problematic for science, and start from the premise that the theory informity of data based on observation is what promotes the objectivity of science. And third, realists should reject the "fact" that the foundations of science must be immune from error and start from the premise that the best evidence is that percepts are substantially veridical and scientific data are substantially trustworthy. That is, starting the debate using the proposed theory, I suggest, may lead toward a resolution of differences, rather than to a confusion of issues, at least that is a possibility—and the hope.

9.4 A FINAL NOTE: FOR A COMMENCEMENT

Controversies in marketing theory continue unabated, and their respective debates continue to evolve. Many of the philosophy debates have been less productive than need be the case. A major reason is that they have been uninformed by the philosophy of science, uninformed by history, and uninformed by reason. The purpose of this book has not been to close the debates, but to argue for the commencement of an informed, reasoned approach to marketing's controversies. The clients of marketing research trust us to deliver our best-informed, best-reasoned efforts. Although they can ask no more from us, they surely deserve no less.

Several decades ago, Philip Kotler and Sidney Levy (1969) proposed that the issue facing nonprofit organizations was not whether they were going to *do* marketing; the issue was whether such organizations were going to do it poorly, or do it well. Likewise for marketing, the issue is not whether we are going to *do* philosophy. Doing philosophy cannot be avoided: Some philosophical position or framework underlies every single controversy on every single issue in every single area of marketing theory and research. The issue is not whether marketing should do philosophy, it is whether we shall do it poorly, or do it well. If this volume helps marketing do it well, its goal will have been achieved. One wonders: Is the goal of doing philosophy *well* visionary or utopian? Hmm. . . .

QUESTIONS FOR ANALYSIS AND DISCUSSION

1. Why has "positivism" received so much attention in the marketing literature, but "realism" so little?
2. How does "naïve" or "direct" realism relate to "foundationalism" and "objectivism"?
3. How long should be the "long" in "long-term success"?
4. Identify a research program in marketing. To what extent is the research program consistent or inconsistent with scientific realism? With positivism? With relativism?
5. What are the advantages for the view that social scientists should, at the same time, be social *researchers*, social *critics*, and social *activists*? What are the disadvantages?
6. Figure 9.1 has a box for "measurement theories." However, there is no box specifically labeled "research design." Should there be? If yes, where should it go? If no, why should there not be such a box?
7. If empirical testing does not "buy us" certainty, as section 9.3.2 maintains, what does it "buy us"? Is Figure 9.1 a "causal" model in the sense of structural equation modeling? If yes, why? If no, what kind of model is it?
8. If there ever is another edition of *Controversy in Marketing Theory*, what new issues should be addressed? What issues should be deemphasized? All comments are welcome, in writing, e-mail, or otherwise.

NOTES

1. This section draws extensively on Hunt (1992a, 1994a).

2. Throughout this section all uses of "see" and perceive" are meant to refer to vision or the results of vision, whereas "view" is meant to be taken as a metaphor for "framework," "model," or "theory."

3. The label "mitigated relativism" is Wylie's (1989) characterization of Bernstein's (1983) position.

REFERENCES

Acton, H.B. 1967. "Idealism." In *The Encyclopedia of Philosophy*, vol. 4, ed. Paul Edwards, 110–18. New York: Free Press.

Adler, Mortimer J. 1985. *Ten Philosophical Mistakes*. New York: Macmillan.

Agazzi, Evandro. 1989. "Naïve Realism and Native Antirealism." *Dialectica* 43, nos. 1–2: 83–98.

Alspector-Kelly, Marc. 2001. "Should the Empiricist be a Constructive Empiricist?" *Philosophy of Science* 68, no. 4: 413–31.

Alston, William P. 1964. *Philosophy of Language*. Englewood Cliffs, NJ: Prentice Hall.

———. 1996. *A Realist Conception of Truth*. Ithaca, NY: Cornell University Press.

Altman, I., and D.A. Taylor. 1973. *Social Penetration: The Development of Interpersonal Relationships*. New York: Holt, Rinehart, and Winston.

Anderson, F.H. 1948. *The Philosophy of Francis Bacon*. Chicago: University of Chicago Press.

Anderson, James C., and David W. Gerbing. 1988. "Structural Equation Modeling in Practice: A Review and Recommended Two-Step Approach." *Psychological Bulletin* 103 (May): 411–23.

Anderson, Paul F. 1982. Comments in "Current Issues in the Philosophy of Science: Implications for Marketing—A Panel Discussion," ed. J. Paul Peter. In *Marketing Theory: Philosophy of Science Perspectives*, ed. Ronald F. Bush and Shelby D. Hunt, 11–16. Chicago: American Marketing Association.

———. 1983. "Marketing, Scientific Progress and Scientific Method." *Journal of Marketing* 47 (Fall): 18–31.

———. 1986. "On Method in Consumer Research: A Critical Relativist Perspective." *Journal of Consumer Research* 13 (September): 155–73.

———. 1988a. "Relative to What?—That Is the Question: A Reply to Siegel." *Journal of Consumer Research* 15 (June): 133–37.

———. 1988b. "Relativism Revidivus: In Defense of Critical Relativism." *Journal of Consumer Research* 15 (December): 403–6.

———. 1989. "On Relativism and Interpretivism—with a Prolegomenon to the 'Why Question.'" In *Interpretive Consumer Research*, ed. Elizabeth Hirschman, 10–23. Provo, UT: Association for Consumer Research.

Angeles, Peter A. 1981. *Dictionary of Philosophy*. New York: Barnes and Noble Books.

Armstrong, J. Scott, and Jerry S. Overton. 1977. "Estimating Nonresponse Bias in Mail Surveys." *Journal of Marketing Research* 14 (August): 396–402.

Arndt, Johan. 1985. "The Tyranny of Paradigms: The Case for Paradigmatic Pluralism in Marketing." In *Changing the Course of Marketing: Alternative Paradigms for Widening Marketing Theory*, ed. N. Dholakia and S. Arndt, 3–26. Greenwich, CT: JAI Press.

Arnould, E.J., and M. Wallendorf. 1994. "Market-Oriented Ethnography: Interpretation Building and Marketing Strategy Formulation." *Journal of Marketing Research* 31, no. 4: 484–504.

Arrow, Kenneth J. 1972. "Gifts and Exchanges." *Philosophy and Public Affairs* 1, no. 4: 343–61.

Asquith, Peter D., and Henry E. Kyburg Jr. 1979. *Current Research in Philosophy of Science.* East Lansing, MI: Philosophy of Science Association.

Ayer, A.J. 1959. *Logical Positivism.* Glencoe, IL: Free Press.

Bagozzi, Richard P. 1974. "Marketing as an Organized Behavioral System of Exchange." *Journal of Marketing* 38 (October): 77–81.

———. 1979. "Toward a Formal Theory of Marketing Exchanges." In *Conceptual and Theoretical Developments in Marketing,* ed. O.C. Ferrell, Stephen Brown, and Charles Lamb, 431–47. Chicago: American Marketing Association.

———. 1980. *Causal Models in Marketing.* New York: Wiley.

———. 1984. "A Prospectus for Theory Construction in Marketing." *Journal of Marketing* 48 (Winter): 11–29.

Baker, G.P., and P.M.S. Hacker. 1984. *Languages, Sense and Nonsense.* Oxford, UK: Blackwell.

Barchas, Isaac D. 1989. "After the Fall." *Academic Questions* 3 (Winter): 24–34.

Barnes, Barry, and David Bloor. 1982. "Relativism, Rationalism, and the Sociology of Knowledge." In *Rationality and Relativism,* ed. Martin Hollis and Steven Lukes, 21–47. Cambridge, MA: MIT Press.

Barney, Jay B. 1990. "The Debate Between Traditional Management Theory and Organizational Economics." *Academy of Management Review* 15, no. 3: 382–94.

Barone, Francesco. 1986. *Il Neopositivismo Logico.* Bari, Italy: Laterza.

Bartels, Robert. 1976. *The History of Marketing Thought,* 2d ed. Columbus, OH: Grid.

Barzun, Jacques. 1991. "Reflections on Teaching and Learning." *Academic Questions* 4 (Spring): 30–40.

Beach, Edward. 1984. "The Paradox of Cognitive Relativism Revisited: A Reply to Jack W. Meiland." *Metaphilosophy* 15: 1–15.

Belk, Russell W.; John F. Sherry Jr.; and Melanie Wallendorf. 1988. "A Naturalistic Inquiry into Buyer and Seller Behavior at a Swap Meet." *Journal of Consumer Research* 14 (March): 449–70.

Belk, Russell W.; Melanie Wallendorf; and J.F. Sherry. 1989. "The Sacred and the Profane in Consumer Behavior—Theodicy on the Odyssey." *Journal of Consumer Research* 16, no. 1: 1–38.

Ben-David, Joseph. 1984. *The Scientist's Role in Society.* Chicago: University of Chicago Press.

Berger, P., and T. Luckmann. 1967. *The Social Construction of Reality: A Treatise in the Sociology of Knowledge.* New York: Doubleday.

Berger, Peter, and Samuel Pullberg. 1966. "Reification and the Sociological Critique of Consciousness." *New Left Review* 35 (January): 56–71.

Bergmann, Gustav. 1957. *Philosophy of Science.* Madison: University of Wisconsin Press.

———. 1967. *The Metaphysics of Logical Positivism.* Madison: University of Wisconsin Press.

Berlin, Brent, and Paul Kay. 1969. *Basic Color Terms: Their Universality and Evolution.* Berkeley: University of California Press.

Bernstein, Richard J. 1983. *Beyond Objectivism and Relativism.* Philadelphia: University of Pennsylvania Press.

Berry, L.L. 1993. "Playing Fair in Retailing." *Arthur Andersen Retailing Issues Newsletter* 5 (March): 2.

Berry, L.L., and A. Parasuraman. 1991. *Marketing Services.* New York: Free Press.

Bhaskar, Roy. 1979. *The Possibility of Naturalism.* Brighton, UK: Harvester Press.

———. 1986. *Scientific Realism and Human Emancipation.* London: Verso.

———. 1993. *Dialectic: The Pulse of Freedom.* London: Verso.

———. 1998. *The Possibility of Naturalism.* 3d ed. New York: Routledge.

Blair, Edward, and George M. Zinkhan. 1984. "The Realist View of Science: Implications for Marketing." In *Scientific Method in Marketing.* Proceedings of the AMA Winter Educator's Conference, ed. P. Anderson and M. Ryan, 26–29. Chicago: American Marketing Association.

Bloom, Alan. 1987. *The Closing of the American Mind.* New York: Simon and Schuster.

Bloomfield, Leonard. 1935. *Language.* London: Allen and Unwin.

Boyd, Richard N. 1984. "The Current Status of Scientific Realism." In *Scientific Realism*, ed. Jarrett Leplin, 41–82. Berkeley: University of California Press.

Braithwaite, Richard B. 1968. *Scientific Explanation.* Cambridge, UK: Cambridge University Press.

Bristor, Julia M., and Eileen Fischer. 1993. "Feminist Thought: Implications for Consumer Research." *Journal of Consumer Research* 19, no. 4: 518–37.

Brodbeck, May. 1962. "Explanation, Prediction, and 'Imperfect' Knowledge." In *Scientific Explanation, Space and Time. Minnesota Studies in the Philosophy of Science*, ed. Herbert Feigl and Grover Maxwell. Minneapolis: University of Minnesota Press.

———, ed. 1968. *Readings in the Philosophy of the Social Sciences.* New York: Macmillan.

———. 1982. "Recent Developments in the Philosophy of Science." In *Marketing Theory: Philosophy of Science Perspectives*, ed. Ronald F. Bush and Shelby D. Hunt, 1–7. Chicago: American Marketing Association.

Brown, Ezra. 1988. "A Fresh Breath of Heresy." *Time*, July 25, 74.

Brown, Harold I. 1977. *Perception, Theory and Commitment.* Chicago: University of Chicago Press.

Brown, James Robert. 1987. "Unravelling Holism." *Philosophy of Social Science* 17, no. 4: 427–33.

Brown, R., and E.H. Lenneberg. 1954. "A Study in Language and Cognition." *Journal of Abnormal and Social Psychology* 49, no. 4: 454–62.

Brubacher, J., and M. Rudy. 1958. *Higher Education in Transition.* New York: Harper.

Buck, R., and R. Cohen. 1971. "PSA 1970: In Memory of Rudolph Carnap." In *Boston Studies in Philosophy of Science*, vol. 8, ed. R. Buck and R. Cohen, 75–90. Dordecht, Netherlands: Reidel.

Bunge, Mario. 1967. *Scientific Research, vol. 2: The Search for Truth.* New York: Springer-Verlag.

———. 1991. "A Critical Examination of the New Sociology of Science, Part I." *Philosophy of the Social Sciences* 21, no. 4: 524–60.

———. 1992. "A Critical Examination of the New Sociology of Science, Part II." *Philosophy of the Social Sciences* 22, no. 1: 46–76.

———. 1998. *Social Science Under Debate: A Philosophical Perspective.* Toronto: University of Toronto Press.

———. 1999. *The Philosophy-Sociology Connection.* New Brunswick, NJ: Transaction.

Bush, Ronald F., and Shelby D. Hunt, eds. 1982. *Marketing Theory: Philosophy of Science Perspectives.* Chicago: American Marketing Association.

Butterfield, H.J. 1958. *The Origins of Modern Science: 1300–1800.* New York: Macmillan.

Bynum, W.F.; E.D. Browne; and Roy Porter. 1981. *Dictionary of the History of Science.* Princeton, NJ: Princeton University Press.

Calder, Bobby J., and Alice M. Tybout. 1987. "What Consumer Research Is . . ." *Journal of Consumer Research* 14 (June): 136–40.

———. 1989. "Interpretive, Qualitative, and Traditional Scientific Consumer Behavior Research." In *Interpretive Consumer Research*, ed. Elizabeth Hirschman, 199–208. Provo, UT: Association for Consumer Research.

Calder, Bobby J.; Lynn W. Phillips; and Alice M. Tybout. 1983. "Beyond External Validity." *Journal of Consumer Research* 10 (June): 112–14.

Carnap, Rudolf. 1932. "The Elimination of Metaphysics Through the Logical Analysis of Language." *Erkenntnis* 2. Reprinted in A.J. Ayer, *Logical Positivism.* Glencoe, IL: Free Press, 1959. (Page numbers in text refer to reprint.)

———. 1934. "On the Character of Philosophic Problems." *Philosophy of Science* 1 (January): 1–25.

———. 1936. "Testability and Meaning." *Philosophy of Science* 3, no. 4: 419–71.

———. 1950. *Logical Foundations of Probability.* Chicago: University of Chicago Press.

————. 1956. "The Methodological Character of Theoretical Concepts." In *The Foundations of Science and the Concepts of Psychology and Psychoanalysis,* Minnesota Studies in the Philosophy of Science, vol. 1, ed. Herbert Feigl and Michael Scriven, 38–76. Minneapolis: University of Minnesota Press.

————. 1962. "The Aim of Inductive Logic." In *Logic Methodology and Philosophy of Science,* ed. E. Nagel, P. Suppes, and A. Tarski, 303–18. Stanford, CA: Stanford University Press.

————. 1966. *Philosophical Foundations of Physics.* New York: Basic Books.

Causey, Robert L. 1979. "Theory and Observation." In *Current Research in Philosophy of Science,* ed. P.D. Asquith and H.E. Kyburg Jr., 187–206. East Lansing, MI: Philosophy of Science Association.

Chalmers, A.F. 1976. *What Is This Thing Called Science?* St. Lucia, Australia: University of Queensland Press.

————. 1990. *Science and Its Fabrication.* Minneapolis: University of Minnesota Press.

Chaudhari, Arjun, and Morris B. Holbrook. 2001. "The Chain of Effects from Brand Trust and Brand Affect to Brand Performance: The Role of Brand Loyalty." *Journal of Marketing* 65, no. 2: 81–93.

Churchill, Gilbert A. Jr. 1979. "A Paradigm for Developing Better Measures of Marketing Constructs." *Journal of Marketing Research* 16 (February): 64–73.

Churchill, Gilbert A.; Neil M. Ford; Steven W. Hartley; and Orville C. Walker Jr. 1985. "The Determinants of Salesperson Performance: A Meta-Analysis." *Journal of Marketing Research* 22 (May): 103–18.

Churchland, Paul M. 1979. *Scientific Realism and the Plasticity of Mind.* Cambridge: Cambridge University Press.

————. 1988. "Perceptual Plasticity and Theoretical Neutrality: A Reply to Jerry Fodor." *Philosophy of Science* 55 (June): 167–87.

Churchland, Paul M., and Clifford A. Hooker. 1985. *Images of Science: Essays on Realism and Empiricism, with a Reply from Bas C. van Fraassen.* Chicago: University of Chicago Press.

Churchman, C. West. 1984. "Early Years of the Philosophy of Science Association." *Philosophy of Science* 51 (March): 20–22.

Cohen, Robert S. 1981. *Herbert Feigl: Inquiries and Provocations: Selected Writings 1929–1974.* Dordrecht, Netherlands: Reidell.

Cole, M., and S. Scribner. 1974. *Culture and Thought: A Psychological Introduction.* New York: Wiley.

Collins, H.M. 1975. "The Seven Sexes: A Study in the Sociology of a Phenomenon, or the Replication of Experiments in Physics." *Sociology* 9, no. 2: 205–24.

————. 1981. "Son of Seven Sexes: The Social Destruction of a Physical Phenomenon." *Social Studies of Science* 11: 33–62.

Comte, August. 1877. *Cours de Philosophie Positive,* vol. 4, 4th ed. Paris: Bailliêre et fils.

Cook, Thomas D., and Donald T. Campbell. 1986. "The Causal Assumptions of Quasi-Experimental Practice." *Synthese* 68: 141–80.

Cooper, Lee G. 1987. "Do We Need Critical Relativism?" *Journal of Consumer Research* 14 (June): 126–27.

Coyne, J.C. 1982. "A Brief Introduction to Epistobabble." *Family Therapy Networker* 6: 27–28.

Crampton, Suzanne M., and John A. Wagner III. 1994. "Percept-Percept Inflation in Microorganizational Research: An Investigation of Prevalence and Effect." *Journal of Applied Psychology* 79, no. 1: 67–76.

Daft, R.L., and A.Y. Lewin. 1990. "Can Organization Studies Begin to Break Out of the Normal Science Straightjacket?" Editorial essay in *Organization Science* 1, no. 1:1–9.

Davidson, Donald. 1973. "On the Very Idea of a Conceptual Scheme." In *Proceedings of the American Philosophical Association, 1973–74,* 5–20. Newark, DE: American Philosophical Association.

Dennett, D.C. 1981. *Brainstorms: Philosophical Essays on Mind and Psychology.* Cambridge, MA: MIT Press.

Denzin, Norman K. 2001. "The Seventh Moment: Qualitative Inquiry and the Practices of a More Radical Consumer Research." *Journal of Consumer Research* 28 (September): 324–30.

Denzin, Norman K., and Yvonna S. Lincoln, eds. 2000. *Handbook of Qualitative Research*, 2d ed. Thousand Oaks, CA: Sage.

Deshpandé, Rohit. 1983. "'Paradigms Lost': On Theory and Method in Research in Marketing." *Journal of Marketing* 47 (Fall): 101–10.

Dholakia, Nikhilesh. 1985. "Opposing Research Camps in Marketing: Rigor vs. Relevance." *Marketing Educator* 4, no. 3: 3.

———. 1988. "Interpreting Monieson: Creative and Destructive Tensions." *Journal of Macromarketing* 8 (Fall): 11–14.

Diamantopoulos, Adamantios, and Heidi M. Winklhofer. 2001. "Index Construction with Formative Indicators: An Alternative to Scale Development." *Journal of Marketing Research* 38 (May): 269–77.

Dickson, Michael. 1995. "An Empirical Reply to Empiricism: Protective Measurement Opens the Door for Quantum Realism." *Philosophy of Science* 62 (March): 122–40.

Donaldson, Lex. 1990. "A Rational Basis for Criticisms of Industrial Organization Economics." *Academy of Management Review* 15, no. 3: 394–401.

Doppelt, Gerald. 1978. "Kuhn's Epistemological Relativism." *Inquiry*. Reprinted in *Relativism: Cognitive and Moral*, ed. M. Krausz and J. Meiland, 113–48. Notre Dame, IN: Notre Dame University Press, 1982.

———. 1986. "Relativism and the Reticulational Model of Scientific Rationality." *Synthese* 69, no. 2: 225–52.

Drake, Stillman, and I.E. Drabkin. 1969. *Mechanics in Sixteenth-Century Italy: Selections from Tartaglia, Benedetti, Guido Ubaldo, and Galileo*. Madison: University of Wisconsin Press.

Durant, Will. 1954. *The Story of Philosophy*. New York: Simon and Schuster.

Dwyer, F. Robert, and Rosemary R. LaGace. 1986. "On the Nature and Role of Buyer-Seller Trust." In *AMA Summer Educators Conference Proceedings*, ed. T. Shimp et al., 40–45. Chicago: American Marketing Association.

Eagleton, Terry. 1991. *Ideology: An Introduction*. London: Verso.

Easton, Geoff. 1998. "Case Research as a Methodology for Industrial Networks: A Realist Apologia." In *Network Dynamics in International Marketing*, ed. P. Naude and P.W. Turnbull, 73–87. Oxford: Elsevier Science.

———. 2002. "Marketing: A Critical Realist Approach." *Journal of Business Research* 55: 103–9.

Edwards, Paul. 1951. "Bertrand Russell's Doubts about Induction." In *Logic and Language*, ed. A.G.N. Flew, 55–79. Oxford: Blackwell.

Einstein, Albert. 1923. *Sidelights on Relativity*. New York: Dutton.

El-Ansary, Adel. 1979. "The General Theory of Marketing: Revisited." In *Conceptual and Theoretical Developments in Marketing*, ed. O.C. Ferrell, Stephen Brown, and Charles Lamb, 399–407. Chicago: American Marketing Association.

Fay, Brian. 1988. "Review of *A History and Philosophy of the Social Sciences* by Peter T. Manicas." *History and Theory* 27, no. 3: 287–96.

Feigl, Herbert. 1965. "Philosophy of Science." In *Philosophy*, ed. R.M. Chisholm. Englewood Cliffs, NJ: Prentice Hall.

———. 1969. "The Origin and Spirit of Logical Positivism." In *The Legacy of Logical Positivism*, ed. Peter Achinstein and Stephen F. Barker, 3–24. Baltimore, MD: Johns Hopkins University Press.

Feigl, Herbert, and Grover Maxwell, eds. 1962. *Scientific Explanation, Space and Time. Minnesota Studies in the Philosophy of Science*, vol. 3. Minneapolis: University of Minnesota Press.

Fenner, Frank, and David White. 1976. *Medical Virology*. New York: Academic Press.

Feyerabend, Paul K. 1962. "Explanation, Reduction, and Empiricism." In *Scientific Explana-*

tion, Space and Time. Minnesota Studies in the Philosophy of Science, vol. 3, ed. Herbert Feigl and Grover Maxwell, 46–48. Minneapolis: University of Minnesota Press.

———. 1965a. "On the Meaning of Scientific Terms." *Journal of Philosophy* 62, no. 2: 267–71.

———. 1965b. "Reply to Criticism." In *Boston Studies in the Philosophy of Science,* ed. P. Cohen and M. Wartofsky, 223–61. New York: Humanities Press.

———. 1970. "Against Method." In *Analysis of Theories and Methods of Physics and Psychology,* ed. Michael Radner and Stephen Winokur, 17–130. Minneapolis: University of Minnesota Press.

———. 1975. *Against Method.* Thetford, UK: Lowe and Brydone.

———. 1977. "Changing Patterns of Reconstruction." *British Journal of the Philosophy of Science* 28, no. 4: 351–69.

———. 1978a. "From Incompetent Professionalism to Professionalized Incompetence—The Rise of a New Breed of Intellectuals." *Philosophy of the Social Sciences* 8 (March): 37–53.

———. 1978b. *Science in a Free Society.* London: Verso.

———. 1982. "Academic Ratiofascism: Comments on Tibor Machan's Review." *Philosophy of Social Science* 12, no. 2: 191–95.

———. 1987a. *Farewell to Reason.* London: Verso, New Left Books.

———. 1987b. "Putnam on Incommensurability." *British Journal of Philosophy of Science* 38, no. 1: 75–81.

Fine, Arthur. 1984. "The Natural Ontological Attitude." In *Scientific Realism,* ed. Jarrett Leplin, 83–108. Berkeley: University of California Press.

———. 1986a. *The Shaky Game.* Chicago: University of Chicago Press.

———. 1986b. "Unnatural Attitudes: Realist and Instrumentalist Attachments to Science." *Mind* 95, no. 1: 149–79.

Firat, A. Fuat. 1989. "Science and Human Understanding." In *AMA Winter Educators Conference,* ed. Terry Childers et al., 93–98. Chicago: American Marketing Association.

Firat, A. Fuat, and Alladi Venkatesh. 1995. "Liberatory Postmodernism and the Reenchantment of Consumption." *Journal of Consumer Research* 22, no. 3: 239–67.

Fiske, Donald W., and Richard A. Shweder, eds. 1986. *Metatheory in Social Science: Pluralisms and Subjectivities.* Chicago: University of Chicago Press.

Flew, Anthony. 1985. *Thinking About Social Thinking: The Philosophy of the Social Sciences.* New York: Blackwell.

Fodor, Jerry A. 1984. "Observation Reconsidered." *Philosophy of Science* 51 (March): 23–43.

———. 1988. "A Reply to Churchland's 'Perceptual Plasticity and Theoretical Neutrality.'" *Philosophy of Science* 55 (June): 188–98.

Fornell, Claes, and Fred L. Bookstein. 1982. "Two Structural Equation Models: LISREL PLS Applied to Consumer Exit-Voice Theory." *Journal of Marketing Research* 19 (November): 440–52.

Fox, John F. 1994. "Review of *Cognitive Realitivism and Social Science* by Diederick Raven, Lieteke van Vucht Tijssen, and Jan de Wolf." *Philosophy of the Social Sciences* 24, no. 4: 506–10.

Friedman, Michael. 1984. "Critical Notice: Moritz Schlick, Philosophical Papers." *Philosophy of Science* 50 (September): 498–514.

———. 1999. *Reconsidering Logical Positivism.* Cambridge: Cambridge University Press.

Fukuyama, Francis. 1995. *Trust: The Social Virtues and the Creation of Prosperity.* New York: Free Press.

Fullerton, Ronald A. 1986. "Historicism: What It Is, and What It Means for Consumer Research." In *Advances in Consumer Research,* ed. M. Wallendorf and P.F. Anderson, 431–34. Provo, UT: Association for Consumer Research.

———.1987. "The Poverty of Ahistorical Analysis: Present Weakness and Future Cure in U.S. Marketing Thought." In *Philosophical and Radical Thought in Marketing,* ed. A.F. Firat et al., 89–103. Lexington, MA: Lexington.

Ganesan, Shankar. 1994. "Determinants of Long-Term Orientation in Buyer-Seller Relationships." *Journal of Marketing* 58 (April): 1–19.

Giere, Ronald N. 1985. "Constructive Realism." In *Images of Science*, ed. Paul M. Churchland and Clifford A. Hooker, 75–98. Chicago: University of Chicago Press.

———. 1988. *Explaining Science: A Cognitive Approach*. Chicago: University of Chicago Press.

Gieryn, Thomas F. 1983 "Boundary-Work and the Demarcation of Science from Non-Science." *American Sociological Review* 48 (December): 370–86.

Gilman, Daniel. 1991. "The Neurobiology of Observation." *Philosophy of Science* 58 (September): 496–502.

Goodman, Nelson. 1965. *Fact, Fiction, and Forecast*. Indianapolis: Bobbs-Merrill.

———. 1978. *Ways of Worldmaking*. Indianapolis: Hackett.

Green, Paul E., and Frank Carmone. 1969. "Multidimensional Scaling: an Introduction and Comparison of Nonmetric Unfolding Techniques." *Journal of Marketing Research* 6 (August): 330–41.

Green, Paul E., and Vithala R. Rao. 1971. "Conjoint Measurement for Quantifying Judgmental Data." *Journal of Marketing Research* 8 (August): 355–63.

Greenwood, John D. 1990. "Two Dogmas of Neo-Empiricism: The 'Theory-Informity' of Observation and the Quine-Duhem Thesis." *Philosophy of Science* S7 (December): 553–74.

———. 1991. *Relations and Representations: An Introduction to the Philosophy of Social Psychological Science*. London: Routledge.

Griffin, David Ray, ed. 1988. *The Reenchantment of Science: Postmodern Proposals*. Albany: State University of New York Press.

Groff, Ruth. 2000. "The Truth of the Matter: Roy Bhaskar's Critical Realism and the Concept of Alethic Truth." *Philosophy of the Social Sciences* 30, no. 3: 407–35.

Gross, Paul R., and Normal Levitt. 1994. *Higher Superstition, the Academic Left and Its Quarrels with Science*. Baltimore, MD: Johns Hopkins University Press.

Grove, J.W. 1985. "Rationality at Risk: Science against Psuedoscience." *Minerva*, no. 3 (Summer): 216–40.

Guthrie, W.K.C. 1962. *History of Greek Philosophy*. Cambridge: Cambridge University Press.

Hacking, Ian. 1982. "Language, Truth, and Reason." In *Rationality and Relativism*, ed. Martin Hollis and Stephen Lukes, 48–66. Cambridge, MA: MIT Press.

———. 1985. "Do We See Through a Microscope?" In *Images of Science: Essays on Realism and Empiricism, with a Reply from Bas C. van Frasssen*, ed. Paul M. Churchland and Clifford A. Hooker, 132–52. Chicago: University of Chicago Press.

———. 1983. *Representing and Intervening: Introductory Topics in the Philosophy of Natural Science*. Cambridge: Cambridge University Press.

Hall, Rupert. 1959. "The Scholar and the Craftsman in the Scientific Revolution." In *History of Science*, ed. M. Clagett, 3–23. Madison: University of Wisconsin Press.

Hamilton, Edith, and Huntington Cairns, ed. 1961. *The Collected Dialogues of Plato*. London: Pantheon Books.

Hanson, Norwood R. 1958. *Patterns of Discovery*. Cambridge: Cambridge University Press.

Harré, Rom. 1984. *Great Scientific Experiments: Twenty Experiments That Changed Our View of the World*. Oxford: Phaidon Press.

———. 1986. *Varieties of Realism*. Oxford: Blackwell.

Harrison, Geoffrey. 1982. "Relativism and Tolerance." In *Relativism: Cognitive and Moral*, ed. M. Krausz and J.W. Meiland, 229–44. Notre Dame, IN: University of Notre Dame Press.

Hausman, D. 1992. *The Inexact and Separate Science of Economics*. Cambridge: Cambridge University Press.

Heath, Timothy B. 1992. "The Reconciliation of Humanism and Positivism in the Practice of Consumer Research." *Journal of the Academy of Marketing Science* 20, no. 2: 107–19.

Heider, E.R., and D.C. Oliver. 1972. "The Structure of the Color Space in Naming and Memory for Two Languages." *Cognitive Psychology* 8 (July): 337–54.

Hempel, Carl G. 1945. "Studies in the Logic of Confirmation." *Mind* 54, no. 1: 1–26; 97–121.

———. 1965a. "Aspects of Scientific Explanation." In *Aspects of Scientific Explanation and*

Other Essays in the Philosophy of Science, ed. C.G. Hempel, 331–496. New York: Free Press.

———, ed. 1965b. *Aspects of Scientific Explanation and Other Essays in the Philosophy of Science*. New York: Free Press.

———. 1970. "Fundamentals of Concept Formation in Empirical Science." In *Foundations of the Unity of Science*, vol. 2, ed. Otto Neurath, Rudolf Carnap, and Charles Morris, 651–745. Chicago: University of Chicago Press.

Hempel, Carl G., and Paul Oppenheim. 1948. "Studies in the Logic of Explanation." *Philosophy of Science* 30: 60–61.

Hendry, Robin F. 1995. "Realism and Progress: Why Scientists Should be Realists." In *Philosophy and Technology*, ed. Roger Fellows, 53–72. Cambridge: Cambridge University Press.

———. 2001. "Are Realism and Instrumentalism Methodologically Different?" *Philosophy of Science* 68 (Proceedings): S25–37.

Heritage, John. 1984. *Garfinkel and Ethnomethodology*. Cambridge, MA: Polity Press.

Herschel, J.F.W. 1830. *Preliminary Discourse on the Study of Natural Philosophy*. London: [n.p.].

Herskovits, Melvile J. 1947. *Man and His Works*. New York: Alfred Knopf.

———. 1972. *Cultural Relativism*. New York: Random House.

Hetrick, William P., and Héctor R. Lozada. 1994. "Construing the Critical Imagination: Comments and Necessary Diversions." *Journal of Consumer Research* 21, no. 3: 548–58.

Hewett, Kelly, and William O. Bearden. 2001. "Dependence, Trust, and Relational Behavior on the Part of Foreign Subsidiary Marketing Operations: Implications for Managing Global Marketing Operations." *Journal of Marketing* 65, no. 4: 51–66.

Hintikka, Jaakko. 1988. "On the Incommensurability of Theories." *Philosophy of Science* 55, no. 1: 25–38.

Hintikka, Jaakko, and I. Niiniluoto. 1979. "An Axiomatic Foundation for the Logic of Inductive Generalization." In *Formal Methods of the Methodology of Science*, ed. M. Prezelecki, K. Szaniawski, and R. Wojcicki, 77–98. Wroclaw, Poland: Ossolineum.

Hirschman, Elizabeth C. 1986. "Humanistic Inquiry in Marketing Research: Philosophy, Method, and Criteria." *Journal of Marketing Research* 23 (August): 237–49.

———. 1989. "After Word." In *Interpretive Consumer Research*, ed. Elizabeth Hirschman, 209. Provo, UT: Association for Consumer Research.

———. 1993. "Ideology in Consumer Research, 1980 and 1990: A Marxist and Feminist Critique." *Journal of Consumer Research* 19, no. 4: 537–56.

Holbrook, Morris B., and Mark W. Grayson. 1986. "The Semiology of Cinematic Consumption: Symbolic Consumer Behavior in 'Out of Africa.'" *Journal of Consumer Research* 13 (December): 374–81.

Holbrook, Morris B., and John O'Shaugnessy. 1988. "On the Scientific Status of Consumer Research and the Need for an Interpretive Approach to Studying Consumption Behavior." *Journal of Consumer Research* 13 (December): 398–402.

Holbrook, Morris B.; Stephen Bell; and Mark W. Grayson. 1989. "The Role of Humanities in Consumer Research." In *Interpretive Consumer Research*, ed. Elizabeth Hirschman, 20–47. Provo, UT: Association for Consumer Research.

Hollis, Martin. 1982. "The Social Destruction of Reality." In *Rationality and Relativism*, ed. M. Hollis and S. Lukes, 67–86. Cambridge, MA: MIT Press.

Hollis, Martin, and Steven Lukes. 1982. *Rationality and Relativism*. Cambridge, MA: MIT Press.

Holt, Douglas B. 1991. "Rashomon Visits Consumer Behavior: An Interpretive Critique of Naturalistic Inquiry." In *Advances in Consumer Research*, vol. 18, ed. R.H. Holman and M. R. Solomon, 57–62. Provo, UT: Association for Consumer Research.

Holton, G. 1970. "Mach, Einstein and the Search for Reality." In *Ernest Mach, Physicist and Philosopher*, ed. R.S. Kohen and R.J. Seeger. Dordrecht, Netherlands: Reidel.

Hooker, C.A. 1985. "Surface Dazzle, Ghostly Depths: An Exposition and Critical Evaluation of van Fraassens' Vindication of Empiricism against Realism." In *Images of Science: Essays on Realism and* Empiricism, ed. Paul M. Churchland and Clifford A. Hooker, 153–96. Chicago: University of Chicago Press.

Hopkins, Donald R. 1983. *Princes and Peasants: Smallpox in History*. Chicago: University of Chicago Press.

Houghton, Walter E. 1957. *The Victorian Frame of Mind*. New Haven, CT: Yale University Press.

Hovland, C.E.; I.L. Janis; and Harold H. Kelley. 1953. *Communication and Persuasion*. New Haven, CT: Yale University Press.

Howell, Roy. 1987. "Covariance Structure Modeling and Measurement Issues: A Note." *Journal of Marketing Research* 24 (February): 119–26.

Hoyningen-Huene, Paul. 1987. "Contexts of Discovery and Contexts of Justification." *Studies in the History and Philosophy of Science* 18, no. 4: 501–5.

Hudson, Laural Anderson, and Julie L. Ozanne. 1988. "Alternative Ways of Seeking Knowledge in Consumer Research." *Journal of Consumer Research* 14 (March): 508–21.

Huff, Lenard C.; Joanne Cooper; and Wayne Jones. 2002. "The Development and Consequences of Trust in Student Project Groups." *Journal of Marketing Education* 24, no. 1: 24–34.

Hull, D. 1975. "Review of Hempel, Kuhn and Shapere." *Systematic Zoology* 24, no. 3: 395–401.

Hume, David. 1911. *A Treatise of Human Nature*. New York: Dutton.

———. 1927. *An Enquiry Concerning Human Understanding*. Chicago: Open Court .

Hunt, Shelby D. 1976a. *Marketing Theory: Conceptual Foundations of Research in Marketing*. Columbus, OH: Grid.

———. 1976b. "The Nature and Scope of Marketing." *Journal of Marketing* 40 (July): 17–28.

———. 1983a. "General Theories and the Fundamental Explananda of Marketing." *Journal of Marketing* 47 (Fall): 9–17.

———. 1983b. *Marketing Theory: The Philosophy of Marketing Science*. Homewood, IL: Richard D. Irwin.

———. 1984. "Should Marketing Adopt Relativism?" In *Scientific Method of Marketing*, ed. Paul F. Anderson and Michael J. Ryan, 30–34. Chicago: American Marketing Association.

———. 1989a. "Naturalistic, Humanistic, and Interpretive Inquiry: Challenges and Ultimate Potential." In *Interpretive Consumer Research*, ed. Elizabeth Hirschman, 185–98. Provo, UT: Association for Consumer Research.

———. 1989b. "Reification and Realism in Marketing." *Journal of Macromarketing* 9 (Fall): 4–10.

———. 1990a. "Commentary on an Empirical Investigation of a General Theory of Marketing Ethics. "*Journal of the Academy of Marketing Science* 18, no. 2: 173–77.

———. 1990b. "Truth in Marketing Theory and Research." *Journal of Marketing* 54 (July): 1–15.

_____. 1991a. *Modern Marketing Theory: Critical Issues in the Philosophy of Marketing Science*. Cincinnati: South-Western.

_____. 1991b. "Positivism and Paradigm Dominance in Consumer Research: Toward Critical Pluralism and Rapprochement." *Journal of Consumer Research* 18 (June): 32–44.

_____. 1991c. "The Three Dichotomies Model of Marketing Revisited: Is the Total Content of Marketing Thought Normative?" In *Proceedings of the 1991 AMA Winter Educators' Conference*, ed. Terry L. Childers et al., 425–30. Chicago: American Marketing Association.

_____. 1992a. "For Reason and Realism in Marketing." *Journal of Marketing* 56 (April): 89–102.

_____. 1992b. "Marketing Is . . ." *Journal of the Academy of Marketing Science* 20 (Fall): 301–11.

———. 1993. "Objectivity in Marketing Theory and Research." *Journal of Marketing* 57 (April): 76–91.

————. 1994a. "A Realist Theory of Empirical Testing: Resolving the Theory Ladenness/ Objectivity Debate." *Philosophy of the Social Sciences* 24, no. 2: 133–58.

————. 1994b. "On Rethinking Marketing: Our Discipline, Our Practice, Our Methods." *European Journal of Marketing* 28, no. 3: 13–25.

————. 1994c. "On the Rhetoric of Qualitative Inquiry: Toward Historically Informed Argumentation in Management Inquiry." *Journal of Management Inquiry* 3 (September): 221–34.

————. 1995a. "On Communication, Probative Force, and Sophistry: A Reply to van Eijkelenburg." *Journal of Management Inquiry* 4, no. 2: 211–13.

————. 1995b. "The Resource-Advantage Theory of Competition: Toward Explaining Productivity and Economic Growth." *Journal of Management Inquiry* 4 (December): 317–32.

————. 2000. *A General Theory of Competition: Resources, Competences, Productivity, Economic Growth.* Thousand Oaks, CA: Sage.

————. 2001. "The Influence of Philosophy, Philosophies, and Philosophers on a Marketer's Scholarship." *Journal of Marketing* 64 (October): 117–24.

————. 2002a. *Foundations of Marketing Theory: Toward a General Theory of Marketing.* Armonk, NY: M.E. Sharpe.

————. 2002b. "Truth and Scientific Realism." Working paper, Marketing Department, Texas Tech University, Lubbock.

Hunt, Shelby D.; Lawrence B. Chonko; and James B. Wilcox. 1984. "Ethical Problems of Marketing Researchers." *Journal of Marketing Research* 21 (August): 309–24.

Hunt, Shelby D., and Robert M. Morgan. 1994. "Relationship Marketing in the Era of Network Competition." *Marketing Management* 3, no. 1: 19–28.

————. 1995. "The Comparative Advantage Theory of Competition." *Journal of Marketing* 59 (April): 1–15.

————. 1996. "The Resource-Advantage Theory of Competition: Dynamics, Path Dependencies, and Evolutionary Dimensions." *Journal of Marketing* 60 (October): 107–14.

————. 1997. "Resource-Advantage Theory: A Snake Swallowing Its Tail or a General Theory of Competition?" *Journal of Marketing* 61 (October): 74–82.

Jacobs, Struan. 1989. "Vindicating Universalism." *Philosophy of the Social Sciences* 19 (March): 75–80.

James, William. 1907. *Pragmatism.* New York: Harper Brothers.

Jaworski, Bernard J., and Deborah J. MacInnis. 1987. "On the Meaning of Data: Historical and Contemporary Perspectives." In *AMA Winter Educators' Conference Proceedings*, ed. R.W. Belk et al., 161–65. Chicago: American Marketing Association.

Jones, Gary. 1981. "Kuhn, Popper, and Theory Comparison." *Dialectica* 35, no. 4: 389–97.

Kant, Immanuel. 1783. *Prolegomena and Metaphysical Foundations of Natural Science.* In *Philosophy of Science*, ed. Joseph J. Kockelmans, 17–27. 1968: New York: Free Press.

Keat, Russell, and John Urry. 1975. *Social Theory as Science.* London: Routledge and Kegan Paul.

Keith, William M., and Richard A. Cherwitz. 1989. "Objectivity, Disagreement, and the Rhetoric of Inquiry." In *Rhetoric in the Human Sciences*, ed. Herbert W. Simons, 195–210. Newbury Park, CA: Sage.

Kekes, John. 1976. *A Justification of Rationality.* Albany: State University of New York Press.

Kerin, Roger A. 1996. "In Pursuit of an Ideal: The Editorial and Literary History of the *Journal of Marketing*." *Journal of Marketing* 60, no. 1: 1–13.

Kitcher, P. 1978. "Theories, Theorists, and Theoretical Changes." *Philosophical Review* 87: 519–47.

Knorr-Cetina, K. 1981. *The Manufacture of Knowledge: An Essay on the Constructivist and Contextual Nature of Science.* Oxford: Pergamon Press.

Knorr-Cetina, K., and Michael Mulkay. 1983. "Introduction: Emerging Principles in Social Studies of Science." In *Science Observed*, ed. K.D. Knorr-Cetina and M. Mulkay. London: Sage.

Kordig, Carl R. 1971. *The Justification of Scientific Change.* Dordrecht, Netherlands: Reidel .

―――. 1980. "Progress Requires Invariance." *Philosophy of Science* 47, no. 1: 141.

Kotler, Philip. 1972. "A Generic Concept of Marketing." *Journal of Marketing* 36 (April): 46–54.

Kotler, Philip, and Sidney Levy. 1969. "Broadening the Concept of Marketing." *Journal of Marketing* 33 (January): 10–15.

Kottenhoff, H. 1957. "Situational and Personal Influences on Space Perception with Experimental Spectacles." *Acta Psychologica* 13: 79–97.

Krips, H. 1980. "Some Problems for 'Progress and Its Problems.'" *Philosophy of Science* 47, no. 4: 601–16.

Kuhn, Thomas S. 1962. *The Structure of Scientific Revolutions*. Chicago: University of Chicago Press.

―――. 1970a. "Reflections on My Critics." In *Criticism and the Growth of Knowledge*, ed. Imre Lakatos and Alan Musgrave, 231–78. Cambridge: Cambridge University Press.

―――. 1970b. *The Structure of Scientific Revolutions*. 2d ed. Chicago: University of Chicago Press.

―――. 1976. "Theory-Change as Structure-Change: Comments on the Sneed Formalism." *Erkenntnis* 10, no. 2: 179–99.

―――. 1977. *The Essential Tension*. Chicago: University of Chicago Press.

Kyburg, Henry E. Jr. 1968. *Philosophy of Science*. New York: Macmillan.

Lakatos, Imre. 1970. "Falsification and the Methodology of Scientific Research Programmes." In *Criticism and the Growth of Knowledge*, ed. Imre Lakatos and Alan Musgrave, 91–196.Cambridge: Cambridge University Press.

―――. 1978. *The Methodology of Scientific Research Programmes*, vol. 1. Cambridge: Cambridge University Press.

Lakoff, George, and Mark Johnson. 1980. *Metaphors We Live By*. Chicago: University of Chicago Press.

Lantz, D., and V. Stefflre. 1964. "Language and Cognition Revisited." *Journal of Abnormal and Social Psychology* 69 (November): 472–81.

Larzelere, Robert E., and Ted L. Huston. 1980. "The Dyadic Trust Scale: Toward Understanding Interpersonal Trust in Close Relationships." *Journal of Marriage and the Family* 42 (August): 595–604.

Latour, B., and S. Woolgar. 1979. *Laboratory Life: The Social Construction of Scientific Facts*. Beverly Hills, CA: Sage.

Laudan, Larry. 1968. "Theories of Scientific Method from Plato to Mach." In *History of Science*, vol. 7, ed. A.C. Cronbie and M.A. Hoskin, 1–63. Cambridge, UK: W. Heffer and Sons.

―――. 1973. "Peirce and the Trivialization of the Self-correcting Thesis." In *Foundations of Scientific Method: The Nineteenth Century*, ed. Ronald N. Giere and Richard S. Westfall, 275–306. Bloomington: Indiana University Press.

―――. 1976. "Discussion: Two Dogmas of Methodology." *Philosophy of Science* 43, no. 4: 585–97.

―――. 1977. *Progress and Its Problems: Towards a Theory of Scientific Growth*. Berkeley: University of California Press.

―――. 1979. "Historical Methodologies: An Overview and Manifesto." In *Current Research in the Philosophy of Science*, ed. Peter D. Asquith and Henry E. Kyburg Jr., 40–54. East Lansing, MI: Philosophy of Science Association.

―――. 1980."Views of Progress: Separating the Pilgrims from the Rakes." *Philosophy of the Social Sciences* 10: 273–86.

―――. 1981a. "A Confutation of Convergent Realism." *Philosophy of Science* 48: 19–49.

―――. 1981b. *Science and Hypothesis*. Dordrecht, Netherlands: Reidel.

―――. 1982. "Commentary: Science at the Bar—Causes for Concern." *Science, Technology, and Human Values* 7 (Fall): 16–19.

―――. 1983. "The Demise of the Demarcation Problem." In *Physics, Philosophy, and Psychoanalysis*, ed. R.S. Cohn and L. Laudan, 111–27. Dordrecht, Netherlands: Reidel.

―――. 1984. *Science and Values*. Berkeley: University of California Press.

————. 1987. "Relativism, Naturalism and Reticulation." *Synthese* 71, no. 2: 221–34.

————. 1990. *Science and Relativism*. Chicago: University of Chicago Press.

Laudan, Larry; Arthur Donovan; Rachel Laudan; Peter Barker; Harold Brown; Jarrett Leplin; Paul Thagard; and Steve Wykstra. 1986. "Scientific Change: Philosophical Models and Historical Research." *Synthese* 69, no. 1: 141–223.

Lavin, Marilyn, and Thomas J. Archdeacon. 1989. "The Relevance of Historical Method for Marketing Research." In *Interpretive Consumer Research*, ed. Elizabeth Hirschman, 60–68. Provo, UT: Association for Consumer Research.

Lenneberg, E. 1967. *The Biological Foundations of Language*. New York: Wiley.

Leong, Siew Meng. 1985. "Metatheory and Metamethodology in Marketing: A Lakatosian Reconstruction." *Journal of Marketing* 49 (Fall): 23–40.

Leplin, Jarrett. 1981. "Truth and Scientific Progress." *Studies in the History and Philosophy of Science* 12, no. 2: 269–91.

————. 1984. *Scientific Realism*. Berkeley: University of California Press.

————. 1986. "Methodological Realism and Scientific Rationality." *Philosophy of Science* 53, no. 1: 31–51.

————. 1997. *A Novel Defense of Scientific Realism*. New York: Oxford University Press.

Levey, G.B. 1996. "Theory Choice and the Comparison of Rival Theoretical Perspectives in Political Sociology." *Journal of Philosophy of the Social Sciences* 26 (March): 26–60.

Levin, Michael E. 1979. "On Theory-Change and Meaning-Change." *Philosophy of Science* 46, no. 3: 407–24.

————. 1984. "What Kind of Explanation is Truth?" In *Scientific Realism*, ed. Jarrett Leplin, 124–39. Berkeley: University of California Press.

————. 1991. "The Reification-Realism-Positivism Controversy in Macromarketing: A Philosopher's View." *Journal of Macromarketing* 11 (Spring): 57–65.

Levitt, Theodore. 1960. "Marketing Myopia." *Harvard Business Review* 38 (July–August): 24–27.

Lincoln, Yvonna S., and Egon G. Guba. 1985. *Naturalistic Inquiry*. Beverly Hills, CA: Sage.

Longman, Kenneth A. 1971. "The Management Challenge to Marketing Theory." In *New Essays in Marketing Theory*, ed. George Fisk, 9–19. Boston, MA: Allyn and Bacon.

Losee, John. 1980. *A Historical Introduction to the Philosophy of Science*. Oxford: Oxford University Press.

Lugg, Andrew. 1986. "Discussion: An Alternative to the Traditional Model? Laudan on Disagreement Consensus in Science." *Philosophy of Science* 53, no. 4: 419–24.

Lukacs, Georg. 1971. *History and Class Consciousness: Studies in Marxist Dialectics*. Cambridge, MA: MIT Press.

Lutz, Richard J. 1989. "Presidential Address, 1988—Postivism, Naturalism and Pluralism in Consumer Research: Paradigms in Paradis." In *Advances in Consumer Research,* vol. 16, ed. Thomas K. Srull, 1–8. Provo, UT: Association for Consumer Research.

Lyons, David. 1982. "Ethical Relativism and the Problem of Incoherence." In *Relativism: Cognitive Moral*, ed. M. Krausz and J. Meiland, 209–25. Notre Dame, IN: University of Notre Dame Press.

MacCormac, Earl R. 1980. *A Cognitive Theory of Metaphor*. Cambridge, MA: MIT Press.

Machan, Tibor R. 1982a. "Anarchosurrealism Revisited: Reply to Feyerabend's Comments." *Philosophy of Social Science* 12, no. 2: 197–99.

————. 1982b. "The Politics of Medicinal Anarchism." *Philosophy of Social Science* 12, no. 2: 183–89.

MacKinnon, Edward. 1979. "Scientific Realism: The New Debates." *Philosophy of Science* 46, no. 4: 501–32.

Maki, Uskali. 1988. "How to Combine Rhetoric and Realism in the Methodology of Economics." *Economics and Philosophy* 4, no. 1: 89–109.

Malinowski, Bronislaw. 1954. *Magic, Science, and Religion*. New York: Doubleday.

Mandelbaum, David G., ed. 1949. *Selected Writings of Edward Sapir in Language, Culture and Personality*. Berkeley: University of California Press.

Manicas, Peter T. 1987. *A History and Philosophy of the Social Sciences*. New York: Blackwell.

Margolis, Joseph. 1983. "The Nature and Strategies of Relativism." *Mind* 42, no. 4: 548–67.

Marsden, David. 2001. "Rethinking Marketing and Natural Science." In *Rethinking European Marketing*: Thirtieth EMAC Proceedings, ed. Einar Breivik, Andreas Falkenberg, and Kjell Gronhaug, 75. Bergen, Norway.

Martin, Laura, and Geoffrey K. Pullman. 1991. *The Great Eskimo Vocabulary Hoax*. Chicago: University of Chicago Press.

Masterman, Margaret. 1970. "The Nature of a Paradigm." In *Criticism and the Growth of Knowledge*, ed. I. Lakatos and A. Musgrave, 59–90. Cambridge: Cambridge University Press.

Maxwell, Grover. 1962. "The Ontological Status of Theoretical Entities." In *Scientific Explanation, Space and Time. Minnesota Studies in the Philosophy of Science*, vol. 3, ed. Herbert Feigl and Grover Maxwell, 3–27. Minneapolis: University of Minnesota Press.

McCloskey, D.N. 1985. *The Rhetoric of Economics, Series in the Rhetoric of the Human Sciences*. Madison: University of Wisconsin Press.

McMullin, Ernan. 1979. "Discussion Review: Laudan's Progress and Its Problems." *Philosophy of Science* 46, no. 4: 623–44.

———. 1984. "A Case for Scientific Realism." In *Scientific Realism*, ed. Jarrett Leplin, 8–40. Berkeley: University of California Press.

———. 1986. "Empiricism at Sea." In *A Portrait of Twenty-Five Years: Boston Colloquium for the Philosophy of Science 1960–1985*, ed. P. Cohen and M. Wartofsky, 121–32. Dordrecht, Netherlands: Reidel.

Meehl, Paul E. 1986. "What Social Scientists Don't Understand." In *Metatheory in Social Science*, ed. Donald Fiske and Richard Shweder, 315–38. Chicago: University of Chicago Press.

Mermin, N.D. 1983. "The Great Quantum Muddle." *Philosophy of Science* 50 (December): 651–56.

Merton, Robert K. 1968. *Social Theory and Social Structure*. New York: Free Press.

———. 1973. *The Sociology of Science*. Chicago, IL: University of Chicago Press.

Mick, David Glen. 1986. "Consumer Research and Semiotics: Exploring the Morphology of Signs, Symbols, and Significance." *Journal of Consumer Research* 13 (September): 196–213.

Moberg, D.W. 1979. "Are There Rival, Incommensurable Theories?" *Philosophy of Science* 46: 244–62.

Monieson, David D. 1988. "Intellectualism in Macromarketing: A World Disenchanted." *Journal of Macromarketing* 8 (Fall): 4–10.

Monroe, Kent B., et. al. 1988. "Developing, Disseminating, and Utilizing Marketing Knowledge." *Journal of Marketing* 52 (October): 1–25.

Moore, George Edward. 1903. "The Refutation of Idealism." Reprinted in *Philosophical Studies*, ed. G.E. Moore, 1–30. London: Trench, Trubuer, and Co., 1992.

Moorman, Christine; Rohit Deshpande; and Gerald Zaltman. 1993. "Factors Affecting Trust in Market Research Relationships." *Journal of Marketing* 57 (January): 81–101.

Morehead, Philip D. 1985. *The New American Roget's College Thesaurus*. New York: Signet, New American Library.

Morgan, Robert M., and Shelby D. Hunt. 1994. "The Commitment-Trust Theory of Relationship Marketing." *Journal of Marketing* 58 (July): 20–38.

Morris, Charles W. 1955. "Scientific Empiricism." In *Foundations of the Unity of Science*, vol. 1, ed. Otto Neurath, Rudolf Carnap, and Charles Morris, 63–75. Chicago: University of Chicago Press.

Muncy, James A., and Raymond P. Fisk. 1987. "Cognitive Relativism and the Practice of Marketing Science." *Journal of Marketing* 51 (January): 20–23.

Munz, Peter. 1987. "Bloor's Wittgenstein of the Fly in the Bottle." *Philosophy of Social Science* 17, no. 1: 67–96.

Murphy, Nancey. 1990. "Scientific Realism and Postmodern Philosophy." *British Journal for the Philosophy of Science* 41, no. 2: 291–303.

Murray, Jeff B., and Julie L. Ozanne. 1991. "The Critical Imagination: Emancipatory Interests in Consumer Research." *Journal of Consumer Research* 18, no. 2: 129–45.

Musgrave, Alan. 1979. "Problems with Progress." *Synthese* 42, no. 3: 443–64.

Nagel, Ernest. 1960. "The Meaning of Reduction in the Natural Sciences." In *Philosophy of Science*, ed. A. Danto and S. Morgenbesser. New York: Meridian Books.

———. 1961. *The Structure of Science*. New York: Harcourt Brace Jovanovich.

Newton-Smith, W. 1981. "In Defence of Truth." In *Philosophy of Evolution*, ed. U. Jensen and R. Harré, 269–94. New York: St. Martin's Press.

Neurath, Otto; Rudolf Carnap; and Charles Morris, ed. 1955. *Foundations of the Unity of Science*, vol. 1. Chicago: University of Chicago Press.

———. 1970. *Foundations of the Unity of Science*, vol 2. Chicago: University of Chicago Press.

Nickles, Thomas. 1985. "Beyond Divorce: The Current Status of the Discovery Debate." *Philosophy of Science* 52 (June): 177–206.

Niiniluoto, Ilkka. 1999. *Critical Scientific Realism*. Oxford: Oxford University Press.

Novick, Peter. 1988. "That Noble Dream: The 'Objectivity Question' and the American Historical Profession." Cambridge: Cambridge University Press.

Olson, Jerry C. 1982. "Towards a Science of Consumer Behavior." In *Advances in Consumer Research*, ed. Andrew A. Mitchell, v–x. Ann Arbor, MI: Association of Consumer Research.

———. 1987. "The Construction of Scientific Meaning." Paper presented at the 1987 Winter Marketing Educators' Conference, American Marketing Association, Chicago.

Orwell, George. 1949. *1984*. New York: Harcourt, Brace and World.

Ozanne, Julie L., and Laurel Hudson. 1989. "Exploring Diversity in Consumer Research." In *Interpretive Consumer Research*, ed. Elizabeth Hirschman, 1–9. Provo, UT: Association for Consumer Research.

Palacios, Joel. 1987. "Slavery Up Among Maranos." *Dallas Morning News* (Reuters).

Palmer, R.E. 1969. *Hermeneutics*. Evanston, WY: Northwestern University Press.

Patterson, Orlando. 1973. "Guilt, Relativism, and Black-White Relations." *American Scholar* 43, no. 1: 26–34.

Paulsen, John. 1910. *Immanuel Kant*. New York: Harper Brothers.

Pechmann, Cornelia. 1990. "Response to President's Column, September 1989." *ACR Newsletter* (June): 5–7.

Peter, J. Paul. 1992. "Realism or Relativism for Marketing Theory and Research: A Comment on Hunt's Scientific Realism." *Journal of Marketing* 56, no. 2: 72–79.

———. 1983. "Some Philosophical and Methodological Issues in Consumer Research." In *Marketing Theory: The Philosophy of Marketing Science*, ed. Shelby D. Hunt, 382–94. Homewood, IL: Richard D. Irwin.

Peter, J. Paul, and Jerry C. Olson. 1983. "Is Science Marketing?" *Journal of Marketing* 47 (Fall): 111–25.

———. 1989. "The Relativist/Constructionist Perspective on Scientific Knowledge and Consumer Research." In *Interpretive Consumer Research*, ed. Elizabeth Hirschman, 24–28. Provo, UT: Association for Consumer Research.

Peter, J. Paul, and Peter A. Dacin. 1991. "Measurement Scales, Permissible Statistics, and Marketing Research." In *AMA Winter Educators' Conference Proceedings*, ed. Terry L. Childers et al., 275–83. Chicago: American Marketing Association.

Phillips, D.C. 1984. "Was William James Telling the Truth?" *Monist* 67 (July): 362–73.

———. 1987. *Philosophy, Science, and Social Inquiry*. Oxford: Pergamon Press.

Pierce, David A., and Larry D. Haugh. 1977. "Causality in Temporal Systems." *Journal of Econometrics* 5 (May): 265–93.

Pinnick, Cassandra L. 1994. "Feminist Epistemology: Implications for Philosophy of Science." *Philosophy of Science* 61, no. 4: 646–57.

Plekhanov, Georgi. 1940. *The Materialistic Conception of History*. New York: Random House.

Podsakoff, Philip M., and Dennis W. Organ. 1986. "Self-Reports in Organizational Research: Problems and Prospects." *Journal of Management* 12, no. 4: 531–44.

Polkinghorne, J.C. 1984. *The Quantum World.* New York: Longman.

Popper, Karl R. 1959. *The Logic of Scientific Discovery.* New York: Harper and Row.

———. 1963. *Conjectures and Refutations*: The Growth of Scientific Knowledge. New York: Harper and Row.

———. [1945] 1966. *The Open Society and Its Enemies.* 5th ed. Princeton, NJ: Princeton University Press.

———. 1972. *Objective Knowledge.* Oxford: Oxford University Press.

———. 1982. *Quantum Theory and the Schism in Physics.* Totowa, NJ: Rowan and Littlefield.

Psillos, Stathis. 1996. "Scientific Realism and the 'Pessimistic Induction.'" *Philosophy of Science* 63, no. 3 (Proceedings): S306–14.

"Purge Toll Under Stalin Revised." 1988. *Dallas Morning News* (Reuters), April 17.

Putnam, Hilary. 1962. "What Theories Are Not." In *Proceedings of the 1960 International Congress*, ed. E. Nagel, P. Suppes, and A. Tarski, 240–51. Stanford, CA: Stanford University Press.

———. 1975. *Mathematics, Matter and Method.* Cambridge: Cambridge University Press.

———. 1979. "Philosophy of Mathematics: A Report." In *Current Research in Philosophy of Science*, ed. P. Asquith and H. Kyburg Jr., 386–89. East Lansing, MI: Philosophy of Science Association.

———. 1981. *Reason, Truth and History.* Cambridge: University of Cambridge Press.

Putnam, L.L. 1993. Comments of Linda L. Putnam in "Ethnography Versus Critical Theory: Debating Organizational Research." *Journal of Management Inquiry* 2: 221–35.

Quine, W.V.O. 1951. "Two Dogmas of Empiricism." *Philosophical Review* 60: 20–43.

———. 1969. "Epistemology Naturalized." In *Ontological Relativity and Other Essays*, ed. W.V.O. Quine, 69–89. New York: Columbia Press.

Rachels, James. 1986. *The Elements of Moral Philosophy.* New York: Random House.

Radcliffe-Brown, A.R. 1952. *Structure and Function in Primitive Society.* London: Cohen and West.

Radner, Daisie, and Michael Radner. 1982. *Science and Unreason.* Belmont, CA: Wadsworth.

Radner, Michael, and Stephen Winokur, ed. 1970. *Analysis of Theories and Methods of Physics and Psychology, Minnesota Studies in the Philosophy of Science*, vol. 4. Minneapolis: University of Minnesota Press.

Raftopoulos, Athanasse. 1995. "Discussion: Was Cartesian Science Ever Meant to be A Priori? A Comment on Hatfield." *Philosophy of Science* 62, no. 1: 150–60.

———. 2001. "Reentrant Neural Pathways and the Theory-Ladenness of Perception." *Philosophy of Science* 68 (Proceedings): S187–99.

Ravetz, Jerome R. 1971. *Scientific Knowledge and Its Social Problems.* Oxford: Oxford University Press.

Reichenbach, Hans. 1938. *Experience and Prediction.* Chicago: University of Chicago Press.

———. 1949. *The Theory of Probability.* Berkeley: University of California Press.

Reisch, George A. 1998. "Pluralism, Logical Empiricism, and the Problem of Pseudoscience." *Philosophy of Science* 65, no. 2: 333–48.

Rescher, Nicolas. 1997. *Objectivity: The Obligations of Impersonal Reason.* Notre Dame, IN, University of Notre Dame Press.

Robertson, T.S., and H.H. Kassarjian, ed. 1991. *Handbook of Consumer Behavior.* Englewood Cliffs, NJ: Prentice Hall.

Rohrlich, Fritz, and Larry Hardin. 1983. "Established Theories." *Philosophy of Science* 50, no. 4: 603–7.

Rokeach, Milton. 1968. *Beliefs, Attitudes, and Values.* San Francisco, CA: Jossey Bass.

Rosenberg, Alexander. 1992. *Economics: Mathematical Politics or Science of Diminishing Returns?* Chicago: University of Chicago Press.

Rotter, Julian B. 1971. "Generalized Expectancies for Interpersonal Trust." *American Psychologist* 26 (May): 443–52.

Rudner Richard. 1966. *Philosophy of Social Science.* Englewood Cliffs, NJ: Prentice Hall.

Russell, Bertrand. 1929. *Our Knowledge of the External World*. New York: New American Library.

―――. 1945. *A History of Western Philosophy*. New York: Simon and Schuster.

Ryan, Michael J., and Julia M. Bristor. 1987. "The Symbiotic Nature of Hermeneutical vs. Classically Generated Knowledge." In *1987 AMA Winter Educator's Conference*, ed. Russell W. Belk et al., 191–94. Chicago: American Marketing Association.

Salmon, Wesley C. 1963. *Logic*. Englewood Cliffs, NJ: Prentice Hall.

Sampson, Geoffrey. 1987. "Imre Lakatos." In *Thinkers of the Twentieth Century*. 2d ed., ed. Roland Turner, 312–13. Chicago: St. James Press.

Sapir, Edward. 1921. *Language: An Introduction to the Study of Speech*. New York: Harcourt, Brace and World.

Sapire, D. 1988. "Jarvie on Rationality and the Unity of Mankind." *Philosophy of the Social Sciences* 18 (December): 497–508.

Sarkar, H. 1981. "Truth, Problem-Solving and Methodology." *Studies in History and Philosophy of Science* 12, no. 1: 61–73.

Sauer, William J.; Nancy Nighswonger; and Gerald Zaltman. 1982. "Current Issues in Philosophy of Science: Implication of the Study of Marketing." In *Marketing Theory: Philosophy of Science Perspectives*, ed. Ronald F. Bush and Shelby D. Hunt, 17–21. Chicago: American Marketing Association.

Sayer, Andrew. 1992. *Method in Social Science: A Realist Approach*. 2d ed. London: Routledge.

Sayers, Brian. 1987. "Wittgenstein, Relativism, and the Strong Thesis in Sociology." *Philosophy of Social Science* 17, no. 2: 133–45.

Scheffler, Israel. 1957. "Explanation, Prediction, and Abstraction." *British Journal for the Philosophy of Science* 7, no. 3: 293–309.

―――. 1967. *Science and Subjectivity*. Indianapolis: Bobbs Merrill.

―――. 1982. *Science and Subjectivity*. 2d ed. Indianapolis: Hackett.

―――. 1986. *Inquiries: Philosophical Studies of Language, Science, and Learning*. Indianapolis: Hackett.

Schlegelmilch, Bodo B. 2002. "Comments." *Journal of Marketing Management* 18, nos. 1–2: 221–27.

Schlick, Moritz. 1934. "Uber das Fundament der Erkenntnis." *Erkenntnis* 4. English translation by David Rynin, in *Logical Positivism*, ed. A.J. Ayer, 209–27. Glencoe, IL: Free Press. (Page numbers refer to English translation.)

Schopenhauer, Arthur. [1818] 1969. *The World as Will and Representation*. New York: Dover.

Schwandt, Thomas R. 1990. "Paths to Inquiry in the Social Disciplines: Scientific, Constructivist, and Critical Theory Methodologies." In *The Paradigm Dialog*, ed. Egon G. Guba, 258–76. Newbury Park, CA: Sage.

Scriven, Michael. 1959. "Explanation and Prediction in Evolutionary Theory." *Science* 130, no. 3: 477–82.

Sellars, Wilfrid. 1963. *Science, Perception and Reality*. New York: Humanities Press.

Shapere, Dudley. 1964. "The Structure of Scientific Revolutions." *Philosophical Review* 73, no. 3: 383–94.

―――. 1966. "The Structure of Scientific Change." In *Mind and Cosmos: Explorations in the Philosophy of Science*, ed. R. Colodny, 41–85. Pittsburgh: University of Pittsburgh Press.

―――. 1982. "The Concept of Observation in Science and Philosophy." *Philosophy of Science* 49 (December): 485–525.

Shapiro, Benson P. 1973. "Price Reliance: Existence and Sources." *Journal of Marketing Research* 10 (August): 286–93.

Shapiro, Edna. 1973. "Educational Evaluation" Rethinking the Criteria of Competence." *School Review* (November): 523–49.

Sherman, Stralford. 1992. "Are Strategic Alliances Working?" *Fortune* (September): 77–78.

Sherry, John F. Jr. 1983. "Gift Giving in Anthropological Perspective." *Journal of Consumer Research* 10 (September): 157–68.

―――. 1991. "Postmodern Alternatives: The Interpretive Turn in Consumer Research." In

Handbook of Consumer Behavior, ed. T.S. Robertson and H.H. Kassarjian, 548–91. Englewood Cliffs, NJ: Prentice Hall.

Sheth, Jagdesh N., and A. Parvatiyar. 1995. "The Evolution of Relationship Marketing." *International Business Review* 4, no. 1: 397–418.

Sheth, Jagdesh N.; David M. Gardner; and Dennis E. Garrett. 1988. *Marketing Theory: Evolution and Evaluation*. New York: Wiley.

Shimp, Terence A., and Subhash Sharma. 1987. "Consumer Ethnocentrism: Construction and Validation of CETSCALE." *Journal of Marketing Research* 24 (August): 280–89.

Short, Thomas. 1988. "'Diversity' and 'Breaking the Disciplines.'" *Academic Questions* 1 (Summer): 6–29.

Shweder, Richard A., and Donald W. Fiske. 1986. "Introduction: Uneasy Social Science." In *Metatheory in Social Science: Pluralisms and Subjectivities*, ed. Donald Fiske and Richard Shweder, 1–18. Chicago: University of Chicago Press.

———. 1989. "Post-Nietzschian Anthropology: The Idea of Multiple Objective Worlds." In *Relativism: Interpretation and Confrontation*, ed. Michael Krausz, 99–139. Notre Dame, IN: University of Notre Dame Press.

Siegel, Harvey. 1980a. "Justification, Discovery, and the Naturalizing of Epistemology." *Philosophy of Science* 47, no. 2: 297–321.

———. 1980b. "Objectivity, Rationality, Incommensurability, and More." *British Journal of the Philosophy of Science* 31, no. 3: 359–84.

———. 1983. "Brown on Epistemology and the New Philosophy of Science." *Synthese* 56, no. 1: 61–89.

———. 1984. "Goodmanian Relativism." *Monist* 67 (July): 66–72.

———. 1985. "What Is the Question Concerning the Rationality of Science?" *Philosophy of Science* 52, no. 4 (December): 517–37.

———. 1986. "Relativism, Truth, and Incoherence." *Synthese* 68 (Fall): 225–59.

———. 1987. *Relativism Refuted*. Dordrecht, Netherlands: Reidel.

———. 1988. "Relativism for Consumer Research? (Comments on Anderson)." *Journal of Consumer Research* 15 (June): 129–32.

———. 1989. "The Rationality of Science, Critical Thinking, and Science Education." *Synthese* 80: 9–41.

———. 1997. *Rationality Redeemed? Further Dialogues on an Educational Ideal*. New York: Routledge.

Silber, John. 1990. "Free Speech and the Academy." *Intercollegiate Review* 26 (Fall): 33–42.

Simons, Herbert W. 1989. "Distinguishing the Rhetorical From the Real: The Case of Psychotherapeutic Placebos." In *Rhetoric in the Human Sciences*, ed. Herbert W. Simons, 109–18. Newbury Park, CA: Sage.

Singh, Jagdip; Roy D. Howell; and Gary K. Rhoads. 1990. "Adaptive Designs for Likert-Type Data: An Approach for Implementing Marketing Surveys." *Journal of Marketing Research* 27 (August): 304–21.

Skipper, Robert, and Michael R. Hyman. 1987. "Evaluating and Improving Argument-Centered Works in Marketing." *Journal of Marketing* 51 (October): 60–75.

Slezak, Peter. 1994. "A Second Look at David Bloor's *Knowledge and Social Imagery*." *Philosophy of the Social Sciences* 24, no. 3: 336–61.

Smith, John K., and Deborah K. Deemer. 2000. "The Problem of Criteria in the Age of Relativism." In *Handbook of Qualitative Research*. 2d ed., ed. Norman K. Denzin and Yvonna S. Lincoln, 877–96. Thousand Oaks, CA: Sage.

Snyder, Paul. 1978. *Toward One Science*. New York: St. Martin's Press.

Stefflre, V.; V. Castillo-Vales; and L. Morley. 1966. "Language and Cognition in Yucatan: A Cross-Cultural Replication." *Journal of Personality and Social Psychology* 4 (July): 112–15.

Steinfatt, Thomas M. 1989. "Linguistic Relativity: Toward a Broader View." In *Language, Communication, and Culture*, ed. S. Ting-Toomey and F. Korzenny, 35–78. Newbury Park, CA: Sage.

Stern, Barbara B. 1989a. "Literary Explication: A Methodology for Consumer Research." In *Interpretive Consumer Research*, ed. Elizabeth Hirschman, 48–59. Provo, UT: Association for Consumer Research.

———. 1989b. "Literary Criticism and Consumer Research: Overview and Illustrative Analysis." *Journal of Consumer Research* 16 (December): 322–34.

———. 1993. "Feminist Literary Criticism and the Deconstruction of Ads: A Postmodern View of Advertising." *Journal of Consumer Research* 19, no. 4: 556–57.

———. 1996. "Deconstructive Strategy and Consumer Research: Concepts and Illustrative Exemplar." *Journal of Consumer Research* 23, no. 2: 136–48.

Sternthal, Brian; Alice M. Tybout; and Bobby J. Calder. 1987. "Confirmatory versus Comparative Approaches to Judging Theory Test." *Journal of Consumer Research* 16 (December): 114–25.

Stewart, Alex. 1998. *The Ethnographer's Method: Qualitative Research Methods*. Thousand Oaks, CA: Sage.

Stove, David. 1982. *Popper and After*. Oxford, UK: Pergamon Press.

Strong, Morgan. 1990. "Playboy Interview: Stephen Hawking." *Playboy* 37 (April): 63–74.

Suppe, Frederick. 1977a. "Afterword—1977." In *The Structure of Scientific Theories*, ed. Frederick Suppe, 614–730. Urbana: University of Illinois Press.

———. 1977b. *The Structure of Scientific Theories*. 2d ed. Urbana: University of Illinois Press.

———. 1984. "Beyond Skinner and Kuhn." *New Ideas in Psychology* 2, no. 1: 89–104.

Suppes, Patrick. 1986. "Book Review, Science and Values." *Philosophy of Science* 53, no. 3: 449–51.

Tarski, Alfred. 1956. *Logic, Semantics, Metamathematics*, trans. J.H. Woodger. Oxford: Clarendon Press.

Theocharis, T., and M. Psimopoulos. 1987. "Where Has Science Gone Wrong?" *Nature* 329 (October 15): 595–98.

Thompson, Craig J. 1990. "Eureka! And other Tests of Significance: A New Look at Evaluating Interpretive Research." In *Advances in Consumer Research*, vol. 17, ed. M. Goldberg, G. Gorn, and R. Pollay, 25–30. Provo, UT: Association for Consumer Research.

———. 1991. "May the Circle Be Unbroken: A Hermeneutic Consideration of How Interpretive Approaches to Consumer Research Are Understood by Consumer Researchers." In *Advances in Consumer Research*, ed. R.H. Holman and M.R. Solomon, 63–69. Provo, UT: Association for Consumer Research.

———. 1993. "Modern Truth and Postmodern incredulity: A Hermeneutic Deconstruction of the Metanarrative of 'Scientific Truth' in Marketing Research." *International Journal of Research in Marketing* 10, no. 3: 325–38.

Thompson, Craig J.; William B. Locander; and Howard R. Pollio. 1989. "Putting Consumer Experience Back into Consumer Research: The Philosophy and Method of Existential-Phenomenology." *Journal of Consumer Research* 16 (September): 133–46.

Time. 1988. July 11: 32.

Trout, J.D. 1998. *Measuring the Intentional World*. Oxford: Oxford University Press.

———. 1999. "Measured Realism and Statistical Inference: An Explanation for the Fast Progress of 'Hard' Psychology." *Philosophy of Science* 66 (Proceedings): S260–72.

Tybout, Alice M.; Brian Sternthal; and Bobby J. Calder. 1983. "Information Availability as a Determinant of Multiple Request Effectiveness." *Journal of Marketing Research* 20 (August): 280–90.

Vallicella, William F. 1984. "Relativism, Truth and the Symmetry Thesis." *Monist* 67 (July): 452–67.

Van Eijkelenburg, Stef. 1995. "On the Rhetoric of Qualitative Methods: A Rejoinder." *Journal of Management Inquiry* 4, no. 2: 209–10.

Van Fraassen, Bas C. 1980. *The Scientific Image*. Oxford: Clarendon Press.

Van Maanan, J. 1993. Comments of John Van Maanan in "Ethnography Versus Critical Theory: Debating Organizational Research." *Journal of Management of Inquiry* 2, no. 2: 221–35.

Venkatesh, Alladi. 1989. "Modernity and Postmodernity." In *AMA Winter Educators' Conference*, ed. Terry L. Childers et al., 99–104. Chicago: American Marketing Association.

Wallendorf, Melanie, and Russell W. Belk. 1989. "Assessing Trustworthiness in Naturalistic Consumer Research." In *Interpretive Consumer Research*, ed. Elizabeth Hirschman, 69–84. Provo, UT: Association for Consumer Research.

Wartofsky, Marx W. 1968. *Conceptual Foundations of Scientific Thought*. New York: Macmillan.

Watkins, John. 1984. *Science and Skepticism*. Princeton, NJ: Princeton University Press.

Watson, James D. 1968. *The Double Helix: A Personal Account of the Discovery of the Structure of DNA*. New York: Atheneum.

Weber, Max. 1947. *The Theory of Social and Economic Organization*. New York: Oxford University Press.

Wensley, Robin. 2002. "Marketing for a New Century." *Journal of Marketing Management* 18, nos. 1–2: 229–37.

Werskey, P.G., ed. [1931] 1971. *Science at the Cross Roads*. London: Verso.

Whewell, William. 1840. "The Philosophy of the Inductive Sciences." Reprinted in *Philosophy of Science*. 1968, ed. Joseph J. Kockelmans, 51–79. New York: Free Press.

Whorf, B.L. 1956. *Language, Thought, and Reality*. Cambridge, MA: MIT Press.

Wilk, Richard R. 2001. "The Impossibility and Necessity of Re-Inquiry: Finding Middle Ground in Social Science." *Journal of Consumer Research* 28 (September): 308–12.

Will, Frederick L. 1981. "Reason, Social Practice, and Scientific Realism." *Philosophy of Science* 48, no. 1: 1–18.

Winch, Peter. 1958. *The Idea of a Social Science and Its Relation to Philosophy*. London: Routledge and Kegan Paul.

———. 1964. "Understanding a Primitive Society." *American Philosophical Quarterly* 1, no. 3: 307–24.

———. 1972. *Ethics and Action*. London: Routledge and Kegan Paul.

Wittgenstein, Ludwig. 1922. *Tractatus Logico-Philosophicus*. London: Routledge and Kegan Paul.

———. 1953. *Philosophical Investigations*, trans. and ed. G.E.M. Anscombe. Oxford: Blackwell.

Worrall, John, and G. Currie. 1978. *The Methodology of Scientific Research Programs: Philosophical Papers of Imre Lakatos*, vol. I. Cambridge: Cambridge University Press.

Wylie, Alison. 1989. "Archeological Cables and Tacking: The Implications of Practice for Bernstein's 'Options Beyond Objectivism and Relativism.'" *Philosophy of Social Science* 19, no. 1: 1–18.

Zaltman, Gerald; Karen LeMasters; and Michael Heffring. 1982. *Theory Construction in Marketing: Some Thoughts on Thinking*. New York: Wiley .

Zaltman, Gerald, and Christine Moorman. 1988. "The Importance of Personal Trust in the Use of Research." *Journal of Advertising Research* 28, no. 5: 16–24.

Zinkhan, George, and Rudy Hirschheim. 1992. "Truth in Marketing Theory and Research: An Alternative Perspective." *Journal of Marketing* 56, no. 2: 80–8.

Zukav, Gary. 1979. *The Dancing Wu-Li Masters*. New York: Bantam.

INDEX

A

a posteriori, 38
a priori, 26, 38
Absolute mind, 41
Absolutism, 102, 112
    vulgar, 102, 258
Academic skepticism, 80–81, 239–40
Acadèmie des Sciences, 25
Acceptance, context of, 152, 160, 161
Adler, Mortimer J., 237
Affirmation, Table of (Bacon), 28
Against Method (Feyerabend), 126, 127, 140
Age of Enlightenment, 26–27
Age of Reason, 26–27
Analytic/synthetic dichotomy, 38, 77
Anderson, Paul
    convergent relativism, 230
    critical relativism, 110, 181, 230
    on Feyerabend, 194, 195
    marketing incommensurability, 228–29
    medical science *vs.* palmistry example,
        191–93
    notions of "science," 189
    PIMS studies, 216
Anomalies, 117
Anthropology, cultural, 98–99, 104
Anti-apriorist thesis, 81
Anti-objectivists, 256–57
Antipositivism, 210–12
Antirealism, 182, 183
"Anything goes" (Feyerabend), 128, 152
Appearance and Reality (Bradley), 43
Approximate truth, 88–89
Aquinas, Thomas, 17

A

Arationality assumption, 103
Aristotle, 15–16, 19
    philosophy after, 16–17
Arndt, Johan, 215
Assumptions, 160
Atom, Mach's opposition to, 47–48
Atomic linguistic expressions, 58–59
Atomism, logical, 56, 65, 70
Awareness, 55
Azande, 107, 108, 134

B

Bacon, Francis, 27–29, 93, 216
Bain, Alexander, 90
Barnes, Barry, 104, 106
Bassi, Agostino, 173
Beach, Edward, 258
Begrisschrift (Frege), 49
Behaviorist theories, of meaning, 58
Beliefs, 90–91, 103, 108
    scientific realism and, 176, 182
    truth and, 222, 225
Ben-David, Joseph, 18, 23
Berkeley, George, 37–38
Bernstein, Richard J., 256, 257
Bias, 28, 254, 263–64
Biochemistry, 109–10
Biology, scientific realism and, 290–91
Bloom, Alan, 100, 138–39
Bloor, David, 104, 106
Boas, Franz, 99
Boole, George, 49
Bosanquet, Bernard, 44

ABOUT THE AUTHOR

SHELBY D. HUNT is the Jerry S. Rawls and P.W. Horn Professor of Marketing at Texas Tech University, Lubbock, Texas. A past editor of the *Journal of Marketing* (1985–87), he is the author of *Foundations of Marketing Theory: Toward a General Theory of Marketing* (2002) and *A General Theory of Competition: Resources, Competences, Productivity, Economic Growth* (2000). He has written numerous articles on competitive theory, macromarketing, ethics, channels of distribution, philosophy of science, and marketing theory. Three of his *Journal of Marketing* articles, "The Nature and Scope of Marketing" (1976), "General Theories and Fundamental Explananda of Marketing" (1983), and "The Comparative Advantage Theory of Competition" (1995) (with Robert M. Morgan) won the Harold H. Maynard Award for the "best article on marketing theory." His 1985 *Journal of Business Research* article with Lawrence B. Chonko, "Ethics and Marketing Management," received the 2000 Elsevier Science Exceptional Quality and High Scholarly Impact award. His 1989 article, "Reification and Realism in Marketing: In Defense of Reason," won the *Journal of Macromarketing* Charles C. Slater Award. For his contributions to theory and science in marketing, he received the 1986 Paul D. Converse Award from the American Marketing Association, the 1987 Outstanding Marketing Educator Award from the Academy of Marketing Science, the 1992 American Marketing Association/Richard D. Irwin Distinguished Marketing Educator Award, and the 2002 Society for Marketing Advances/Elsevier Science Distinguished Scholar Award.